Do the Geneva Conventions Matter?

Do the Geneva Conventions Matter?

EDITED BY MATTHEW EVANGELISTA
and
NINA TANNENWALD

OXFORD
UNIVERSITY PRESS

OXFORD
UNIVERSITY PRESS

Oxford University Press is a department of the University of Oxford. It furthers the University's objective of excellence in research, scholarship, and education by publishing worldwide. Oxford is a registered trade mark of Oxford University Press in the UK and certain other countries.

Published in the United States of America by Oxford University Press
198 Madison Avenue, New York, NY 10016, United States of America.

CIP data is on file at the Library of Congress
ISBN 978–0–19–937977–4 (hbk)
ISBN 978–0–19–937978–1 (pbk)

CONTENTS

LIST OF TABLES

ACKNOWLEDGMENTS

This volume is the result of collaboration between the Watson Institute for International Studies at Brown University, Cornell University's Judith Reppy Institute for Peace and Conflict Studies, and the Peace Research Institute Frankfurt (PRIF), Germany. Funding was provided by those institutions, as well as through a seed grant from the Mario Einaudi Center for International Studies at Cornell, the Cluster of Excellence of the Goethe-University Frankfurt's initiative on "The Formation of Normative Orders," and a Policy-Connect grant from the US International Research and Exchange Board (IREX). We are grateful for the support of Michael Kennedy and Nicolas van de Walle, then directors of the Watson Institute and Einaudi Center, respectively, and to Harald Müller and Klaus-Dieter Wolf of PRIF.

Each chapter of this volume has gone through several revisions. An initial authors' workshop was held at Cornell in November 2007. A second workshop was held in Frankfurt in October 2008, and a third at the Watson Institute in June 2010. In addition, we organized a panel at the annual meeting of the International Studies Association in March 2011, where several of the authors presented their drafts. Oxford University Press carried out a review process that produced valuable comments addressing legal, political, and historical aspects of the volume. Three colleagues deserve special mention and gratitude for their thorough reading at various stages of all of the chapters: Benjamin Valentino at the Cornell workshop, Alexander Downes at Watson, and Judith Reppy—whose efforts equaled those of a third editor, but who refused the title—as we were preparing the final project for submission to Oxford. Elaine Scott and Sandra Kisner provided their usual excellent administrative support for the Cornell workshop, and Sandy edited and prepared the manuscript for review with skill and patience. Thanks to Larissa Eltsefon for her research at Cornell on the European Court of Human Rights and Russian crimes in Chechnya and to Huss Banai for serving as rapporteur of the Brown workshop.

Many colleagues contributed to the success of this volume (we take sole responsibility for any failures), by preparing papers or serving as discussants at our workshops in Ithaca, Providence, or Frankfurt. With apologies if we have overlooked anyone, we offer our thanks to Olivier Barsalou, Arnulf Becker, Doug Blum, Michael Bothe, Reuben E. Brigety II, Lothar Brock, Steven Burg, Holly Case, Neta Crawford, Nicole Deitelhoff, Janina Dill, Molly Clark Dunigan, Marco Duranti, David Engerman, Jennifer Erickson, Chip Gagnon, Abbott Gleason, Burke Hendrix, Jean-Charles Jauffret, Oliver Jütersonke, Stefan Kadelbach, Colin Kahl, David Kaiser, Elke Krahmann, Bernd Kubbig, Ricardo Larémont, George A. Lopez, Katherine McCoy, Richard Miller, Zina Miller, Naz Modirzadeh, Karl Mueller, Muna Ndulo, Jelena Pejic, Pablo Policzer, Jody Prescott, Mary Roldán, Gabor Rona, Yael Ronen, Frederik Rosen, Hans Peter Schmitz, Ulrich Schneckener, Sabrina Schulz, Mark Selden, Michael Shin, Henry Shue, Tamara Taraciuk, Sidney Tarrow, Ramesh Thakur, Salvador Tinajero, Nick Turse, Michel Veuthey, Isaiah Wilson III, and David Wippman. We are grateful to David McBride, our editor at Oxford, and to his colleagues Kathleen Weaver, Emily Mackenzie, Claire Silbey, and Rajakumari Ganessin. We thank Jehad Nga for permission to use his extraordinary photo for our book's cover. The editors owe their biggest debt of gratitude to the authors for their patience and willingness to undertake multiple revisions to keep their chapters up to date—which, for some topics, entailed tracking a moving target.

LIST OF CONTRIBUTORS

Elizabeth Grimm Arsenault is a visiting assistant professor in the Security Studies Program at Georgetown University.

Eyal Ben-Ari is an anthropologist who is director of the Kinneret Center for Society, Security and Peace in Israel.

Raphaëlle Branche is professor of modern history at the University of Rouen (France). She works mainly on colonial violence and laws of war during colonial warfare.

Amichai Cohen is a professor of international law at the Ono Academic College, Israel, and a senior fellow at the Israel Democracy Institute.

Sahr Conway-Lanz is a historian in the Manuscript Division of the Library of Congress and author of *Collateral Damage: Americans, Noncombatant Immunity, and Atrocity after World War II.*

Renée de Nevers is an associate professor in the Department of Public Administration and International Affairs at The Maxwell School at Syracuse University.

Matthew Evangelista is President White Professor of History and Political Science at the Department of Government, and director of the Judith Reppy Institute for Peace and Conflict Studies, Cornell University.

Mark Kramer is director of Cold War Studies at Harvard University and a senior fellow of Harvard's Davis Center for Russian and Eurasian Studies.

Giovanni Mantilla is assistant professor of international studies at Centro de Investigación y Docencia Económicas (CIDE) in Mexico City. He has held post-doctoral fellowships at Princeton University's Niehaus Center for Globalization and Governance and Brown University's Watson Institute for International Studies.

R. Craig Nation has been professor of strategy and director of Russian and Eurasian Studies at the US Army War College in Carlisle, Pennsylvania, since 1996.

Gary D. Solis, PhD, a retired US Marine, has taught the law of war for more than twenty years.

Nina Tannenwald is director of the International Relations Program and faculty fellow at the Watson Institute for International Studies and senior lecturer in the Department of Political Science, Brown University.

Anicée Van Engeland is a senior lecturer in international security and law at Cranfield University and author of *Civilian or Combatant? A Challenge for the 21st Century.*

Siobhán Wills, professor of law at the Transitional Justice Institute, Ulster University, and senior fellow of the Higher Education Authority, UK, researches protection of civilians, peacekeeping, and use of force; a documentary she produced on the UN Stabilization Mission in Haiti (funded by the Arts and Humanities Research Council, UK) premiered in 2017.

1

Assessing the Effects and Effectiveness of the Geneva Conventions

NINA TANNENWALD

Introduction

In recent years, the Geneva Conventions, once mainly the province of legal scholars and professional do-gooders, have become the subject of increasing public discussion in the context of 9/11 and the so-called war on terror. The four Geneva Conventions of 1949 and the two Additional Protocols of 1977, along with a set of earlier agreements going back to 1864, are the definitive written source of international humanitarian law, or what we colloquially call the laws of war. They codify the standards that the countries of the world have set for the humane treatment of prisoners of war and noncombatants during armed conflict. They represent the assertion that even in wartime there are limits to what counts as acceptable behavior. With the accession of South Sudan in January 2013, all states are parties to the 1949 conventions (somewhat fewer adhere to the Protocols), and many of the Conventions' provisions are considered customary law.[1] It is the first time in modern history that a treaty has achieved universal acceptance.

Although humanitarian practitioners argue strongly for the value of these conventions in limiting the violence of war, trends in recent decades raise serious questions about their actual effectiveness. In the 1990s, concern about civilian victims of war steadily increased. Armed forces engaged in internal conflicts in places such as the former Yugoslavia, Rwanda, and Tajikistan seemed

[1] Theodore Meron, "The Geneva Conventions as Customary Law," *American Journal of International Law* 81, no. 348 (1987). Note that 196 states (including, as of April 2014, the aspiring state of Palestine) are parties to the Conventions, 171 are parties to Additional Protocol I, and 166 are parties to Additional Protocol II. The United States has not joined either Protocol.

deliberately to target civilians, calling into doubt the relevance of the Geneva prohibitions. In the first decades of the 21st century, the rise of fundamentalist Islamic terrorism targeting civilians, and the subsequent response of the United States emphasizing preventive war and setting aside portions of the Geneva Conventions, posed new challenges for the humanitarian law regime. Many recent conflicts evoke perennial questions of how regular armed forces should deal with guerrilla armies whose success depends on blending into the civilian population. The behavior of Russian troops in Chechnya in 1999 and of Israeli forces combating Hezbollah in 2006 and Hamas in 2008–2009 and again in 2014 involved indiscriminate attacks against civilian targets that appeared aimed at punishing civilians for their support for rebel groups. The behavior of both government and rebel troops in brutal civil wars in Democratic Congo, Sudan, Sierra Leone, Sri Lanka, Libya, and Syria further contributes to a disturbing picture of the Conventions as either irrelevant or invoked hypocritically, leading to the question of whether they really serve to constrain state behavior.

At the same time, it is also clear that US troops in Iraq and Afghanistan operate under extensive legal guidelines that shape the rules of engagement and the conduct of operations.[2] The official Rules of Engagement for US forces in Iraq, leaked by Wikileaks in 2008, detailed an extensive set of rules designed to protect civilians. For example, all attacks except those in self-defense or active pursuit with a reasonable possibility of harming thirty or more civilians needed approval from the US secretary of defense.[3] William Arkin, the military analyst for the *Washington Post*, argued that the rules were "so meticulous and sensitive to civilians" that it would actually benefit the United States to publicize them rather than keep them secret.[4] In Afghanistan, US commanders progressively tightened the rules of engagement in order to protect civilians, to the open grumbling of some soldiers and conservative critics who felt this excessively restricted soldiers' ability to defend themselves. Yet some Iraq war veterans reported that the rules of engagement were often "thrown out the window," especially as the level of threat increased. They testified before Congress that they had witnessed and participated in widespread misconduct toward civilians in Iraq, including unwarranted killings of Iraqi civilians and mistreatment of detainees, that was met with indifference or encouragement by commanding officers.[5] More than a decade earlier, Human Rights Watch and Greenpeace found that the United

[2] Colin Kahl, "How We Fight," *Foreign Affairs* (November/December 2006).

[3] "U.S. Consolidated Rules of Engagement for Iraq," 2005, document available at https://www.wikileaks.org/wiki/US_Rules_of_Engagement_for_Iraq; David Isenberg, "War By the Rules in Iraq," *Asia Times*, February 12, 2008. The number 30 was apparently subsequently lowered even further.

[4] William Arkin, "Iraq Rules Need More Airing," *Washington Post*, February 4, 2008.

[5] "Iraq Vets Recount Concerns over Rules of Engagement," *PBS Newshour*, May 28, 2008.

States had generally complied with the Geneva Conventions during the 1991 Persian Gulf War.[6] In short, there may be some good news about the Geneva Conventions, but what exactly is it?

This volume examines how the Geneva Conventions matter. It brings together an interdisciplinary group of authors from political science, sociology, anthropology, history, and international law to analyze the impact of the Geneva Conventions in concrete empirical cases. The volume focuses on the period since 1949 as the era of the "modern" Geneva Conventions when, following the tremendous destructiveness of two world wars, support for the incorporation of both humanitarian and human rights norms into international law expanded greatly. This introductory chapter lays out a framework for analyzing the effects and effectiveness of the Geneva Conventions, identifies key themes, and develops some preliminary hypotheses that are applied in the empirical chapters. The following chapter provides a historical overview of the development of the Conventions, focusing on the issues that proved controversial during negotiation and how they were resolved. Many of those issues deal with internal conflict, irregular warfare, and the treatment of civilians. The ten empirical chapters then examine the role of the Geneva Conventions in specific historical cases that brought such issues to the fore. The concluding chapter draws together and assesses the findings from the empirical cases.

This is a question-driven, not a theory-driven, inquiry, and we draw on an eclectic array of theoretical tools. Nevertheless, our analysis engages particularly the law and society literature in sociology on compliance within organizations, the constructivist literature in international relations on persuasion and socialization, and legal scholarship on "internalization." A central question is to what extent, and under what conditions, does symbolic or "ritual" compliance (e.g., incorporation into military manuals and military training) translate into actual compliance on the battlefield? We also seek to move beyond issues of compliance and effectiveness to examine the question of *effects* more broadly, including indirect effects (on behavior, norms, identity, and institutions) and unintended consequences.

This chapter proceeds in several steps. In the first part, I elaborate on the challenge of assessing the impact of the laws of war. I then describe the Geneva Conventions as an international regime—its core principles and norms, the mechanisms by which it operates, and the particular challenges it faces. The

[6] Reported in Stephanie Carvin, *Prisoners of America's Wars: From the Early Republic to Guantanamo* (Oxford: Oxford University Press, 2010), p. 134. Carvin concludes that the first Gulf War may have been the "most legalistic war in history," p. 139. For a detailed analysis, see Adam Roberts, "The Laws of War in the 1990–1991 Gulf Conflict," *International Security* 18, no. 3 (Winter 1993–1994): 134–181.

chapter then reviews theoretical arguments in the literature about the effectiveness and impact of the laws of war. It develops a theoretical framework regarding the issue of compliance with and internalization of norms that informs the analysis conducted in the empirical cases. This framework is employed by authors of the empirical chapters to assess how "internalized" (or not) the Geneva Conventions are in the practices of the countries analyzed in the volume. Finally, the chapter concludes by laying out the plan of the rest of the book.

A note on terminology: the modern laws of war are a combination of so-called Geneva law and Hague law. As the following chapter on the history of the Conventions spells out in greater detail, "Geneva" law focuses on protecting the "victims" of armed conflict. "Hague" law is concerned with the rules of combat and the legality of weapons—what is often referred to as the means and methods of warfare—whose original purpose was the protection of armed forces from unnecessary suffering. In recent years, the distinction between the two bodies of law has blurred and, indeed, has lost much of its meaning. This is due in part to the rising concern with human rights as a subject of international regulation, and because both Hague and Geneva law have expanded to the point where their concerns overlap. They are collectively now known as the "law of armed conflict" (LOAC)—the common usage among military lawyers—or "international humanitarian law" (IHL)—the more common usage among humanitarian practitioners and academics. In this volume we use the phrases "laws of war" or IHL interchangeably, while still giving primary emphasis to the Geneva Conventions, which focus on protecting noncombatants, as the core of this regime.

The State of Knowledge

Despite the widespread acceptance of the Geneva Conventions norms in principle, we lack systematic understanding of the overall effectiveness or effects of this regime. A vast literature on IHL now exists. But much of it is written by legal scholars and humanitarian actors, assessing gaps and ambiguities in the law, given the changing nature of war, and proposing ways to strengthen it.[7] While humanitarian actors have provided extensive reporting on violations and compliance in numerous cases of armed conflict, systematic social science assessments of the consequences and impact—positive or negative—of this body of rules and practices are scarce. The few systematic assessments that do exist focus

[7] The International Review of the Red Cross is a leading example. See also David Wippman and Matthew Evangelista, eds., *New Wars, New Laws? Applying Laws of War in 21st Century Conflicts* (Ardsley, NY: Transnational, 2005).

primarily on Western cases.[8] The growing social science literature on the causes of genocide and intentional killings of civilians generally devotes little attention to the role of the laws of war (perhaps the conclusion seems too obvious in these cases).[9] Quantitatively oriented scholars have begun to conduct statistical research on the impact of IHL on state behavior during war, but the findings are still preliminary. Such studies are useful for discerning patterns or trends but generally are unable to probe causal mechanisms very deeply.[10] Historians, for their part, have devoted almost no attention to the history of the laws of war. As one historian observed, "the history of the field barely exists."[11]

One reason, perhaps, for this lack of systematic attention is that the effectiveness of the regime overall is supremely difficult to assess. Ideally, to know whether the Geneva regime has saved civilian lives and reduced state violence, we would need to know a counterfactual—what would have happened in the absence of the regime—and this is nearly impossible to know. Even in the many instances where those acting on humanitarian grounds have clearly enjoyed successes—in delivering medical care to conflict zones, in improving conditions of prisoners of war, or even in ending wars through the use of force (as in Bosnia, Kosovo, or Libya)—such successes often seem dwarfed by the scale of the humanitarian violations that either preceded or continued to take place around them, leading to the impression that the successes are highly contingent.

Certainly the statistical trends in civilian casualties are difficult to interpret. Historically, the treatment of civilians in warfare has been harsh, but as the means and methods of warfare have become more sophisticated, the effects on the civilian population have become even more pronounced. Since the end of World War II, civil wars of one form or another have been the predominant form of armed conflict, and the civilian casualties in some of these disputes have reached catastrophic proportions. Analysts disagree, however, to what extent

[8] Michael Howard, George J. Andreopoulos, and Mark R. Shulman, *The Laws of War: Constraints on Warfare in the Western World* (New Haven, CT: Yale University Press, 1994); Carvin, *Prisoners of America's Wars*.

[9] Benjamin A. Valentino, *Final Solutions: Mass Killing and Genocide in the 20th Century* (Ithaca, NY: Cornell University Press, 2005); Michael Mann, *The Dark Side of Democracy: Explaining Ethnic Cleansing* (New York: Cambridge University Press, 2005); Alexander Downes, *Targeting Civilians in War* (Ithaca, NY: Cornell University Press, 2008); Alex J. Bellamy, *Massacres and Morality: Mass Atrocities in an Age of Civilian Immunity* (Oxford: Oxford University Press, 2012).

[10] Benjamin Valentino, Paul Huth, and Sarah Croco, "Covenants without the Sword: International Law and the Protection of Civilians in Wartime," *World Politics* 58, no. 3 (April 2006): 339–377; Alyssa K. Prorok and Benjamin J. Appel, "Compliance with International Humanitarian Law: Democratic Third Parties and Civilian Targeting in Interstate War," *Journal of Conflict Resolution*, published online March 18, 2013, pp. 1–28.

[11] John F. Witt, "The Dismal History of the Laws of War," *U.C. Irvine Law Review* 1, no. 3 (September 2011): 897.

civilians have become the major victims of war. In the view of many humanitarian actors, "civilian population displacement and casualties have increasingly become the purpose rather than a by-product of war."[12] In recent decades, analysts and international organizations have often cited the appalling statistic that since the 1990s civilians have made up 80–90 percent of war victims, as compared with an estimated at 5 percent in World War I. However, others argue that this figure rests on shaky ground. The *Human Security Report*, a large-scale effort to analyze trends in warfare, has criticized this statistic as unreliable, describing the 9:1 civilian-military casualty ratio was an "urban myth."[13]

Governments themselves rarely keep statistics on civilians they have killed in an enemy country. Despite extensive work in war zones by humanitarian actors and academics, massive obstacles to gathering accurate data on civilian casualties, along with differences in methodologies for calculating them, mean that all the statistics are highly uncertain. Do casualties include just those killed or those wounded as well? What about the (much larger) number of people who die from war-exacerbated disease and malnutrition? In many cases, accurate data is simply not available.

Certainly since World War I, when an estimated 5 percent of the war victims were civilians, the trend in civilian casualties has been upward. Scholars estimate that about 50 percent of the casualties in World War II were civilians, and analysts tend to agree at least that, since then, civilian deaths have outnumbered military deaths in conflicts. It is unclear how the Geneva Conventions, which more or less coincide with the period following World War II, have affected this trend. Did they have no effect (as the upward trend in the casualty statistic would superficially suggest) or, alternatively, would things have been worse without the Geneva Conventions?

Because of the enormous difficulties in developing accurate statistics, the effort to seek universal civilian–military casualty ratios, as Adam Robert suggests, may be "flawed," and analysts should focus instead on specific wars.[14] We follow this advice in this volume. The even more difficult question of what proportion of civilian victimization is a war crime as compared with merely a result of "collateral damage" is an important topic that gets at "permissive" effects of the Geneva Conventions, an issue I take up further in what follows.

[12] Randolph Martin, "An Introduction to NGO Field Security", in *Emergency Relief Operations*, ed. Kevin M. Cahill (New York: Fordham University Press, 2003), p. 227.

[13] Adam Roberts, "Lives and Statistics: Are 90% of War Victims Civilians?" *Survival* 52, no. 115 (June–July 2010). It is possible, however, that some conflict situations have something close to a 9:1 ratio. Two likely cases are the government-supported mass killings in Cambodia in 1975–1979 and in Rwanda in 1994. See Roberts, pp. 47–48.

[14] Ibid.

The Geneva Conventions as an International Regime

International regimes are "arrangements created to solve more or less well-defined problems that make their way onto the international political agenda."[15] More concretely, they are "social institutions consisting of agreed upon principles, norms, rules, procedures and programs that govern the interactions of actors in specific issue areas."[16]

The Geneva Conventions qualify as a regime in this sense. They are what Oran Young has described as a "negotiated regime," characterized by "conscious efforts to agree on their major provisions, explicit consent on the part of individual participants, and formal expressions of the results."[17] The Geneva regime consists of a set of treaties on IHL with a nongovernmental organization (NGO)—the International Committee of the Red Cross (ICRC)—as their central "guardian." Other organizations, including United Nations (UN) humanitarian and human rights agencies, and human rights groups such as Human Rights Watch and Amnesty International, play active roles in support of the regime, though this may sometimes depend on the consent of states.

At the core of the regime are the four Conventions concluded in 1949, as well as the two Additional Protocols, concluded in 1977. The latter further elaborated the protections afforded by the 1949 agreements and extended them to a wider range of military situations, including those that arise from civil war and revolutionary insurgency. Also forming part of the regime are a long line of treaties extending back to the Brussels Declaration of 1874, the first attempt to spell out the legal rights of noncombatants in war, as well as customary law.

The four 1949 agreements were negotiated in the aftermath of the atrocities and devastation of World War II, which made obvious that laws protecting noncombatants in war needed strengthening. During the war, the firebombing of cities, the deportation and murder of civilians in concentration camps, and the use of atomic bombs on Japan resulted in the deaths of millions of civilians and incalculable suffering. The agreements negotiated in 1949 updated the terms of three earlier treaties and added a new, fourth treaty. They focus on the treatment of enemy forces who are wounded or taken prisoner and of civilians who fall into the hands of the enemy or are living in occupied territory.

[15] Oran Young, *Governance in World Affairs* (Ithaca, NY: Cornell University Press, 1999).

[16] Marc A. Levy, Oran Young, and Michael Zürn, "The Study of International Regimes," *European Journal of International Relations* 1, no. 3 (September 1995): 274.

[17] Oran Young, "Regime Dynamics: The Rise and Fall of International Regimes," in *International Cooperation* (Ithaca, NY: Cornell University Press, 1989), p. 86.

The first Convention, first concluded in 1864 and updated several times, deals with treatment of wounded and sick combatants. The second Convention, first concluded in 1906 and significantly revised in 1949, deals with the wounded and sick at sea. The third, first adopted in 1929 and likewise replaced by the 1949 revisions, deals with the treatment of prisoners of war. The fourth Geneva Convention, entirely new in 1949, defines humanitarian protections for civilians in a war zone and outlaws the practice of total war. It grew out of the universal condemnation of the Nazis' treatment of civilians during World War II. An additional innovation was so-called Common Article 3 (because it is common to all four Conventions), which prohibited a set of practices not previously part of the laws of war, including the use of torture and degrading treatment, as well as violations of legal due process.

At the time the 1949 Conventions were drawn up, the legislators were principally concerned with wars between states. As civil wars and wars of national liberation began to command growing international attention in subsequent decades, states negotiated the 1977 Additional Protocols to fill the gaps left by the Conventions and to extend some humanitarian protections to wars *within* states. In 1993, the UN Security Council adopted a report from the secretary-general and a commission of experts which concluded that the Geneva Conventions had passed into the body of customary international law, thus making them binding on nonsignatories to the Conventions whenever they engage in armed conflicts.[18]

Violations of these treaties constitute war crimes, with individuals subject to trial and punishment for violations. The Geneva regime thus installed a criminal justice approach—defining and punishing violations by individuals—to replace the traditional state practice of collective punishment of an adversary. Since World War II, war crimes law has been applied by national courts and military tribunals, though sometimes inadequately. Beginning in the 1990s, several ad hoc international tribunals (e.g., for Rwanda and the former Yugoslavia) were established, as well as a permanent International Criminal Court, to prosecute gross violations of human rights and the laws of war. Finally, at the sharp end of the spear, since the end of the Cold War, the UN Security Council has with increasing if irregular frequency engaged in enforcement action to halt severe abuses of human rights and uphold humanitarian law.

Key Principles and Rules

The basic purpose of the laws of war is to provide some restraints on the waging of war and to protect noncombatants as far as is compatible with "military

[18] *Report of the Secretary-General Pursuant to Paragraph 2 of Security Council Resolution 808* (1993), UN Doc S/25704, 3 May 1993, p. 9.

necessity" and public order. Two basic principles lie at its core: discrimination and proportionality. The principle of *discrimination* (or distinction) requires parties to an armed conflict to distinguish at all times between civilians and soldiers, and between civilian and military objects, and to direct their military operations only at the latter. The principle of *proportionality* requires that a balance be struck between the achievement of a military goal and the costs in terms of civilian lives. Attackers must balance the concrete and direct military advantage of an attack against the risk of harm to civilians. Needless to say, this becomes an especially tricky judgment call when the line between military forces and civilian groups is increasingly blurred, as it is in many guerrilla and civil wars.

The Conventions spell out in great detail the obligations of combatants toward each other and toward civilians caught in the conflict zone. The six main treaties contain over five hundred articles in total, covering everything from defining a prisoner of war to specifying those cultural heritage sites that should be spared during conflict. The rules require, among many other things, that prisoners of war and civilians in occupied territory be treated humanely, that the lives and property of citizens of neutral states be respected, and that reasonable force be used against targets. Hospitals and cultural sites cannot be attacked. Enemy soldiers accused of war crimes must be given fair trials. Military forces must keep order and supply public services in occupied areas. Truces must be respected. Beyond the Conventions themselves, another set of rules ("Hague" law) governs the types of weapons that can be used, forbidding dum-dum bullets, certain types of fragmentary explosives, blinding lasers, poison gas, and other weapons believed to be inhumane.

The regime is thus quite formalized, with the primary norms taking the form of legal documents to which states formally adhere. Experts from the ICRC have written extensive commentaries on humanitarian law that clarify and expand on these general principles. Most states have incorporated these obligations into domestic law, where they are reflected in national legislation and military manuals.[19]

Additional Characteristics

Several additional characteristics of the regime are worth noting. First, the Geneva regime differs from more widely studied international regimes in economic and security issue areas in that private individuals were its key instigators. Henry Dunant, a Swiss financier, horrified by the abysmal conditions of wounded

[19] The ICRC maintains a country-by-country database of national implementation including national legislation, military manuals, and court cases.

soldiers at the battle of Solferino in 1859, founded the ICRC with like-minded colleagues as a private relief organization. They held the first international conference in 1863, drafted the first international convention on humanitarian law, and persuaded states to adhere. Later, the ICRC was a prime mover behind the negotiation of the 1949 Conventions and the subsequent 1977 Protocols. The ICRC initiated the negotiations, convened by the Swiss government. It wrote the working drafts, and ICRC experts took part in all meetings in an advisory capacity. The ICRC continues to play a leading role as a "moral entrepreneur" and a regime promoter. But it is a private, not an international, organization, and states neither control it nor appoint its staff. It is often well out ahead of states in its views of what the law requires and what constitutes customary law.[20]

A second important characteristic of the regime, one common to human rights as well, is the huge imbalance in the regime between setting standards and enforcing those standards. International humanitarian law depends largely on national action for its implementation. It lacks reliable and effective means for enforcing its provisions or for monitoring or assessing their implementation. According to one observer, IHL "define[s] principles that purport to be universal, indivisible, and timeless yet are to be carried out through ad hoc mechanisms that possess none of these attributes."[21] The ICRC has no power or means to enforce the laws of armed conflict. At best, it can complain to the party at fault, though even this is often done in private. There are no reporting requirements under the Geneva Conventions or the Protocols—as there are for many of the human rights conventions—and each state is responsible for ensuring its own compliance. The laws of war are thus much more thinly institutionalized than the human rights regime.

The ICRC, along with other humanitarian NGOs, works hard through its private interventions with states parties to improve compliance.[22] Today, however, thanks in part to 24-hour news and social media, much of the pressure for compliance is quite public. The issue of noncompliance with humanitarian law is often a highly politicized feature of many contemporary armed conflicts. As recent conflicts in Israel-Palestine, Sri Lanka, and Syria illustrate, disputes over compliance with humanitarian law may become matters of heated diplomacy

[20] Leah M. Nicholls, "The Humanitarian Monarchy Legislates: The International Committee of the Red Cross and Its 161 Rules of Customary International Humanitarian Law," *Duke Journal of Comparative and International Law* 17, no. 223 (2006–2007).

[21] Edward Luck, "The Enforcement of Humanitarian Norms and the Politics of Ambivalence," in *Civilians in War*, ed. Simon Chesterman (Boulder, CO: Lynne Rienner, 2001), p. 205.

[22] William O'Neill, "Gaining Compliance without Force: Human Rights Field Operations," in Chesterman, *Civilians in War*, p. 94.

among states at the United Nations and other international forums, and in bilateral relations.

Nonetheless, despite the generally thinly institutionalized nature of the laws of war, the last quarter-century has witnessed significant development in enforcement procedures. These include new international criminal courts with jurisdiction over IHL, noted earlier, and increasing activity by national courts under principles of universal jurisdiction. In addition, the profession of military lawyering has expanded, and the UN Human Rights Council has increasingly investigated violations of the laws of war.[23] The increasing but uneven willingness of the Security Council to authorize enforcement action on behalf of humanitarian goals under Chapter VII of the UN Charter (so-called humanitarian intervention), as witnessed in Bosnia, Libya, and elsewhere, represents a new development in the enforcement of humanitarian norms. However, its ad hoc and inconsistent nature—as witnessed in the lack of response to humanitarian crises in Rwanda, Darfur, and Syria—must be counted as a weakness of the Geneva regime.

A third characteristic of the Geneva regime is that the discourse of the regime is one of moral duty, obligation, and appropriate behavior rather than of state self-interest and advantage. As Martha Finnemore has emphasized, at the founding of the regime in the 1860s, state leaders and private citizens articulated the reasons for adherence in terms of Christian morality.[24] Henry Dunant framed his appeal in terms of responsibilities of Christian gentlemen and civilized nations. Leaders justified decisions to sign and comply on the basis of religious and moral duties borne by civilized nations. Citizens embraced the Conventions for similar reasons.[25] This discourse is sustained by the central role of the ICRC as the "moral entrepreneur" of the regime. This is not to say that self-interest is absent. Reciprocity (the fear of reprisals) has clearly played a role in encouraging state and nonstate actor compliance with IHL, although not in all cases. Reflecting the moral discourse, signatories of the 1949 Geneva Conventions (unlike the earlier Hague treaties) are bound by the terms of the convention even if the adversary is not party to the treaty.

Finally, a fourth feature of the regime is that, in humanitarian affairs, nonstate actors are often big players, whether as perpetrators of abuses, sources of relief,

[23] Amichai Cohen and Yuval Shany, "Beyond the Grave Breaches Regime: The Duty to Investigate Alleged Violations of International Law Governing Armed Conflict," *Yearbook of International Humanitarian Law* 14 (December 2011): 37–84.

[24] Martha Finnemore, "Rules of War and Wars of Rules: The International Red Cross and the Restraint of State Violence," in *Constructing World Culture: International Nongovernmental Organizations since 1875*, ed. John Boli and George M. Thomas (Stanford, CA: Stanford University Press), pp. 152–153.

[25] Finnemore, "Rules of War," p. 164.

or mediators of disputes. In addition to the prominent role of the ICRC itself, these include armed groups, peacekeepers, and private military contractors, among others. They may not have seats at the UN or be parties to relevant treaties, but the extent of their cooperation on the ground may determine whether the Geneva rules are observed.

In sum, the Geneva regime is based on both moral principles and self-interest, widely subscribed to norms at the rhetorical level, but largely national implementation. I now turn to some of the challenges it faces.

Challenges for the Geneva Conventions

The goal of protecting noncombatants in war faces numerous challenges. The main challenge is the ability and will of belligerents to conduct discriminate warfare. Several factors, including technology and the changing nature of warfare, have made this more difficult over the years. However, the rules of the Geneva Conventions themselves leave significant discretion in the hands of military decision-makers.

Technology cuts both ways in terms of preserving the distinction between soldiers and civilians. Some kinds of weapons technology have made it easier to attack civilians and have contributed to blurring the line between combatants and civilians. In the 20th century, the development of the submarine (and its torpedo) and the airplane made it possible to reach beyond the front lines to apply pressure on an enemy's population, food supply, and economy and to destroy people's morale by attacks on places of work, railway lines, ports, and workers' homes. This practice reached its apex with the development of nuclear weapons, the most indiscriminate weapon the world has ever known. Nevertheless, much indiscriminate warfare rages in the absence of modern weapons—as we know from the conflicts in Rwanda or Sierra Leone, where massacres were often carried out with machetes—while advanced technology, such as precision-guided weapons, can also help sustain the laws of war by reducing "collateral damage." However, beyond the major powers, most nations do not have access to precision-guided weapons.

The most significant challenge to the practice of discriminate warfare is the *changing nature of war*. Traditionally, the actors the Geneva regime was designed to address were states and their professional standing armies. Today, however, civil wars predominate, and most armed conflicts involve one or more nonstate armed groups that are not parties to the Conventions. Guerrilla warfare, insurgency and counterinsurgency, and terrorism and counterterrorism have contributed to the deterioration of the practice of distinguishing between civilians and combatants in armed conflict. The Algerian struggle for independence from France from 1954 to 1962, in which both the Algerian National Liberation Front and the French army employed terror tactics targeting civilians, epitomized this trend. More recently, the trademark brutality of the Tamil Tigers guerrilla group fighting for independence from Sri Lanka provoked an equally brutal response by the Sri Lankan military, with catastrophic consequences for civilians, in the bloody 2009 defeat of the Tigers.

Uncertainty about how to characterize perceived "terrorist" adversaries creates difficulties for states in applying the Conventions. Many argue that, today, conventional armies that seek to adhere to the rules of war are disadvantaged and are under pressure to circumvent or change the rules. Debates over whether the US prisoners held at Guantanamo from the war against Al Qaeda and the Taliban in Afghanistan enjoyed any rights under the Geneva Conventions or whether the Palestinian police force in Gaza should be considered a civilian or military actor (and therefore a legitimate target for the Israeli military) illustrated the pressure on the rules. In 2006, the US Supreme Court made clear that the United States was not free to set aside the Geneva Conventions even when dealing with terrorists and that, at a minimum, the basic humanitarian provisions of Common Article 3 applied.[26] Although the ICRC continues to insist that Geneva rules recognize only two categories—combatants and civilians—and that there is no "third category" (as the Bush administration sought to create with its invention of the label "unlawful enemy combatant"), pressure is increasing for creating a special set of rules for dealing with terrorists.[27]

Finally, the Geneva rules themselves contain some weaknesses. Perhaps the biggest challenge facing the Geneva norms is the argument of "military necessity." This, by its very nature, is subjective. Everything hangs on a decision by a military leader as to what he or she judges to be needed.[28] To commanders in the field, military necessity becomes a particularly attractive line of argument if an action of dubious legality holds out the prospect of saving their soldiers' lives. Further, what counts as a legitimate military objective is often difficult to determine in contemporary conflicts, where the objective is often not complete military defeat of an enemy state but rather the attempt to force a particular regime to comply with certain specified requirements. Finally, some scholars argue that the notion of "collateral damage" actually creates a huge loophole for civilian victimization during war. While the term refers to the unavoidable deaths of noncombatants as a side effect of a legitimate military strike, critics argue that contemporary militaries increasingly treat the notion of collateral damage as an endlessly elastic concept. They stretch it to justify the rising "incidental" deaths

[26] *Hamdan v. Rumsfeld* (2006).

[27] Amitai Etzioni, "Terrorists: Neither Soldiers Nor Criminals," *Military Review* (July/August 2009).

[28] Howard et al., *The Laws of War*, p. 218.

of civilians, to the point where it can no longer be regarded as providing any real protection of civilians.[29]

Further, the Geneva Conventions mainly address the obligations of "attackers." They say much less about obligations of "defenders" (e.g., the practice of hiding fighters or weapons among the civilian population). For the armed forces, the norm that noncombatants' lives and property should be respected is paramount. But the noncombatants have an obligation as well, namely, not to take advantage of their immunity to engage in hostile acts.

In sum, technology, the changing nature of war, and weaknesses in the Geneva rules themselves all pose challenges for the effective operation of the humanitarian regime.

Theoretical Perspectives on the Laws of War

The existing literature in international relations and international law offers several theoretical arguments about the laws of war that help to illuminate dynamics in the empirical cases.

Realism

Realists, who focus on the role of material power in world affairs, are generally skeptical that the laws of war have any real constraining effect on state behavior. Realists tend to endorse the tragic words of Cicero: "in time of war, law falls silent." States will always put their vital interests first and will quickly set aside the law if it conflicts with those interests. The laws of war are especially fragile as they have the arguably utopian task of constraining combatants in the heat of battle. As soon as state interests and military necessity dictate, the law is easily brushed aside.

Recent cross-national quantitative studies support this pessimistic view of the laws of war, finding "no evidence that signatories of international treaties on the laws of war are significantly less likely to kill civilians in war than are nonsignatories."[30] Other research suggests that, as the costs of war go up, the incentives to target civilians go up as well. In an important study, Alexander Downes argues that as wars grow more costly, governments, including liberal democracies,

[29] Bruce Cronin, "Reckless Endangerment Warfare: Civilian Casualties and the Collateral Damage Exception in International Humanitarian Law," *Journal of Peace Research* 50, no. 2 (March 2013): 175–187; and Valerie Epps, "Civilian Casualties in Modern Warfare: The Death of the Collateral Damage Rule," *Georgia Journal of International and Comparative Law* 41 (Winter 2013).

[30] Valentino et al., "Covenants without the Sword," p. 2.

prefer to target enemy civilians as a way to reduce the costs to their own soldiers. Desperation to win and save lives on a state's own side as a war drags on leads the state to push the costs of war onto enemy civilians. Because democracies are more sensitive to costs, they are actually more likely than nondemocracies to target civilians when war becomes costly.

Downes's analysis is sobering. However, most of his case studies date from before the 1949 Geneva Conventions. They thus leave open the question of whether, and how, the Conventions have influenced state behavior since 1949. The dynamic he identifies appears to enjoy some measure of popular support, however. According to a 1999 survey by the ICRC, overwhelming majorities of people in all types of societies and cultures believe that purposefully targeting civilians or failing to discriminate between combatants and noncombatants is wrong. But when their state actually gets into a fight, these attitudes change: People become willing to breach the laws of war and sacrifice the lives of enemy civilians if doing so promises to ensure the survival of their own state or preserve the lives of their soldiers.[31]

Thus the key realist insight is that as the costs of war go up, the pressure to bend or jettison the rules increases. The case studies in this volume provide ample evidence for this general dynamic. For realists, the main mechanisms of compliance with the laws of war are expediency and the employment of power, force, and coercion to enforce compliance by others. The primary restraints on civilian victimization are a low-cost war, a shorter rather than longer war, and deterrence (the expectation that a battlefield action will be met with a punishing response) rather than any normative factors.[32]

Liberalism

The liberal perspective on international relations emphasizes the key role of rational self-interest in explaining both the origins of and compliance with the laws of war. Liberals note that the laws of war grew out of the self-interest of states. The laws originated out of concerns of military officers with the condition and treatment of their soldiers on the battlefield. Only later did such laws expand to include the protection of civilians. According to liberals, the rise of the laws of war provides evidence against the realist claim that "anything goes." States have an interest in maintaining some restraints on the uses of violence, since unrestrained warfare is costly and inefficient. War that is simply an orgy of murderous,

[31] International Committee of the Red Cross, *The People on War Report: ICRC Worldwide Consultation on the Rules of War* (October 1999).

[32] Downes, *Targeting Civilians in War.*

unrestrained violence can be self-defeating. Effectiveness in war is linked to discipline: states with unrestrained armies have often found that their goals cannot be achieved without enforcing discipline. Harsh tactics can backfire. The rape and pillage of towns could turn a population against an occupying army. As liberals note, "Restraint is not only humane, it is militarily advantageous."[33]

In the rationalist strand of liberal theory, the ability to reciprocate (or retaliate) is the key mechanism encouraging compliance, and it makes the laws of war "self-enforcing."[34] Other factors encouraging compliance include concerns about one's international reputation and various political costs, including potential loss of domestic or allied support, the threat of judicial trials for war crimes, and the risk of adverse publicity from the press or NGOs.[35] Thus Secretary of State Colin Powell argued in an internal memo in 2002 that the United States should comply with the Geneva Conventions in the war on terror because it would encourage reciprocal humane treatment of US soldiers captured by others.[36]

Even if national policy supports compliance, however, individual soldiers can violate the rules. Further, in the rationalist view, since nonstate armed groups cannot ratify the Conventions, "they cannot clearly signal their intentions or formally engage their reputations."[37] This helps explain the lower levels of compliance with the laws of war in conflicts between states and nonstate actors. Thus, according to the legal scholar Eric Posner, the United States disregarded the laws of war in the conflict with Al Qaeda while largely complying with them ("albeit with notable exceptions") in the simultaneous conflict with Iraq. US leaders were not concerned that Al Qaeda could retaliate and therefore felt free to set aside the Geneva Conventions.[38]

More generally, rationalists would argue that the self-enforcing nature of the laws of war helps explain the pattern of universal adherence to the Geneva Conventions, compared with the more checkered adherence to human rights treaties. When the Conventions were first opened for signature in 1949, all five members of the Security Council signed them. By 1960, 114 countries had ratified the Conventions. Today, adherence is universal. Human rights treaties, in

[33] Carvin, *Prisoners of America's Wars*, p. 7.

[34] James D. Morrow, "When Do States Follow the Laws of War?" *American Political Science Review* 20, no. 3 (August 2007): 559–572.

[35] Andrew T. Guzman, *How International Law Works: A Rational Choice Theory* (New York: Oxford University Press, 2008).

[36] Memorandum from Colin Powell, Secretary of State, to Counsel to the President and Assistant to the President for National Security Affairs (January 26, 2002).

[37] Kenneth W. Abbott, "International Relations Theory, International Law, and the Regime Governing Atrocities in Internal Conflicts," *American Journal of International Law* 93 (1999): 370.

[38] Eric A. Posner, "Human Rights, the Laws of War, and Reciprocity," John M. Olin Law and Economics Working Paper No. 537, University of Chicago Law School, September 2010.

contrast, which regulate how states treat their own citizens, do not enjoy the same degree of support. The United States, for example, along with many nondemocratic states, is not party to numerous important human rights conventions. Rationalists dismiss any kind of legitimacy explanation for the difference between the two cases, arguing instead that it is best explained by the fact that the laws of war are reciprocally enforced while human rights treaties are not.[39]

A second strand of liberal theory links state behavior to domestic regime type and state-society relations generally. This approach emphasizes both the role of domestic structures and the domestic political process as key factors explaining whether states follow international law.[40] Much of this literature argues that democracies, which tend to uphold human rights, humanitarian values, and the rule of law at home, are also more likely to abide by their international legal commitments than are autocratic regimes.[41] This perspective would expect that democracies are more likely to comply with the laws of war than nondemocracies. Some scholars emphasize the role of domestic institutions in internalizing norms and thereby promoting compliance with them.[42] Others have highlighted the role of treaty ratification in mobilizing domestic actors to lobby for compliance.[43] Most of this work has focused on human rights rather than IHL, however, and thus must be extrapolated to IHL.

Constructivism

Constructivist and transnational legal process approaches emphasize the key role of norms, identity, and discourse in world affairs. Constructivists argue that war is a cultural and social practice. How one fights is highly regulated and also connected to conceptions of identity. For constructivists, humanitarian law is the product of private political action and social values—not of rational calculations about reciprocity. As noted earlier, the founding of the ICRC, which involved a key role for individuals and civil society groups, and placed moral concerns at the forefront, was a very un-realist development. For constructivists, state behavior is not bound by fixed interests; rather, as values and identities shift, so will humanitarian practices. Even as states pursue their interests, they do so within a normative structure.

[39] Ibid.

[40] Anne-Marie Slaughter, "International Law in a World of Liberal States," *European Journal of International Law* (1995).

[41] Beth A. Simmons, "Compliance with International Agreements," *Annual Review of Political Science* (1998): 75–93.

[42] Harold Hongju Koh, "Why Do Nations Obey International Law?" *Yale Law Journal* 106, no. 8 (June 1997).

[43] Beth A. Simmons, *Mobilizing for Human Rights: International Law in Domestic Politics* (New York: Cambridge University Press, 2009).

Constructivists argue that the Geneva Conventions are not merely regulative norms that restrict the behavior of states but rather, along with the rise of human rights, are constitutive of a new international normative order created after 1945 that places individuals at its center.[44] The Conventions create a new set of expectations—or norms—about appropriate state action regarding how states treat individuals.

In the constructivist view, law influences state behavior through the process of norm internalization, which may involve mechanisms of socialization, persuasion, and acculturation.[45] Transnational advocacy groups and epistemic communities play a key role in promoting norms and values to states and non-state actors.[46] Government officials, including judges and military lawyers, norm entrepreneurs, and advocacy groups, generate patterns of activity that are internalized into the domestic structures of states, thus eventually creating self-enforcing compliance with the law.[47]

There are two competing constructivist claims about the role of identity as a compliance mechanism for the laws of war. The first is the "standard of civilization" argument, which emphasizes, "it's about who *they* are." Constructivists hold that the Geneva Conventions have become a core element of the "standard of civilization," a script for what constitutes a "civilized state." The laws of war are part of a broader discourse—a set of practices—of the society of states that defines what it means to be a civilized member of the international community. One of the requirements of being a civilized state is participation in the regulation of warfare, which began among European states in the 19th century. Along with other requirements, the laws of war helped define a notion of civilization by which Europeans distinguished between those nations that were members of the civilized world and those outside: "barbarians" or "savages."[48] Only those capable of complying with the rules were considered members of the community of nations and thus entitled to all its privileges and benefits. Others, the "uncivilized," were ostracized, and the restraints of the laws of war could be dispensed with in any battle against the barbarians.[49]

[44] Sonia Cardenas, "The Geneva Conventions and the Normative Tenor of International Relations," in *The Geneva Conventions under Assault*, ed. Sarah Perrigo and Jim Whitman (London: Pluto Press, 2010); Ruti Teitel, *Humanity's Law* (New York: Oxford University Press, 2011).

[45] Ryan Goodman and Derek Jinks, "International Law and State Socialization: Conceptual, Empirical and Normative Challenges," *Duke Journal of International Law* 54, 983 (2004–2005).

[46] Margaret Keck and Katherine Sikkink, *Activists beyond Borders: Advocacy Networks in International Politics* (Ithaca, NY: Cornell University Press, 1998).

[47] Koh, "Why Do Nations Obey International Law?"

[48] Gerrit Gong, *The Standard of Civilization in International Society* (Oxford: Clarendon, 1984).

[49] For evidence, see Howard et al., *The Laws of War*.

Thus at one level the standard of civilization is a set of regulative norms governing warfare. At the same time, compliance with these norms helps define the collective identities of actors in the system: the "civilized" and the "uncivilized." This perspective would predict that adversaries who perceive the other as "uncivilized" would fight with less restraint and more brutality, whereas adversaries who perceive each other as cultural equals in some sense would be more restrained in battle. Scholars have found evidence for this dynamic in the wars between colonists and natives in Colonial America and elsewhere, where Europeans conducted much less restrained wars than when fighting other Europeans. The barbarity of the conduct of the World Wars in Europe and Asia, however, called the civilizational explanation of restraint into doubt, because atrocities were committed on all sides, including against people who were members of the same ostensibly civilized society.

The contemporary war on terror has revived elements of this "civilization" discourse, where beliefs are often widespread that "terrorists" and "rebels" who intentionally flout the laws of war are undeserving of legal protections. The Bush administration's justification for employing "cruel, inhuman, and degrading treatment" against members of Al Qaeda turned on the fact that these individuals were foreign nationals held abroad but also that they had, in the words of Secretary of Defense Donald Rumsfeld, "declared war on civilization." According to the administration, the United States could do it to "them" because "they" are different from "us."

A competing identity mechanism of compliance with the laws of war makes the opposite claim: that it is about *who we are* rather than who they are. In this view, compliance with international law is the result of processes of socialization, internalization, and acculturation; complying with the laws of war becomes part of a state's identity. This mechanism would predict that states would comply with the laws of war even in the face of violations by the adversary. This mechanism was captured by Arizona Senator John McCain's famous statement in November 2005 to the US Senate arguing why the United States should not engage in torture: "It's not about who they are. It's about who we are." McCain was defending his amendment to a defense appropriations bill that would bar US officials from inflicting "cruel, inhuman, and degrading treatment" on detainees in the war on terror. Terrorists are "the quintessence of evil," he said. "But it's not about them; it's about us. This battle we're in is about the things we stand for and believe in and practice. And that is an observance of human rights, no matter how terrible our adversaries may be."[50] In November 2011, US President Barack Obama, responding to a question about waterboarding, echoed such

[50] Foster Klug, "McCain: Torture Ban Protects U.S. Image," Associated Press, November 14, 2005.

views. "Waterboarding is torture," he said. "It's contrary to America's traditions. It's contrary to our ideals. That's not who we are. That's not how we operate. We don't need it in order to prosecute the war on terrorism. And we did the right thing by ending that practice."[51]

Critical Theory

Finally, for critical theorists, the primary effect of the laws of war is to legitimize military violence. Critical theorists focus on the role of law in practices of power and domination. In their view, the laws of war "have been formulated deliberately to privilege military necessity at the cost of humanitarian values." According to Chris af Jochnick and Roger Normand, "the laws of war impose no substantive restraints on pre-existing customary military practices," but rather mainly serve to legitimize war as a practice.[52] Thus critics charge that "military necessity," rather than serving as any kind of limiting condition on the use of force, is instead an endlessly flexible concept, which many commanders simply interpret as mere "utility"—anything useful or advantageous in war. A more subtle line of argument holds that the humanitarian law corpus provides a framework for "an economy of violence," in which the calculation, balancing, and application of military violence takes place. Within this framework of balancing and calculation, almost any military practice can be defended as a "lesser evil" than some other undesirable outcome.[53] Further, the categories of "civilian" and "combatant" on which IHL rests are productions of power, not inherent categories, and thus reflect the interests of states that can maintain professional standing armies.[54]

In short, by promoting the illusion that war can be fought humanely, the laws of war make it easier to launch a war and to justify the violence of war to oneself and others. The practice of humanitarian intervention epitomizes this situation, critical theorists argue. By providing a justification for violating state sovereignty, humanitarian intervention often creates worse outcomes for civilians.[55]

[51] CBS News, "John McCain Hits GOP Hopefuls over Waterboarding," November 14, 2011.

[52] Chris af Jochnick and Roger Normand, "The Legitimation of Violence: A Critical History of the Laws of War," *Harvard International Law Journal* 35, no. 49 (Winter 1994).

[53] Eyal Weizman, *The Least of All Possible Evils: Humanitarian Violence from Arendt to Gaza* (London: Verso, 2012), p. 13.

[54] Helen M. Kinsella, *The Image before the Weapon: A Critical History of the Distinction between Combatant and Civilian* (Ithaca, NY: Cornell University Press, 2011).

[55] Mahmood Mamdani, "The New Humanitarian Order," *The Nation*, September 29, 2008.

One problem with the radical critical view is that its deep pessimism about the laws of war makes it unclear what one should do about the situation. Should we simply let war be as destructive as possible so people will do away with it? This does not seem a tenable approach. Further, the critical perspective also overlooks that the laws of war have changed over time. For example, while Jochnick and Normand's claim that the laws of war basically codified customary law is true with respect to the early Hague conventions, the 1949 Geneva Conventions banned absolutely practices that had been widespread only a few years earlier during World War II, including most of the traditional tools used by occupying armies to punish civilian resistance (such as reprisals, deportations, taking of hostages, collective punishments, inhuman internment, torture, and the resettling of a belligerent population on occupied territory).[56] Today some military practices are entirely prohibited (such as the use of chemical weapons).

Nevertheless, the critical perspective raises important questions about the permissive nature of key concepts of the laws of war (such as military necessity or collateral damage). It also reminds us that notions of "legitimate violence" are often shaped by power.

Explaining Compliance

We draw on these theoretical perspectives to provide a framework for analyzing how the laws of war matter in specific cases. It is useful to distinguish among three concepts: compliance, effectiveness, and effects. *Compliance* is the degree of conformity between the requirements of treaty, law, or rule and the behavior of those subject to the requirements. *Effectiveness* refers to the efficacy of a given rule or rules to solve the political problem that it is intended to address. Even with perfect compliance, for example, some rules could simply be ineffective.

Finally, the notion of *effects* refers to the broader consequences of a law, treaty, or regime that goes well beyond simply the notion of compliance. Effects are much broader, and can be more diffuse and indirect than simply behavioral compliance with the rules. Here we can think in terms of *regulative, constitutive,* and *permissive* effects. In this section I consider the issue of compliance and in the next section I turn to effectiveness and effects.

Determining what counts as compliance is often the subject of significant dispute. Efforts to assess compliance with specific laws face difficulties in specifying

[56] Karma Nabulsi, "Evolving Conceptions of Civilians and Belligerents: One Hundred Years after the Hague Peace Conferences," in Chesterman, *Civilians in War*, pp. 19–20.

measurements and gathering accurate data. Nevertheless, the actors themselves, including humanitarian NGOs, international organizations, and states regularly make pronouncements about compliance and produce reports full of assessments about compliance with the laws of war.

Compliance is not simply a matter of matching observed behavior to a stable rule, however. Rather, the key starting point is interpretation. Compliance is a political act—a matter of interpretation by political actors. Legal rules are always subject to interpretation. Whether others accept one's claims of "compliance" in a specific instance is a political, not simply legal, decision. As legal scholars argue, "legal agents bargain in the shadow of the law." Further, international law compliance may engage a wide range of actors.[57]

Compliance is, in other words, a process of social construction. Sociologists of law have analyzed the social construction of law within organizations. Organizations interpret, mediate, construct, and ultimately shape the meaning of the law. This is especially true when the terms of the law are vague. As Lauren Edelman and Shauhin Talesh argue, "The nature of organizational compliance is best illustrated not by a compliance versus noncompliance dichotomy, but rather by a processual model in which organizations construct the meaning of both compliance and the law."[58]

With regard to Geneva Conventions, this approach would focus on the military (or a peacekeeping force or private military contractors) as an organization—including its organizational culture and interests—and how it constructs compliance with the laws of war. Here the sociologists' notion of *symbolic* or *ritual compliance* may capture an important dynamic. This refers to the development of organizational institutions and practices that seem like efforts to comply but in the end may have little effect on the actual outcome.[59] The efforts, in other words, are more symbolic than substantive. An example of symbolic compliance would be the Israeli military's practice of dropping leaflets during the 2009 Gaza War to warn Palestinian civilians to flee. It seemed like an act of compliance with the laws of war—and was presented as such by the Israeli Defense Forces—but it was actually largely meaningless when the Gaza borders were blocked and civilians had nowhere to flee.

[57] Robert Howse and Ruti Teitel, "Beyond Compliance: Rethinking How International Law Really Matters," *Global Policy* 1, no. 10 (May 2010): 127–135.

[58] Lauren B. Edelman and Shauhin A. Talesh, "To Comply or Not to Comply—That Isn't the Question: How Organizations Construct the Meaning of Compliance," in *Explaining Compliance: Business Responses to Regulation*, ed. Christine Parker and Vibeke Lehmann Nielsen (Cheltenham, UK: Edward Elgar, 2011), p. 103.

[59] Lauren B. Edelman, "Legal Ambiguity and Symbolic Structures: Organizational Mediation of Civil Rights Law," *American Journal of Sociology* (1992).

Mechanisms of Compliance

From the review of the theoretical literature, we can summarize several mechanisms of compliance: coercion, reciprocity, internalization, socialization, and persuasion. In the case of *coercion*, threats and material incentives largely drive the upholding of IHL. The classic example is carrots and sticks wielded by great powers. This argument says nothing about whether the norms are internalized by the actor. In this situation one can get behavioral compliance with a rule without internalization (e.g., external pressure on a government to arrest war crimes suspects and hold trials). *Reciprocity*—the rationalist mechanism of compliance—emphasizes the prospect of reciprocal treatment of ones' soldiers or civilians on the battlefield. The laws of war tend to erode (or be violated) in circumstances where one side lacks the ability to reciprocate or the laws end up favoring one side.[60] But even reciprocity does not seem to be all that powerful a motivating restraint for many kinds of conflicts. Consider civil wars, for example, where the prospect of reciprocal treatment does not seem to work very well as a restraint.

These first two mechanisms are instrumental forms of compliance. They operate on the basis of narrowly defined self-interest and external incentives (punishment or rewards). While they may promote behavior consistent with a rule, they do not involve any deep or internalized belief about the intrinsic value of the laws themselves. In contrast, compliance may result from processes of *internalization*, where norms become deeply held values and become institutionalized in domestic institutions and practices. Harold Koh has offered a model of norm internalization in which international law does not become domestic law simply by means of a formal act of legislation. Rather, it is a collective effort involving both transnational and domestic political actors. It is through a social and political process on the part of politicians, judges, civil society, public opinion, and, increasingly, scrutiny by international organizations and transnational NGOs that international law becomes part of domestic discourse and organizational practice. The iterative process of gradual norm internalization, through political and social action, reconstitutes the interests and identities of the participants. In short, state identities change through the internalization of norms.[61]

Applying this approach to the Geneva Conventions, we would look for evidence of the process by which the laws of war become part of national legislation and of a nation's military law, soldiers are trained in IHL, and a real effort is made to implement them on the battlefield in the event of an armed conflict. Further, we would want to see evidence of an enforcement and accountability process in the event of a violation of the Conventions. Finally, we would want to see

[60] Posner, "Reciprocity," p. 5.

[61] Harold Koh, "Why Do Nations Obey International Law?" p. 2646.

evidence that adherence to the laws of war has become part of a state's identity, that is, that decision-makers express a need to be viewed as acting in accord with ethical beliefs widely held within the state or with internationally agreed norms.

Internalization may come about through processes of socialization and persuasion. *Socialization* may take several forms. Scholars of the world policy school of sociology hold that the international state system is a social system that contains "scripts" for what it means to be a modern, civilized state. Social pressures impel actors to adopt these scripts—socially legitimated attitudes, beliefs, and behaviors. The evidence for this mechanism is when states adopt a policy or practice without there being a particular domestic task or constituency for it. International socialization may also be accomplished through state emulation of other successful states, which are praised for conforming to prevailing norms or condemned for deviating from them. Arguments from social psychology suggest that states adopt norms with an eye to a reference group: they may comply with the norms but without internalizing them (though internalization may follow later). These kinds of socialization mechanisms may help to explain the universal ratification of the Geneva Conventions, even by states that demonstrate little domestic capacity or interest to actually comply with the rules on the battlefield. It may also help to explain partial internalization of norms.

Finally, *persuasion* refers to a process by which actors become convinced of the truth, validity, or appropriateness of norms. This is an argument about social or individual learning. It involves not simply superficial adoption of a norm or behavioral conformity, but rather internal acceptance of the substantive value of the norm.[62]

Following Koh, we can thus think of a spectrum of compliance ranging from (1) coincidence, or matching by chance; to (2) conformity, or matching only when convenient and with little sense of obligation; to (3) compliance, matching to gain incentives or avoid punishment; to (4) internalization, that is, matching due to an actor's internal acceptance of the norm as part of its value system.[63]

In this volume, we are especially interested in the links between compliance and internalization, and assessing degrees of internalization. This is especially important in light of the recent experiences of the United States in the war on terror—where norms such as the prohibition on torture turned out to be less deeply internalized in US domestic institutions than we had assumed. How do norms become internalized in the domestic practices and institutions of a state or a nonstate actor in specific cases? How easily can they unravel under pressure? It is worth noting that the ICRC itself seeks only behavioral compliance with

[62] Martha Finnemore and Kathryn Sikkink, "International Norms Dynamics and Political Change," *International Organization* (1998).

[63] Koh, "Why Do Nations Obey International Law?" pp. 2600–2601, n.3.

the laws of war, not internalization.[64] Nevertheless, we are interested in looking at how processes of compliance and internalization work in concrete cases, how they may fail to work, and how they get undone.

Beyond Compliance: Explaining Effects and Effectiveness

In addition to compliance, we are also interested in the broader effects of the Geneva Conventions. Law is not simply a set of rules, it is a process for resolving social conflicts. The impact of the law cannot be measured purely by compliance but also by how legal requirements shift normative expectations. The laws of war serve as a framework for moral contestation and debate about ends and means. For example, international law may shift in whole or in part decision-making, interpretative, and/or legitimating power from one set of elite actors to another (e.g., from diplomats, foreign policy analysts, and military planners to legal professionals such as judges, lawyers, and law professors).[65] Our chapters suggest that in the domain of humanitarian law, the rise of the profession of military lawyers, especially after the Vietnam War, has had significant effect in promoting compliance with the laws of war.

With respect to the actual effectiveness of the regime in protecting noncombatants, the evidence suggests that the Geneva regime has indeed influenced the way at least some states and some nonstate actors fight wars, and thereby has contributed to saving civilian lives. The modern laws of war have had a very palpable impact on the shape of war over the past century, both in terms of the conduct of combatants in conflict and the fact that war crimes law was still applied through the post–World War II period through national courts and military tribunals. Specifically, the most fundamental effect of the regime has been on discourse and identity. The regime provides the moral framework and categories in which the obligations of states during war are discussed, justified, and assessed. Both state practice and policymakers' discourse—as reflected, for example, in debates over the abuses of the Saddam Hussein regime and US practices with regard to prisoners from the war on terror—indicate that, for the international community today, the Geneva Conventions provide the relevant framework—even if acknowledged in the breach—about the proper way to fight war.

[64] Steven R. Ratner, "Persuading to Comply: On the Deployment and Avoidance of Legal Argumentation," in *Interdisciplinary Perspectives on International Law and International Relations: The State of the Art*, ed. J. L. Dunoff and M. A. Pollock (New York: Cambridge University Press, 2013).

[65] Howse and Teitel, "Beyond Compliance," p. 130.

At the same time, the Geneva principles have become part of the discourse of the "standard of civilization" by which states justify their identity as "civilized" members of the international community. To put it in more conceptual terms, the regulative effect of the Geneva rules is to constrain how militaries fight wars and to reduce state violence. The constitutive effects are to constitute identities of civilized states and the practice of "civilized war."

At the same time, the regime has produced a series of side effects and some unintended consequences. First, it has given rise to scores of humanitarian actors and aid and relief organizations that now compete in the "business" of humanitarianism. Second, it can confer political standing on insurgent groups that agree to observe humanitarian rules in a conflict, thereby influencing the politics of the conflict (something from which humanitarianism is supposed to remain aloof). Third, the most significant effect, perhaps, is that it has helped to legitimize war on behalf of humanitarian ends, an ironic outcome for a movement based on the belief that war is horrible. These are important constitutive effects of the Geneva regime.

In addition to the regulative and constitutive effects, the Geneva regime has also given rise to "permissive" effects—the unintended consequences of the operation of a norm.[66] The most prominent permissive effects are the notions of "military necessity" and "collateral damage." Under the guise of such concepts, military actors can potentially inflict large numbers of civilian casualties while in principle remaining within the letter of the law.

We examine both the effects and effectiveness of the Geneva Conventions. We ask, What effects does the Geneva Conventions regime have? How does it bring about these effects, and under what circumstances does it do so? A central question is effectiveness—whether the regime achieves its desired goal of restraining the violence of states and protecting noncombatants. Has the Geneva regime influenced behavioral outcomes in a systematic way? There are many challenges to examining compliance and beyond, and we do not claim that it is an easy task or that we will get it exactly right. But it is an important one.

Research Design and Plan of the Book

The rest of the volume consists, first, of an overview of the evolution of the Geneva Conventions following World War II. It then provides a close examination of a number of countries, particularly those that have faced the most

[66] See Nina Tannenwald, *The Nuclear Taboo* (New York: Cambridge University Press, 2007), pp. 46–47.

challenging circumstances, in order to explore the conditions under which the Geneva constraints succeeded or failed. Countries confronting the threat of terrorism or guerrilla insurgencies are especially worth studying. But so are armies engaged in peacekeeping operations or "humanitarian interventions" that face unexpected armed resistance. Do the armed forces show restraint and make an extra effort to protect the civilians whose interests they are supposed to serve? Or do they put a priority on protecting themselves, given that placing soldiers in harm's way for altruistic motives, when there is no clear national interest, might not play well at home? The latter mode of thinking, evident in NATO's intervention in Kosovo, for example, led to high-altitude bombing (to protect pilots) with extensive damage to civilian infrastructure and a worsening of the plight of refugees and peaceful citizens.

In addition to considering different types of *armed conflict*, the volume examines a range of types of *countries*, varied by size, by region of the world, and by distance from the traditions of European warfare that formed the basis of contemporary laws of war. In all of these cases a central question is to what extent, and under what conditions, symbolic or "ritual" compliance with the Geneva Conventions (for example, incorporation into military manuals and military training) translates into actual compliance on the battlefield.

Many of the volume's chapters covering different types of armed conflicts and types of countries examine the behavior not only of state armies but also of armed nonstate actors: guerrilla insurgents and terrorists, most prominently. Two other categories of nonstate actors raise particular issues of relevance to the laws of war and come in for detailed discussion in chapters of their own: peacekeeping forces and private security contractors. The volume is thus organized into three major sections, following the background chapter on the development of the Geneva Conventions: (1) three chapters are devoted to the behavior and practice of the United States, a superpower whose postwar major military engagements cover the entire period from the signing of the Geneva Conventions to the present (with wars in Korea, Vietnam, Afghanistan, and Iraq); (2) five chapters cover a selected set of other countries that have been involved in military conflicts that pose significant challenges to the application of the Geneva Conventions (France in Algeria, Russia in Chechnya, the wars of Yugoslav secession, Israel in the Occupied Territories, and Iran); and, finally, (3) a chapter each is devoted to peacekeeping forces and private military companies. While no volume can be entirely comprehensive, this set of cases illuminates how the Geneva Conventions have operated in a variety of military contexts and with regard to a variety of actors.

This set of in-depth case studies engages in process tracing on how the Geneva Conventions came to be adopted and internalized (or not) in each country, and how and whether their principles were actually reflected in the state's military practice in concrete instances. The authors were asked to address a uniform set of questions about their case, as well as issues unique to each case. The chapters on nonstate actors identify the numerous difficulties in applying the Geneva Conventions to actors hardly imagined at the time the original treaties were designed, but who play increasingly prominent roles in contemporary conflicts.

Our authors take a relatively broad approach to the Geneva Conventions and in some cases treat them as shorthand for a general conception of international humanitarian law. This move has both theoretical and empirical grounding. Our goal is to take a broad, social science, rather than a formally legal, approach to assessing the influence of the laws of war. The approach of the study is thus not a legalistic one of specifying particular provisions of the Geneva Conventions and evaluating article by article which states comply with which provisions and how. Rather, we seek to analyze international humanitarian law more broadly conceived and consider how it influences state behavior across a range of possibilities, only one of which is strict compliance with the letter of the law.

The Geneva Conventions in part codify long-standing customary international law and have come to symbolize humane behavior on the battlefield, with effects that are not tightly connected to actors' precise knowledge of specific provisions. Thus, depending on the analysis, in some cases it will be appropriate and necessary for authors to specify certain provisions of the Geneva Conventions. In other cases, however, our authors do not parse chapter and verse of the law but rather treat the Geneva Conventions as a moral idea that may have spillover effects on actor behavior beyond the strict letter of the law. As an empirical matter, most of the actors on the battlefield cannot parse the law, and our research suggests that actors themselves, including the ICRC, often treat the Conventions as a stand-in for a general conception of humane behavior on the battlefield.

To set the stage for the case studies, in chapter 2, Giovanni Mantilla surveys the negotiating history, and subsequent development, of the Geneva Conventions and Additional Protocols. He traces the influence of the Cold War context on the Conventions and explains why the treaties look the way they do. He also reviews the practice of states with regard to the Conventions, including the pattern of formal adhesion by the states parties to the treaties and measures to incorporate the laws into domestic practice.

In chapter 3, Sahr Conway-Lanz considers the role of the Conventions in the Korean War. The Korean War broke out in 1950, less than a year after the drafting of the 1949 Conventions, and ended in a stalemate in 1953, just over two years *before* the United States signed and ratified them. To what extent did US practices adhere to the newly codified norms of warfare and to what extent did they diverge? To what degree did the reservations placed on US ratification of the treaties depend on the experience of the Korean War? How did that experience, in turn, influence US behavior in subsequent wars, in Vietnam, in particular?

Can one still identify a legacy of the Korean War experience in current US practice and debates on compliance with the laws of war?

In chapter 4, Gary Solis analyzes US behavior in the Vietnam War. The US armed forces in Vietnam provide a good example of an army under pressure from an irregular guerrilla enemy with extensive support among the civilian population. Historians and journalists—and Solis's own prior work—have produced excellent investigations of war crimes committed on the ground, and the assessment of the legality of the campaign of aerial bombardment is quite extensive. Less systematic attention has been paid to the US troops' training in and adherence to the laws of war, even in the context of guerrilla combat. The genesis of high-level decisions could also use further exploration. According to Prugh's 1975 study, for example, US forces accorded Viet Cong detainees the status of prisoner of war—in effect, adhering to a norm that was yet to be codified into law (with the 1977 Geneva Protocols). This chapter explores the rationale for such decisions and the overall impact of the Vietnam experience on subsequent US military practice.

In chapter 5, Elizabeth Grimm Arsenault addresses the US wars in Iraq and Afghanistan. US compliance with the laws of war in these conflicts appeared to vary with the particular subject matter. Legal specialists assessed the legality of virtually every proposed target, for example, to monitor adherence to norms governing aerial bombardment. In addition, the Rules of Engagement for Iraq emphasized that military force must be highly discriminant to protect civilians and civilian infrastructure. These guidelines nevertheless allowed for dramatic failures. The aerial attacks, siege, and invasion of Fallujah in November 2004, carried out in retaliation for the killing of US private security contractors, were particularly destructive of civilian life and property—not least because the focus of the initial assault was the Fallujah General Hospital.[67] Treatment of detainees posed particular problems, owing in part to the ambiguous status of combatants who did not clearly fit the Geneva requirements for prisoners of war, but also to the belief that conventional restraints should not apply to the exceptional circumstances that obtain in the "global war on terror." US legal experts flagrantly overlooked the minimum standards of treatment guaranteed to all individuals—terrorists and insurgents, included—under Common Article 3.

Despite this erratic pattern of compliance with the Geneva Conventions, the United States increased its sensitivity to both civilian casualties and

[67] Richard W. Miller, "Civilian Deaths and American Power: Three Lessons from Iraq and Afghanistan," in *The American Way of Bombing: Changing Ethical and Legal Norms, from Flying Fortresses to Drones*, ed. Matthew Evangelista and Henry Shue (Ithaca, NY: Cornell University Press, 2014), ch. 8; Neta C. Crawford, *Accountability for Killing: Moral Responsibility for Collateral Damage in America's Post-9/11 Wars* (New York: Oxford University Press, 2013), pp. 288–293.

prisoner treatment as a result of the tactical shift from counterterrorism operations to counterinsurgency operations. The tactical considerations of counterinsurgency—employing restraint to avoid creating more insurgents—rendered humane treatment a central objective of the military missions, even if not always achieved. In this view, compliance with the Geneva Conventions, avoiding excessive force, and treating captured individuals humanely was supposed to challenge Al Qaeda's narrative, to diminish terrorist recruitment, and to lessen the likelihood of producing a new generation of jihadists on the battlefield.

In chapter 6, Raphaëlle Branche analyzes the French army during the Algerian war of independence and in the aftermath. The French Army confronting the anticolonial rebellion in Algeria in the 1950s is a good candidate case for the study of a traditional army engaging a rebellion dependent on guerrilla and terrorist tactics. Two recent developments have led to considerable discussion of this case in France. The first was the open admission by senior military officers of the extent to which torture was a routine technique employed by the French armed forces and police to break the resistance. The second was the revelation of the abuses by US troops at Abu Ghraib and elsewhere that led to considerable soul-searching by the French about their country's own past practices. These events have inspired work by historians, including joint Algerian-French efforts, to unearth relevant information. How could France, which signed the Geneva Conventions in 1949 and ratified them by mid-1951, have so clearly violated their provisions within less than a decade? Have the recent discussions led to a strengthening of the French commitment to the Conventions? Branche addresses these questions, drawing on her extensive archival research in French and Algerian sources. She finds sources of restraint in French military behavior less in the Geneva Conventions themselves than in a commitment to individual responsibility and honor, a relatively recent development linked to French attitudes toward human rights as much as humanitarian law.

Chapter 7 takes up the case of Russia. Its armed suppression of the movement for autonomy in Chechnya offers an important case for exploring the influence and limits of pressure from international institutions for compliance with the laws of war. Post-Soviet Russia became party to a number of international and European human-rights conventions in the early 1990s, but proceeded to violate many of them, along with the Geneva Conventions, in its brutal war against Chechnya later in the 1990s. Subsequent efforts by the international community to persuade the Russian government to adhere to its commitments met with limited success. This chapter, by Mark Kramer, after reviewing the Soviet legacy, details how the Russian government trains its armed forces in the laws of war and why that training has proved inadequate to the task of fighting an insurgency with links to international terrorism. It considers why the Russian government did not declare a "state of emergency" in the course of combating the insurgency in Chechnya—a move that would have made the government less susceptible to charges of violating provisions of the European Convention of Human Rights, which allows for a degree of derogation under such circumstances. In this respect, Russia's practice has become the norm in contemporary antiterrorist operations, in that many governments suspend the normal functioning of law without invoking the (temporary) emergency provisions for doing so that are often provided for in their constitutions and international legal instruments. Kramer's assessment of Russian compliance with the laws of war and its human-rights obligations draws on extensive documentary evidence as well as field work and interviews in Chechnya and in Moscow. Its conclusions are pessimistic indeed.

In chapter 8, Eyal Ben-Ari and Amichai Cohen analyze the case of Israel. Israel has been subject to particular scrutiny in its adherence to the laws of war, both from inside and outside the country. The status of the occupied territories is particularly controversial, in that the Israeli government does not accept the judgment of much of the international legal community on its obligations there. Israel is also unusual in the degree to which its domestic public opinion has engaged the moral and legal arguments about torture of suspected terrorists. The Israeli Supreme Court is unique in the extent to which it has been willing to investigate and judge specific practices of physical and mental coercion during interrogation for compliance with international law. The practice of targeted assassination of suspected organizers of attacks, including suicide bombing, has also come under scrutiny. From outside the country, Israel faced criticism for deployment of cluster munitions and for targeting civilians in its attack against Hezbollah forces in Lebanon, even though Israel did not sign the 2008 convention on cluster munitions. How do the Israeli Defense Forces and Israeli government deal with emerging norms against specific weapons and practices? Do they try to attain a status of "persistent objector" to norms that they argue infringe on Israel's ability to defend itself, or do they gradually move toward compliance?

In chapter 9, Craig Nation analyzes the case of the former Yugoslavia. The Yugoslav National Army, by most accounts, was a highly trained and disciplined force before the country's breakup and descent into civil war. This chapter examines how soldiers came to engage in atrocities and deliberate attacks against civilians and sheds light on the limits of formal training and the circumstances that can lead to abandonment of basic principles of humanitarian law. This case also examines the procedures for inculcating in the successor armies of Bosnia and Croatia, for example, humanitarian norms of warfare and the role that international organizations and other states play in such efforts.

In chapter 10, Anicée Van Engeland analyzes the adherence of Iran to the Geneva Conventions, particularly during the challenging circumstances of the ten-year war between Iran and Iraq. How has Iran understood its commitment both in theory and in practice? How has the Iranian government articulated this commitment and to what degree, if at all, has it actually attempted to comply with the Conventions? Iran signed the Geneva Conventions in 1949 and ratified them in 1957 under the Western-oriented shah. Following the 1979 Islamic revolution, however, Iranian leaders asserted the primacy of Islamic conceptions of humanitarian law. During the Iran-Iraq war, both sides flagrantly violated the Geneva Conventions, and the major powers tended to overlook those violations. How did Iranian leaders justify the violations and their military conduct generally during the war? How did the war influence subsequent Iranian thinking and practice regarding the Geneva Conventions?

Van Engeland argues that Iran's position on humanitarian law has evolved since the end of the conflict with Iran. There is a greater openness to involvement by the ICRC in training and disseminating information about the Geneva Conventions and increased participation by Iranian jurists and academics in international conferences devoted to humanitarian law. Yet the Islamic Republic of Iran still insists that Islamist interpretations of the laws of war supersede IHL. Van Engeland claims that this is not of major concern for the most part, given the degree of overlap between the two bodies of law. But where there are serious discrepancies, she argues for a greater appreciation by the international legal community for the religious sources of humanitarian law and a willingness of Iranian interpreters of Islamic law to favor interpretations that coincide with IHL. Such changes would, in her view, facilitate internalization of humanitarian norms.

Chapter 11 focuses on private military and security companies. The increasing prevalence of private security forces in Iraq and Afghanistan has raised concerns about the rules of engagement under which they operate and about accountability for crimes they might commit. In this chapter, Renée de Nevers lays out the main legal issues and various proposals for bringing such forces into a coherent regulatory regime. She homes in on the question of the private contractors' status—the key to understanding their relationship to the Geneva Conventions. Are private security forces civilians or are they combatants? If the latter, private contractors engaged in hostilities would be designated unlawful combatants, because they do not serve as regular armed forces in a chain of command or in militia units attached to the state's army. They could be targeted by enemy troops during conflict, and, if captured, could be subject to prosecution for unlawful belligerency. Because the current state of international humanitarian law does not accommodate private security forces adequately, much of the effort to regulate their behavior has come in the form of voluntary rules formulated by associations of private security companies in consultation with international organizations and states. De Nevers's chapter concludes by exploring the positive and negative features of this emerging solution.

In chapter 12, Siobhán Wills focuses on peacekeeping forces. The status is similar in some ways to that of private security forces, because under normal circumstances they do not fall under the regime of the Geneva Conventions: Soldiers deployed in multinational peacekeeping forces are expected to keep the peace rather than engage in hostilities and should therefore enjoy the protected status of civilians. With the increasingly volatile situation in postconflict areas, peacekeeping troops have been obliged to use force in self-defense or to engage in offensive action to protect the civilian population. The creation by the United Nations in 2013 of an Intervention Brigade deployed to the Democratic Republic of the Congo put the unit's members in a legal gray area between armed forces that are party to a conflict and neutral peacekeepers who should avoid direct participation in hostilities. Ultimately, Wills advocates "development of a specific regime of international criminal accountability for peacekeepers, applicable regardless of whether or not there is an armed conflict," but she acknowledges "considerable practical as well as political hurdles that would need to be overcome" and little prospect for such an outcome in the foreseeable future.

In the concluding chapter, Matthew Evangelista draws together the findings of the volume. His chapter offers an assessment of the status of the Geneva Conventions as a normative regime and how the regime matters. By and large the country case studies support the intuition that states fighting guerrilla insurgencies and adversaries who rely on terrorist attacks would face challenges in adhering to the laws of war—not least because of the absence of the mechanism of reciprocity that rationalist explanations credit for restraint in warfare. Yet, in some respects, many cases exhibit more compliance than the rationalist accounts would anticipate, and the concluding chapter summarizes the various reasons our authors adduce. In exploring mechanisms of noncompliance as well as compliance, Evangelista finds promising the disaggregation of the process that some of the authors have undertaken—from the top political and military authorities to the individual soldier—and he highlights some of the counterintuitive insights that emerge. Again drawing on the material from the case studies, he analyzes the influence of a number of factors on states' compliance. Contrary to much of the conventional wisdom, he claims that the international system—powerful states and institutions—serves not only as a constraint on human-rights abuses and war crimes but also sometimes as an enabler. The role of courts in the process of socialization and internalization of norms also comes under scrutiny in his conclusions, as he finds on the basis of comparative analysis of the country cases, less influence than one might have expected. Evangelista's chapter concludes with some reflections on the methodological challenges facing scholars who seek to assess the impact of the Geneva Conventions and IHL generally.

Conclusion

This project engages a topic critical to international peace and security: whether laws and norms restraining the use of force matter and under what conditions. The laws of war are one of the few bulwarks, however fragile, against the unrestrained violence of states. It is imperative that we have an accurate understanding of exactly what role these Conventions have played since 1949. Empirically, this volume deepens our understanding of how the Geneva Conventions have influenced, or failed to influence, state behavior in specific instances. Conceptually, it expands our knowledge of the role of norms in restraining state violence, and factors that contribute to compliance with norms. Finally, from a policy perspective, it helps to illuminate the prospects for strengthening normative and institutional constraints on the destructiveness of war in the future, in an effort to protect human rights even in the most extreme circumstance.

2

The Origins and Evolution of the 1949 Geneva Conventions and the 1977 Additional Protocols

GIOVANNI MANTILLA

Why does international humanitarian law (IHL) look the way it does? This chapter traces the development of the 1949 Geneva Conventions from their origins in pre-1949 treaty law through the 1977 Additional Protocols and to the present. I treat IHL as an international regime born out of a contentious mix of interest, values, and emotions grounded in the traumatic episodes leading to its revision. Put otherwise, IHL is an international sociopolitical construct marked by history at different global junctures, in complex but discernible ways.

The first part of the chapter provides a short background of treaty law up to 1949. The sections that follow examine the negotiation of the 1949 Conventions and the Additional Protocols in the 1970s in depth. The concluding remarks reflect on the chapter's general findings and on the recent, post-1977 developments in the field of IHL.

The 19th-Century Origins of International Humanitarian Law

The IHL regime as we know it today evolved over time and in parts, beginning in the mid-19th century. Sometimes called the "Geneva Convention" in singular, the Conventions of 1949 are in reality four distinct agreements that emerged at diverse historical moments. The First Convention was the landmark treaty that inaugurated the trend of codified (or "positive") international law to protect the victims of war. European powers negotiated the First Convention in 1863–1864 after the Battle of Solferino (a bloody conflict during the Italian reunification wars) on the call of the Swiss nongovernmental organization now known as the International Committee of the Red Cross (ICRC), led by the businessman-cum-humanitarian Henry Dunant. That Convention sought mainly to provide for humane treatment of wounded and sick *soldiers* on land, in this sense designating them the original "war victims."[1] The Second Convention, which extended protections to wounded and sick combatants at sea, was adopted in 1899 and then revised in 1907 (both times at The Hague). The Third Convention, dealing with prisoners of war (POWs), was first negotiated in 1929 with World War I as its key precipitating event, although work on it had begun around 1906.[2] The first three conventions protected combatants no longer able to fight—*hors de combat* is the legal term from French—because of their wounds or because they surrendered and became prisoners. Only the Fourth Convention, protecting (as we will see) *certain* types of civilians, may be said to have been "new" in 1949, although formative drafts dated from the 1930s. States' relatively late adoption of treaty rules to safeguard civilians contrasts with current popular perception giving them pride of place under IHL.

Separate from the Geneva-based lineage of law just described stood The Hague Conventions of 1899 and 1907, which deal with multiple aspects of states' conduct while engaged in hostilities with one another, and the use of certain weapons.[3] The Hague Conventions were negotiated largely on the initiative of governments in the second half of the 19th century (notably the Russian Empire and the United States) and had the Netherlands as their official "guardian" state (the equivalent of Switzerland, as the home of the ICRC, for Geneva law).

For nearly a century the Hague Conventions were taken to constitute "the law of war" proper, heeding a lasting (but now outdated) distinction between the regulation of combat practices among combatants and the victim-centered (hence humanitarian) law of Geneva. Notably, whereas Geneva law was revised, updated, or complemented several times since 1864, usually in the aftermath of major war atrocity, for various reasons states managed to resist changes or additions to the Hague Conventions until the 1970s. That decade, as this chapter describes, pressure from nongovernmental advocates and certain governments

[1] For contrasting views on the origins of the First Convention, see Martha Finnemore, "Norms and War: The International Red Cross and the Geneva Conventions," in *National Interests in International Society* (Ithaca, NY: Cornell University Press, 1996); John F. Hutchinson, *Champions of Charity: War and the Rise of the Red Cross* (Boulder, CO: Westview Press, 1996).

[2] For a detailed history of this period, see Pierre Boissier, *From Solferino to Tsushima* (Geneva: Henry Dunant Institute, 1985).

[3] They also contained (brief and underdeveloped, but seminal) references to the respect for non-combatants and prisoners of war, later complemented through the Geneva Conventions.

forced the hand of governmental stalwarts and produced its de facto "merger" with (or semiabsorption by) the humanitarian law of Geneva. Since 1977, the official separation of the two bodies of law has lost much of its traction and become instead a curious historical artifact.

Alongside the Hague and Geneva Conventions, during the pre-1949 period states created additional treaties dealing with specific weapons, such as the 1925 Protocol that bans the use of asphyxiating gases, poison, and bacteriological warfare. Further weapons regulations emerged in early 1980s, a trend that has continued into the 1990s through the present.

The Development of International Humanitarian Law after World War II

The 1949 Geneva Conventions are now virtually universal agreements that all states in the world have ratified. They also constitute international customary law, from which no state can derogate. The 1977 Additional Protocols I and II, having garnered over 170 and 165 ratifications each, are now also widely accepted treaties, and the ICRC and legal scholars argue that large portions of the Protocols also have acquired customary status.[4]

Important levels of contemporary consensus, however, conceal the difficulties that arose at the time of these instruments' making. The purpose of this chapter is to provide a general overview of IHL and its development since World War II. Rather than provide detailed explanations of all of the outcomes of the negotiations, I provide an illustrative genealogy of IHL, highlighting how variation in historical context, legal protagonists, and motivation has shaped this international regime in complex, counterintuitive ways.

Specifically, I outline the major political "cleavages" that emerged during negotiations in the 1940s and 1970s and their impact. In so doing, I focus on three general areas of the law of most interest to the readers of this volume: the protection of combatants and POWs/captured fighters, the protection of noncombatants, and the mechanisms for implementation and enforcement of the law.

[4] Countries such as the United States dispute parts of the Protocols and have not ratified them. Despite this, the United States considers much of the Protocols to be customary law. See Michael J. Matheson, "The United States Position on the Relation of Customary International Law to the 1977 Protocols Additional to the 1949 Geneva Conventions," *American University International Law Review* 2, no. 2 (1987): 419–431.

The 1940s Revisions: The Red Cross Leads the Way

The development of the 1949 Geneva Conventions was driven largely by a nongovernmental "norm entrepreneur," the ICRC, which rallied states around the need to create or improve standards of humane conduct during armed conflict. These ICRC efforts occurred after the unprecedented horrors of World War II, which became an auspicious condition to spark a conversation among governments of very different political persuasions.

With its lived experience of the war, the ICRC began campaigning to revise the Geneva Conventions in early 1945, months before the war's end.[5] It assumed many responsibilities, with states' acquiescence. These included drawing lists of issues to consider, preparing draft language, and organizing formal and informal debates (in public and private) with government delegates and National Societies of the Red Cross and Red Crescent, separately or jointly. Three key preparatory meetings were held in 1946–1948, on which the ICRC disseminated reports (and additional studies) looking to generate consensus on matters big and small. This manner of proceeding allowed the Swiss humanitarian organization to simultaneously assess *and* shape the attitudes of key actors toward ideas for new law, amounting to a powerful (and usually underestimated) mechanism of "socializing" influence.[6]

The project involved in particular updating the three existing Geneva Conventions (on wounded and sick soldiers and sailors, and on POWs) and creating a brand new treaty for civilians. Yet for this to occur a core group of states needed to be brought on board. The ICRC sought initial buy-in from the major powers (the United States, the United Kingdom, the Soviet Union, China, and France), without which it knew the project of legal revamping might not fly.

Luckily, most great powers responded enthusiastically. The United States expressed readiness, since internally the Department of the Army was already conducting a review of the POW Convention's performance in order to identify areas for improvement.[7] The French were keen to take advantage of the

[5] For an expanded discussion of the ICRC's leading role behind the 1940 revisions, see Catherine Rey-Schyrr, *De Yalta à Dien Bien Phu: Histoire du Comité International de La Croix-Rouge, 1945–1955* (Geneve: Georg Editeur, 2007), 237–288.

[6] In practice the ICRC becomes indispensable to states at the same time that it wields major influence over the draft law. The success of this practice lies in the ICRC's subtle political prowess of sustaining an image of independence and neutrality. This ability, and the important tensions it presupposes, are well explained in David P. Forsythe, *The Humanitarians: The International Committee of the Red Cross* (Cambridge: Cambridge University Press, 2005).

[7] R. McDonald Gray, Colonel, GSC, to General Paul, January 1947. Report: "Revision of Geneva Conventions Relating to Prisoners of War," in "Gray's Reports," Administrative Division, Mail and Records Branch, Geneva Convention, 1946–1949, Record Group 389 (Records of the Office of the Provost Marshall General), Entry 437, Box 670, US National Archives at College Park, College Park, MD (NACP hereafter.)

psychological impact of a painful war experience that they feared might soon recede to develop new and improved international legal protections for civilians, POWs, and more controversially, resistance movements.[8] The British were more skeptical at first, and while accepting the ICRC request, they demanded that states' collective energies should first focus on remaking the Conventions to benefit the *military* wounded, sick, and captured, and to leave civilian protections for later.[9] Precedence, they thought, should be given to those fighting on the frontlines. Although the USSR was unresponsive for years out of deep hostility toward the ICRC over an allegedly lackluster performance and anti-Communist bias during the Spanish Civil War (and toward Soviet POWs during World War II), it eventually made a momentous appearance at the treaty-making Diplomatic Conference in 1949. China seemed to come on board without much hassle. After securing great power involvement, the ICRC summoned sixteen states to the 1947 meeting of government experts. By 1948 participation was open to all member states and societies of the International Red Cross Conference (56 attended), and in 1949 almost the entirety of the states (63) existing at the time flocked to the Diplomatic Conference.[10]

A few nations from Africa and Asia participated in 1949, but at this time the newly decolonized states from these regions were few (e.g., India, Pakistan, Lebanon, and Burma). As a result, unlike later revisions in the 1970s, in the 1940s the making of the law largely rested on the shoulders of the United States and Western and Eastern Europe (including the Soviet Bloc), with some role for Arab countries such as Egypt.

The 1940s Revisions: The Substance

The revision of the three Geneva Conventions and the creation of a new one for civilians in 1949 were momentous. The process was often acrimonious, and most of its crucial outcomes intensely hard-fought due to the different views states (or groups of states) held over how far humanitarian law should temper state

[8] Note "Prochaines Conférences en vue de la révision des Conventions de Genève," Direction des Unions Internationales, Ministère des Affaires Étrangères, République Française, May 24, 1947, in folder labeled "Revision des Conventions de Genève," in Unions Internationales, Periode 1944–1964, Box 159, National Diplomatic Archives of France, La Courneuve.

[9] The National Archives of the United Kingdom (TNA hereinafter), PRO FO 369/3592/K17349. Therefore, contrary to common belief, support for the idea of issuing new international law to protect civilians during war after the Holocaust was not unquestioned even in the West.

[10] The gradual convocation raises potential critiques of "preferential treatment" given by the ICRC to certain countries. Although at a general level this seems a valid criticism, I see the practice as an uneasy, pragmatic balance between the organization's need to garner necessary "buy-in" from powerful gatekeepers in order to increase the success of the revisions process.

sovereignty and military necessity. Despite important ICRC influence throughout, it was states that ultimately shaped the terms of the negotiated law. States' motivations and interaction, determinative of the Conventions' substance, can be explained as a mix of self-interest, emotion, and concern for morality and legitimacy.

The level of controversy varied across the four agreements. By the late 1940s the First and Second Conventions (protecting the wounded and sick on land and sea, respectively) were several decades old and had undergone various rounds of renewal. Therefore, although time-consuming and important, their 1940s revision did not elicit extreme tensions. Gaps and problems had been identified, but most changes were seen as "technical" improvements lacking in political connotation. Major changes introduced in 1949 related to better guarantees for persons attached to the military, such as medics and chaplains. Increased respect for merchant vessels and their crews was also inserted in the revised law, as were regulation on the markings and protection of then-new technologies such as medical aircraft.[11]

Bigger clashes awaited elsewhere. Reconstructing the POW (or Third) Convention produced intense quarreling. States debated a plethora of modifications after the harrowing experience of the recent war, including specifying the types of work prisoners could be required to perform, clarifying the duration of their status and treatment during transfer/repatriation after the end of hostilities, and deciding whether they forfeited humane treatment due to allegations of crimes committed prior to capture.

Of all of the proposed changes to the Third Convention, perhaps the most contentious was the extension of POW status and protection to so-called partisans, that is, members of organized resistance groups fighting against foreign occupation. The controversy around partisans illustrates one of the two major political cleavages that emerged during the 1940s revisions, namely the chasm between the "Liberated" (France and others in Western Europe, along with Eastern European countries) and "Liberator" countries (the United States and the UK, in particular). While the former group—given its traumatic experience of occupation—were resolved (or at least reasonably inclined) to introduce humanitarian protections that modified traditional doctrines of state sovereignty and military necessity, the latter were far less so. Yet securing humanitarian treatment for partisan groups was essential for France as well as the Eastern

[11] I cannot devote proper attention to these important issues, but recommend Raymond T. Yingling and Robert W. Ginnane, "The Geneva Conventions of 1949," *American Journal of International Law* 46, no. 3 (1952): 393–427; Jean S. Pictet, "The New Geneva Conventions for the Protection of War Victims," *American Journal of International Law* 45, no. 3 (1951): 462–475; G. I. A. D. Draper, *The Red Cross Conventions* (New York: Praeger, 1958).

European countries, whose partisans had suffered gruesome repression in Nazi hands and were considered heroes. The voice of the "Liberated" resonated strongly in Geneva, not least because former resistors now sat in positions of power, including in the French team studying revisions to the law.

The Americans and the British felt differently. These states hesitated to grant POW protections and a veneer of legitimacy to partisans (whom they viewed as guerrilla fighters) without introducing strict requirements, including the control of some portion of territory. The Liberated countries pushed back insistently against any restrictive conditions, finding them both unsympathetic (given their own experience) and unrealistic (since partisans were bound to emerge whether occupiers wanted it or not, necessitating regulation).

Although the United States and the UK were hardly of one mind across the entire range of issues, both resented the allegedly "naïve" and "sentimental" attitude of their traumatized, war-fearing European peers. They sharply criticized the "Liberated" countries in private for showing an "extreme tendency" to rely on international law "as a means of eliminating evil from the minds of men."[12] As a 1947 US secret report acidly put it, the formerly occupied countries seemed so bent on tying the hands of future occupiers and adding humanitarian guarantees to the revised POW Convention that, "relatively speaking, next time they [the Liberated] wanted to be sitting on satin cushions and fed peaches and cream."[13]

The divide between Liberators and Liberated permeated many other aspects of the negotiations. Yet interestingly, the great powers did not get their way on the partisans issue. Despite being terribly annoying to the American and British, the persistent, emotion-laden attitude of the Liberated countries often proved effective, and the Third Convention was revised to include protections for resistance movements in international conflict, without the requirement of territorial control the UK and United States desired.

The power of the Liberated countries lay not only in their ability to find allies/sympathizers and wield numerical majorities (although this seemed to be a necessary condition). The firsthand testimony they brought to the table relied on extraordinary moral authority that was hard for their more powerful peers to brush off completely. Tellingly, American and British confidential reports contain arguments that their delegates could not make in public without looking bad. Chief among them was the suggestion that through their enthusiastic legal humanitarianism, these European countries were actually acting against Western interests (and in the case of France, against its own interest). In other

[12] Report on the 1947 ICRC Conference, by Albert E. Clattenburg Jr., Chairman of the United States Delegation, to the Secretary of State, August 26, 1947, Central Decimal File 1945–1949, 514.2 Geneva, RG 59, Box 2386, NACP.

[13] Ibid.

words, while the United States and the UK saw themselves as potential future *occupiers*, and therefore wanted to preserve the legal advantage granted to occupiers, France and the Eastern Europeans wore on their sleeves the scars of past and future *victims* of occupation, and thus fought to enhance protection for resistance movements.

These positions and outcomes discredit claims that states negotiate humanitarian (or any other) conventions "behind a veil of ignorance over future war."[14] Instead, diverse groups of states adopted positions based on their experiences in past wars as well as differing expectations of whom they may be fighting in future conflicts.

Early Cold War tensions provided the second "cleavage" that influenced the 1940s revisions. Although some states behind the Iron Curtain attended the preparatory meetings, the Soviet Union itself refused participation until a week and a half before the Diplomatic Conference in April 1949. This attitude produced much anxiety in the West, especially among the French, who (unlike the Americans and British) were convinced that the absence of the USSR would imperil the consensus behind the Conventions. Upon arriving in Geneva in mid-April 1949, however, Soviet diplomats displayed attitudes that defied any predictions: Instead of sabotaging the proceedings, USSR delegates were articulate, well prepared, and even cooperative. Other delegates were surprised, but the British predicted, "the honeymoon cannot last."[15]

And so it was. The Soviets had come to Geneva determined to pose as beacons of "extreme" humanitarianism. Their goal, as it soon became clear in various other international forums, was to shame Western countries strategically through inflated rhetoric and the (likely insincere) support of demanding international standards. In this way the Soviets and their Eastern bloc allies aimed to embarrass the West, especially the United States and the UK, by highlighting the inconsistency between their professed liberal-democratic worldview and their conservative stance toward progressive international law.[16]

If successful, the concrete benefits of this strategy for the Soviets would go beyond mere shaming. One the one hand, it could generate moral credit potentially fungible into political capital in the global struggle for "hearts and minds." On the other, it stood a chance of forcing the West to accept stringently binding

[14] As proposed in James D. Morrow, "The Laws of War, Common Conjectures, and Legal Systems in International Politics," *Journal of Legal Studies* 31, no. 1 (2002): 541–560.

[15] Robert Craigie, Head Delegate of the United Kingdom Delegation to the Diplomatic Conference, Despatch (*sic*) No. 1, May 4, 1949, to Ernest Bevin, Secretary of State for Foreign Affairs, Foreign Office, London, TNA PRO FO 369/4149/K4590.

[16] Ilya Gaiduk, *Divided Together: The United States and the Soviet Union in the United Nations, 1945–1965* (Stanford, CA: Stanford University Press, 2013), 248.

international standards of restraint in war, which could in turn translate into battlefield advantage for the USSR.

Assessing these suspicions vis-à-vis the Soviet position in 1949 will require future research in Russian archives, but historians studying the ideological competition between the Soviet Union and the West have noted just how important the "scramble" for political allegiance was for both sides during the early Cold War.[17] Cold War politicking is thus fundamental for understanding the shape of the 1949 Conventions. The fact that Soviet diplomats' "humanitarian" stance was probably a political ploy should not distract from its actual effects in advancing IHL in progressive ways, however. This is well illustrated by what was perhaps the most radical breakthrough of this episode of revisions: the extension of the Geneva Conventions, for the first time ever, to internal conflicts or "armed conflicts not of an international character," as they came to be known.

The Extension of International Humanitarian Law to Internal Conflicts

The omission of internal conflict under the law of war had been obvious for decades, but in the aftermath of the bloodbath of the Spanish Civil War, the ICRC and various National Red Cross Societies were determined to address this gap in the law.[18] Luckily, despite the delicate nature of this issue, in the 1940s a host of states (beginning with Norway in 1946–1947) seemed willing to consider it, enough for it to become a subject of heated debate since the early preparatory meetings.

When the Diplomatic Conference opened in 1949 the negotiating states were faced with a particularly ambitious draft text (the product of a two-year preliminary discussion between governments, the ICRC and National Red Cross Societies) that proposed to apply the *entire* text of the four Conventions, in all their complexity, to internal conflicts. The ICRC and various countries including Switzerland and Norway strongly supported this version, yet the idea utterly displeased great powers such as the United States, the UK, and France as well as wartorn China and Greece. The skeptical argument was, in short, that without stiff safeguards that assured rebel commitment and compliance with the rules of war, the application of the Conventions to internal war was a "step in the dark," and something of a "fantastical" idea.[19] An equally important corollary of

[17] Robert J. McMahon, ed., *The Cold War in the Third World* (New York: Oxford University Press, 2013), 3.

[18] For the full story of the development of IHL for internal conflicts, see: Giovanni Mantilla, "Under (Social) Pressure: The Historical Regulation of Internal Armed Conflicts through International Law" (PhD Diss., University of Minnesota, 2013).

[19] TNA: PRO FO 369/4142/K406.

this concern was the fact that introducing new law on internal conflicts might legitimize current rebels and empower future ones, something that struck the British and the French as plainly self-defeating.[20]

At the turn of the decade, the British and French were troubled by a specific concern: rebellion in their colonies. The UK already faced troubles in Malaya, as did the Dutch in Indonesia and the French in Morocco and Tunisia. If rebels and their supporting communities benefited from the protection of international law, this might have some real and uncomfortable consequences for colonial powers. Likewise for Greece and China, which faced communist uprisings, and for the United States, which sympathized with its European imperial allies and actively worked to repel communism in Greece. The British were especially mortified to see that the idea had acquired an important degree of political and moral support.[21]

After a careful consideration of risks and benefits, the various opponents of the idea came to the 1949 Conference ready to either tighten the language (the United States and France) or to nix it altogether (Britain). But as expected, they met resistance. On the "pro-change" side stood a vocal group, formed mainly by Scandinavian countries and Switzerland, alongside a few Latin Americans (Mexico and Uruguay). These states showed few qualms about offering unilateral guarantees of good treatment to captured rebels, claiming that "some of them may have a reputable character," presumably those fighting in the name of democracy.

Although influential, the "pro-change" alliance lacked the votes needed to cajole their powerful counterparts into acceptance. Little did they know that their view would find its strongest echo in the Soviet bloc, which since the first debate on the issue forcefully lashed out against the conservative West. In some pointed speeches Soviet delegates decried Western (allegedly liberal) powers' stance toward the bloodiest types of armed conflicts, "civil and colonial wars [which] were . . . characterized by cruelty of all kinds."[22] They put the UK, United States, France, and others in a bind by essentially asking, "What would Henry Dunant do?"

By amplifying the humanitarian claims of the "pro-change" group and furnishing it with symbolic-political force, the USSR provided the push needed to

[20] For other work on the British attitude also supporting this view, see William I. Hitchcock, "Human Rights and the Laws of War: The Geneva Conventions of 1949," in *The Human Rights Revolution: An International History*, ed. Akira Iriye, Petra Goedde, and William I. Hitchcock (New York: Oxford University Press, 2012).

[21] See Mantilla, "Under (Social) Pressure," ch. 3.

[22] *Final Record of the Diplomatic Conference of Geneva of 1949, Volume II-B* (Bern: Swiss Federal Political Department, 1963), 14.

corner Western skeptics. After some insistence, the Americans and the French eventually gave in. The British, feeling publicly derided, anxiously requested a change in instructions from London. But neither France nor the UK had a genuine change of heart. Instead, archival records show how both labored jointly behind the scenes to make the definition of "armed non-international conflict" (in what became Article 3 common to all four Conventions) vague enough to leave embattled states an interpretive escape, and to limit its contents to selected provisions they cynically considered "innocuous."

Although the damage done via ambiguity was notable, in historical hindsight (and as later chapters suggest) Common Article 3 has had crucial merits. For one, it clearly legitimated the invocation of IHL in conflicts occurring within states' borders. Moreover, although a systematic survey of its practical effects and effectiveness is still lacking, it seems to have provided a legal resource for humanitarian access and even acted as a source of restraint in some cases. Finally, since the 1990s, Common Article 3 has acted as the crucial legal bedrock in the growing trend toward accountability for atrocities committed in internal conflicts. I return to these points further below.

New Rules for Protecting Civilians: The Fourth Geneva Convention

Beyond the introduction of internal conflicts, another tremendous innovation in 1949 came with the codification of rules to protect civilians. As we have seen, this was one of the most pressing issues on the agenda after World War II. States opted to focus on creating protections for two concrete types of civilians, not surprisingly the two kinds most victimized by the Nazis: those living under an occupying power, and foreign nationals living in the territory of a state waging war against their home country (hence known as "enemy" civilians).[23] The construction of the Fourth (or Civilians) Convention was an arduous task, and the resulting 159-article treaty was a major watershed in the history of IHL. Among other things, the treaty prohibited transfers and evacuations from occupied territory; murder, torture, and many other types of brutality; and laid out rules on the treatment of interned persons.[24]

Yet, impressive though it was, the Fourth Convention was only a partial achievement.[25] Like much of IHL, its provisions were tempered by language

[23] States' treatment of their own citizens became the subject of the human rights regime.

[24] For a digestible longer description of the Fourth Convention, see Frits Kalshoven and Liesbeth Zegveld, *Constraints on the Waging of War: An Introduction to International Humanitarian Law* (Geneva: ICRC, 2001), 61–70.

[25] For another excellent discussion of the politics behind the 1940s revisions, see Geoffrey Best, *War and Law since 1945* (New York: Oxford University Press, 1994), ch. 5.

allowing for exceptions on the (malleable) grounds of "military necessity," or were made conditional on belligerents' capabilities. Perhaps the most glaring omission of all was states' refusal to insert legal limits on their combat practices in order to reduce civilian suffering. Protecting "enemy" civilians or those living in occupied territory was critical, but what about those exposed to aerial bombardment or weapons of mass destruction? From a humanitarian perspective, all civilians not actively participating in hostilities merit protection. Still, instead of codifying the customary norms of civilian immunity, or what are now known as the principles of distinction and proportionality, all the negotiating states could agree on in 1949 was to allow for the creation of optional protective zones where noncombatants and the wounded and sick could be gathered as refuge from the dangers of war.

On this point Soviet participation was again momentous in 1949. Protecting civilians from "indiscriminate" warfare was not absent from debates in Geneva, but it happened to be the Communists who were peddling it under the broad banner of prohibiting nuclear and chemical weapons alongside other means of exterminating civilians and their property. The political context was less than conducive to success, however. At the same time that the Soviets tried to delegitimize others' recourse to nuclear weapons, they were working to "go nuclear" themselves in order to balance the Americans. And to a West beholden to the idea of "total war," and for which the use of nuclear weapons and conventional aerial bombardment seemed to have played a crucial factor in winning the war, the notion of making such practices illegal was obnoxious, unrealistic and, coming from the Soviets, obviously strategic and hypocritical.

In the end, the West managed to contain Soviet pressures successfully. Since weapons control and the regulation of combat practices had traditionally been a "Hague" matter, as soon as the Soviet delegates introduced their proposal, the United States and UK quickly rallied votes against the initiative behind the scenes, publicly arguing that although eliminating the scourge of war and harsh methods of warfare was not without merit, it exceeded the mandate of the Geneva conference. This procedural argument effectively helped them win the day without looking antihumanitarian, at least too overtly.[26]

As shown later, although the 1949 process did not produce all the protections for civilians from warfare that seemed necessary, pressure to achieve such protections continued to grow. Despite setbacks, codification of the principles of distinction and proportionality mentioned previously finally emerged through the 1977 Additional Protocols.

[26] Ibid., 110–114.

Monitoring and Enforcement

Until 1929, beyond the private diplomacy of the ICRC, IHL lacked an official institutional form of international monitoring and enforcement. That year states codified a mechanism called "Protecting Powers" in the then-brand-new POW Convention.[27] Protecting Powers were third-party, neutral states mutually accepted by belligerents to care for their interests and imperiled citizens. During World War II, Sweden and Switzerland acted as Protecting Powers to several belligerents, to good effect.[28] Although in 1949 the ICRC and many states tried to improve the Protecting Powers system and add other enforcement and monitoring mechanisms, most efforts ultimately foundered during negotiations.[29] Yet a crucial outcome nonetheless emerged: the establishment of a system to account for serious violations ("grave breaches") of the Conventions.

Major powers from both sides of the Iron Curtain disliked the idea of strengthening the Protecting Powers system and declined to be legally obligated to accept external oversight on the battlefield (or for the USSR, any oversight at all). Despite efforts from Switzerland and Sweden to strengthen its role, as Geoffrey Best argues, the Protecting Power "was left with a lot of things to do and to ensure that others did, but no larger power than to 'scrutinize' what went on in some sort of 'co-operation' with the host belligerent."[30] Although in appearance the 1949 Conventions make Protecting Powers mandatory, in practice state consent and respect for state security became impediments to their automatic or effective operation. Likewise, an "enquiry procedure," proposed to facilitate the investigation of alleged violations, was made optional and has therefore to date not been used.

On the upside, the ICRC's traditional ability to perform humanitarian activities during war was respected and expanded, including during noninternational conflict. ICRC activities and "soft" monitoring have in rare cases of particularly egregious state behavior led to public shaming, most recently against the United States' treatment of prisoners in Afghanistan, as Elizabeth Arsenault discusses in

[27] Protecting Powers have a longer history. For an excellent if now outdated overview, see David P. Forsythe, "Who Guards the Guardians: Third Parties and the Law of Armed Conflict," *American Journal of International Law* 70, no. 1 (1976): 41–61.

[28] Best, *War and Law since 1945*, 148.

[29] Ibid., 156–157.

[30] Ibid., 149–150. Attempts were made to ensure that if belligerents failed to reach an agreement on a potential Protecting Power, the ICRC or another humanitarian organization should substitute for it. This, however, was not a role the Swiss organization desired to perform, as it might compromise its neutrality and jeopardize its humanitarian right of access or "initiative" enshrined elsewhere in the Conventions (and in the Statutes of the Red Cross Movement.) The ability of the ICRC to act as substitute Protecting Power of last resort was inserted, not without provoking an infamous reservation from the Soviet Union.

her chapter. Yet despite representing a form of external scrutiny and diplomatic pressure, the ICRC's protective role during armed conflict is conceptually different from an institutionalized procedure of supervision or denunciation.

Criminal prosecution was another mechanism that could facilitate the enforcement of the Conventions. Since the Conventions were being negotiated after the Nuremberg and Tokyo trials, a reasonable expectation existed that states would make violations to the new treaties "war crimes," and to introduce some sort of adjudication mechanism. The ICRC was sympathetic to the idea, and at the initial intergovernmental meetings many states seemed supportive, including the United States and especially France.

Ultimately, high hopes were dashed. Various arguments prevented radical breakthroughs. First, as with weapons prohibitions, major Western states insisted that Red Cross–steered Conferences were not the proper forum for making decisions on international penal law, which beyond violations of the law of war was seen to include the thorny political issue of defining the crime of aggression. For most participants this question fell indisputably within the province of the newborn United Nations (UN) organization. Second and related, the postwar mood of promoting international peace and security made it seem incongruous that the very organization created to keep the peace would expend its efforts on the repression of atrocities committed in future wars. Although the UN International Law Commission was tasked with the preparation of a "Draft Code of Offences Against the Peace and Security of Mankind," quick agreement was not expected in the increasingly contentious environment of the late 1940s (and was in fact not achieved until the 1990s, with the Rome Statute creating the International Criminal Court). Third, with few exceptions, to most states in the 1940s the creation of an international tribunal or a panel of experts to supervise the Conventions seemed like an undesirable pipe dream. Even a proposal to designate the International Court of Justice as impartial arbiter fell flat.[31]

After watering down the early strong proposals involving international enforcement, in 1949 states managed to agree that domestic courts should bear the responsibility of trying alleged violators of the Geneva Conventions, regardless of the nationality of the perpetrators or of the territory where the acts were committed. To mete out punishment, states were asked to pass the necessary (domestic) legislation criminalizing specified acts against the Conventions, and either to bring suspects before their tribunals or to authorize their extradition, according to a principle now known as "universal jurisdiction." This was in fact another example of legal-political compromise: Although from the perspective of state sovereignty universal jurisdiction was a "risky" concession to

[31] See ibid., 142–158.

international law, its realization remained within states' own grip. There was an important measure of innovation here, credited to the work of the ICRC and the pressure of countries like Monaco and Denmark.

A final, accountability-related debate from 1949 involved how to treat violations of the Conventions. How would acts against the Convention be called? Should every infraction be considered and punished with equal force, or only violations of distinct gravity?

The United States and the UK opposed language referring to "war crimes," which harked back to Nuremberg, and seemed inappropriately dramatic. The Soviets, for their part, liked the vivid label as well as the idea of making *every* violation of the Conventions a crime, even the minor infractions, something intensely opposed by the Western camp. In particular, the Americans and British feared that the Soviet bloc countries would use any alleged violation to the Conventions as an excuse to deny due protection to Western POWs (whom the USSR would already consider guilty of the crime of aggression). To solve the impasse, states agreed to the strong but less controversial label of "grave breaches," which was to include a specific set of particularly gruesome violations, including "willful killing, torture or inhuman treatment, including biological experiments [and] willfully causing great suffering or serious injury to body or health."[32] In the 1970s states complemented this list of acts through the Additional Protocol I, labeled them "war crimes," and in the 1990s—most notably through the International Criminal Court—states made these and other types of violations of IHL internationally enforceable.

Interlude: 1949–1968

Soon after the 1949 Conference the new Geneva treaties had garnered demonstrable formal support from every corner of the globe. All the great powers ratified them in the 1950s, and by 1960 most existing states had accepted their validity.[33] Over time, as new states cropped up due to decolonization in Africa and Asia, they too sought membership in the Geneva system.

[32] Ibid., 164.

[33] For the story behind United States and United Kingdom ratification, see Giovanni Mantilla, "Conforming Instrumentalists: Why the United States and the United Kingdom Joined the 1949 Geneva Conventions," *European Journal of International Law* (forthcoming). The USSR ratified with various reservations that invalidated POW protections for alleged violators of the Conventions, and the authority of Protecting Powers and the ICRC. These reservations deeply upset Western powers, but did not prevent their ratification. The controversy resurfaced in conflicts involving Communist states, however, and during the 1970s negotiations, as seen later.

The Geneva Conventions entered into force during the Korean War, but none of the belligerents in that conflict ratified them until after the armistice. Yet, as Sahr Conway-Lanz points out in the next chapter, the experience of the war helped grant the Conventions a certain legitimacy, particularly in American eyes. Unfortunately, the inadequacy of the Conventions to contain harm to civilians during that conflict and subsequent ones was evident. Concern deepened with special regard to two thorny issues: the limitation of the effects of indiscriminate weaponry on civilian populations, and various matters relating to internal violence.

On the one hand, the ICRC was alarmed by the growing belief among actual or potential belligerents that civilian immunity in an era of total war was something of a mirage. Though aware of the risk of falling prey to Soviet propagandistic efforts to prohibit war and certain weapons, the Swiss organization refused to stand aside, and was particularly concerned that states seemed in no rush to update the Hague Conventions.

On the other hand, the ICRC knew the vague text of Common Article 3 would not easily become operative in practice. It feared that states experiencing internal violence would argue—no matter the conflict's intensity—that it did not rise to the level of a "non-international conflict" and therefore was not a matter for international law. Unfortunately, this particular suspicion quickly became a reality, as internal armed violence intensified or erupted in Southeast Asia, North and East Africa, Eastern Europe, and Latin America, but governments invoked the norm of state sovereignty to prevent international scrutiny.[34] As a result, the ICRC faced tremendous obstacles in effectively persuading or pressing most conflict-ridden states to abide by the international humanitarian standards they had just signed.

The ICRC thus set out to remedy two specific gaps in the immediate aftermath of the 1949 Conventions: limitations on indiscriminate warfare affecting civilians, and the treatment of political prisoners in internal situations of violence. Its chosen method was to hold meetings of government and legal experts in Geneva, whose results could be disseminated and used as a basis for progressive interpretation and development of the Geneva law. As explained later, valuable though they were, the results of these efforts remained nonbinding on states, and by 1967 the prospect of formal legal extensions were dim.

Two rounds of consultations (in 1954 and 1956) and much private correspondence with governments and National Societies of the Red Cross and Red Crescent on the issue of indiscriminate warfare produced a set of "Draft Rules for the Limitation of Dangers Incurred by the Civilian Population in Time of War," which in essence sought to enshrine into treaty law the notions that (1) the

[34] For the longer story and full references, see Mantilla, "Under (Social) Pressure," ch. 4.

choice of methods of combat was not unlimited; (2) the civilian/combatant distinction should be upheld and guide states' combat practices; and (3) states should refrain from using weapons with uncontrollable consequences.

Although the ICRC believed the Draft Rules were only codifying customary principles, the initiative died a sad death in 1957, when in the context of the Nineteenth International Conference of the Red Cross, the United States and other NATO powers conspired behind the scenes to sabotage it. Publicly, the old formalistic argument was rehearsed against the proposed Rules: the UN, not the Red Cross, was the proper forum to discuss warfare ("Hague") regulations. Yet the actual underlying reason was clear: Western states had no interest in banning nuclear weapons and aerial bombardment through humanitarian law, and efforts to that end were perceived as unrealistic and, coming from the Soviets, hypocritical. All the ICRC could do in the face of such resistance was to keep alive the spirit of the initiative in the form of "soft" resolutions, hoping that over time states might be willing to endorse them as treaty law. As the rest of the chapter describes, this would only occur some two decades later.

Presaging similar resistance, the ICRC decided not yet to push for an additional treaty on the issue of internal armed violence and the protection of political prisoners. Instead it organized expert dialogues in Geneva in which the majority of experts (a mix of legal scholars, diplomats, and military lawyers) debated and agreed that the definition of "non-international conflict" contained in Common Article 3 should be given broad interpretation, and that even in cases believed to fall outside of its purview, states should feel bound to respect the humanitarian principles of the Conventions and to allow the Red Cross to perform its protective role toward all categories of political detainees. All this seemed palatable to states, as long as there was no binding law. By 1967, however, legal strengthening of this sort had stalled.

Yet a brief ten years later, in 1977, states concluded not one but two (binding) Additional Protocols to the Geneva Conventions. What had changed?

Several conditions helped spur governments to consider a further expansion of IHL. First, although states did not denounce Common Article 3 (instead they failed to uphold it in part or in full), the atrocities witnessed in the 1950s and 1960s in internal conflicts in Kenya, Algeria, Morocco, Laos, Rhodesia, the Congo, and Nigeria, among others, demonstrated its inadequacy. Second, nongovernmental actors beyond the ICRC mobilized to press for new and improved law. The International Commission of Jurists, especially, through its secretary-general Seán MacBride, persuaded a small group of states to spark debate within the UN on the topic of "human rights in armed conflict."[35] Third,

[35] For more on the reopening of IHL revisions at this time, see Keith Suter, *An International Law of Guerilla Warfare: The Global Politics of Law-Making* (New York: St. Martin's Press, 1984); Mantilla, "Under (Social) Pressure."

decolonization and the attendant expansion of membership within the UN opened the door to issues important to the new postcolonial nations, including humanitarian law. Fourth, the escalation of the war in Vietnam in 1965 gradually fostered a changed (progressive) US attitude toward the law. The last two conditions had a lasting impact on the evolving debate about IHL. I return to them shortly.

Strengthening the Conventions: The 1977 Additional Protocols

Most armed conflicts after World War II were not waged between states but inside them (or their "dependent territories"). National liberation struggles and threats of secession in Africa and Asia, communist revolutions and ensuing tensions in Eastern Europe, and variously motivated uprisings and coups d'état in Latin America all posed drastic challenges to a body of law that focused almost entirely on interstate war and was therefore profoundly unequipped to deal with internal conflicts. Indeed, of hundreds of provisions negotiated in 1949, only Common Article 3 offered some hope as a potential legal response to proliferating internal atrocities.

Unfortunately, as we have seen, that Article alone proved insufficient to confront an extremely complex reality. First, partly due to its ambiguous (non) definition of internal conflict, embattled states rarely recognized Common Article 3 as applicable to their respective cases. Prominent cases of nonapplication included the UK in Kenya and Cyprus, and France in Algeria—the subject of Raphaëlle Branche's chapter. Second, Common Article 3 contained only very general principles of humane treatment for wounded and sick, persons not actively engaged in combat, or to captured fighters of any stripe (to whom it did not confer POW status or protections). Third, Common Article 3 (like the rest of the articles in all four of the Geneva Conventions) remained silent regarding limitations on the conduct of hostilities and military practices like aerial bombardment that gravely affected civilians. Fourth, it did not expressly cover the low-level violence seen in so-called internal disturbances or tensions.

Discussion on the revision of the Geneva Conventions increased after 1968 with the adoption of various resolutions within the UN, but the "official" preparatory process began in earnest in 1971 at the behest of the ICRC. To pave the way for a Diplomatic Conference, the Swiss organization once more conducted research and organized events with government experts, National Red Cross and Red Crescent Societies, one International Conference of the Red Cross, and multiple other formal and informal encounters with various audiences between 1971 and 1973. Although by this point organized civil society (e.g., advocacy by nongovernmental organizations—NGOs—and lawyers' groups) had grown relative to previous episodes of revision, treaty making remained in essence controlled by states.

States, for their part, approached and justified the impetus toward revamped law from very different vantage points. If the cleavages of the 1940s seemed intense, the stark divergence of ideas and interests seen in the 1970s constituted a truly explosive cocktail, which, without actually derailing negotiations, made the Additional Protocols a troubled product of this historical period. My goal in what follows is to substantiate this claim.

Without doubt, the political circumstance that most shaped this episode of revisions was decolonization. Between 1945 and 1965, after arduously fighting or negotiating their way out of dependent status from their (mostly but not exclusively European) masters, most of the formerly "non-self-governing" or colonial territories in Africa and Asia acquired statehood and UN membership.[36] Put in percentage terms, in 1950 new states represented 8.33 percent of the UN system, in 1960 33.3 percent, and in 1967 45.5 percent. This "revolution in sovereignty" fundamentally changed the dynamics within (near) universal-membership international institutions and processes including, as we will see, the revision of IHL. Most importantly, the West found it increasingly harder to command voting majorities and thus was forced to listen and compromise with an emerging "Third World" that could no longer be tamed.[37]

Newly decolonized states' most cherished project was to further the global struggle for national liberation in Africa and Asia, in addition to undermining white minority rule in Southern Africa, and to support Palestine against Israeli occupation. Pursuing this in the context of IHL involved at least two goals: (1) to heighten the legitimacy of national liberation in existing international law (and as a crucial corollary, to further undermine colonialism, racism, and occupation); and (2) to practically enhance the status of so-called freedom fighters, who in terms of protection and risk were considered at a formal disadvantage vis-à-vis the colonizers' armies.

At the same time, the decolonized world clung fervently to the idea of national sovereignty and nonintervention.[38] Many of the new regimes were

[36] Not all the new states were former colonies, for example, Israel.

[37] For an excellent recent overview of this process, see Roland Burke, *Decolonization and the Evolution of International Human Rights* (Philadelphia: University of Pennsylvania Press, 2010). For the experience of decolonization wars in Algeria and Kenya, see Fabian Klose, *Human Rights in the Shadow of Colonial Violence: The Wars of Independence in Kenya and Algeria* (Philadelphia: University of Pennsylvania Press, 2013).

[38] For more on the 1970s revisions, see Mantilla, "Under (Social) Pressure," ch. 5.

trying to consolidate their rule against domestic contenders through violent, authoritarian means. This led them, quite unsurprisingly, to reject the idea of inviting scrutiny or creating international rules that might interfere with how they managed social upheaval and secessionist threats at home. All this meant that the newly independent world was as passionate about expanding protections and lending legitimacy to national liberation and "freedom fighters" (to colonial powers' detriment) as it was allergic to new law dealing with any other type of internal conflicts.

In the latter attitude they were not alone: though far from fierce anticolonialists, Latin American states were in the 1970s fragile and increasingly authoritarian (Argentina, Uruguay, Brazil, Chile, among others) or conflict ridden (Colombia) internally, hence deeply inimical to onerous humanitarian rules tying their hands. Similarly, Arab states supporting Palestine stood by the principles of self-determination and antioccupation but resented interference in their domestic, authoritarian practices.

Cold War dynamics again worked to shape states' approaches to the revision of IHL in the 1970s, though not entirely coinciding with what transpired in 1949. An element of continuity lay in the Soviet bloc's continued support of decolonization and self-determination in the prolonged struggle for hearts and minds against a morally compromised West. American intervention in Southeast Asia and lingering European colonialism were obvious rhetorical whips put to good use by the communists. But in other aspects, Soviet and Western views now coincided and produced some collaboration. The potential regulation or prohibition of nuclear weapons was a case in point. Neither the Americans nor the Soviets desired to engage in multilateral negotiation on this topic within the increasingly overcrowded and politicized (read: unpredictable) forum of the UN General Assembly, much less within the framework of IHL, as negotiation efforts progressed elsewhere via nuclear-specific instruments and forums.[39] The era of détente thus had some impact on the transformation of IHL, though not enough to suggest deep, across-the-board convergence between the United States and the Soviet Union.

Third, after the mid-1960s, the Vietnam War undermined the United States' conservative gatekeeping approach toward the laws of war. US leaders grew increasingly concerned after 1965 about the fate of American soldiers captured by North Vietnamese and Vietcong forces, which viewed Americans as guilty of aggression, hence undeserving of humanitarian protection. The

[39] The topic of weapons eventually became decoupled (or *mostly* decoupled) from the process of the Protocols and instead carried through a parallel "spin-off" process that concluded in 1979–1980.

US government's initial strategy of demanding respect or reciprocity under the POW Convention or under Common Article 3 bore no fruit. As a result, as Gary Solis describes in his chapter, US leaders began to view an extension of POW treatment to all captured troops (regardless of whether the conflict was internal or interstate) as desirable, in the hope that as far as "the law in the books" was concerned, the Communists could not muster excuses. Additionally, in a clear policy reversal after the 1968 My Lai massacre (in which American soldiers killed over three hundred unarmed Vietnamese civilians) became public in 1969, the United States gained an interest in improving the legal protection of civilians from the dangers of hostilities. An incensed domestic public opinion and renewed congressional pressure became critical forces for transforming US attitudes toward human rights in armed conflict. Finally, the United States took an interest in strengthening the mechanisms of legal monitoring and enforcement within IHL, believing that the failings of the law ultimately had less to do with lack of regulation than with lack of respect for them.

Interestingly, the West was fractured in its attitudes to revisions, especially vis-à-vis internal conflicts.[40] Colonial powers like Portugal, the UK, and France continued to oppose quite fiercely any special consideration of national liberation in international law. But like the newly independent states, they too were wary of increased legal interference in internal conflicts below a high threshold. (The British were especially obsessed with preventing any new law from applying in Northern Ireland.) In contrast, Canada and the United States, less beholden to fears of internal armed unrest, expressed support for a treaty extending Common Article 3 to apply automatically to as many situations of internal conflict as possible.

As in the 1947–1949 negotiations, perhaps the most radical Western dissenters were the Scandinavians. While the Norwegians staunchly supported the cause of national liberation, the Swedish were the most adamant promoters of weapons limitations and prohibitions in the framework of IHL. Norway and Sweden caused the rest of the Western group many headaches, sometimes to good or "progressive" effect. Indeed, Sweden's pathbreaking forceful diplomacy behind the regulation and/or prohibition of conventional weapons produced initial results in the late 1970s and continues to this day.

[40] In what follows I use the term "West" or "Western Group" to refer to North America and Western Europe. This said, at times the Western Group extended to Australia, New Zealand, and even Turkey and Japan. Latin American states, though located in the Western Hemisphere, usually constituted a separate, semicohesive group during discussions about humanitarian law in the 1970s.

The Diplomatic Conference, 1974–1977: Dynamics and Outcomes

In 1973, after nearly three years of intense discussion among states, the ICRC, and other actors, governments agreed that two draft Protocols (on international and internal conflicts) could serve as an acceptable baseline for formal negotiations. The First Session of the Diplomatic Conference on the Reaffirmation and Development of International Humanitarian Law Applicable in Armed Conflicts (CDDH) thus opened on February 20, 1974. In attendance were all the state parties to the Geneva Conventions. Of 126 delegations that came to the First Session, 64 were African and Asian, and only 29 North American and Western European. The CDDH thus resembled the near-universal membership of the UN. Three more official sessions and several encounters on the side were eventually necessary to complete the two Protocols. The process vastly exceeded the intensity and acrimony of the 1949 negotiations, and the fate of the treaties, especially of Protocol II, was uncertain until the final weeks of the Conference in 1977.

The Protocols are not merely small additions to the original Conventions but rather codify principles and concepts that are today viewed as central to IHL. Most important was the long-overdue codification of protection for civilians from the dangers of hostilities, particularly the principles of distinction, proportionality, and precaution that have come define the law of war as we today know it. Protocol I (applicable to interstate and national liberation conflict) was made particularly strong in this regard; although, as I discuss later, the Protocols are less than watertight in this respect, this should not detract from the fact that they do contain guidelines (previously absent in treaty law) likely to narrow military arbitrariness and thereby decrease harm caused to civilians. Crucially, the incorporation of these principles in the 1970s Protocols dissolved the historical separation between Geneva and Hague law, which had—on more than one occasion—acted as an excuse for blocking legal development. I return to these innovations shortly.

With some exceptions, it is generally acknowledged that both Protocols develop the substance of existing law in the right direction. Protocol I updated the 1949 rules on the protection of medical aircraft, an otherwise "unsexy" but still essential part of the law. Both Protocols also featured an important list of minimum "fundamental guarantees" to all those detained or not actively involved in conflict. Protocol I created measures to account for the missing in action and the dead. And whatever its weaknesses, Protocol II complemented and enriched Common Article 3 in matters as crucial as the protection of civilians and civilian objects, and of medical personnel, transport and units, among others.

That being said, from a more demanding humanitarian standpoint (say, the ICRC's initial aspirations) the 1970s process fell far short of expectations. This was manifest not only in the many instances of "watering down" but especially in the extreme polarization over certain political issues, to the detriment of war victims' protection. Although politics is always constitutive of international law and institutions, in the 1970s the atmosphere seemed especially charged, unfortunately tilting the balance of negotiations toward the preservation of sovereignty and the instrumentalization of the new law. The vignettes that follow seek to illustrate this point.

National Liberation and Freedom Fighters

The most heated debate of the entire CDDH focused on whether to make the First Protocol applicable to national liberation wars (from colonialism, occupation, or racism) alongside international armed conflicts. From the perspective of the African, Asian, and Arab states this was a legitimate and long overdue adjustment of humanitarian law to principles increasingly accepted within the UN.[41] Yet as noted, for most of the West this change presupposed unacceptable consequences, including the vindication of specific motives for waging violence within a body of law long agnostic to ideas of "just" or "unjust" war. In addition, this legal change would entail the application of the *entire* Geneva Conventions (and Protocol I) to those types of conflicts, at a minimum raising doubt as to whether and how liberation movements (as nonstate actors) could participate in and comply with formal and extremely demanding treaties.[42]

Compounding this general innovation was that of securing enhanced treatment for "freedom fighters" via the attribution of POW status and protection. Alleging a bias in the existing law, the new "Afro-Asian" states argued that the requirements set out in the Third Geneva Convention for combatant/POW status should be relativized or eliminated, especially those forcing combatants to distinguish themselves from the civilian population at all times through a distinctive sign, or by carrying arms openly. The delegates of Third World countries and their sympathizers rejected these older requirements because they seemed both unrealistic and damaging to the struggle for self-determination. Specifically, by forcing freedom fighters to make themselves distinguishable at all times, existing IHL allegedly made them into easy targets of colonial, racist, and occupation armies. This, in their view, needed to change, allowing freedom

[41] See, for example, Georges Abi-Saab, "Wars of National Liberation and the Laws of War," in *International Law: A Contemporary Perspective*, ed. Richard A. Falk, Friedrich V. Kratochwil, and Saul H. Mendlovitz (Boulder, CO: Westview Press, 1985), 410–437.

[42] These are only two of the many objections Western states raised in debate.

fighters to wage violence without depriving them of POW status and protection upon capture.

From the perspective of (most of) the West, however, these changes implied unacceptable and almost scandalous political and legal effects. After all, POWs are usually given a heroic status denied to others, such as rebels, criminals, or terrorists. But the potential legal consequences under IHL went farther. First, the attribution of POW status to freedom fighters would activate the manifold benefits of the 143-article-long Third Geneva Convention, including detailed guidelines on internment, work, food, clothes, and even rights to recreation and canteens. Second, it might invite third-party scrutiny through the operation of Protecting Powers. Third, it would trigger judicial benefits denied to rebels under domestic criminal law. And fourth, it entailed the risk of increasing harm to civilians, since relaxing freedom fighters' duty to make themselves distinguishable in conflict inevitably generated confusion as to who was an "active fighter," affecting belligerents' ability or will to respect civilian immunity at all times.

Intense Western opposition to the formal inclusion of national liberation in Protocol I failed. With supporting votes from most Socialist, Arab, and Latin American states, in the 1974 session the decolonized world managed to impose their wish to extend the First Protocol to anticolonial, antioccupation, and antiracist conflicts. This development, though not set in stone until Plenary approval in 1977, threatened to break up the entire Conference.

Surprisingly, after prolonged private anxiety and debate, the Western group ultimately opted for acquiescing to the Third World, wishing to avoid a dramatic exit that could prove socially and legally costly. Yet Western states' acquiescence did not rest on a sincere change of heart about the appropriateness of the innovation, but rather out of concern for their social image (in private the British stated that they did not want to appear racist).[43] Western delegations' nervousness was also allayed once a quietly inserted reciprocity clause in Protocol I promised to ensure that no national liberation movement could formally accede to the instrument. Finally, Western states bet on the likelihood that national liberation would soon wane, thus making the prickly provision irrelevant.[44]

Similarly, the protection of freedom fighters as POWs and the associated loosening of fighters' obligation to distinguish themselves at all times were successfully inserted into Protocol I. Interestingly, this was as much the outcome of Third World pressure as it was of ICRC liaison and American-led behind-the-scenes negotiation. According to Jacques Moreillon, then-ICRC director of

[43] TNA: PRO FCO 61/1233.

[44] Article 96, para. 3., which makes the application of the Protocol and the Geneva Conventions conditional on the de jure and de facto compliance of the national liberation movement, something the West thought nearly impossible.

law and principles, sometime between the 1975 and 1976 session ICRC officials contacted the US head delegate George Aldrich and provided him with the legal formulas through which the United States in Vietnam (and the French in Algeria before it) had allowed for the application of POW *treatment* (and in the American case, *status*) to most detained "irregulars," so long as they had been carrying arms openly before and during military engagements. (Gary Solis and Raphaëlle Branche discuss these issues in more detail in their respective chapters.) Aldrich then used this template as a basis for a compromise text that set out the conditions under which combatants could receive POW status and offered "POW-like" treatment to anyone who was captured while carrying arms openly.[45]

Importantly, in American eyes this text contained various critical ambiguities that the Western group believed could ultimately serve to deny POW status to freedom fighters. The working text recognized that although "there are situations in armed conflicts where, owing to the nature of the hostilities an armed combatant cannot . . . distinguish himself" from the civilian population, a combatant could retain his status as long as he carried his arms openly "during each military engagement" and "during such time as he is visible to the adversary while he is engaged in a military deployment preceding the launching of an attack in which he is to participate." The ambiguities related specifically to the meaning of two words within the text: "deployment" and "protection." While from the Third World perspective this passage would be given generous interpretation (the obligation of distinction operating only immediately prior to executing an attack), the US delegation believed a restrictive interpretation could prevail, covering "all the period of time (and distance in space)" elapsed between guerrilla members or groups leaving their posts until the attack took place, thereby allowing for wide governmental latitude to target them.[46]

These ambiguities were probably not evident to the Norwegians, Algerians, Vietnamese, Egyptians, or Palestinians, to whom the compromise text appeared

[45] For firsthand corroboration the American delegation's role in the drafting of this article, see George H. Aldrich, "Some Reflections on the Origins of the 1977 Geneva Protocols," in *Studies and Essays on International Humanitarian Law and Red Cross Principles in Honour of Jean Pictet*, ed. Christopher Swinarski (The Hague: Springer, 1984), 1143; George H. Aldrich, "Prospects for United States Ratification of Additional Protocol I to the 1949 Geneva Conventions," *American Journal of International Law* 85, no. 1 (1991): 1–20; George H. Aldrich, "The Laws of War on Land," *American Journal of International Law* 94, no. 1 (2000): 42–63. On the role of the ICRC in persuading the French and the United States to treat and/or consider captured rebels as POWs in Algeria and Vietnam respectively, and the importance of these experiences for the drafting of Article 42/44 of the First Protocol, see Edwina Morgan, "The Protection of 'Irregular' Combatants: An Enduring Challenge for Humanitarian Action" (MAS Thesis, Geneva Center for Education and Research in Humanitarian Action, 2011), 49–50, 76–77; David P. Forsythe, *The Politics of Prisoner Abuse: The United States and Enemy Prisoners after 9/11* (Cambridge: Cambridge University Press, 2011), 19.

[46] TNA: PRO FCO 58/1127.

satisfactory. Despite fierce British resistance on this point, most Western group states acquiesced to the US view, and by the end of negotiations, no Western state voted against. Although this innovation was defended by the American delegation to the CDDH as a pragmatic compromise, it became one of the main reasons why the US government ultimately declined to sign or ratify Protocol I.

The Protection of Civilians

In stark contrast to years prior, few delegations in the 1970s dared to publicly suggest that better rules for protecting civilians during hostilities were unnecessary; a "general desire" to achieve them was clear.[47] The difference between states' positions was one of degree: how far should regulation go? Some, including controversial players like North Vietnam, insisted on the absolute prohibition of harm against civilians, civilian property, facilities containing dangerous materials, or the natural environment. To powerful others, including most of the Western group with the United States at the helm, this seemed not just illusory, but insincere and politically driven.

The question here as elsewhere was where to strike the balance between military necessity and civilian immunity, privileging the latter without obstructing the former "too much."[48] On balance it appears that the final articles on civilian (and related) protections turned out less awkward than they could have been, stating unequivocally in various places that civilian populations and civilian objects should not be directly or deliberately targeted nor terrorized; that attacks should be directed only against military objectives; and that civilians are defined as all those who are not combatants or who are not actively participating in hostilities. Importantly, Protocol I also enshrines the principle of proportionality, which refers to the idea that attacks should not exceed the level required to weaken or destroy the enemy's military strength, or otherwise said, that a lawful attack becomes unlawful if it may be expected to result in injury or damage disproportionate to the military advantage sought.[49] Codification of these and other principles and measures of precaution impinging on the conduct of hostilities constituted a step forward in the history of IHL. The prohibitions of starvation as a method of warfare and of "target area" aerial bombardment are notable examples of the various critical changes made in the 1970s.[50]

[47] Forsythe, "Who Guards the Guardians" 138.

[48] George H. Aldrich, "Establishing Legal Norms through Multilateral Negotiation: The Laws of War," *Case Western Reserve Journal of International Law* 9 (1977): 13.

[49] Ibid., 11.

[50] Note, however, that the language used regarding protections for civilians and related objects varies from the comprehensive Protocol I to the much leaner Protocol II. I elaborate on this point further in what follows.

Yet it is also clear that these rules as negotiated retain various definitional and textual flaws, that they allow for the possibility of civilian harm via collateral damage, and that good faith interpretation is inevitably required to ensure, for example, that assessments as to what constitutes a "deliberate" attack or a military "advantage" are not abused.[51] Optimistically, the US head delegate at the Diplomatic Conference, George Aldrich, acknowledged in 1981 that these rules "contain sufficient flexibility and recognition of the pressures and confusion of combat so that conscientious and properly trained officers who try to apply them on the basis of available information should be able to do so without either undermining the success of their mission or running the risk of committing war crimes."[52] More skeptically, as Helen Kinsella has noted, the uncertainty and indeterminacy that pervade the distinction between combatants and civilians allows for discourses of innocence, civilization, and gender to operate as the lenses through which their meaning is deciphered in practice.[53] Stiff controversies between legal and military experts endure to this day on crucial parts of the 1970s law, most recently regarding the meaning of the phrase "unless and for such time as they take a direct part in hostilities," which determines the potential lawful targeting of civilians participating in conflict.[54]

Supervision and Enforcement

Historically, one of the areas of IHL that has proven most stubborn to develop is that of external supervision and enforcement. The Protecting Powers system revamped in 1949 had worked only in a handful of occasions, and the refusal of belligerents to accept a substitute organization (such as the ICRC) had hindered the widespread operation of the mechanism. The hope in the 1970s was to transform it such that its automaticity could be definitely guaranteed.

Unfortunately, this goal proved lofty. The same hostility of the Communist bloc toward the idea of automatic external monitoring, especially of the ICRC, remained alive and well. Although the adopted text introduced a clearer Protecting Power appointment procedure and seemingly mandated the

[51] Best, *War and Law since 1945*, 270.

[52] George H. Aldrich, "New Life for the Laws of War," *American Journal of International Law* 75, no. 4 (1981): 778.

[53] Helen M. Kinsella, *The Image before the Weapon: A Critical History of the Distinction between Combatant and Civilian* (Ithaca, NY: Cornell University Press, 2011).

[54] Ryan Goodman and Derek Jinks, "The ICRC Interpretive Guidance on the Notion of Direct Participation in Hostilities under International Humanitarian Law: An Introduction to the Forum," *New York University Journal of International Law and Politics* 42, no. 3 (2010): 637–640.

automatic appointment of a substitute, its wording in fact conditioned the latter to the consent of the detaining power.[55]

Another attempt at bringing in a strong measure of outside monitoring came with the proposal (from Denmark, Sweden, and New Zealand), for an International Fact-Finding Commission, to be composed of fifteen members "of high moral standing and acknowledged impartiality," and charged among others with investigating alleged grave breaches or other serious violations of the 1949 Conventions or of Protocol I. The original intent was to make the Commission mandatory, but in the face of Soviet bloc obstinacy and to the chagrin of its supporters, the mechanism was ultimately subjected to belligerents' consent.

Finally, in the 1970s states agreed to expand the original list of grave breaches and serious violations of the Conventions and of the First Protocol, including many of the new rules they were creating on civilians, POWs, and historic monuments. They also finally agreed to call violations of IHL what they are—"war crimes." In this sense, the CDDH developed existing law in a progressive manner. The backstory is more complicated, however.[56] In short, the list of grave breaches became the object of contention between Communist (especially North Vietnam) and Western countries (led by the United States), the former wanting it to be lengthy and detailed, and the latter pushing back fiercely on aspects they found unreasonable. In the 1970s, as in 1949, it was evident that Socialist states saw the creation of war crimes as an opportunity to shame their political opponents and as means to deny them humanitarian treatment. The final list of grave breaches and serious violations appears to have been a compromise between the US and Soviet delegations, the latter ostensibly acting as a moderating force on its satellites.

The United States succeeded in neutralizing (at least nominally) the communist ploy of justifying exceptions to IHL on the grounds of "aggressive war," through wording to that effect in Protocol I's preamble. However, the United States insisted, successfully, on the insertion of intent (or "willful commission") as a way to raise the evidentiary bar in war crimes allegations.

In the 1970s states agreed to develop existing criminal law in international, but not internal, conflicts. Although the contemporary observer is accustomed to hearing of war crimes allegations and trials in places like Rwanda and the former Yugoslavia, just four decades ago the great majority of states considered the idea

[55] See Forsythe, "Who Guards the Guardians."

[56] For other analysis of the CDDH's contributions, see: Antonio Cassese, "A Tentative Appraisal of the Old and the New Humanitarian Law of Armed Conflict," in *The New Humanitarian Law of Armed Conflict*, ed. Antonio Cassese (Naples: Editoriale scientifica, 1979), 461–501.

of criminal responsibility in the context of internal war ludicrous. The era of transitional justice had not yet begun, and at the end of hostilities rebels were thought to either deserve treatment as traitors, or to be given amnesty. As a result, making violations of Protocol II "war crimes" was not a consideration of the CDDH, leaving a critical gap filled only years later. In general, as explained further below, despite the fact that internal conflicts had arguably been the key motivating force behind the revision of IHL in the late 1960s, the majority of negotiating states at the CDDH ultimately left them in relative legislative darkness.

Protocol II

As noted, the atmosphere of decolonization (and the deeper revolt against old Western/imperial structures that underpinned it) put the spotlight on two very specific forms/sites of "internal" conflict: wars of liberation/self-determination and opposition to racist (white minority) rule in Southern Africa. Facing internal challenges, the great majority of the new states in Africa and Asia were at best uninterested in further regulating nonliberation internal conflicts. The rollback of democracy in Latin America pointed in the same direction, Socialist and Arab states thrived on repression, and insecure major powers such as Britain and France had little to gain and much to fear from higher standards that tied their hands and might embolden opposition at home (and, for the British, in Northern Ireland).

This charged environment produced the early death of the ICRC's wish to include low-intensity armed revolt ("tensions" or "disturbances") in IHL. It also buttressed the view that if new rules emerged for nonliberation internal conflicts, they could only apply in major civil wars in which the rebel parties were well-organized armies that controlled territory and that stood a chance to actually respect the law through a disciplined chain of command. For the majority coalition (formed by the Third World, Socialist states, Latin American, and Arab countries) these requirements promised simultaneously to keep Protocol II at bay except in the *really* bad cases (think the Nigerian or Spanish civil wars), striking an apparent balance between self-interest and humanitarianism.

A few states distanced themselves from this sovereignty-protecting mindset. In particular, the Scandinavians, the United States, and Canada argued publicly and privately for the need to create expansive rules with wide applicability to both state and nonstate actors. Their insistence came to naught, however, and stringent conditions of application were inserted for Protocol II (control of territory, level of organization and responsible command, an ability to conduct sustained and concerted military operations) in 1975, subject to Plenary review.

Although the United States eventually began to see the substance of the Second Protocol as a lost cause (or the inevitable casualty) of the Conference, the Canadians fought to keep Western interest alive in it and to seek a compromise with its detractors. The Scandinavians, however, mobilized intensely to make sure that the contents of both Protocols remained as similar as possible. The skeptical majority found this unacceptable and by the close of the Conference's Third Session in 1976, it was evident that the draft Protocol II (with extensive humanitarian protections and high threshold of application) was in jeopardy, unlikely to be adopted a year later.

Concerned not to let Protocol II fall through the cracks, it appears that Canada, the ICRC, and a limited number of "enlightened" moderates in the Third World coalition, especially Pakistan (and possibly Egypt) labored to construct a version of the Protocol that could prove acceptable to the majority, retaining the high threshold but also severely trimming the contents of the draft under negotiation.[57] When the time for the Protocols' final adoption came in 1977, the Pakistani delegate introduced a treaty-long "amendment" (among others, cutting provisions such as the assurance of quarter, the delay of the death penalty, or the provisions allowing the ICRC and similar humanitarian organizations to offer their services), and after an article-by-article Plenary review, and not without grumbling from the extremists on both sides in the room, this "gentleman's agreement" became Protocol II.[58]

This succinct look at the CDDH allows for the inference that in the 1970s very few states seemed to be negotiating on the basis of a genuine, broad humanitarianism that would expand the law in ways that tamed their sovereignty and security concerns. Instead, most states sought changes to the law that would enhance their positions, while not unduly constraining their future military operations. The 1970s revisions certainly produced crucial hard-won humanitarian achievements. Yet beyond this and behind the veil of the Protocols' adoption "by consensus" in 1977 lies the fact that many of their outcomes were the product of uneasy compromises, insincere acquiescence, and textual ambiguities. In other words, while the Additional Protocols introduced major innovations into IHL, many of those innovations seemed to rely only on a thin layer of diplomatic consent rather than on substantive, thick political consensus.

[57] Mantilla, "Under (Social) Pressure," ch. 6.

[58] Notable articles retained (in modified form) due to pressure from the ICRC, Scandinavian states, Austria, and the Holy See, were those related to the protection of the civilian population, the protection of objects indispensable to the survival of the civilian population and the protection of works and installations containing dangerous forces.

From Contention to Acceptance: Post-1977 Developments

Despite the slight veneer of agreement, over time Additional Protocols I and II have become widely accepted treaties, with 194 and 166 ratifications respectively. Many of the principles they embody, though initially controversial, seem to have taken root, even in the initially hesitating West.[59] At the very least, many of their principles now seem publicly and privately unquestionable in a way that they were not a half-century ago. This suggests that, despite the troubled negotiation of these rules, with the passage of time and through various pathways the Protocols have in large part been "decoupled" from their origins and entered the realm of well-accepted international norms and law.[60] As explored in the following chapters, military training, judicial proceedings, and external pressure, among other mechanisms, have to some extent (and with important variation) disseminated key IHL principles and rules among state and nonstate actors, international organizations, and the general public.

Indeed, the 1970s revisions themselves spurred further movement toward progressive developments almost immediately.[61] Many participants and observers of those negotiations, including the ICRC and legal scholars from various latitudes, were on the whole disappointed with the CDDH's outcomes. The lesson they drew was that international conferencing was not the best method to develop the law, given the plethora of conflicting state interests, the risk of forced compromise, and the pull toward a low common denominator. In effect, since the late 1970s, developments of the law via alternative routes such as scholarly interpretation or judicial precedent (both are instances of *opinio juris*) have proliferated. It was thanks the International Court of Justice's *Nicaragua* 1986 decision that Common Article 3 came to be considered basic customary law for all types of conflicts, a point later reaffirmed through the creation and work of the International Criminal Tribunals for the Former Yugoslavia (ICTY) and Rwanda (ICTR). Equally important, an opinion of the Appeals Chamber of the ICTY (in the *Tadić* case) introduced international criminal law in internal conflicts through recourse to customary law, a gesture that was later "hardened" in

[59] The US government attitude toward ratification of the Protocols is complicated. Despite the fact that in 1977 the delegation at the Conference counted its results as a success, years later the Reagan administration decided to publicly decry Protocol I as "terrorist law" due to its treatment of national liberation wars and prisoners of war. This story is well and bitterly told by its principal protagonist, George Aldrich, in "Prospects for United States Ratification of Additional Protocol I."

[60] Critical views may persist on this point, given lamentably lackluster compliance patterns. Yet the law as such has not lost its legitimacy, quite the contrary.

[61] See Mantilla, "Under (Social) Pressure," ch. 6.

the Rome Statute of 1998 that created the International Criminal Court (ICC). Most recently, an extensive ICRC study has declared most rules of treaty-based IHL as customary. Although not devoid of controversy among states and lawyers, this turn to custom, courts, legal, and scholarly interpretation has extended IHL in interests of justice and to the benefit of war victims.[62]

In addition, normative change and growth since 1977 have been due to at least three other factors: changing political structures around the world, persistent atrocities, and the proliferation and strengthening of nongovernmental organizations and advocacy networks dedicated to human rights, humanitarian, or human security issues. First, the end of the Cold War and of formal empire, alongside the spread of democracy and the formation of security communities in Europe and elsewhere contributed to forging a political climate far less inimical to the diffusion of liberal norms, including improved humanitarian standards to mitigate internal atrocities. Second, the recurrence of gross IHL violations in the early 1990s served as demonstration effect and motive for tackling the inadequacy of received legal norms and mechanisms, facilitating institutional and ideational innovation.

Third, the rising "soft" power of principled practitioner or advocacy nongovernmental organization networks capable of creating new alliances and cajoling states, shaping their interests or altering their cost-benefit calculations has produced success even in the daunting task of prohibiting weapons or creating permanent criminal courts through international treaty-making.[63] A strong "human security network" has hugely amplified the opportunity for norm entrepreneurship in the humanitarian legal field, harnessing the enduring authority and stature of the ICRC but also going beyond it.[64] Through the passing of resolutions, and (often controversial) reporting and inquiry missions, regional courts and commissions, and UN bodies and agencies such as the Human Rights Council and the Security Council, have become key protagonists and practitioners of IHL. Increasingly, as the world has witnessed a convergence between humanitarian law, human rights law, and criminal law (what some now term "atrocity law"),[65] it appears that IHL has gone from

[62] See Theodor Meron, "The Humanization of Humanitarian Law," *American Journal of International Law* 94 (2000): 239–278.

[63] Maxwell A. Cameron, Robert J. Lawson, and Brian W. Tomlin, *To Walk without Fear: The Global Movement to Ban Landmines* (Oxford: Oxford University Press, 1998); Michael J. Struett, *The Politics of Constructing the International Criminal Court: NGOs, Discourse, and Agency* (New York: Palgrave Macmillan, 2008); John Borrie, *Unacceptable Harm: A History of How the Treaty to Ban Cluster Munitions Was Won* (New York: United Nations Publications, 2009).

[64] Denise Garcia, "Humanitarian Security Regimes," *International Affairs* 91, no. 1 (2015): 55–75.

[65] Ruti G. Teitel, *Humanity's Law* (Oxford: Oxford University Press, 2011); David Scheffer, *All the Missing Souls: Personal History of the War Crimes Tribunals* (Princeton: Princeton University Press, 2013).

comprising a restricted "monoculture" of experts to an "ecosystem" of norms and institutions.

This portrait is rosier than reality, however. The attacks and aftermath of 9/11 posed a profound challenge to the core of IHL, and the discourse and practice of terrorism (and counterterrorism) challenged the venerable regime in important ways. Notably, some insisted on the existence of categories of persons not protected by the law ("illegal enemy combatants"), raising doubts about IHL's adequacy in the contemporary world. Prolonged detention, targeted killings, and unmanned aerial vehicles (drones) have further raised doubts about IHL's robustness and validity. And debate is ongoing regarding the legal responsibilities of "new" actors, including peacekeepers, peacebuilders, business corporations, and private security companies, as the chapters by Siobhán Wills and Renée de Nevers discuss.

Yet when seen in the long historical trajectory, challenges to the law (either via new methods of war or after egregious instances of noncompliance) are not only *not* anomalous, but in fact act as a constant source of normative regeneration. Of course, contingency and politicization are also recurrent ingredients of any process of legal development. In particular, a sizable group of actors (including states) must agree to mobilize behind new revisions or additions. At present, however, renewed tensions stemming from Russia, and the persistence of myriad conflicts in the Middle East and Africa (with overt and covert involvement by multiple parties) make the prospect of swift or robust legal development unlikely.

Yet this chapter illustrates that it is precisely under challenging political conditions that some of IHL's most basic principles have emerged or become extended, albeit painstakingly, over time. The turmoil of Cold War and colonial/decolonization politics explains some of the most surprising rules (and silences or disappointments) of the Geneva Conventions and the Additional Protocols. Great power experience and interests explain the development of robust protections in many areas, especially the treatment of the wounded, sick, and shipwrecked, and of POWs, but also why IHL lacked strong criminal provisions until the 1990s, or why controversial parts of it (the provisions for internal conflict and national liberation war, for instance) are notoriously vague or ineffectual. Developing and non-Western countries have made their own varied imprints on IHL, helping expand protections to all victims of conflict in 1949, or in a more politicized direction, as in 1977 through Additional Protocol I and national liberation conflict. For their part, the ICRC, Scandinavian countries, and Switzerland have consistently been the critical IHL "entrepreneurs" in the direction of victim-centered humanitarianism. On the basis of this overview, it seems appropriate to conclude that international and domestic political forces, both normative and military, progressive and conservative, have shifted and mixed over time to shape the law in interesting and sometimes counterintuitive ways, as the chapters that follow attest. This pattern will undoubtedly continue into the future. Given the continuing transformation of armed conflict and its proliferation, scholars would do well to devote more thoughtful historically grounded and theoretically eclectic analysis to this most important international regime. The case studies that make up the remainder of this book are intended to do so.

3

The Struggle to Fight a Humane War

The United States, the Korean War, and the 1949 Geneva Conventions

SAHR CONWAY-LANZ

The newly expanded Geneva Conventions on the protection of war victims experienced a troubled start during the Korean War. Along with the People's Republic of China and the regimes in North and South Korea, the United States struggled to put into practice these new international humanitarian laws. Many had expected the US armed forces to be exemplary in their adherence to the conventions in Korea. Confronted by the pointed questioning of a reporter from the New York *Daily Worker* in the first weeks of the war, the secretary-general of the United Nations, Trygve Lie, retorted, "Don't you know that the United States Army has always adhered to the Geneva Convention—always when they have been in action?"[1] These expectations were well founded on the United States' past record of leadership in advancing the laws of war as well as the publicly stated intentions of American leaders. From early in the Korean War, US officials repeatedly criticized the North Koreans, and then the Chinese, for violating the conventions and refusing to cooperate with the International Committee of the Red Cross (ICRC), reinforcing the idea that the United States fully embraced the agreements.

However, the experience of the war revealed the severely limited protections that the new conventions could offer to war victims and exposed a number of areas in which Americans failed to comply with the humanitarian laws' strictures. Difficulties in controlling the movements of refugees resulted in first an informal understanding, and then specific orders from American commanders, to fire on civilians in order to prevent them from approaching American positions. Largely silent on restrictions for aerial bombardment or the use of

[1] *New York Times*, July 15, 1950.

indiscriminate weapons, the 1949 Geneva Conventions allowed the United States to employ methods that destroyed entire cities and towns on the Korean peninsula, including a firebombing campaign that harmed countless noncombatants. Although not publicly exposed during the war, US officials also prevented the ICRC from inspecting atrocious conditions in civilian refugee camps and hospitals. Finally, the United States had difficulties conforming to the conventions in its adopted policies on the repatriation of prisoners of war (POWs) and its handling of violent conflicts in its POW camps. While the harm from bombing reflected gaps in the Geneva Conventions' protections, the rest of this harm to war victims resulted from failures to comply with the laws, motivated by overriding military and political interests. What constituted a violation of the conventions was often hotly disputed and ambiguous, but the harm Americans inflicted on refugees and POWs were instances in which experts in international humanitarian law, often ICRC representatives, at the time identified as deviations from the Geneva laws.

Even though the conventions had gaps and American interests overrode their provisions at times, the laws were not simply fig leafs obscuring raw power. The Geneva Conventions did provide limited but concrete protections and moreover underwent a process of legitimatization for Americans and a broader international community during the Korean War that laid a foundation for the future expansion and internalization of humanitarian protections. In 1955, the United States chose to ratify the conventions that had gained a new visibility during the war. The visibility came through the formal incorporation of the conventions' protections into American military training and military justice system during the war, but even more through public controversy that urged protections for war victims and increased pressures on leaders. The public prominence and legitimacy of the conventions was also reinforced by the propaganda charges and countercharges of the two conflicting sides, which sought to paint the other as the inhumane combatant violating the decent norms of the international community.

The New Geneva Conventions

At the outset of the Korean War, people like Secretary Lie had good reasons to expect that the United States would follow the new Geneva Conventions scrupulously. The United States had long been an innovator and active participant in the construction of modern international humanitarian law and the codification of the rules of warfare. In 1863, the United States established one of the earliest national codes of the laws of war when the US Army issued its General Order No. 100, "Instructions for the Government of Armies of the United

States in the Field," more commonly called the "Lieber Code" after its primary author, the legal scholar Francis Lieber. American representatives participated in the international conferences that produced the first Geneva Convention on the sick and wounded in 1864, the 1899 and 1907 Hague laws, and the subsequent updates of the Geneva Conventions including the 1929 Convention on POWs. With the exception of several of the Hague Conventions on international arbitration and permissible weapons, the US Senate adopted all of these treaty obligations.

World War II deepened American engagement with the international laws of war. Revulsion at German and Japanese atrocities gave impetus to the 1942 Allied War Crimes Declaration and 1943 Moscow Declaration, which pledged the Allies to try the perpetrators of war crimes. After the war, the United States took a leading role prosecuting war crimes at the international tribunal at Nuremberg and the International Military Tribunal for the Far East. The ICRC proposed that revision of the Geneva Conventions could mitigate the types of crimes that the Germans and the Japanese had committed during World War II and so led an initiative in the fall of 1945 to organize international support for updated agreements. American officials also saw this potential in revised conventions and became involved in the ICRC's initiative at an early stage. The US delegates participated in preliminary informal discussions at Geneva in April 1947 and continued discussion at the Seventeenth International Red Cross Conference in Stockholm in August 1948. The US negotiators actively participated in the 1949 Geneva conference that produced the new conventions, and the United States signed the agreements at the conference's conclusion.[2]

The 1949 conventions introduced a number of major changes in international humanitarian law and a host of minor revisions. Two primary innovations addressed harm to war victims that the Axis had been guilty of during World War II: repression of civilians in occupied areas and refusal to offer protections to partisan fighters. The 1949 revisions produced an entirely new convention on the "Protection of Civilian Persons in Time of War," which was primarily concerned with the humane management of civilian populations in occupied territories and offered a variety of protections against collective punishment, pillaging, inhumane internment, and other forms of arbitrary violence toward

[2] Draft memorandum, J. V. Dillion to Raymond Yingling, February 15, 1950, box 673, Provost Division, Record Group (hereafter RG) 389, National Archives, College Park, MD (hereafter NA); William H. McCahon, "Report of the United States Delegation, Diplomatic Conference for the Establishment of International Conventions for the Protection of War Victims at Geneva, Switzerland, April 21–August 12, 1949," n.d., box 2385, 514.2, Central Decimal Files 1945–1949, RG 59, NA.

civilians at the mercy of an occupying army. The primary change to the POW convention was language that defined a legitimate combatant more precisely and acknowledged that resistance fighters who conformed to a few simple practices deserved the same protections under the convention as regular soldiers. Another major addition incorporated into all four conventions was a brief but significant common article concerning civil wars, which laid out general principles of the humane treatment of those placed *hors de combat*. Besides this common article, little changed in the 1949 revisions for the other two conventions on the care of sick and wounded on land and in the sea.[3]

Although central to all of the Geneva Conventions, the idea of noncombatant immunity—the principle that those not participating in combat should be sheltered from its violence—was largely expressed implicitly in the 1949 treaties. The agreements were overwhelmingly concerned with detailed provisions that offered protections to various types of noncombatants—the sick and wounded, POWs, civilians—but did not prominently articulate the general principle of distinction between combatants and noncombatants nor the responsibility to protect noncombatants from harm. Ironically, the clearest statement of these principles appeared in the rump common article concerning civil wars, an article kept brief because more detailed provisions for these conflicts "not of an international character" proved too controversial for the states negotiating the conventions.

Moreover, the treaties were largely mute on a significant threat to noncombatants: indiscriminate violence from increasingly destructive weapons. The Hague laws, untouched since 1907, had more to say in this area of restrictions on inhumane methods of warfare, but the updated Geneva laws avoided this area almost entirely even though the Hague and Geneva laws had often overlapped in the past. At the 1949 Geneva conference, the Americans and the British opposed the inclusion of restrictions on bombing as well as the Soviet Union's attempts to use the treaty to outlaw atomic weapons. Two of the American negotiators later wrote, "It is to be emphasized that these 'grave breaches' do not constitute restrictions upon the use of modern combat weapons. For example, modern warfare unfortunately and often may involve the killing of civilians in proximity to military objectives, as well as immense destruction of property."[4]

[3] Geoffrey Best, *Humanity in Warfare* (New York: Columbia University Press, 1980), 290; Jean S. Pictet, "The New Geneva Conventions for the Protection of War Victims," *American Journal of International Law* 45, no. 3 (July 1951): 462–475.

[4] Geoffrey Best, *War and Law since 1945* (New York: Clarendon, 1994), 115–116, 204–205; conference minutes, July 7, 1949, 514.2, Central Decimal Files 1945–1949, RG 59, NA; Raymund T. Yingling and Robert W. Ginnane, "The Geneva Conventions of 1949," *American Journal of International Law* 46, no. 3 (July 1951): 427.

The Korean War

When the North Korean People's Army swept into the southern half of the Korean peninsula on June 25, 1950, igniting the Korean War, the United States quickly committed its armed forces to the humanitarian principles of the Geneva Conventions. The 1949 treaties had not technically entered into force at the start of the war,[5] and the US Senate had not yet ratified the conventions. However, the US State Department quickly assured the ICRC that the United States would be guided by the humanitarian principles of the conventions. General Douglas MacArthur, commander of the American and UN forces in Korea, publicly pledged that his soldiers would adhere to the conventions in their conduct of the war, a promise the South and North Korean governments soon also made.[6]

As a civil conflict, the Korean War posed challenges for the Geneva laws written almost entirely with interstate warfare in mind, especially for the American participants unfamiliar with and often unsympathetic to Korean culture and society. With Koreans fighting on both sides, sometimes as guerrillas, Americans and other members of the UN coalition had difficulties identifying enemy combatants and distinguishing them from innocent civilians. The recent political division of the Korean peninsula also raised questions of state allegiance for individual Koreans. With the governments of both the North and South making claims on each other's territory, clear definitions for concepts central to the Geneva Conventions such as "occupied territory" and "protected persons" could be elusive. In contrast, as a coalition war, the Korean War placed added pressures to conform to international agreements. As the dominant member of the UN coalition, the United States had incentives to seek legitimacy through its observance of the Geneva Conventions as well as clear political interests in mollifying any ally who raised concerns about American deviation from the agreements.

As the war began, the US armed forces already had in place many institutional practices that aligned with the earlier Geneva Conventions and the revised 1949 agreements. The US field manual on the laws of land warfare from 1940, *FM 27-10 War Department Field Manual: The Laws of Land Warfare*, was the doctrinal manual in use during the Korean War. It was based on earlier Geneva and Hague law as well as the Lieber Code and contained many provisions similar to the 1949 Geneva Conventions. The manual included requirements for the protection of civilians and POWs. Provisions banned wanton destruction and the harming of POWs, and stated that a universal recognition existed that hostilities

[5] The treaties came into force on October 21, 1950.

[6] Memorandum, Charles Runyon to Louis J. Halle, June 28, 1954, with attachment "Background Memorandum Concerning the Application of the 1949 Geneva Conventions," n.d., box 75, Lot 61D53, Bureau of Public Affairs 1944–1962, RG 59, NA; *New York Times*, July 5, 1950.

were restricted to armed forces and that civilians must not be harmed in life, liberty, or private property without cause. However, other provisions allowed for the killing of noncombatants when it was "incidentally unavoidable" in armed conflict and for the destruction of property, both on the grounds of military necessity. The manual contained little concerning aerial bombing except that it forbade the bombardment of undefended places, which American military lawyers interpreted to mean a place that a military force could occupy without firing a shot. This meant the prohibition did not apply to any target behind enemy lines.[7]

Even though the American officials who helped negotiate the conventions tended to minimize the changes that the 1949 agreements introduced as simply reflecting custom in civilized societies like the United States,[8] the US armed forces took measures to further incorporate the new Geneva laws into their military justice system and their training programs during the Korean War. After World War II, the American military undertook an extensive effort to reform and standardize its two separate systems of military justice in the Navy and the Army. The result was the 1950 Uniform Code of Military Justice. Having been worked out while the Geneva Conventions were being negotiated, the new uniform code implemented many of the protections that the agreements required. The code included sanctions against American service members for crimes such as murder, rape, assault, and theft committed in the midst of war. The Geneva Conventions required signatories to provide instruction in the conventions and Americans made some progress in this during the Korean War. For example, in July 1951, the Department of the Army issued Training Circular No. 22 "Training in the Geneva Conventions of 1949." The circular introduced a three-hour course of instruction to ensure familiarity with the conventions and convey to all military personnel an understanding of the basic rules of warfare and of the rights of war victims.[9]

Refugees

Almost immediately after the outbreak of the war began the difficulties adhering to the conventions in practice. Only weeks into the war, American armed forces encountered problems handling Korean refugees. The military's response

[7] *Law of Land Warfare: Judge Advocate General School, Text No. 7* (Ann Arbor, MI: Judge Advocate General's School, 1945), 40–41.

[8] Yingling and Ginnane, "The Geneva Conventions of 1949," 393–427.

[9] William G. Downey Jr., "Training in the Geneva Conventions of 1949," *American Journal of International Law* 46, no. 1 (January 1952): 143–144.

to these troubles resulted in first a widespread informal understanding, and later explicit orders, to fire on civilian refugees as a last resort in order to control their movements. This policy produced documented instances in which American soldiers shot and killed unarmed men, women, and children. Both the killings and the orders arguably violated the injunction of Article 32 of the civilian convention prohibiting "any measure of such a character as to cause the physical suffering or extermination of protected persons in their hands," certainly ICRC representatives had such concerns. However, military alarm over the refugees interfering with military transportation and posing a threat to American forces crowded out any considerations that the policy might be a war crime. The desperate circumstances of the Americans' retreat before the North Korean offensive and difficulties telling friend from foe among Koreans only made the challenges for Americans worse.

In the first month of the war, as the North Korean forces advanced down the peninsula, tens of thousands of civilians moved southward along with the retreating American units. These refugees clogged roads and interfered with military transportation. American soldiers also came to believe that the flow of refugees constituted a more direct military threat to them by providing opportunities for North Korean soldiers to infiltrate UN lines disguised as civilians.[10] Although it appears unlikely that large numbers of North Korean soldiers were actually using infiltration tactics to attack US forces from behind,[11] American commanders treated infiltration by the enemy, disguised as refugees, as a problem of major proportions. Guerrillas assisting the North Koreans may have also contributed to these fears of infiltrators.[12] This fueled a climate of distrust of all Korean civilians. A State Department advisor to the South Korean government on the refugee problem told the *New York Times* that during the summer fighting American soldiers had developed a tendency to regard all Korean civilians near the battle zone as the enemy.[13]

To address the problems that refugees posed for their forces, US commanders established in late July a strict policy to control the movements of civilians. At a meeting on July 25, representatives of the South Korean government, the American embassy, the National Police, and the Eighth Army decided on a comprehensive policy to control refugee movements. The orders sent out the

[10] *Report of the No Gun Ri Review* (Washington, DC: US Department of the Army, Inspector General, 2001), 33–35.

[11] Robert L. Bateman, *No Gun Ri: A Military History of the Korean War Incident* (Mechanicsburg, PA: Stackpole, 2002), 71–75; Charles J. Hanley, Sang-Hun Choe, and Martha Mendoza, *The Bridge at No Gun Ri: A Hidden Nightmare from the Korean War* (New York: Henry Holt, 2001), 79–80.

[12] Bruce Cumings, *The Origins of the Korean War*, Vol. 2, *The Roaring of the Cataract, 1947–1950* (Princeton, NJ: Princeton University Press, 1990), 686–690; Bateman, *No Gun Ri*, 74–75, 79–80.

[13] *New York Times*, September 1, 1950.

following morning said that no refugees would be permitted to cross battle lines at any time, and the movement of all Koreans in groups was to cease immediately. Each division would be assigned National Police liaison officers to assist in clearing any area of civilians who would interfere with operations.[14]

Although the orders did not explicitly authorize the use of lethal force against refugees as a last resort to control their movements, substantial evidence indicates that this was how the orders were understood by frontline soldiers and officers as well as the highest levels of the Eighth Army. A July 24 entry in the communications log of a frontline regiment recorded a liaison officer's interpretation of the emerging refugee control policy. The entry read, "No refugees to cross the frontline. Fire everyone trying to cross the lines. Use discretion in case of women and children."[15] Each commanding general of the three US divisions fighting in Korea in late July was reported by either journalists, Army historians, or the division's own daily journal to have ordered their troops to fire on refugees to control their movements.[16]

However, the strongest evidence of a general understanding that lethal force might be deemed necessary to control refugees can be found in a July 26 letter from the American ambassador to Korea John J. Muccio to Dean Rusk, the assistant secretary of state for Far Eastern affairs. The letter addressed the refugee control problem and recounted the decisions made at the July 25 meeting at Eighth Army headquarters. Ambassador Muccio wrote that the problem had developed "a serious and even critical military nature" and that he was writing because the military was "necessarily" making decisions about the problem that threatened to have repercussions in the United States. The letter described the military problems of clogged roads and infiltration that the movements of refugees caused. Muccio then listed his impressions of the July 25 meeting's decisions, and the first read, "Leaflet drops will be made north of U.S. lines warning the people not to proceed south, that they risk being fired upon if they do so. If refugees do appear from north of U.S. lines they will receive warning shots, and if they then persist in advancing they will be shot." The letter also reported that refugees would be warned that no group could move south unless so ordered and then only under police control. All movement of Korean civilians had to end at sunset or those moving would "risk being shot when dark comes."[17]

[14] *No Gun Ri Review*, 23–24.

[15] Ibid., 26–27.

[16] O. H. P. King, *Tail of the Paper Tiger* (Caldwell, ID: Caxton, 1962), 358–359; Roy Appleman, *South to the Naktong, North to the Yalu* (Washington, DC: Office of the Chief of Military History, Department of the Army, 1961), 291; HQ journal, July 26, 1950, 25th Infantry Division, Command Reports, 1949–1954, RG 407, NA.

[17] Muccio to Rusk, July 26, 1950, box 4266, 795.00, Central Decimal Files 1950-54, RG 59, NA. For a closer examination of the US refugee control policy and harm to refugees, see Sahr

What happened near the village of No Gun Ri on the very day Ambassador Muccio sent his letter demonstrated the danger that the strict refugee control policy posed for Korean civilians. Despite thorough investigations by the Associated Press, the US Department of Defense, South Korea's Ministry of Defense, and representatives of the Korean survivors, many questions remain about what precisely happened at No Gun Ri. According to Korean witnesses, US soldiers evacuated five hundred to six hundred villagers from their homes on July 25, 1950. Heading south on the morning of July 26, the villagers reached an American roadblock, where they were stopped by US troops and ordered onto railroad tracks above the road. Tired and hungry, the refugees sat and ate while American soldiers inspected their belongings and found no weapons among them. Shortly afterward, airplanes appeared overhead and strafed and bombed the villagers on the tracks killing 50–150 of them. Many of the survivors scrambled for cover into twin tunnels running beneath the railroad tracks. There they crouched to avoid periodic gunfire that riddled the tunnel entrances for at least a day. This small arms fire killed another 60–300 villagers.[18] The Defense Department report from its investigation in 2001 offered a different version of events, but did agree with the Korean witnesses that, as a result of US actions, Korean civilians were killed and injured in the vicinity of No Gun Ri in the last week of July. Soldiers from the American battalion near No Gun Ri reported to investigators shooting in the direction of refugees, either as a warning to keep them from moving or because they believed gunfire was coming from the direction of the refugees.[19]

The killings at No Gun Ri were unique primarily in the thoroughness of the subsequent investigations and confirmation by all sides of the deaths of Korean civilians at the hands of American soldiers. Many other Koreans suffered from American policies on controlling refugees. Although the issue of whether the deaths at No Gun Ri resulted from a direct order from American officers remains disputed,[20] US commanders did give orders to fire on refugees starting only days after No Gun Ri. Investigative reporting by the Associated Press has documented that American commanders gave direct orders to fire on refugees later in the summer of 1950 as the UN forces fought along the Naktong River in southeastern Korea. A communications log from a battalion of the 1st Cavalry Division recorded an officer's August 9 order to "shoot all refugees coming across the

Conway-Lanz, "Beyond No Gun Ri: Refugees and the United States Military in the Korean War," *Diplomatic History* 29, no. 1 (January 2005): 49–81.

[18] *No Gun Ri Report*, i–ii, 139–141, 153, 147, 190. See also Koo-Do Chung, *The Truth of the No Gun-Ri Massacre* (Taejeon: The Committee for Unveiling Truth about the No Gun-Ri Massacre, 2002).

[19] *No Gun Ri Report*, i, vii, ix–x, xiv–xv, 131–132.

[20] Conway-Lanz, "Beyond No Gun Ri," 49–81.

river."[21] In late August, the division commander General Hobart R. Gay ordered his artillery to fire on all refugees, according to unit journals.[22] Also during the fighting along the Naktong river, the journal of the 35th Regiment of the 25th Infantry Division stated, "Any refugees approaching our defensive position will be considered to be En[emy] and will be disperwde[*sic*] by all availlabe[*sic*] fires including Art[illery]."[23]

This trend culminated in explicit orders issued from the top US commander in Korea during a second refugee crisis in the winter of 1951, after the Chinese had entered the conflict. Out of concerns similar to those of the summer of 1950 over infiltration and the hampering of transportation, General Matthew B. Ridgway issued a series of orders intended to manage this second tide of refugees. With the communist forces threatening to retake Seoul, Ridgway issued a January 2 order that refugees not be permitted to pass through forward positions nor along main roads and bridges. This time the commander of the Eighth Army explicitly authorized his troops to shoot refugees who violated the movement restrictions. Ridgway passed instructions to General Charles D. Palmer of the 1st Cavalry Division that his military police were first to fire over the heads of refugees who attempted to use Route 1, the main road out of Seoul, and as a last resort to fire at them. A day earlier the Eighth Army headquarters had issued an even more sweeping directive to "stop all civilian traffic in any direction." It instructed subordinate commands that "responsibility to place fire on them to include bombing rests with you." Apparently this order was difficult to implement, because the 1st Cavalry Division resorted to threatening its officers with a $100 fine for allowing any civilians to pass through the front lines.

On January 4, leaflets were dropped warning civilians that further crossing of the Han River south of Seoul was prohibited and anyone attempting to cross would be fired on. The Army's official history of the Korean War said that no firing was necessary to enforce the ban on crossing the river. However, the directive to prevent civilians from crossing front lines by fire, if necessary, appears to have remained in effect through the spring of 1951. In June, intelligence officers from the 2nd Infantry Division were recommending a modification of this policy, in

[21] Communications log, August 9, 1950, 1st Battalion, 8th Cavalry Regiment, 1st Cavalry Division, RG 338, NA.

[22] Journal, August 29, 1950, Artillery Command, 1st Cavalry Division, RG 338, NA; journal, August 29, 1950, HQ 61st Field Artillery Battalion, 1st Cavalry Division, RG 338, NA.

[23] Journal, August 17, 1950, 35th Infantry Regiment, 25th Infantry Division, Command Reports, 1949–1954, RG 407, NA. See also Bateman, *No Gun Ri*, 127; "Men at War: The Ugly War," *Time*, August 21, 1950, 20–22; John Osborne, "Report from the Orient: Guns Are Not Enough," *Life*, August 21, 1950, 77–85.

part "due to the hesitancy on the part of the younger officers to fire directly upon groups of old men, women, and children."[24]

How many, if any, Korean refugees were shot by US troops during the winter fighting will probably never be known, but at least one American officer claimed after the war that his revulsion at harming innocent civilians led him to choose not to fire on refugees even though it put his men at greater risk. Refugees were pressing in on a roadblock held by this infantry captain's company, and his troops were urgently requesting permission to fire on them. The captain understood that if disguised enemy soldiers were mingled among the civilians, they would be in the rear of his company in the morning. Despite this fear, the officer could not bring himself to order the shooting of the women and children who made up most of the group of refugees.[25]

The orders to fire on refugees and the resulting deaths did not attract much public attention during the Korean War. A North Korean newspaper made vague charges about Americans killing two thousand civilians in Yongdong county, the district that contained No Gun Ri.[26] However, the Americans involved in the severe refugee control policy did display a sensitivity to the norm against harming civilians even in the absence of a public spotlight, as evidenced by the concern expressed in Ambassador Muccio's letter, the communication log's recommendation to "use discretion" in the case of women and children, and the captain's refusal to fire on refugees.

Certainly, there were voices beyond the Americans' communist adversaries ready to question US methods in the war. Working behind the scenes as it usually did, the ICRC by the early fall of 1950 was cautioning the United Nations about the fighting in Korea. The ICRC wrote, "From information we received it appears certain frontline fighters on both sides Korean conflict are insufficiently informed fundamental principles of humanitarian conventions leading to derogations to conventions and especially actions contrary to respect due to red cross emblem." The committee also reiterated that "non-combatants especially women children shall never be attacked but always respected and humanely treated."[27] Many of the Koreans harmed by the American policy to

[24] Billy C. Mossman, *Ebb and Flow: November 1950–July 1951* (Washington, DC: US Army Center of Military History, 1990), 196, 202, 204; Matthew B. Ridgway, *The Korean War: How We Met the Challenge* (Garden City, NY: Doubleday, 1967), 95–96; message, EUSAK to X Corps et al., January 1, 1951, Command Reports, 1949–1954, RG 407, NA; journal, January 3, 1951, HQ 2nd Battalion, 8th Cavalry Regiment, 1st Cavalry Division, Command Reports, 1949–1954, RG 407, NA; memorandum to CO 38th Infantry, June 29, 1951, 2nd Infantry Division, Command Reports, 1949–1954, RG 407, NA.

[25] Donald Knox, *The Korean War: An Oral History* (San Diego: Harcourt, 1985), 657.

[26] Cumings, *Origins of the Korean War*, 706.

[27] Message, ICRC to Executive Assistant to UN Secretary General, n.d. [c. October 19, 1950], box 4380, 800.571, Central Decimal Files 1950–1954, RG 59, NA.

fire on refugees may have arguably not qualified as "protected persons" under the conventions because those refugees may not have been in areas controlled by American soldiers—"in the hands" of American soldiers as the language of the civilian convention puts it—something only much more research might be able to establish for particular cases. Nevertheless, either because of an additional gap in the Geneva Conventions or a deviation from them, the laws failed to protect civilian refugees effectively during the Korean War.

Bombardment

While the United States deviated from the Geneva Conventions on the protection of refugees largely out of public view, the use of American airpower generated numerous accusations of atrocious harm to war victims from communist adversaries as well as more muted expressions of concern about indiscriminate destruction from allies. The 1949 Geneva Conventions were largely silent on protections for war victims against bombardment. Article 32 of the civilian convention forbade extermination and physical suffering of civilians but made no specific mention of bombing, and American military lawyers argued that the conventions' protections did not apply to civilians behind enemy lines except in very specific situations like the protections of Article 18 that shielded hospitals from attack. Otherwise, the civilian convention only proposed voluntary establishment of safety zones where noncombatants could be sheltered from the effects of war.

Lacking a formal legal basis, criticism of the bombing reflected the broader international norm that opposed harm to noncombatants in war. The 1949 Geneva Conventions that inadequately embodied this norm left practices like bombing, a serious threat to the norm, largely unrestricted. Although American officials did display a certain level of sensitivity to protecting civilians from US firepower and did implement some measures to protect them, the bombing inflicted terrible destruction and suffering on Korean civilians. After an initial policy of restraint, US forces embarked on a firebombing campaign that incinerated cities, towns, and villages. Even when Americans did attempt to discriminate between combatants and noncombatants their efforts were complicated by the challenges of identifying the enemy in a civil war.

Public protests against "barbarous" American attacks on civilians emanating from North Korea and its supporters put Americans on the defensive from the very start of the war. *Pravda* reported that a June 29 attack on railyards in the North Korean capitol of Pyongyang destroyed many houses and left a "considerable number" of victims among the civilian population of the city. On August 8, the Soviet representative Yakov Malik introduced a draft resolution to the UN

Security Council condemning American attacks. The resolution claimed that "the bombing by the United States armed forces of Korean towns and villages, involving the destruction and mass annihilation of the peaceful civilian population, is a gross violation of the universally accepted rules of international law." Two weeks later the North Korean minister of foreign affairs accused the United States of a "flagrant violation" of the Geneva Conventions through the alleged bombing of hospitals and ambulances.[28]

UN allies voiced more muted concerns about the bombing, and these concerns were echoed at times in the American press. In August, British officials worried that the Far East Air Force (FEAF) intended to commence saturation bombing with the object of leveling entire cities. Indian Prime Minister Jawaharlal Nehru expressed concern in a press conference that innocent persons might be killed and unnecessary damage done in the UN bombing. He argued against the tactic of heavy bombing, which he believed created future problems.[29] Concerns about protecting civilians from bombing appeared in a variety of American publications, spanning the Jesuit magazine *America* to the conservative newsletter *Human Events* to the Air Force Association's magazine *Air Force* and the *Washington Post*. In one of his columns, Walter Lippmann cautioned that the United States had to convince its allies that America could defend a friendly nation without destroying it. He believed that a year of bombing Korea could only result in a "pyrrhic" victory: "We shall not have proved that we can contain aggression but only that we can wreck a country while the aggressor is trying to enslave it."[30]

With concern over world opinion mounting, American leaders gave clear assurances that the United States was using violence discriminately in Korea. "The problem of avoiding the killing of innocent civilians and damages to the civilian economy is continually present and given my personal attention," General MacArthur reassured the United Nations.[31] At a September 6 news

[28] Message, Moscow Embassy to Secretary of State, June 30, 1950, box 4263, 795.00, Central Decimal Files 1950–1954, RG 59, NA; *United Nations Security Council Official Records*, August 8, 1950, 5th year, 484th mtg., S/PV.484, 20; message, New York to Secretary of State, August 21, 1950, box 4380, 800.571, Central Decimal Files 1950–1954, RG 59, NA.

[29] Memorandum of conversation, Philip C. Jessup, August 18, 1950, box 4267, 795.00, Central Decimal Files 1950–1954, RG 59, NA; memorandum of conversation, George W. Perkins, August 18, 1950, box 4267, 795.00, Central Decimal Files 1950–1954, RG 59, NA; notes on Cabinet meeting, James E. Webb, August 18, 1950, box 4267, 795.00, Central Decimal Files 1950–1954, RG 59, NA; message, New Delhi Embassy to Secretary of State, August 18, 1950, box 4267, 795.00, Central Decimal Files 1950–1954, RG 59, NA; *New York Times*, August 19, 25, 1950.

[30] Robert A. Graham, "Strategic Bombing," *America*, September 9, 1950, 612; Henry Beston, "Soliloquy on the Airplane," *Human Events* 7, no. 42 (October 18, 1950): 1–4; "Brickbat," *Air Force* 33, no. 11 (November 1950): 6; *Washington Post*, August 17, September 12, 1950.

[31] *New York Times*, September 3, 1950. See also "Report of the United Nations Command Operations in Korea," *U.S. Department of State Bulletin*, October 2, 1950, 534–540; "Fifth Report

conference, the secretary of state Dean Acheson also denied the accusation that UN forces were "bombing and killing defenseless civilians." Acheson said that UN air strikes in Korea had been "directed solely at military targets of the invader" and that these targets were "enemy troop concentrations, supply dumps, war plants, and communication lines." The secretary accused the North Koreans of compelling civilians to labor at military sites, using peaceful villages to hide tanks, and disguising their soldiers in civilian clothes.[32]

Official sensitivity to harming civilians translated into more than just attention to maintaining a scrupulous public image. Concern for sparing civilians generated individual actions and general policies that provided some real protection for Korean noncombatants. Initially, General MacArthur refrained from launching a campaign of firebombing attacks against North Korean cities and towns. Although this policy stemmed from concern over provoking a wider war with the Soviets rather than from deference to the Geneva Conventions or its humanitarian principles,[33] it did temporarily spare civilians. During this initial phase of the air campaign against North Korean forces, American bombers did conduct precision strikes, against industrial targets, that attempted to avoid civilian structures. One classified Air Force report describing an attack on the main industrial complex at Chinnampo said virtually all bombs struck the target areas or open spaces and that negligible damage was inflicted on nearby housing.[34] The FEAF told the press that it was attempting to reduce civilian casualties. Reporters wrote that US pilots were under orders not to strafe anyone on the roads unless they were positively identified as military. A Fifth Air Force public relations officer described for the press the procedures that pilots were supposed to use to avoid strafing refugees: "To separate refugees from soldiers we have certain criteria. For instance, if they carry things on their heads, they are women. If they are in white and we haven't seen them change clothes, they are refugees. But if the Army reports they are troops in disguise, we strafe them."[35]

In practice, distinguishing enemy soldiers from civilians was much more difficult. During the North Korean retreat after the Inchon landing, a Navy pilot

of the U.N. Command Operations in Korea," *U.S. Department of State Bulletin*, October 16, 1950, 603–606.

[32] "North Korea Slanders U.N. Forces to Hide Guilt of Aggression," *U.S. Department of State Bulletin*, September 18, 1950, 454.

[33] Sahr Conway-Lanz, *Collateral Damage: Americans, Noncombatant Immunity, and Atrocity after World War II* (New York: Routledge, 2006), 84–87.

[34] "Annex to Summary of Air Situation in Korea, August–December 1950," vol. 1, box 209, Korean Daily Reports April 1951–July 1953, Office of the Deputy Director for Estimates, Directorate of Intelligence, Office of the Deputy Chief of Staff for Operations, RG 341, NA.

[35] *New York Times*, January 10, 1951. See also, "Out of Korea by Christmas?" *U.S. News and World Report*, September 29, 1950, 16–19; *New York Times*, July 5, 1950.

complained to intelligence officers about the problem of identifying civilians. "Commie soldiers may turn around and walk south as soon as they hear us coming," he said. "Hell, how can we tell a real refugee from a disguised soldier when they're all moving south?"[36] The difficulties of identifying civilians from the air resulted in attacks on Koreans who were most likely refugees or farmers and led to the belief among at least a few American officers that pilots were under orders to strafe civilians early in the war. A July 31, 1950, mission report from the 35th Fighter Bomber Squadron recorded a strafing of a sand bar in a river where people and foxholes were seen. Pilots reported that the "people appeared to be evacuees." An operations report summary from the aircraft carrier the USS *Valley Forge* the same month described a similar attack. A Navy plane strafed a group of fifteen to twenty people dressed in white. After the first pass, the pilots decided that the people seemed to be civilians and groups sighted subsequently were investigated without firing. They all appeared to be peasants working in their fields. The Valley Forge operations report explained that the attack on the civilians had resulted from information from the Army that "groups of more than eight to ten people were to be considered troops, and were to be attacked."

An Air Force colonel who had recently arrived in Korea in late July 1950 quickly came to believe that the Fifth Air Force had a policy of strafing civilian refugees. In a memorandum to Brigadier General Edward L. Timberlake with the subject line "Policy on Strafing Civilian Refugees," the colonel wrote that because of concerns about enemy soldiers infiltrating American lines disguised as refugees, the "army has requested that we strafe all civilian refugee parties that are noted approaching our positions." He continued, "To date, we have complied with the army request in this respect." It is not clear whether the policy was implemented widely and the purpose of the colonel's memorandum was to recommend that this policy be discontinued because of potentially embarrassing publicity, but at least the colonel was convinced that American pilots were expected to strafe Korean civilians.[37]

In early November 1950, when UN soldiers first fought with Chinese units, the UN Command adopted a policy of the purposeful destruction of cities in enemy hands. The FEAF began incendiary raids against urban areas reminiscent

[36] "Out of Korea by Christmas?" *U.S. News and World Report*, September 29, 1950, 16–19. See also Walter Karig, "Korea—Tougher to Crack than Okinawa," *Collier's*, September 23, 1950, 24–25, 69–70.

[37] Mission report, 35th Fighter Bomber Squadron, July 31, 1950, US Air Force Historical Research Agency; action summary, U.S.S. Valley Forge, July 25, 1950, Korean Combat Action Reports for Carriers, Naval Aviation History Office; memorandum, Turner C. Rogers to Timberlake, July 25, 1950, Office of the Deputy Chief of Staff for Operations, Fifth Air Force, RG 342, NA. See also mission report, 35th Fighter Bomber Squadron, July 20, 1950, US Air Force Historical Research Agency.

of World War II, and MacArthur spoke of making the remaining territory held by the North Koreans a "desert."[38] Unlike the summer retreat of 1950, Washington did not restrain MacArthur, likely because the wider war feared earlier had already broken out, with the Chinese instead of the Soviets. The new firebombing campaign reflected little restraint out of a concern for protecting war victims beyond a publicly professed sensitivity to destroying hospitals.

Sinuiju was one of the first cities to be destroyed. The FEAF showered 500 tons of incendiary bombs on more than one square mile of the city's built-up area, destroying 60 percent of the city. The Air Force press release assured that the aiming points for the bombers were away from hospital areas. In General Emmett O'Donnell's report on the work of his bombers, he declared, "the town was gone." Other towns were to follow. By November 28, Bomber Command reported that 95 percent of the town of Manpojin's built-up area was destroyed, for Hoeryong 90 percent, Namsi 90 percent, Chosan 85 percent, Sakchu 75 percent, Huichon 75 percent, Koindong 90 percent, and Uiju 20 percent. One B-29 bombardier said that with the switch to the use of incendiaries in November the bombers had "completely wiped out innumerable cities in North Korea." The destruction continued into the winter as Chinese forces compelled the UN soldiers to retreat south. As UN units withdrew from the major North Korean cities, those cities too became targets. On December 30, the FEAF commander Lieutenant General George E. Stratemeyer informed his subordinates that they had the authority to "destroy" Pyongyang, Wonsan, Hamhung, and Hungnam, four of North Korea's largest cities. The FEAF conducted the attacks without warning to the civilian population and purposefully avoided publicizing the strikes. The firebombing of North Korean towns that commenced in November made meaningless the earlier claims by the FEAF that their bombing operations avoided the destruction of residential areas.[39]

General Stratemeyer demonstrated a single-mindedness in carrying out the incendiary campaign even at the risk of unwanted destruction. Stratemeyer's staff pointed out to him how reported sites of POW camps, hospitals, and prisons would be vulnerable to incendiary attack. The Air Force commander later wrote in his diary about the danger to these sites, "Whether vulnerable or not,

[38] Memorandum of conversation, Muccio, November 17, 1950, *Foreign Relations of the United States* (hereafter FRUS) 1950, vol. 7, 1175.

[39] Robert Futrell, *The United States Air Force in Korea, 1950–1953*, rev. ed. (Washington, DC: US Government Printing Office, 1983), 221–223, 226; *New York Times*, November 9, 1950; William T. Y'Blood, ed., *The Three Wars of Lt. Gen. George E. Stratemeyer: His Korean War Diary* (Washington, DC: Air Force History and Museums Program, 1999), 269, 371–372; interview transcript from 98th Bomb Group, November 30, 1950, box 905, Project Decimal File 1942–1954, Directorate of Plans, Office of the Deputy Chief of Staff for Operations, RG 341, NA; Conrad C. Crane, *American Airpower Strategy in Korea, 1950–1953* (Lawrence: University of Kansas Press, 2000), 63.

our target was to take out lines of communication and towns." Stratemeyer sent orders to the Fifth Air Force and Bomber Command "to destroy every means of communications and every installation, factory, city, and village."[40]

Actions of the UN naval and ground forces added to the civil destruction on the Korean peninsula during the winter of 1950–1951. The Navy systematically destroyed the port city of Wonsan with more than a year of daily naval bombardment and in another incident shelled hundreds of civilian refugees on a crowded beach at Pohang. The Eighth Army repeatedly requested air strikes for close air support that simply named South Korean cities instead of any specific military target within the cities.[41]

As the vulnerability of the civilian population to American bombing became increasingly evident, the ICRC urged additional measures that US leaders found unacceptable. In April 1951, Paul Ruegger, president of the ICRC, urged the creation of safety zones in Korea to protect women, children, and old people from the ravages of the war as Article 14 of the civilian convention urged. The following year the idea of safety zones was raised in both the United Nations and the Consultative Assembly of the Council of Europe. An Air Force letter to the secretary of state explained some of the American objections to the safety zones. It said that communist guerrillas in South Korea might use the zones to provide themselves with immunity, and the United Nations would require a guarantee through neutral supervision that safety zones in North Korea were not contributing to the war effort. However, the North Korean and Chinese governments, suspicious of the International Committee's neutrality, refused to allow ICRC observers into their countries. Without neutral observers, which the civilian convention recommended, the US government found the proposal for safety zones in North Korean controlled areas unacceptable. The Air Force letter failed to explain why ICRC or other neutral supervision for safety zones in South Korea could not prevent their feared exploitation by communist guerrillas.[42] The closest the United States came to establishing safe zones was implementing a sporadic policy of warning civilians of impending air attacks through leaflets,

[40] Y'Blood, *Stratemeyer Diary*, 258–261.

[41] *New York Times*, March 30, 1951; "Korean Release Unnumbered," December 17, 1951, box 5, Korean War Communiques and Press Releases 1950–1951, Office of the Chief of Information, RG 319, NA; "Korean Release Unnumbered," December 19, 1951, box 5, Korean War Communiques and Press Releases 1950–1951, Office of the Chief of Information, RG 319, NA; *Washington Post*, April 14, 2007; message, CG FEAF to CG EUSAK, September 28, 1950, box 905, Project Decimal File 1942–1954, Directorate of Plans, Office of Deputy Chief of Staff for Operations, RG 341, NA.

[42] Paul Ruegger, "Press Conference Statement," April 9, 1951, box 4380, 800.571, Central Decimal Files 1950–1954, RG 59, NA; *New York Times*, July, 23, September 27, 1952; K. R. Kreps to Secretary of State, April 20, 1951, box 879, 014, Project Decimal File 1942–1954, Directorate of Plans, Office of Deputy Chief of Staff for Operations, RG 341, NA.

radio broadcasts, and loudspeaker-equipped airplanes. However, American military planners also favored the warning program for its anticipated psychological effects of demoralizing enemy civilians and convincing them to abandon their war-related jobs.[43]

Without sufficient protections for civilians from UN firepower, the fighting devastated Korea. By the summer of 1951, when the front had stabilized around the 38th parallel, the hostilities had ruined large areas of the Korean peninsula both north and south, and the human toll was terrible. Quantification of the suffering of Korean civilians is a poor reflection of what the war put them through, but some numbers can give an idea of the scale. In the summer of 1951, the UN Command estimated that five million Koreans had left their homes and become refugees. The South Korean government reported in August 1952 the complete destruction of over 400,000 civilian houses and 8,700 primary schools. Estimates of the number of civilians killed in the entire war range from 244,000 to 990,000 for South Korea. North Korea would continue to suffer from UN air attacks and naval bombardment until the end of the war. UN bombardment destroyed or forced underground virtually all of the North's heavy industry. By the end of the war, eighteen of twenty-two major cities in North Korea had been at least half obliterated according to damage assessments by the US Air Force. The North Korean government has never published estimates of civilian deaths in the war but more than one million killed has been an estimate common among historians who have studied the conflict. Charles R. Joy, the head of the CARE mission in Korea, summarized his impression of the destruction left by the war. He wrote, "In twelve successive years of relief work in different parts of the world I have never seen such destitution and such wider spread misery as I have seen here."[44]

[43] HQ USAF, *An Evaluation of the Effectiveness of the United States Air Force in the Korean Campaign* (Barcus Report), vol. 5, 102–103, box 906, Project Decimal File 1942–1954, Directorate of Plans, Office of the Deputy Chief of Staff for Operations, RG 341, NA; transcripts, "Voice of the Free Peoples of World," July 7–9, 11, 12, 15, 16, 19, 20, 21, 23, 26, 1950, box 2539, 511.95, Central Decimal Files 1950–1954, RG 59, NA; First Radio Broadcast and Leaflet Group, "Plan for Psychological Warfare Operations Designed to Support the United Nations Air Force," June 12, 1952, box 20, General Correspondence 1952, Psychological Warfare Section, General Headquarters, Far East Command, RG 338, NA; "Plan for Psychological Warfare Operations in Support of Air Attack Program," July 7, 1952, box 7, General Correspondence 1952, Psychological Warfare Section, General Headquarters, Far East Command, RG 338, NA; "Reports of U.N. Command Operations in Korea: Sixty-Fifth Report for the Period March 1–15, 1953," *U.S. Department of State Bulletin*, July 13, 1953, 52–53.

[44] *New York Times*, August 2, 9, 1951; "Statistical Tabulation Explaining the Overall Status of Damage Suffered during the Course of the War of June 25, 1950," August 12, 1952, box 4283, 795.00, Central Decimal Files 1950–1954, RG 59, NA; Alan R. Millett, "Casualties," *Encyclopedia of the Korean War*, ed. Spencer C. Tucker et al. (Santa Barbara, CA: ABC-CLIO, 2000), 100–101; Crane, *American Airpower Strategy in Korea*, 168; David Rees, *Korea: The Limited War* (New York: St. Martin's, 1964),

The vast scale of destruction in Korea became a story for American journalists[45] and around the world. The attention generated criticism of American bombing from several quarters. Predictably, communist charges were the most shrill. In June 1951, Soviet UN Ambassador Yakov Malik submitted an inflammatory report to the Security Council authored by the Women's International Democratic Federation. The conclusion of the report accused the United States of conducting a "merciless and methodical campaign of extermination" in violation of the rules of warfare laid down in the Hague and Geneva conventions, a campaign that surpassed the atrocities of the Nazis in occupied Europe. The US ambassador to the United Nations, Warren Austin, dismissed the report as malicious propaganda. Austin assured that US forces in Korea were under orders to obey the Geneva and Hague conventions.[46]

Communist adversaries were not the only critics. American peace activists challenged the tactics of American soldiers in Korea as too destructive. The National Council for the Prevention of War and the Fellowship of Reconciliation condemned the obliteration of Korean communities and harm to civilians in their publications.[47] Religious periodicals like the *Christian Century, Commonweal,* and *Catholic World* expressed concern over the role the US military played in devastating Korea.[48] Books by I. F. Stone and the British correspondent Reginald Thompson charged the US armed forces with indiscriminately harming noncombatants, and the American mainstream press occasionally placed some

460–461; Cumings, *Origins of the Korean War,* 748; Charles R. Joy, "May Discursive Report: Korea," June 6, 1952, box 48, Joy Papers, Andover Harvard Theological Library (hereafter AHTL).

[45] For examples, see "Does U. S. Face Endless War in Korea?" *U.S. News and World Report,* May 4, 1951, 22–23; "Korean War: The Big Losers," *U.S. News and World Report,* July 13, 1951, 19–20; "Tragedy of Korea," *Newsweek,* July 9, 1951, 30; "The Forgotten People," *Time,* July 16, 1951, 22–24.

[46] United Nations Document S/2203, June 19, 1951; *New York Times,* July 3, 1951; "Charges of Atrocities in Korea Called Propaganda to Discredit U.N. Action," *U.S. Department of State Bulletin,* July 30, 1951, 189–190. The North Koreans and Chinese also used the armistice negotiations as a forum for criticizing US bombing as inhumane. See message, CINCUNC to JCS, July 29, 1951, box 33, Geographic File 1951–1953, RG 218, NA; message, CINCUNC to JCS, August 14, 1951, box 33, Geographic File 1951–1953, RG 218, NA; message, CINCUNC to Dept of the Army for G3 and JCS, August 15, 1951, box 33, Geographic File 1951–1953, RG 218, NA.

[47] Frederick J. Libby, "Plans for Peace," *Peace Action* 17, no. 9 (September 1951): 2; Alfred Hassler, "Cops in Korea," *Fellowship* 16, no. 9 (September 1950): 4–8; Alfred Hassler, "Call Off the Cops!" *Fellowship* 17, no. 3 (March 1951): 1–5; Helen Mears, "The Voices of America," *Fellowship* 17, no. 9 (September 1951): 6–7; "Is There a Lesser Evil?" n.d., box 3, series A-5, section II, Fellowship of Reconciliation-USA Papers, Swarthmore Peace Collection.

[48] "Faith, Morals and War," *Christian Century,* April 4, 1951, 422–423; "Korea Must Be Rebuilt," *Christian Century,* August 8, 1951, 907–908; H. C. Francis, "Modern War," *Commonweal,* February 16, 1951, 470–472; S. D. Newberry, "Delectable Slaughter," *Catholic World,* May 1952, 127. Also see "Outlook for Korea," *Commonweal,* November 28, 1952, 187; "Not Inconvenienced," *Christian Century,* March 11, 1953, 292.

blame on US policy for the suffering of the Korean people.[49] A few conservatives and strong anticommunists such as Senator Robert Taft and Upton Sinclair also criticized American methods of warfare in Korea as too destructive.[50]

Refugee Camps

The devastation inflicted by American bombing contributed to another humanitarian challenge that the new Geneva Conventions had been updated to address, the need to provide for displaced war refugees. The more than five million refugees that the war created imposed a staggering burden on the UN coalition and the South Korean government. The United States undertook extensive relief efforts to aid the refugees and had notable successes in preventing the human suffering from becoming much worse. However, the war effort came first and military and political interests overrode protections for displaced civilians in a number of areas. Atrocious living conditions developed in the refugee camps, and these conditions prompted the UN Command to refuse to cooperate with the ICRC in carrying out their full responsibilities under the conventions.

The United States did much to ameliorate the enormous suffering of Koreans displaced by the fighting. The UN Command established the UN Civil Assistance Command Korea (UNCACK) to handle aid to the civilian population. Its public health programs had dramatic successes in reducing the number of deaths from typhoid, typhus, and smallpox, and its food distribution program prevented widespread famine. The US government and private charitable organizations also cooperated to establish the relief organization American Relief for Korea (ARK), which by June 1952 had delivered more than $2 million in relief aid to Korean civilians to supplement US government aid.[51]

[49] I. F. Stone, *The Hidden History of the Korean War* (New York: Monthly Review Press, 1952), 143, 179, 236, 256–258, 265; Reginald W. Thompson, *Cry Korea* (London: Macdonald, 1951), 42, 44, 53–54, 74, 89, 91, 114, 125, 143, 148; Freda Kirchwey, "Liberation by Death," *Nation*, March 10, 1951, 215–216; Walter Sullivan, "Rebuilding Shattered Korea," *Nation*, February 2, 1952, 107–109; Harold L. Ickes, "Sherman's Hell; Korea's Hell," *New Republic*, March 3, 1951, 18; E. J. Kahn Jr., "Letter from Korea," *New Yorker*, April 21, 1951, 122–125; *Washington Post*, February 24, 1951; *New York Times*, March 3, 1951.

[50] *New York Times*, January 6, 1951, June 25, 1952; Robert A. Taft, *A Foreign Policy for Americans* (Garden City, NY: Doubleday, 1951), 12; Upton Sinclair radio scripts, August 20 and, September 3, 1950, *The Right Wing Collection of the University of Iowa Libraries, 1918–1977*, microfilm collection (Glen Rock, NJ: Microfilming Corporation of America, 1977), C35.

[51] Appleman, *South to the Naktong*, 670; Albert E. Cowdrey, *The Medics' War* (Washington, DC: Center of Military History, United States Army, 1987), 327; George Barrett, "Preview in Korea—The Task of Relief," *New York Times Magazine*, August 19, 1951, 10; *New York Times*, July 14, 1951; "Reports of U.N. Command Operations in Korea: 58th Report for the Period November

Nonetheless, for American officials unsurprisingly, the war effort came before aid to Korean refugees. This sense of priorities was acknowledged in the press. As a *Saturday Evening Post* article put it, the UNCACK axiom was "the war must be won, above all other considerations, and anything done for the people of Korea must come second to that necessity."[52] Because of military priorities, the UN Command required that all donations from the private relief agencies be distributed by UNCACK in conjunction with the South Korean government. Several of the relief agencies believed that the UNCACK monopoly on the distribution of aid hindered them from making their maximum contribution to assisting the refugees.[53]

While the United States government poured soldiers, weapons, and money into Korea to prevent the North Koreans and the Chinese from expelling the United Nations from the peninsula, it did not provide sufficient resources to avoid atrocious conditions at the refugee camps in which homeless Koreans found shelter. Chinese intervention created a refugee crisis for the UN Command that surpassed the one at the outbreak of the war. Ensuring the health and welfare of these hundreds of thousands of fleeing Koreans would have been extremely difficult during the winter months of 1950 and 1951, when UN forces were scrambling to halt the Chinese advance. It is difficult to see how deplorable conditions in refugee camps thrown up to accommodate this human flood could have been avoided initially.

However, terrible conditions in refugee camps persisted for more than a year after the initial crisis of the Chinese invasion had ended. The South Korean government was directly responsible for the management of the refugee camps, but the UN Command and US government did not do everything they could have to ameliorate the suffering they had helped to create. Press coverage at times prodded American officials into doing more. Greg MacGregor of the *New York Times* in late July filed a dramatic story about the conditions in the Koochon refugee camp near Seoul, which he called "a blot on the United Nations' record in Korea." The camp overflowed with 37,000 refugees. Some were North Koreans forced out of their homes and into the camp by UN forces concerned about espionage and enemy exploitation of the civilian population, and some were South

16–30, 1952," *U.S. Department of State Bulletin*, May 11, 1953, 692–693; "Information Bulletin No. 61," July 12, 1952, box 1, Unit Histories and Command Reports, Public Information Office, Far East Command, RG 349, NA.

[52] William L. Worden, "What Must We Do about Korea Now?" *Saturday Evening Post*, December 15, 1951, 32–33, 93–101. See also *New York Times*, December 29, 1950.

[53] *New York Times*, January 18, 1952; Harold E. Fey, "Let the Churches Help Korea!" *Christian Century*, February 13, 1952, 190–192; Charles R. Joy, "CARE Conference Report: Korea, Summary of Activities from December 1st, 1951 to August 1st, 1952," box 48, Joy Papers, AHTL; Edgar S. Kennedy, *Mission to Korea* (London: Derek Verschoyle, 1952), 108–109.

Koreans trying to move north back to their former homes in the Seoul area. In the camp, army tents designed to house four soldiers were crowed with as many as forty men, women, and children. Some of the less fortunate had to camp in the open. The camp hospital was staffed by five doctors and eighteen nurses with facilities for about 120 patients. On the day MacGregor visited, the hospital contained 817 patients with many lying on grass mats on the floor. MacGregor wrote that the people "are forced to live worse than any animal kept by an American farmer." The UN public welfare officer responsible for the area had tried to do what he could to rectify the situation. Recently, he had ordered 200 more tents, but he complained that official red tape delayed his requests and hindered his efforts. Within a week of MacGregor's story, the UN Command had undertaken greater efforts to relieve the situation at Koochon. Tents were delivered, and half the camp's population was forced south to other better-equipped refugee camps, despite the refugees' reluctance to move further from their former homes.[54]

Other camps had problems, though. E. J. Kahn reported in the *New Yorker* about poor conditions in a refugee camp near Pusan and noted that UN camps for POWs maintained much better living conditions. William Worden writing in the *Saturday Evening Post* conceded that the camps were "horrible, by Western standards," but, professing his detestation of what he thought communist rule to be, he claimed that the camps were "a thousand times better than the real horror from which North Koreans in particular have fled."[55]

The continuing poor conditions in South Korean refugee camps prompted the UN Command to avoid its full responsibilities under the Geneva Conventions. In February 1951, representatives of the ICRC complained that the UN Command was not fully applying the conventions. They specifically avoided accusing the UN Command of violating the conventions but claimed that the command was not providing transportation and authorization to visit areas such as refugee camps and hospitals so that the ICRC could carry out its responsibilities under the conventions. According to ICRC representatives, the UN Command was only cooperating with them in the application of the POW convention and not the other three conventions. The State Department entered into a prolonged dialogue with the UN Command and the Defense Department in an attempt to obtain the military's full cooperation with the ICRC. After the State Department had made several unsuccessful attempts to instruct the UN Command to cooperate on all four conventions, Assistant Secretary of State John D. Hickerson wrote to the secretary of defense. Hickerson argued that the State Department considered it "essential that this Government obtain from the

[54] *New York Times*, July 21, 29, 1951.

[55] E. J. Kahn Jr., "Letter from Korea," *New Yorker*, June 30, 1951, 60–66; Worden, "What Must We Do about Korea Now?", 32–33, 93–101.

International Committee a clean bill of health with respect to the treatment of civilians as well as prisoners of war." Ridgway's headquarters had to allow Red Cross representatives to fulfill their role as neutral observers to do this.

Military leaders, however, feared that the ICRC would not give a clean bill of health on the treatment of civilians. In early 1952, Secretary of the Army Frank Pace Jr. wrote to the secretary of defense that if the UN Command allowed ICRC inspections under the fourth convention, they would reveal the deplorable conditions existing in civilian hospitals and refugee camps managed by the South Korean government. Published reports of these conditions would cause worldwide criticism and condemnation of the UN Command, the United States, and the United Nations, he believed.

Attached to Pace's memorandum was an extract from a report by the chief physician of the hospital ship *Jutlandia*, a Danish vessel dispatched to assist the UN effort in Korea. The extract described the terrible conditions in one refugee camp that an ICRC investigation might uncover. The camp, one of several just south of the Han river, contained between 50,000 and 70,000 refugees who had been left to their own initiative to procure shelter against the elements on a bare patch of ground. The camp "hospital" consisted of a structure resembling an open shed under which 600 to 700 lay and sat. Some rested on bare earth while others lay on rush mats soaked with urine and feces.

The *Jutlandia*'s chief physician described the scene at the hospital as an "inconceivable sight." In one corner lay cases of small pox, most of them children whose faces were almost unrecognizable because of large festering wounds. Scattered elsewhere he noted patients with typhoid fever, dysentery, typhus, tetanus, or leprosy. The doctor called the hospital "a disgrace for the U.N." He credited the Korean doctors at the camp with heroic efforts, but they could neither obtain sufficient food nor medicine for these suffering people. Despite the difficulties of war, the doctor felt that thousands of people should not be dying in Korea because they did not have access to modern medicines, and he believed that poor administration and the lack of cooperation among the different UN relief organizations was an essential cause of the misery.

Because of concerns that such conditions would be exposed to public scrutiny, the UN Command and the Department of Defense refused to accredit ICRC representatives except under the POW convention. As a compromise, the Defense Department suggested that ICRC delegates not be "accredited" or "recognized" but instead "invited" to join a guided inspection tour "prescribed by" the UN Command. The delegates would then be required to make their reports to the UN Command, which would have the opportunity to comment on them before they were forwarded to the United Nations. The State Department refused the proposals because it did not believe they would be acceptable to the ICRC, "since they are inconsistent with its necessary freedom of action as an impartial humanitarian organization." Unable to reach a compromise, the situation remained unresolved. Representatives of the ICRC were not accredited under three of the four Geneva Conventions, and this lack of accreditation deprived them of the necessary access to transportation and relevant areas.

Despite the UN Command hampering the Red Cross inspections into such conditions, the International Committee never publicized the command's obstructionism. A confidential ICRC report in July 1952 continued to protest the failure to provide adequately for three to four million refugees who were "slowly dying." However, the Defense Department's conscious suppression of information about miserable conditions at refugee camps and the United States' failure to apply fully three of the four Geneva Conventions in the Korean War went unchallenged in public.[56]

Prisoners of War

While the United States had a better record of cooperating with the ICRC on the POW convention, that convention's application during the Korean War encountered its own problems. Americans made a big show of touting their compliance with the POW convention and the norms it represented, and condemning their adversaries for committing atrocities against prisoners. American leaders reckoned serious breaches of the POW convention—murder of prisoners, torture, forced marches, beatings, and inadequate food—a central charge in their public campaign against their communist opponents. Indeed, the investigation of enemy war crimes by the US military during the Korean War and the publicity surrounding those investigations exceeded the efforts undertaken

[56] Memorandum of conversation, "Relations of International Committee of the Red Cross with Unified Command in Korea," February 14, 1951, box 4380, 800.571, Central Decimal File 1950–1954, RG 59, NA; memorandum of conversation, "Relations of International Committee of the Red Cross with Unified Command in Korea," 3:00 p.m., February 14, 1951, box 4380, 800.571, Central Decimal File 1950–1954, RG 59, NA; memorandum, Charles Runyon to Louis J. Halle, June 28, 1954, with attachments "Background Memorandum Concerning the Application of the 1949 Geneva Conventions," n.d., letter, Hickerson to Secretary of Defense, November 21, 1951, letter, William C. Foster to Secretary of State, February 15, 1952, letter, Hickerson to Secretary of Defense, April 21, 1952, and letter, Marshall S. Carter to Secretary of State, May 15, 1952, box 75, Lot 61D53, Bureau of Public Affairs 1944–1962, RG 59, NA; memorandum, Robert M. Lee to Hoyt Vandenberg, January 31, 1952 with attachments memorandum, Pace to Secretary of Defense, January 11, 1952, and "Extract of Report by Chief Physician on Hospital Ship 'Jutlandia,'" box 903, 383.6, Project Decimal File 1942–1954, Directorate of Plans, Office of Deputy Chief of Staff for Operations, RG 341, NA; message, Tokyo Embassy to Secretary of State, December 5, 1951, box 4380, 800.571, Central Decimal Files 1950–1954, RG 59, NA; message, CG KCOMZ to CINCUNC, July 30, 1952, box 808, Security Classified General Correspondence 1952, Adjutant General Section, RG 500, NA.

during World War II, when most attention to these issues occurred after the end of hostilities. Early in the war, the US armed forces publicly warned the North Koreans against violating international humanitarian law. On August 19, 1950 General MacArthur warned Kim Il-Sung, "I shall hold you and your commanders criminally accountable under the rules and precedents of war." As concern among the UN Command grew about potential North Korean atrocities in the wake of the UN counteroffensive in September 1950, MacArthur approved the establishment of a War Crimes Section at Eighth Army Headquarters in October 1950 to begin investigations of enemy war crimes.[57] By this time, atrocities against US soldiers had become a common story in the American press.[58] In November, public attention in the United States and abroad to the atrocity charges increased significantly when the head of the Eighth Army War Crimes Section, Colonel James N. Hanley, announced to reporters that the North Koreans had murdered over 5,700 American soldiers.[59] While Hanley's figures were later questioned, even by his commanders, Hanley's revelation and other reports from Korea created an international uproar and generated thousands of letters to Congress.[60]

Communist brutality toward POWs continued as a common theme of US propaganda throughout the war. Between the start of the war and October 1951, a third of all the public reports that the UN Command submitted to the United Nations included mention of mistreatment of prisoners. The military's public information officers passed along photographs to the press suggesting the enemy's savagery but censored photographs that might indicate crimes by UN forces. Censorship criteria stated, "Photos of UN troops and POWs dead or alive which suggest or hint actual or possible atrocious acts, or other violations of the Geneva Convention by UN forces will not be passed."[61] After the war, the heated accusations of atrocity continued. In late 1953, US Ambassador to the United Nations Henry Cabot Lodge presented the alleged communist crimes against POWs to the United Nations, and Senator Joseph McCarthy held congressional hearings on the subject, giving another highly visible venue for

[57] US Senate, Committee on Government Operations, *Korean War Atrocities: Report* (Washington, DC: US Government Printing Office, 1954), 2; US Senate, Committee on Government Operations, *Korean War Atrocities: Hearing*, 83rd Cong., 1st sess., pt. 1, 8–9, pt. 3, 150.

[58] See, for example, *New York Times*, September 29, 30, 1950, October 6, 14, 23, 1950.

[59] Message, Chief of Staff, U.S. Army to CINCFE, November 15, 1951, FRUS 1951, vol. 7, 1137.

[60] William Stueck, *The Korean War: An International History* (Princeton, NJ: Princeton University Press, 1995), 245; Senate Committee on Government Operations, *Korean War Atrocities Report*, 1.

[61] Steven Casey, *Selling the Korean War: Propaganda, Politics, and Public Opinion in the United States, 1950–1953* (New York: Oxford University Press, 2008), 280; "Press Advisory Division Censorship Criteria," [1951], box 35, Subject Files 1949–1951, Office of the Chief of Information, Office of the Chief of Staff, Office of the Supreme Commander for the Allied Powers, RG 331, NA.

hyperbolic rhetoric. At the hearings, General Ridgway called the North Korean and Chinese armies the "most brutal and ruthless in the modern history of warfare."[62]

Although the atrocity charges had political utility for the United States in garnering sympathy in the international community, and Americans had their own deviations from the Geneva Conventions, the accusations of communist war crimes was not simply cynical hypocrisy. The Chinese, and especially the North Koreans, did mistreat UN POWs. The United States also held its own soldiers accountable for brutality against war victims. The US military enforced its Uniform Code of Military Justice during the Korean War, which agreed in many of its particulars with the Geneva Conventions. Americans tried their own individual soldiers before military courts martial for crimes similar to those of which they accused the North Koreans and Chinese. Courts martial tried and convicted American soldiers of murder, rape, assault, theft, and other crimes committed against Korean civilians. Of convictions that were appealed, three concerned the murder of POWs. In one case, a private was sentenced to life at hard labor for shooting an apparently sleeping Korean whom the soldier thought was a communist and unconvincingly claimed was reaching for a grenade. The two other cases concerned another murder. A lieutenant and two airmen were accused of killing a captured Korean who had been apprehended trespassing at a bomb depot. The lieutenant who ordered the shooting and the airman who actually shot the prisoner were found guilty. The other airman had his court-martial overturned by the Supreme Court because he had been discharged from the Air Force when he was tried. Besides these three cases, most of the murders by American soldiers that were appealed concerned killings that were committed in connection with other criminal activity like rape or theft. However, one concerned the murder of a civilian by a soldier improperly carrying out his military assignment. A private was convicted of shooting a five-year-old girl while trying to chase her away from bunkers he was maintaining.[63] Although it is difficult to judge whether these few convictions constituted adequate enforcement and the case of the acquitted airman demonstrated that the American system of military justice had gaps that interfered with holding individuals accountable, these courts martial did demonstrate that the US armed forces enforced seriously some of the protections provided for under the Geneva Conventions.

Although the US military upheld the POW convention in its cooperation with the ICRC and its exercise of its military justice system, American compliance with the convention was not complete. In two areas, the international

[62] Senate Committee on Government Operations, *Korean War Atrocities Hearings*, pt. 1, 4.

[63] *Court Martial Reports*, vol. 2, 213–219, vol. 14, 742–786, vol. 16, 638–674.

community questioned US adherence to the POW convention: repatriation of prisoners and the methods used to suppress violence that broke out in POW camps. Unlike the issues surrounding the civilian refugee camps, the problem of repatriation and the POW camp violence did attract public attention and became another arena in the Cold War propaganda battles between the United States and the communists.

As the two sides began armistice negotiations in July 1951 to end the war, US leaders realized they had a problem with the repatriation provision of the POW convention. Article 118 of the convention spelled out in plain language that all POWs should be repatriated quickly after the end of hostilities. Nevertheless, American officials began offering numerous arguments publicly and privately for why prisoners held by the United Nations should be treated differently from the injunctions of Article 118 and allowed to decide themselves whether they wanted to be repatriated. Publicly and in internal discussions, American officials and their supporters presented the dilemma in moral terms. They claimed that many of the Koreans and Chinese captured fighting for the communists were in fact anticommunists who would violently resist being repatriated, especially since they feared retribution from communist governments. The civil war in Korea and recent civil war in China made these claims plausible, except that there was no easy way to assess the individual sentiments of the prisoners. Although UN forces guarded and ostensibly administered the camps, groups of communist and anticommunist inmates came to dominate separate compounds, exposing prisoners to various forms of coercion in proclaiming their loyalties. Moreover, in private discussions, US officials revealed the political and military interests that could be furthered by deviating from Article 118 and supporting a policy of "non-forcible repatriation." The Joint Chiefs of Staff expressed concern that forcible repatriation would undermine American psychological warfare efforts both in Korea and the Cold War in general. US Army officials in charge of psychological warfare operations worried that a policy of forcing prisoners to repatriate unwillingly would reduce the incentive to surrender to UN forces in the future. Although left unstated in records of these discussions, a large number of prisoners supposedly willing to resist violently their repatriation to the People's Republic of China and North Korea could also be viewed as a humiliating repudiation of the communist system.[64]

[64] Memorandum, JCS to Secretary of Defense, August 8, 1951, FRUS 1951, vol. 7, 792–793; memorandum, Robert A. McClure to Chief of Staff, U.S. Army, July 5, 1951, box 8, Bureau of Public Affairs, 1944–1962, Lot 57D459, RG 59, NA; memorandum by Chief of Staff, U.S. Army, n.d., box 8, Bureau of Public Affairs 1944–1962, Lot 57D459, RG 59, NA; memorandum of conversation, January 17, 1952, box 8, Bureau of Public Affairs 1944–1962, Lot 57D459, RG 59, NA; Stueck, *Korean War*, 252.

The question of repatriation became a central and publicly prominent obstacle to concluding an agreement in the armistice negotiations for more than a year. The Chinese made repeated public protests at the truce talks and elsewhere over the US refusal to conform to the Geneva Conventions.[65] Although the two sides did eventually conclude a negotiated settlement of the repatriation issue that theoretically provided for neutral screening of prisoners in order to allow them to profess their loyalties free from coercion, this screening proposal barely worked in practice. Over twenty thousand Korean and Chinese prisoners were never repatriated. Korean prisoners were simply released in South Korea while thousands of Chinese prisoners were shipped to Taiwan. The United States could claim that repatriation to Taiwan was a legal solution under the Geneva Conventions, since Taiwan could be "officially" considered part of China, but only with such legalistic contortions could one view US policy on repatriation as conforming to the POW convention.[66]

Lax control of the POW camps and tensions over repatriation contributed to the outbreak of violence among the internees. The measures US armed forces used to suppress the violence and reestablish control provoked further questions about American adherence to the Geneva Conventions. A series of violent confrontations started in the POW camps in early 1952. In February, additional screening of prisoners sparked a riot in a camp on Koje-Do in which UN forces battled prisoners armed with makeshift weapons, killing 77 prisoners and wounding more than 140. In May, POWs took hostage the American commander of the camps on Koje-Do and held him for several days. To win his release without further violence, his replacement issued a public statement that lent some credibility to concerns that the United States was not fully meeting its obligations under the Geneva Conventions. The statement said, "I do admit that there has been instances of bloodshed where many PW have been killed and wounded by UN Forces. I can assure in the future that PW can expect humane treatment in this camp according to the principles of International Law." The Communist negotiators at the truce talks exploited the statement, and UN efforts to reassert control of the compounds on Koje-Do and elsewhere resulted in further violence, which culminated in ICRC protests over US methods.

Days after the hostage incident, a hospital camp near Pusan housing prisoners receiving medical treatment saw a clash between inmates with handmade

[65] Stueck, *Korean War*, 252; Rosemary Foot, *A Substitute for Victory: The Politics of Peacemaking at the Korean Armistice Talks* (Ithaca, NY: Cornell University Press, 1990), 96–97; Callum A. MacDonald, *Korea: The War before Vietnam* (New York: Free Press, 1986), 159.

[66] Walter Hermes Jr., *Truce Tent and Fighting Front: October 1951–July 1953* (Washington, DC: Office of the Chief of Military History, Department of the Army, 1966), 137, 496.

spears and barbed-wire flails and soldiers who used tanks, tear gas, and concussion grenades. US forces killed one inmate and wounded dozens. Over this clash, the senior ICRC delegate privately protested to American leaders. He argued that the use of concussion grenades and the withholding of food and water from the rioting POWs were infringements of the Geneva Conventions. The State Department acknowledged to the American consul in Geneva that the deprivation of food and water was a "technical" violation but dismissed the delegate's conclusion that the use of concussion grenades was excessive, pointing out that the delegate was not a "military man." A more senior ICRC official agreed with his colleague's objection to the use of the concussion grenades, since they were not normally used in riot control. However, this senior Red Cross official, according to the State Department, also appeared to appreciate "the inapplicability of certain portions of the Geneva Convention to the control of large oriental masses." While the ICRC may have quietly advocated for protections for Korean war victims, racial prejudice may have restrained their humanitarian efforts at times.

Although the ICRC raised its objections behind closed doors, the violence in the prison camps created a public spectacle as well. The conflicts attracted widespread media attention. At the truce talks, the communists accused the United States of "tearing up the Geneva Convention" in its treatment of prisoners.[67] The Joint Chiefs of Staff described communist propaganda on this issue as a "hate America" campaign exploiting the allegations of atrocities against POWs, spurred in particular by events on Koje-Do. In return, Secretary of State Acheson reiterated charges against the communists for refusing to comply to the POW convention including their failure to publish lists of individual POWs held, their refusal to allow the ICRC to inspect their camps or render services to the prisoners, and their neglect of making known when prisoners were sick or wounded and the location of POW camps.[68] Deadly clashes continued through the rest of 1952, resulting in dozens of additional prisoner deaths, more public scrutiny, and further private ICRC objections.[69]

[67] Foot, *Substitute for Victory*, 118–121; Hermes, *Truce Tent*, 233–262, 404–407; "War in Korea," *Time*, June 2, 1952, 23–24; memorandum, U. Alexis Johnson to Young, May 28, 1952, box 8, Bureau of Public Affairs 1944–1962, Lot 57D459, RG 59, NA; message, Secretary of State to US Consul, Geneva, June 23, 1952, box 903, 383.6, Project Decimal Files, Air Force Plans, RG 341, NA; "Geneva Primer," *Time*, May 26, 1952, 30.

[68] Message, JCS to CINCFE, June 5, 1952, box 60, National Security Policy Subject Files 1950–1957, Lot 62D385, RG 59, NA; press conference, July 16, 1952, *Press Conferences of the U.S. Secretaries of State, 1922–1974*, microfilm collection (Wilmington, DE: Scholarly Resources, 1974), reel 12.

[69] Message, McClure to CINCFE, January 22, 1953, box 757, Chronological File 1949–1954, Office of Security Review, Office of the Assistant Secretary of Defense for Legislative and Public Affairs, RG 330, NA; *Washington Post*, December 17, 1952; *New York Times*, December 22, 1952.

Legitimation of the Conventions

In the United States' first war since the 1949 Geneva Conventions had been signed, Americans struggled to fight a humane war and uphold the new humanitarian standards. American actions had contributed to extensive harm to refugees, POWs, and civilians in Korea, stemming from both gaps in the conventions and deviations from the agreements. This record of harm raises the question of the relevance and effectiveness of the Geneva Conventions, especially since so many expected American practices to conform to the laws and the United States did formally incorporate the laws into the training and military justice system of its armed forces. The new Geneva Conventions had a tragically flawed start in the Korean War.

However, the war's legacy was not simply one of failure for the Geneva treaties. The United States and the international community did not abandon the problematic agreements. Indeed, formal implementation of the Geneva Conventions continued after the end of the Korean War, with the United States ratifying the agreements in 1955 and the US Army issuing a new doctrinal manual on the laws of war in 1956 that reflected the 1949 conventions. Soviet ratification of the Geneva Conventions in May 1954 revived American interest in the agreements. Almost immediately after the Soviet ratification, the Department of Defense sent a letter to the State Department requesting that it end its objection to the ratification of the four Geneva Conventions. President Harry S. Truman had submitted the Geneva Conventions to the Senate in April 1951, but the State Department had asked that ratification of the treaties be postponed during the Korean War. Besides pointing out that ratification of the conventions could simplify military planning, the Defense Department letter raised the political disadvantage that the country would face if it remained the sole great power not a party to the Geneva Conventions of 1949. France had ratified them; Britain was in the process of ratifying them; and now the Soviet Union had recently become a party to them.

State Department officials initially hesitated to move on the treaty because they feared that US action during the Korean War had not been entirely consistent with the conventions. Once they studied this issue more closely, they uncovered the UN Command's lack of compliance with the convention on civilians during the war as well as the problems of complying with the POW convention. Yet concerns over the propaganda advantage that the Soviet Union would reap if the United States did not follow their lead pushed aside the liability that the US government had had difficulties fulfilling its responsibilities in the only American war since the agreements had been drafted. The Senate Foreign Relations Committee held hearings on the conventions in June 1955, and the full Senate ratified the treaty the following month. The United States deposited its ratification and thus formally adhered to the conventions on 2 August 1955. The United States submitted two reservations from the treaty that concerned copyright of the Red Cross symbol and the exercise of the death penalty in occupied areas, but these reservations fail to reflect the true legacy of American experience in the Korean War.[70]

The 1956 US Army field manual on the laws of war embodied this legacy more clearly and was another significant effort that furthered the formal implementation of the Geneva Conventions. Reflecting the updated conventions, the manual added a new chapter specifically devoted to the treatment of civilians and in another chapter stated, "it is a generally recognized rule of international law that civilians must not be made the object of attack directed exclusively against them." However, the manual also reflected the military interests that the experience of the Korean War had shown could override protections for war victims. For example, it more narrowly interpreted the restriction on bombarding undefended places by stating that factories producing military supplies, warehouses storing them, and transportation facilities moving them as well as places used to accommodate troops could be attacked.[71]

Together the US ratification of the Geneva Conventions and the revisions to the Army's law of war manual reflected an even larger legacy of the Korean War experience for Americans and a wider international community. Struggle with the Geneva Conventions was part of a broader process of international consensus-building on minimizing the destructiveness and human costs of war. The most easily realized part of the consensus was reflected in the relatively noncontroversial convention provisions that governments around the world agreed conformed to their military and political interests and their notions of military necessity, such as the immunity of doctors and hospitals from attack or the hundreds of mundane regulations for the humane operation of internment camps for POWs and civilian detainees. The protections for war victims that clashed the most with perceived military and political interests failed to even make it

[70] Memorandum by Jesse M. MacKnight, May 18, 1954, box 75, Bureau of Public Affairs 1944–1962, Lot 61D53, RG 59, NA; memorandum of meeting by Louis J. Halle, June 10, 1954, box 76, Bureau of Public Affairs 1944–1962, Lot 61D53, RG 59, NA; memorandum, Charles Runyon to Louis Halle, June 25, 1954, box 75, Bureau of Public Affairs 1944–1962, Lot 61D53, RG 59, NA; memorandum, Charles Runyon to Louis Halle, June 28, 1954, with attachment "Background Memorandum Concerning the Application of the 1949 Geneva Conventions," n.d., box 75, Bureau of Public Affairs 1944–1962, Lot 61D53, RG 59, NA; US Senate, Committee on Foreign Relations, *Geneva Conventions for the Protection of War Victims: Hearings*, 84th Cong., 1st sess.; *New York Times*, July 7, 1955.

[71] *FM 27-10 Department of the Army Field Manual: The Law of Land Warfare* (Washington, DC: Department of the Army, 1956), 16, 19, 98–137.

into the 1949 conventions, like noncombatant protections from bombing, or only appeared in the conventions in the form of voluntary provisions, such as safety zones for civilians.

However, the Geneva Conventions did more than simply codify accepted military practice that national armed forces would have implemented in pursuit of their own interests even without the international agreements. The treaties also included aspirational provisions that at times conflicted with political interests and ideas of military necessity and reflected either broader humanitarian sentiments or international compromises. These provisions were not always practiced, but the states that had negotiated and signed the 1949 conventions had formally agreed to them. American divergences from the conventions in the Korean War placed a public spotlight—or threatened to—on a number of these aspirational provisions that were overridden at times by perceived needs. Americans endured public controversy surrounding their mistreatment of POWs, and US leaders worried about the exposure of their use of lethal force against refugees and their failures to provide for Koreans who found themselves in refugee camps. The ICRC can also be seen as pushing the aspirational nature of the Geneva Conventions by stretching their applicability during the Korean War to humanitarian concerns, like harm to refugees not clearly in the hands of a combatant force, that stricter interpretations of the laws might dispute.

Although the United States made significant deviations from Geneva standards, this lack of compliance did not render the Geneva Conventions impotent. Indeed, the conventions actually gained a broader international legitimacy during the Korean War. Not only did the United States ratify the agreements in 1955, but so would major powers like the Soviet Union, the United Kingdom, and France in the 1950s. As the propaganda battles of the Korean War showed, the Geneva Conventions and the whole issue of inhumane warfare became another arena for the international political competition of the Cold War. Each side could charge the other with atrocities and curry sympathy in the international community, but those atrocity charges could have a boomerang effect. The accusations introduced the political trap of hypocrisy if the accuser was exposed as perpetrating similar crimes. The more the United States accused the North Koreans and Chinese of the murder and mistreatment of POWs, the more likely others would hold Americans to those standards.

The process of formally incorporating the Geneva Conventions into doctrinal manuals, training, and the military justice system may have also helped a variety of individual Americans to internalize the treaties' humanitarian standards, even if the formal process might be an empty ritual for many of the political and military leaders implementing it. At times, American leaders may have cynically implemented the conventions only as a screen for US interests, but others, including some American officials, might have come to believe sincerely in their provisions.

This process of internalization is extremely difficult to measure, but what is more discernable was the public controversy and pressure that the Korean War generated around the conventions. As the controversies surrounding the bombing of civilians and sympathy for the plight of refugees and POWs illustrated during the conflict, the pressure on US officials did not only come from communist propagandists. Other governments, the press, and nongovernmental organizations like relief agencies, churches, and peace groups expressed their concern about the conventions and the broader norms that reinforced the agreements. This public pressure and acceptance of the conventions often stemmed from expressions of support for the wider norm of noncombatant immunity.[72]

Although the Geneva Conventions certainly incorporated aspects of this norm into its provisions, the treaties themselves were not a particularly clear or compelling presentation of general principles like noncombatant immunity. The conventions were concrete and specific, and, while this may have made them politically practical as agreements between states, this may also have been one of the 1949 conventions' greatest limitations. Without clear statements of normative principles, the agreements had less potential to rally public support and mobilize transnational public sentiment and networks of nongovernmental organizations emerging after World War II. This may have hampered the internalization of the conventions' humanitarian principles for individuals as well. The conventions do not make compelling reading even when compared to the Hague laws that preceded them or the 1977 Additional Protocols to the Geneva Conventions, which at least contained preambles and frequent statements of general principle. The ICRC also saw its role not as a public pressure group but as a discreet and neutral intermediary, rarely employing public criticism or advocacy to bolster the conventions. The 1949 conventions were best suited to closed-door wrangling among diplomats rather than public advocacy in the court of world opinion.

The 1949 treaties had one other major failing related to the norm of noncombatant immunity. After World War II, the massive fire power of modern weapons, from napalm to nuclear arms, was arguably the single greatest threat to noncombatants, and the 1949 Geneva Conventions barely offered any protections from this danger. The Americans and British had succeeded in keeping such protections out of the Geneva treaties, but the Korean War experience demonstrated the extent of this danger. The United States encountered criticism over its bombing and other widely destructive methods of warfare, and after the war the ICRC

[72] For an examination of Americans' engagement with the norm of noncombatant immunity, see Conway-Lanz, *Collateral Damage*.

saw potential for further expanding Geneva protections against such threats. The general trajectory of the Geneva Conventions in the 20th century had been one of expansion. One of the major innovations of the 1949 conventions was moving beyond protections for the sick and wounded and POWs to protecting civilians in occupied territory. In 1955, the ICRC circulated its draft rules on the protection of civilian populations from the dangers of indiscriminate warfare. These rules sought to expand Geneva law further, into the realm of protecting all civilians of combatant nations whether in occupied territory or still defended by their own armed forces. Enemy civilians behind an adversary's frontlines were precisely the people most vulnerable to bombing and the increasingly destructive weapons of war that could kill over long distances and wide areas as the Korean War, like World War II, had starkly demonstrated. This moved Geneva law into another area formerly governed only by the Hague laws, which imposed very limited restrictions on weapons and methods of war. The expansion held out the potential for much greater protection for war victims since harm from indiscriminate weapons was much more pronounced in the types of armed conflict that followed World War II, like the many civil wars where the notions of occupied territory and protected persons lost much of their meaning, with both sides claiming legitimate political control of the same territory and populations. This expansion also converged with the growing international support for the norm of noncombatant immunity and therefore promised much more potential for mobilizing public sentiment on behalf of the Geneva Conventions.

This expansion, however, was hotly contested, precisely because of its potential conflicts with military and political interests. For example, the president of the American Red Cross, Ellsworth Bunker, argued against the draft rules because they would enlarge the scope of Red Cross activities into areas that he believed only militaries should be allowed to judge. He pointed out that citizen civilians of a belligerent state had not been previously included in the category of people deserving of protections. He suggested that they had not because unlike the sick and wounded, POWs, and occupied civilians, they were not clearly rendered incapable of assisting in the conduct of hostilities. Bunker viewed protections for citizen civilians as a military issue that the Red Cross societies were not qualified to judge. While views similar to Bunker's gained widespread support, they did not prevent the expansion of the Geneva Conventions in this area. The draft rules were not implemented quickly, but elements of these rules and much greater protections for all civilians from bombardment and indiscriminate destruction in war were incorporated into the 1977 Additional Protocols to the Geneva Conventions.[73]

[73] Bunker to Leopold Boissier, November 7, 1955, box 21, Operations Control Board Central Files, Dwight D. Eisenhower Library.

Although controversial, this expansion of civilian protections may have been made more tolerable to many Americans because of another legacy of the Korean War concerning the norm of noncombatant immunity. In the decade after World War II, Americans debated and redefined noncombatant immunity as they struggled to reconcile their armed forces' increasingly destructive methods of warfare with traditional protections for war victims. The new prominent attitudes toward noncombatant immunity stressed the importance of intention in rationalizing harm to noncombatants. Only the intentional targeting and killing of noncombatants was considered illegitimate, unintentional harm—what would later be called "collateral damage"—was a regrettable but tolerable cost of war. This redefinition of noncombatant immunity and the growing significance of intention is a separate story,[74] but one that may help explain American tolerance for the expansion of civilian protections in the 1977 Additional Protocols. The Additional Protocols expanded on the restrictions on methods of warfare found in the Hague laws and added limitations on targeting that stressed prohibitions on intentional attacks against noncombatants and nonmilitary targets.

These restrictions on intentional attacks paralleled attitudes that had solidified among Americans in the decade after World War II, even though the Additional Protocols and these types of restrictions continued to be controversial, among Americans in particular. The United States refused to ratify the Additional Protocols in the 1980s, but the US armed forces have since come to acknowledge that some provisions of the Additional Protocols have become customary international law.[75] While American discussions of noncombatant immunity and the Geneva Conventions were often separate dialogues during the Korean War because the treaties failed to engage and articulate the norm of noncombatant immunity adequately, these conversations increasingly converged as the Additional Protocols incorporated and expressed many of the sentiments that Americans had engaged during their deliberations over noncombatant immunity.

Despite expectations that the United States would be exemplary in its application of the new 1949 Geneva Conventions, the Korean War demonstrated the serious problems that Americans had adhering to these humanitarian standards and the severely limited protections that these new treaties provided. American forces at the outbreak of the Korean War did not internalize Geneva standards as well as many had thought, and the effectiveness of the conventions was low in actually mitigating harm. The protections for war victims were undermined

[74] This story is told in Conway-Lanz, *Collateral Damage*.

[75] *Operational Law Handbook* (Charlottesville, VA: International and Operational Law Department, Judge Advocate General's Legal Center and School, 2009), 14.

both by serious gaps, as in the case of bombing, and by deviations, as in the cases of handling refugees and POWs. Even with the deviations that inflicted terrible harm, American compliance with the conventions was substantial in the sense that US armed forces adhered to most of the specific provisions of the agreements throughout the war.

More importantly, though, Americans did not discard the Geneva Conventions in the wake of their troubled experiences during the Korean War. Instead, the war helped to legitimize and lay the foundation for the further internalization of the new laws through their formal implementation, the public controversy they generated, and the boomerang effect of atrocity accusations. The United States' implementation of the Geneva Conventions may have been flawed during the Korean War, but the treaties were part of a broader international consensus-building process that helped to spread humanitarian norms.

4

America, the 1949 Geneva Conventions, and War Crime Courts-Martial in the Vietnam Conflict

GARY D. SOLIS

Introduction

The Vietnam conflict (1965–1973) was a defining moment in American history. Today, it provides a window through which to examine America's commitment to the law of war and the Geneva Conventions. From a distance of forty-five years, we see a commitment enforced by courts-martial. Alongside that enforcement we also recall incidents of shameful disregard for the law of war.

What was America's engagement with the 1949 Geneva Conventions in Vietnam? How did the law of war become incorporated into the ethos our armed forces? Was the American military's observance of the Geneva Conventions a genuine commitment, or was it merely symbolic—exhortations in manuals to be parroted in training while battlefield misconduct was rampant? Were war crime courts-martial mere show trials imposing negligible punishments? What was expected and enforced on Asian battlefields nearly half a century ago?

The murky answers to such questions are neither clear nor consistent, neither "yes" nor "no."

Law of War Training during the Vietnam War

Today, military training in the requirements of Geneva is continuous and pervasive. Today, America's combatants are better trained in the law of war than ever before. During the Vietnam conflict that training was neither as well taught nor as well executed as it might have been.

Military lawyers—judge advocates—are graduates of civilian law schools who have passed some state's bar examination. During the Vietnam fighting, newly appointed Army judge advocates attended additional three-month legal training courses in Charlottesville, Virginia. Marine Corps judge advocates attended a similar school in Newport, Rhode Island. In addition, many Army judge advocates later attended a yearlong "career course" that entailed far more study of the law of war and the 1949 Geneva Conventions than did their initial training. It was with such backgrounds that military lawyers were assigned tours of duty in Vietnam; twelve months "in country" for Army lawyers, thirteen for Marines.

Not only judge advocates received law of war training. Whether an infantry officer, a pilot, artilleryman, or supply specialist, every commissioned officer in every branch of the US armed forces received (and still receives) formal training in the law of war and the Geneva Conventions during postcommissioning schooling. Every enlisted man and woman in every service branch received law of war training during "boot camp" and, often, in subsequent military specialty training, as well.

> Long before U.S. troop units were engaged in combat in Vietnam, the Army had included in its training programs material designed to inculcate in the troops a knowledge of their rights and obligations under the Geneva Conventions of 1949. Army Regulation 350-216 . . . placed upon the commanding General, Continental Army Command, the responsibility of incorporating within appropriate training programs periods of instruction designed to insure that all members of the Army were familiar with the 1949 Geneva Conventions. The soldier's first introduction to the Geneva Conventions was during basic training, where he received two hours of formal instruction, followed by a test, the results of which were noted on his record. During advanced individual training, instruction in the Geneva Conventions was integrated with other subjects and principles were applied during field exercises. . . . In Vietnam, Geneva Conventions training was intensified and became more formalized as troop strength increased.[1]

A series of Department of Defense directives required continuing rudimentary law of war training, even in the South Vietnam combat zone. General William C. Westmoreland, commander of all US forces in South Vietnam for most of

[1] George S. Prugh, *Law at War: Vietnam—1964–1973* (Washington, DC: Department of the Army, 1975), 74–75.

the conflict, later wrote, "I required that all men entering Vietnam be indoctrinated in . . . provisions of the Geneva Convention on handling of prisoners of war. Having taught a course on the Geneva Convention and the laws of war at the Command and General Staff College . . . I was sharply conscious of the responsibilities they placed on field commanders."[2]

An Army judge advocate assigned to the Military Assistance Command–Vietnam (MAC-V) found that the Saigon office of the senior military lawyer, MAC-V's staff judge advocate, had six "divisions," one of which was the international law division, the law of war specialists.[3] Grandiose as the title sounded, the division actually consisted of a single judge advocate. In early days there were only four lawyers in the entire office.[4] But the office anticipated the growth it would soon see.

Army Colonel George S. Prugh, the staff judge advocate on the MAC-V staff, was an exceptionally able and humane officer. He later rose to the grade of major general and became the judge advocate general of the Army. His monograph, *Law at War: Vietnam—1964–1973*, is an excellent record of early US law of war activities in South Vietnam. Prugh wrote of the international law "division":

> This division rendered opinions on international law for the command, including . . . the Geneva Conventions of 1949, and the Laws of War. It maintained files of investigations of alleged war crimes and atrocities committed by or against U.S. military or civilian personnel in Vietnam. It assured that prisoners of war who had been captured by U.S. troops and turned over to the Vietnamese government for detention were being provided the legal rights accorded them by the Geneva Conventions. The International Affairs Division provided instruction to newly assigned MACV personnel in the Geneva Conventions and Code of Conduct.[5]

Prugh later noted that, as in most armed conflicts, international law proved inadequate to fully protect victims on both sides of the insurgency. The law of war was not completely ineffective, however. That was due in large part to the continuous training that US military personnel received on the subject in the combat zone.

[2] William C. Westmoreland, *A Soldier Reports* (New York: Da Capo/Doubleday, 1976), 286.

[3] Prugh, *Law at War*, supra, note 1, at 9.

[4] Frederic L. Borch, *Judge Advocates in Combat: Army Lawyers in Military Operations from Vietnam to Haiti* (Washington, DC: Office of the Judge Advocate General/ Center of Military History, 2001), 10.

[5] Prugh, *Law at War: Vietnam*, supra, note 1, at 12.

The Practice of Law in Vietnam

The practice of law in South Vietnam was not easy for judge advocates or for enlisted legal clerks. Long before the Internet, the bound volumes of military appellate opinions available at stateside legal offices were unobtainable in Vietnam except at one or two headquarters locations. Few judge advocates had access to those headquarters. The Uniform Code of Military Justice (UCMJ) is the military's criminal code applicable to all branches of US armed forces. It requires that virtually any court-martial have a verbatim record of the trial for purposes of appellate review. In Vietnam, to meet that requirement, military court reporters employed electric-powered belt, or reel-to-reel, tape recorders in conjunction with a closed-mask microphone. A back-up recording on a second machine was always made. Typed records of trial, with four carbon copies, were produced by long-suffering court reporters on manual typewriters. There were no electric typewriters or copy machines in Vietnam in the mid-1960s. Erasures in the four-carbon record of trial involved a torturous labor-intensive process. Vietnam's hot, humid, and dusty climate ensured problems at every step of the mechanized recording process. Gasoline-powered generators were located in most base camps where courts-martial were convened. But generators often broke down, electric current for recorders was lost, and, the required verbatim record no longer possible, trials came to an abrupt halt. Paper clips rusted so quickly they could only be used once. Broken recording machines had to be sent to the Philippines for repair.[6] Illegal drugs the prosecution wished to offer in evidence were sent to the closest forensic laboratory, also in the Philippines, for analysis. Essential witnesses were sometimes wounded or killed. Despite administrative "legal holds," military witnesses often were returned to the United States when their tours of Vietnam duty were completed, leaving both the prosecution and defense without vital witnesses at trial. Finding Vietnamese witnesses and bringing them to the court-martial's location was an adventure. There were no addresses or named streets in Vietnamese villages, let alone telephones, in rural areas where war crimes were committed. Arranging a meeting with a Vietnamese witness was difficult when the witness had never owned a calendar, clock, or wristwatch. The temporal length of an event was related by rural Vietnamese witnesses in terms of cigarettes: "The soldiers fired at my village for two cigarettes." Vietnamese interpreters were rare. Competent interpreters were very rare.

[6] Gary Solis, *Marines and Military Law in Vietnam, Trial by Fire* (Washington, DC: GPO/USMC, 1990), 29–31.

Judge advocates had no dedicated transportation. No other unit's vehicles were assigned to meet the legal section's needs. That lack made the location of witnesses, witness interviews, and site views difficult. Prosecutors and defense counsel were reduced to hitching unscheduled rides on any jeep, truck, or helicopter going their way. In April 1970, the only judge advocate killed in the Vietnam War, Army Captain Howard Andrews, died when the helicopter in which he was hitching a ride to see a soldier client, crashed on takeoff.[7]

For the first year after the 1965 troop buildup, and several months beyond that, courts-martial were often held in large tents with dirt floors, subject to monsoon rains, coastal winds, searing heat, and enemy fire. For about a year, when there was a shortage of junior Marine Corps infantry officers, Marine judge advocates were "volunteered" for duty as combat platoon leaders and company commanders. Two were wounded while serving in that capacity.[8]

Yet, throughout the entirety of the conflict, from the 1965 troop buildup until the last judge advocates left country in 1971, thousands of Army and Marine Corps courts-martial were completed in-country, many involving grave breaches of the Geneva Conventions. The Conventions were seldom mentioned at trial; there was no need. Instead, the UCMJ article corresponding to the alleged war crime was charged, defended, and decided.

The UCMJ became federal law in May 1950, bringing courts-martial into the mainstream of contemporary law.[9] It replaced the Army and Air Force's Articles of War, the Navy's Articles for the Government of the Navy, and the Coast Guard's Disciplinary Laws, with a single criminal code applicable to all armed force branches. The UCMJ was not intended as American compliance with the Geneva Convention requirement that ratifying states enact domestic legislation criminalizing grave breaches. But, as to US combatants, it neatly met that requirement. In fact, today most Geneva Convention High Contracting Parties comply with the domestic legislation requirement through their military justice system. US legislation criminalizing grave breaches committed by civilians would have to wait until passage of the 1996 War Crimes Act.[10]

War crimes were anticipated in South Vietnam, of course. MAC-V Directive 20-4, in April 1965, was the first directive addressing the subject.[11]

[7] Frederic L. Borch, *Judge Advocates in Vietnam: Army Lawyers in Southeast Asia, 1959–1975* (Ft. Leavenworth, KS: US Army Command & General Staff College Press, 2003), 102.

[8] One Marine judge advocate was awarded the Navy Cross while serving as an infantry officer, another the Silver Star. A senior Marine judge advocate who had been a fighter pilot in World War II earned a Distinguished Flying Cross in Vietnam.

[9] PL 506, 81st Congress, c 169, sec. 1, 64 Stat. 108, 50 USC (chap. 22) §§ 551–736.

[10] 18 U.S. Code § 2441.

[11] MAC-V Directive 20–24, "Inspections and Investigations: War Crimes," dated 20 April 1965.

The Geneva Conventions were cited as the directive's driving force.[12] Throughout the conflict, Directive 20-4 was regularly updated and reissued. It applied to all armed service branches deployed in South Vietnam. In paragraph 5.a., the directive read, "It is the responsibility of all military personnel having knowledge or receiving a report of an incident or of an act thought to be a war crime to make such incident known to his commanding officer as soon as practicable." It was this requirement to report known or suspected war crimes that later was the basis for charging senior officers, including Brigadier General John W. Donaldson, an infantry brigade commander, and Major General Samuel W. Koster, the division commander in the My Lai case.[13] "This decision to penalize the failure to report a war crime applied to all levels of command."[14]

Judge advocates, focused on the UCMJ offense that corresponded to the particular war crime involved, often did not think about the fact that they were prosecuting or defending Geneva Convention grave breaches. Murdering a prisoner, for example, was charged not as a war crime but as a violation of UCMJ Article 118, murder. The term "war crime" might not be uttered throughout the entire court-martial. The rape of a Vietnamese villager in US custody, a "protected person" under the law of war,[15] was simply charged as a violation of UCMJ Article 120, rape. By prosecuting grave breaches under their corresponding UCMJ articles the US was complying with the Conventions' mandate to punish those committing grave breaches of the laws and customs of war. Nor was the court-martial's verdict merely the expression of America's military law. "The military court, by punishing the acts, executes international law even if it applies . . . its own military law."[16] Some battlefield offenses, of course, were so clearly law of war violations that they were seen to be grave breaches and argued as such during trial.

[12] "1. PURPOSE. This directive provides uniform procedures for the collection and perpetuation of evidence relative to war crimes incidents and . . . possible violations of the Geneva Convention of 12 August 1949 For the Protection of War Victims."

[13] The two generals were indeed *charged*, but that is misleading. Koster, charged in 1970 with covering up My Lai war crimes, was administratively reduced in grade to brigadier general and his Distinguished Service Medal revoked. In June 1971, Donaldson was charged with killing six Vietnamese civilians and assaulting two others by rifle fire from his helicopter. Court-martial charges against both officers, however, were dropped before trial.

[14] Borch, *Judge Advocates in Vietnam*, supra, note 7, at 35: "Koster's failure to obey MAC-V Directive 20-4 while commanding the Americal Division was part of the legal basis for the adverse administrative action against him."

[15] 1949 Geneva Convention IV, Art. 4. "Protected person" is an individual status enjoying specific rights and requiring specific duties of the holding power.

[16] Hans Kelsen, *Peace through Law* (Chapel Hill: University of North Carolina Press, 1944), 77.

Enemy Prisoners in the Vietnam War

An example of the military's commitment to the law of war was the treatment accorded enemy prisoners. From the first days of the US troop buildup in Vietnam, senior American commanders evidenced a concern that captured enemy fighters be treated in accordance with the Geneva Conventions.

> In September [1965] the Commanding General, Fleet Marine Force, Pacific, Lieutenant General Victor H. Krulak, contacted Major General Walt [commander of U.S. forces in I Corps, the northern-most area of South Vietnam], saying, "I am anxious that all of our people are made fully aware of their obligations under the Geneva Convention as to the treatment of prisoners."[17]

Krulak, the senior Marine officer in the Pacific, which included the Vietnam theater, emphasized the point four months later, when he ordered, "Ensure that every officer in the chain of command knows the rules, the reasons for the rules, and the penalties for their violation, and then accept no compromise at all."[18]

The Army, if anything, evidenced an even stronger concern for prisoners. In 1975, Colonel Prugh wrote about POWs in terms that General David Petraeus might have uttered in regard to Afghanistan in 2010:

> The application of the Geneva Conventions . . . to captives in the Vietnam War was complicated by the perplexing legal nature of that conflict. In the classic sense, the conventions presume a declared state of war between two or more sovereign states, each fielding a regular army fighting on a readily identifiable battlefront. Virtually none of those classic conditions existed in the Vietnam conflict.[19]

Initially, the individual status of captured enemy fighters—North Vietnamese Army troops, main force Vietcong (VC), local force VC, and "unattached" farmers with weapons, was further complicated by the questionable status of the conflict. Was the war an international armed conflict in which the Geneva Conventions applied in their entirety? Or was it a noninternational armed conflict in which the basic protections of Convention common Article 3, alone, applied?[20] Logic

[17] Solis, *Marines and Military Law in Vietnam*, supra, note 6, at 34.

[18] Ibid.

[19] Prugh, *Law at War: Vietnam*, supra, note 1, at 61.

[20] Ibid., at 63. In early 1965, the United States took the position that the conflict was an international armed conflict with the Geneva Conventions applying in full.

suggested an international conflict, the Democratic Republic of Vietnam (the north) versus the Republic of Vietnam (the south) aided by the United States. If it was an international armed conflict, all of Geneva applied, including prisoner of war (POW) provisions; if a noninternational conflict, the POW convention was inapplicable. But there is no supranational body that decides such things, and logic does not always prevail in international politics. The MAC-V's resolution of the POW issue illustrates a commitment to not just the letter of Geneva but also its spirit.

There was little question that captured North Vietnamese Army (NVA) soldiers were POWs. Captured VC guerrillas, however, were viewed by our South Vietnamese allies as criminals to be tried and heavily sentenced upon their inevitable conviction for violation of South Vietnam's criminal code. As viewed by the United States, in an international armed conflict the VC did not qualify for POW status because they did not fight while displaying the required "fixed distinctive sign recognizable at a distance."[21] Still, the US military was hesitant to turn over captured VC to the South Vietnamese, as had been agreed, since "Under Article 12 [of the Geneva 1949 POW convention] the United States retained responsibility for treatment of its captives . . . even after transfer of the captives to the South Vietnamese."[22] As General William Westmoreland wrote, "Having long experienced the calculated cruelty and terrorism of the Viet Cong—parading the severed head of an official through a village was commonplace—some South Vietnamese saw little point in observing niceties with prisoners of war."[23] Additionally, executions of VC by the South Vietnamese had resulted in retaliatory executions of American prisoners by the VC.

> The Saigon government insisted that the Geneva Convention was inapplicable and that captured enemy personnel were not entitled to prisoner of war status. Thus, those guerrillas who did survive capture in the field . . . were imprisoned "in provincial and national jails along with political prisoners and common criminals."[24]

A solution was announced by MAC-V in late 1965: Enemy personnel captured by US forces would not be turned over to the Vietnamese:

> The Commander, U.S. Military Assistance Command, Vietnam, established a policy that all suspected Viet Cong captives taken by U.S. forces

[21] A requirement imposed by 1949 Geneva Convention III, Art. 4A. (2).

[22] Prugh, *Law at War: Vietnam*, supra, note 1, at 62.

[23] Westmoreland, *A Soldier Reports*, supra, note 2, at 244.

[24] Borch, *Judge Advocates in Vietnam*, supra, note 7, at 19.

> were to be treated initially as prisoners of war by the capturing unit . . . irrespective of the type of [enemy] unit to which they belonged.[25]

In practice, POW treatment of captured VC continued for as long as the individual was held by US forces. "Contact with the representatives of the International Committee of the Red Cross [ICRC] and collection of data on prisoners, their apprehension and disposition, became important."[26] Important not only as evidence of US humane treatment of enemy captives but also as a showing of American intent to abide by the spirit of the Geneva Conventions. As a result of ICRC contacts by the US military, "between 1964 and 1975 ICRC delegates made 620 visits to places of detention in South Vietnam (prisoner-of-war camps and hospitals, screening centers, interrogation centers, correctional institutions and civilian prisons.)"[27] The US humanitarian priority for POWs continued through the war.

The enemy's application of the third Geneva Convention respecting POWs was quite different.

> Though the North Vietnamese had acceded to the Geneva Convention of 1949, which holds that prisoners of war are "victims of events" who merit "decent and humane treatment," they followed the Soviet lead in making an exception for "crimes against humanity"—their portrayal of the U.S. bombing of their country.[28]

Throughout the conflict, the ICRC was not represented in Hanoi and its delegates were not allowed into North Vietnam.[29] The mistreatment and torture of American prisoners by their North Vietnamese captors is well documented. The ICRC notes, "Until the Paris agreements of January 1973 and the repatriation of American prisoners of war, [North Vietnam] rejected all offers of services by the ICRC, asserting that as the victim of a war of aggression waged by the United States, [North] Vietnam was not bound to apply the Third Geneva Convention to American prisoners of war."[30] Even if captured Americans were not considered by the North to be POWs, their unlawful treatment was prohibited by the Fourth Geneva Convention, regarding civilians. That is because, in the law of war, there

[25] Prugh, *Law at War: Vietnam*, supra, note 1, at 65.

[26] Ibid., at 116.

[27] François Bugnion, *The International Committee of the Red Cross and Protection of War Victims* (Oxford: ICRC/McMillan, 2003), 634.

[28] Stanley Karnow, *Vietnam: A History* (New York: Viking Press, 1983), 655, see also 446, 620.

[29] Bugnion, *The International Committee of the Red Cross*, supra, note 27, at 436, 513, and 589.

[30] Ibid., at 446.

are but two classifications of individuals on the battlefield: combatants and civilians. If US captives were viewed as lawful combatants they merited POW status and treatment in accord with the third Convention; if not viewed as combatants they were necessarily civilians protected by the fourth Convention, as well as common Article 3, which requires humane treatment of all who are *hors de combat*.[31]

The ICRC delegate in Saigon said of the US decision to treat all captives as POWs:

> The MACV instruction . . . is a brilliant expression of a liberal and realistic attitude. . . . This text could very well be a most important one in the history of humanitarian law, for it is the first time . . . that a government goes far beyond the requirements of the Geneva Convention in an official instruction to its armed forces.[32]

That was high praise for the military's commitment to the principles of Geneva, demonstrating more than a symbolic compliance with the letter of the Conventions. Thereafter, in 1966, the Army built POW camps in Ben Hoa, Pleiku, Da Nang, and Can Tho. In 1968, a camp was opened on Phu Quoc Island, off the coast of Cambodia, and another for female POWs was opened at Qui Nhon. Prisoners under eighteen years of age were concentrated in the Ben Hoa camp. By the end of 1971, the six camps held 35,665 prisoners, all treated as POWs.[33] Policies and procedures for ICRC inspection team visits to the camps were set forth in a MAC-V directive.[34] These policies are rarely mentioned in postwar accounts that recount American involvement in Vietnam in negative terms.

In 1977, after years of Geneva meetings and negotiations, two Protocols Additional to the 1949 Geneva Conventions resulted. The first 1977 Additional Protocol applies to international armed conflicts. It has been ratified by more than 170 of the world's 194 states. The United States, however, refuses to ratify either Protocol.[35] A principal US argument against ratification of Additional

[31] 1977 Additional Protocol I, Art. 50.1. "A civilian is any person who does not belong to one of the categories of persons [entitled to POW status].

[32] Prugh, *Law at War: Vietnam*, supra, note 1, at 66.

[33] Ibid., at 67–68.

[34] MAC-V Directive 190-6, International Committee of the Red Cross Inspections of Detainees and Prisoners of War Facilities" (8 January 1961). The directive reads, in part, "4. *Policy*. a. All personnel detained will be extended the full protection of the Geneva Conventions of 12 August 1949. b. The Saigon delegation of the ICRC is recognized as the authority on the Geneva Conventions and is authorized to inspect all detainee/PW facilities in the RVN. c. Violations of the Geneva Conventions are considered serious breaches of international law and every effort will be made by commanders and advisors [to South Vietnamese units] to ensure full compliance."

[35] In 2011, the Obama administration submitted 1977 Additional Protocol II, relating to noninternational armed conflicts, to the Senate for ratification. No action has, so far, followed.

Protocol I relates to its Article 44. That provision requires ratifying states to give captured enemy fighters who do not meet all four of the traditional requirements for POW status[36] to nevertheless provide captured enemy fighters "protections equivalent in all respects to those accorded to prisoners of war." Some ask, "But is that not what you did in the Vietnam war—treat captured North Vietnamese guerrillas as POWs?" Yes, we did, but the United States is apparently unwilling to assume a written international obligation to do so.

My Lai and More

As long as nations at war give high-powered weapons to young men, war crimes will follow. That is not cynicism so much as a recognition of history. Every conflict has its war crimes. As the US Supreme Court has noted, "In the Armed Forces, as everywhere else, there are good men and rascals, courageous men and cowards, honest men and cheats."[37]

Throughout the Vietnam conflict the commitment of the United States' military to the Geneva Conventions cannot be seriously questioned. The aggressive prosecutions of soldiers and Marines accused of war crimes continued through the war and after, with prosecutions convened and completed in the United States. Sentences imposed at war crime courts-martial by military juries were often severe—confinement at hard labor for life in the cases of at least fifteen Marines, alone.[38] Sentences of twenty, thirty, and fifty years were not uncommon.

That does not suggest that the US commitment to the laws and customs of war was so effective as to end their violation, or that it led to the prosecution of every war crime. No law will deter the lawless. No domestic criminal code ends civilian criminality and no military code or order, no matter how aggressively enforced, will end war crimes. An example is the My Lai massacre, America's most infamous Vietnam war crime.

On 16 March 1968, Task Force Barker, a cobbled-together temporary unit from the Army's 23rd Infantry (Americal) Division, was to engage and destroy elements of the 48th Local Force Battalion, said by US intelligence reports to be located at Son My village. The reports were wrong. There were no enemy fighters in My Lai on that day.

[36] Be commanded by someone responsible for his subordinates; have a fixed distinctive sign recognizable at a distance; carry arms openly; and conduct operations in accordance with the laws and customs of war. 1949 Geneva Convention III, Art. 4A. (2).

[37] *Ball et al. v. United States,* 366 U.S. (1961), 393, 401.

[38] Gary Solis, "Military Justice, Civilian Clemency: The Sentences of Marine War Crimes in South Vietnam," *Transnational Law and Contemporary Problems* 10, no. 11 (Spring 2000): 74–75.

My Lai is one of several hamlets that make up the village of Son My. My Lai is itself made up of six "subhamlets" designated on US maps as My Lai 1 through My Lai 6. My Lai was also known to the Vietnamese as Tu Cung, and to Americans as "Pinkville" because of its color overlay on military maps. Army 2nd Lieutenant William L. Calley's 1st platoon of Company C, 1st Battalion, 11th Light Infantry Brigade, was a mere twenty-five men strong. It was to assault the enemy forces in My Lai-4. Other similarly small Company C platoons had related missions in nearby locations. The Company was commanded by Captain Ernest Medina, who, throughout the morning of the events in My Lai, was present in an adjacent field.

Throughout the 1st platoon's assault on My Lai-4, no enemy troops were encountered, no enemy fire received. The sole American casualty was Private Herbert Carter, who accidentally shot himself in the foot with his own pistol. During that March morning the platoon, at Calley's direction and often with his involvement, murdered approximately 350 unarmed, unresisting old men, women, and children. A precise number of victims has never been authoritatively determined. Besides the murders, Calley's soldiers raped, gang raped, sodomized, and sexually mutilated numerous Vietnamese women and girls. "The American public never understood the full horror of My Lai—the rapes, tortures, and mutilations that were committed."[39]

Nor was Calley's platoon alone in its criminality. The Army's principal My Lai investigator, three-star general William Peers, reported that in the neighboring village of My Khe Lieutenant Thomas K. Willingham's platoon murdered "a large number of women and children (as few as 38 but possibly over 90)."[40]

Televised postwar interviews of surviving soldiers of Calley's platoon reveal saddened old men, remorseful but asserting a lack of guilt; they were victims, too, they profess; victims of the military, they assert, hardened by images of (inevitably) dead best friends, fearful of the possible consequences of not obeying orders. But, as ethicist Michael Walzer writes, "it has been argued on behalf of these soldiers that they acted, not in the heat of battle (since there was no battle) but in the context of a brutal and brutalizing war." Walzer rightly rejects such self-serving excuses: "This was not a fearful and frenzied extension of combat, but 'free' and systematic slaughter, and those men that participated in it can hardly say that they were caught in the grip of war."[41] Nor was the assault on My Lai-4 undertaken by soldiers looking for "payback" for the combat deaths of

[39] Michael Bilton and Kevin Sim, *Four Hours in My Lai* (New York: Viking, 1992), 334.

[40] William R. Peers, *The My Lai Inquiry* (New York: W.W. Norton, 1979), 197. The Peers investigation was by far the most thorough and comprehensive of the four Army investigations of the My Lai incident.

[41] Michael Walzer, *Just and Unjust Wars*, 3rd ed. (New York: Basic Books, 1977), 309, 310.

their fellows. In the four and-a-half months Company C had been in Vietnam, five of their number had been killed, one by a sniper, the other four by mines. In 1968, in that area of South Vietnam, five KIAs in 110 days was a decidedly modest number.

Horrific as events in My Lai-4 were, they were immediately covered up by senior Army officers, some of whom were present, observing the event from command helicopters overhead. Other officers received oral or written reports of what had happened. Falsified reports of the operation's success led an unknowing General Westmoreland to congratulate the Task Force for its excellent performance.

It was a year later that a young Vietnam veteran, by then discharged from the Army, became disturbed by My Lai-4 accounts he heard from service buddies. His efforts to alert the press unsuccessful, Ronald Ridenhour wrote twenty-three identical letters to congressmen, the secretaries of state and defense, the Secretary of the Army, and the Chairman of the Joint Chiefs of Staff. Finally revealed, My Lai became international news. Lieutenant General Peers's investigation followed. It was a serious, well-funded, fully staffed inquiry. Finally concluding his report, the general, a decorated combat infantryman of three wars, charged four officers and nine enlisted men with committing war crimes in My Lai-4 and recommended their courts-martial. He additionally charged twelve officers with covering up events in My Lai-4 that they knew of, or should have known of, and recommended that they be court-martialed, as well. The charged officers included a two-star and a one-star general, two colonels, and a lieutenant colonel. The constant training and repeated written orders to observe the law of war had failed; from infantry privates to the major general commanding the division, the law of war had been violated at My Lai-4, atrocities concealed, and lies sworn to.

The military legal proceedings that followed—and did not follow—showed the US military justice system at its worst. Of the twenty-five officers and men charged with crimes in, or related to My Lai, only six went to trial. Five of the six who went to trial were acquitted, including Captain Medina, the company commander who, from fields closely adjacent to My Lai-4, heard the firing of US weapons all morning. He professed to have no idea what was happening.

Lieutenant Calley, alone, was convicted, found guilty of the premeditated murder of twenty-two civilian villagers and the assault with intent to murder of a two-year-old child. Clearly, he murdered many more than the number of which he was convicted. At the time, Calley was often portrayed in American media as a scapegoat. But a scapegoat is an innocent who is sacrificed. Calley was no innocent. Many uninformed civilians objected that the Army trained Calley to kill then, when he did kill, the Army tried him for murder. But Calley and his platoon were never trained to kill unarmed and defenseless civilian old men, women and children, to gang rape young girls, and mutilate the living and dead. The military jurors who convicted him, who had themselves served in Vietnam, recognized Calley for what he was. They sentenced him to dismissal from the Army, loss of all pay and allowances, and confinement at hard labor for life.[42] It was the maximum punishment they could impose.

Calley's conviction, however, was soon undermined and diminished by the very system that imposed it. The general who ordered the court-martial to be convened reduced Calley's confinement to twenty years, as was within his lawful authority. While Calley's conviction progressed through the military appellate system, he was ordered not to a stockade but, with the intervention of President Richard Nixon, to comfortable on-base officers' quarters, where he received frequent visitors, including a girlfriend who sometimes cooked for him. Then the secretary of the Army further cut Calley's confinement, as permitted by federal law, to ten years. At about the same time, in a collateral attack on the military conviction, a Georgia federal district court overturned Calley's conviction, then was itself reversed by the Federal Court of Appeals. By then, Calley had served a third of his twice-reduced court-martial sentence and was eligible for parole, which was promptly granted by the secretary of the Army. Calley served a total of four and-a-half postconviction months in the Fort Leavenworth stockade, and three years and five months under house arrest.[43]

As egregious as was American military conduct at My Lai, there were heroes there, too. Few have heard of Privates First Class Dennis Bunting and James Dursi, who refused Calley's orders to fire on groups of unarmed civilians. Specialist Robert Maples also refused, even as Calley stood before him with his rifle pointed at him. Sergeant Michael Bernhardt refused, as well. Warrant Officer Hugh C. Thompson, pilot of a small three-man observation helicopter, was appalled at what he was witnessing in My Lai from the air. Twice he landed his helicopter to pick up wounded Vietnamese and flew them to US military medical units.[44] Upon seeing a small group of running Vietnamese pursued by a clutch of American soldiers, and knowing what was about to happen, Thompson landed his helicopter between the two groups. He got out to intercept the soldiers and, astoundingly, told his door gunner, Specialist Lawrence M. Colburn, that if the American soldiers fired on the Vietnamese, Colburn was to open fire

[42] *U.S. v. Calley*, 48 CMR 19 (USCMA, 1973).

[43] Bilton and Sim, *Four Hours in My Lai*, supra, note 39, at 383–385.

[44] Peers, *The My Lai Inquiry*, 71.

on the Americans. Thompson then ensured the soldiers held their fire while another helicopter landed at Thompson's behest and evacuated the civilians to a safe location.

What of the nineteen who were never tried for their My Lai crimes? The charges against twelve officers accused by General Peers were dismissed for lack of evidence. Several of the dismissals were granted even before the military version of a civilian preliminary hearing—an Article 32 investigation—was held. How could the senior officers dismissing the charges know there was insufficient evidence without a preliminary hearing to determine the evidence available, one wonders? Those dismissals of charges have never been explained. Charges against seven enlisted soldiers were similarly dismissed. Charges against two of the twelve officers, both of them chaplains who were told of My Lai-4 but failed to forward the war crime reports they received, were never referred to courts-martial, at the direction of the secretary of the Army.

One might ask of My Lai, "Of what effect, then, were the training, the orders and directives?" General Peers wrote of the outcome, "part of the problem was rooted in the lackadaisical manner in which the training was handled."[45] In an official Army history, the Army JAG Corps' historian agrees:

> Particularly damning was the [Peers] report's finding that Law of War training in Calley's unit was deficient with regard to the proper treatment of civilians and the responsibility for reporting war crimes. Almost immediately, senior members of the Judge Advocate General's Corps began examining ways to correct this deficiency.[46]

Yes, one can point to inadequate training, "caused in part by the pressure to ready troops for combat in Vietnam,"[47] but My Lai also represents a failure of battlefield and higher command leadership plus, in cases other than Calley's, prosecutions of questionable effectiveness.[48] Feckless presidential politics played a role, as well.[49]

[45] Ibid., at 230. Peers added, "Even accepting these training deficiencies . . . there were some things a soldier did not have to be told were wrong—such as rounding up women and children and mowing them down, shooting babies out of mothers' arms, and raping."

[46] Borch, *Judge Advocates in Combat*, 30.

[47] Guenter Lewy, *America in Vietnam* (New York: Oxford University Press, 1978), 331.

[48] Mary McCarthy, *Medina* (New York: Harcourt Brace Jovanovich, 1972), 6–7, 58–59.

[49] Michael R. Belknap, *The Vietnam War on Trial* (Lawrence: University Press of Kansas, 2002), 198–202, 208, 224, detailing President Nixon's inappropriate and possibly illegal involvement in directing Calley's place of confinement with an eye to public opinion and election politics.

But My Lai was a one-off, contrary to the assertions of a few overwrought authors.[50] As most writers accurately report,[51] no other crime committed by American service members in Vietnam compares.

Counting War Crimes

How many war crimes were committed in Vietnam by American forces? It is a question without an answer. The Department of Defense did not require the armed services to record war crime numbers. To have done so would have raised

[50] Two notably one-sided accounts: Deborah Nelson, *The War behind Me* (New York: Basic Books, 2008), and Bernd Greiner, *War without Fronts* (New Haven, CT: Yale University Press, 2009). Nelson spends much of her book painting herself as an intrepid and savvy investigator confronting power. Military officers, military lawyers, and military law enforcement personnel are portrayed as duplicitous, incompetent, or craven (p. 39: a long-retired officer refuses her interview "through clenched teeth"; p. 47: "[General] Westmoreland moved swiftly to contain the scandal"; p. 57: career military officers in Vietnam were "ticket punchers"). Her Vietnam veteran sources, however, are uniformly truthful, reliable—and likable (p. 45: a friendly informant has "rosy cheeks, and a strong chin"; p. 128: a Vietnamese source has "a graceful walk and unwavering gaze."). Nelson accepts, and quotes without question, her sources' recitations of 35-year-old events, no matter how implausible the account (p. 28: a colonel in "full dress uniform" "from Washington D.C." appears without notice to question a former soldier about long-past war crime allegations; p. 36: apparently unaware of the lengthy administrative processes necessary to issue military transfer orders, Nelson writes that a soldier is questioned and "that night" receives orders transferring him cross-country "effective immediately"; p. 55: ignorant of how white phosphorous munitions work, a soldier relates seeing U.S. C-130 (!) aircraft dump fuel on an infirmary, followed by white phosphorous bombs to ignite the fuel). With clear unawareness of the issues, legal and otherwise, that might prevent a combat zone court-martial prosecution, or an effective crime investigation, Nelson persistently castigates military officials, judge advocates, and combat commanders for the number of cases not tried. To denigrate military war crime cases that *were* tried, she compares military conviction rates with Stateside Justice Department conviction rates (pp. 142–143). Nelson misstates both the number of soldiers charged with, and tried for, My Lai crimes (p. 147). Her ignorance of the workings of universal jurisdiction (p. 149–151), as well as what constitutes a war crime (p. 204, fn. 9), is deep. Lest the reader mistake her position, she uses the word "massacre" repeatedly—at one point twenty-five times in seven pages (pp. 130–137), and labels a chapter, "A My Lai a Month." These and other issues negate the value of legitimate issues Nelson does raise.

The Greiner book, as lacking in balance, nuance, and perspective as Nelson's, also portrays My Lai as the Vietnam norm, and US combatants as "useless," and "disposable," (p. 129), habitually empowering themselves through random killings (pp. 124–142).

[51] Among the authoritative and balanced accounts of the Vietnam conflict, including the criminal misconduct of American combatants, are Michael Sallah and Mitch Weiss, *Tiger Force* (New York: Back Bay Books, 2006), a solidly researched, well-written Pulitzer Prize–winning exposé of the murderous rampage of a rogue US Army unit. Similarly authoritative volumes are Lewy's excellent *America in Vietnam*; Ronald H. Spector, *After Tet* (New York: Free Press, 1993); and Belknap, *The Vietnam War on Trial*.

an impossible requirement. A definition of what constitutes a "war crime" is not universally agreed on. Should war crime allegations that were administratively disposed of be included? Does the question refer to war crimes, whatever their definition, that resulted in court-martial conviction, or also to offenses that were charged but did not result in conviction, or even trial? Or does the question simply refer to war crimes that actually took place? (The latter, of course, is an unknowable quantity.) The variables are many.

Figures are sometimes offered that purport to quantify the number of Vietnam war crimes, but all are suspect, including "official" tallies. W. Hays Parks, an internationally respected American law of war expert, offers a partial accounting.[52] Guenther Lewy, a similarly respected academic, lists numbers pertaining only to the Army.[53] Colonel Fred Borch, the Army JAG Corps' historian, has published what are essentially Lewy's numbers.[54] Aubrey Daniel, the eminently effective judge advocate who prosecuted Calley, offers still other war crime numbers.[55] The figures most often cited are those tallied by General Prugh in his monograph. He was in-country early enough to have captured war crime numbers from the beginning of the troop buildup, and he was senior enough to have required the reporting of war crime numbers through the end of the conflict. However, because he was an Army officer he had no access to, or authority to require, numbers from the Marine Corps, the other American armed force engaged in ground combat. Thus, the Prugh numbers, even if correct in every particular, are significantly skewed to the low side. The Department of Defense has never published Vietnam war crimes numbers because it does not have them. Ultimately, the number of Vietnam war crimes cannot even be estimated with accuracy.

It is not surprising that My Lai remains the war crime remembered by many Americans and much of the world. It is often overlooked that the enemy North Vietnamese committed their own atrocities. The NVA massacre of noncombatants at Hue, for example, makes My Lai appear a minor event by comparison. But there were no cameramen or Ridenhour-like reporters to reveal the NVA's murder of 5,000 noncombatants in Hue.

At 0200 on 31 January 1968, as the Tet offensive began, two NVA infantry regiments and supporting units entered Hue, the ancient capital of Vietnam. Months before, NVA intelligence troops had pretargeted South Vietnamese

[52] W. Hays Parks, "Crimes in Hostilities," Part I, *Marine Corps Gazette* (August 1976), 16.

[53] Lewy, *America in Vietnam*, supra, note 47, at 348.

[54] Borch, *Judge Advocates in Vietnam*, supra, note 7, at 35. In Borch's excellent history, *Judge Advocates in Combat*, supra, note 4, at 21–22, he notes additional figures.

[55] Aubrey M. Daniel III, "The Defense of Superior Orders," *University of Richmond Law Review* 7, no. 3 (Spring 1973): 477–495.

officials, military personnel, politicians, and foreigners. Within two hours the city, except for the Citadel, was captured. For the next twenty-six days US Marines and South Vietnamese soldiers fought brutal house-to-house battles to re-take Hue. Two hundred sixteen Marines and soldiers died and 1,364 more were wounded, along with an estimated 5,100 NVA and VC troops who were killed. The forgotten atrocity was the unresisting unarmed civilian victims of the NVA, including children, who were shot, clubbed, strangled, buried alive, and bludgeoned to death with shovels.[56] "Paradoxically, the American public barely noticed these atrocities, preoccupied as it was by the incident at My Lai."[57] Three thousand bodies were recovered from mass graves, another 2,000 were never found. "Communist murders and terrorism against 'traitors,' 'tyrants,' and 'reactionaries' seldom received much attention except when carried out in a particularly striking manner, as when six hundred Viet Cong troops wielding Russian-made flamethrowers attacked the Montagnard hamlet of Dak Son in Phuoc Long Province, killing more than 250 people."[58]

The ICRC rejected the idea of the disadvantaged guerrilla forced to employ terrorist tactics: "There are those who feel that they cannot do without terrorism. . . . The ICRC considers that, as is the case with torture, which is in a way the countermeasure against terrorism, such acts should be explicitly prohibited."[59] That explicit rejection of terrorism is contained in Geneva Convention IV, Relative to the Protection of Civilian Persons, Article 33: "All measures of intimidation or of terrorism are prohibited."[60]

The Military's Post-Vietnam Law of War Program

There was one positive outcome of My Lai. "The My Lai massacre and the resulting Department of Defense creation of a Law of War program . . . required the Army's legal corps to take primary responsibility for ensuring that "the Armed Forces of the United States shall comply with the law of war in the conduct of military operations."[61]

[56] Karnow, *Vietnam*, supra, note 28, 529–534. Also: The Vietnam Archive, Texas Tech University, Special Collections Library, The Douglas Pike Collection, Unit III: War Atrocities. U.S. Mission in Vietnam, "A Study: Viet Cong Use of Terror," (March 1967), 7.

[57] Karnow, *Vietnam*, 530.

[58] Spector, *After Tet*, supra, note 51, at 206.

[59] International Committee of the Red Cross, *Conference of Government Experts on the Reaffirmation and Development of International Humanitarian Law Applicable to Armed Conflicts*, vol. 2, part 2, (Geneva: ICRC, 1972), 14.

[60] Terrorism is also specifically prohibited in 1977 Additional Protocol I, Art. 51 (2), as well as Additional Protocol II, Arts. 4 (2) (d) and 13 (2).

[61] Borch, *Judge Advocates in Vietnam*, supra, note 7, at 121.

The My Lai–inspired law of war program is detailed in an Instruction from the Chairman of the Joint Chiefs of Staff. Titled, "Implementation of the DOD Law of War Program," the Instruction lays out "military doctrine and guidance for all aspects of joint employment and activities of the Armed Forces."[62] It establishes policy for a law of war program for all military branches and directs that the "Armed Forces of the United States will comply with the law of war during all armed conflicts, however such conflicts are characterized, and . . . [they] will comply with the principles and spirit of the law of war during all other operations."[63] That language announces that the United States will apply the mandates of the law of war, the 1949 Geneva Conventions in their entirety, along with other international agreements, whether the conflict is international in nature, or is internal (noninternational). The full panoply of the laws of war customarily do not apply in noninternational conflicts—rebellions, insurgencies, revolutions, and civil wars. For US forces, now they do.

The Instruction requires each of the armed forces to establish "An effective program designed to prevent violations of the law of war."[64] In compliance, the Department of Defense established a law of war program and the subordinate armed forces, in turn, did so as well.[65] These programs are not optional and they are not suggestions. They are orders to be obeyed by every armed service branch. Each Law of War Program directive, instruction, and order specifies the commanders who are responsible for implementing the law of war program for his or her service branch and what the program shall consist of. Today's Marine Corps order, the most complete of all the services, is thirty-four pages in length.

Combat Zone Trials, Stateside Clemency

One sometimes reads, perhaps in an indignant editorial, of a violent criminal's parole after serving but a brief portion of his trial-imposed prison sentence. Outraged letters to the editor follow. More frequently, however, the parole of civilian prisoners goes unreported and unremarked. In the American military justice system similar circumstances of release prevail. As trial lawyers know, even after appeals are exhausted, the court's verdict is not the end of the case.

[62] CJCSI 5810.01B, dated 25 March 2002, para. 1. Purpose.

[63] Ibid., para. 4.a., Policy.

[64] Ibid., at para. 4.a.(2).

[65] Department of Defense Directive 2311.01E, of 9 May 2006. The Marine Corps' program complying with the DOD Directive is contained in Marine Corps Order 3300.4, of 20 October 2003; the Navy's program in compliance in SecNav Instruction 3300.1B, of 27 December 2005; the Air Force program in Air Force Policy Directive 51–54, of 26 April 1993. All are available online.

Table 4.1 **Court-Martial Convictions Involving Vietnamese Victims, 1965–1973**

Offense	*ARMY*	*NAVY*	*USMC*	*USAF*
Murder	41	3	27	0
Rape	25	1	16	0
Mutilation of a corpse	2	0	1	0
Manslaughter	26	2	15	1

Source: Parks, "Crimes in Hostilities," supra, note 52, at 18.

In the military trial system, parole and clemency are the last act, unannounced, unreported, and unknown to the public.

As noted, no official record of US war crimes exists. There is, however, an authoritative all-service record of convictions for serious offenses involving Vietnamese victims—although not all such offenses are necessarily war crimes. One soldier whose case figures in the totals, for example, was convicted of murdering a Vietnamese drug dealer.[66] The unofficial tables that follow are based on Department of Defense and Department of the Army figures.

Other war crime tabulations said to be from official sources vary in various ways. There is no way of determining which are accurate, if any.[67] What can be said is that "official" tabulations cover only a portion of the war,[68] or fail to reflect a reliable source.[69]

What of those war crimes that were prosecuted? What punishment was imposed on those who were convicted, most often for the murder of Vietnamese noncombatants? How likely was a military jury to impose punishment upon one of their own?

In Vietnam, courts-martial convicted 122 US combatants of the murder or manslaughter of Vietnamese noncombatants; ninety-five soldiers and twenty-seven Marines (Table 4.1). No single record of the sentences to confinement that were actually served has been found, although there *is* a record of the confinement served in the Marine Corps cases (Table 4.2).

[66] *U.S. v. Stamats*, 45 CMR 765 (ACMR, 1971).

[67] E.g., Daniel, "The Defense of Superior Orders," supra, note 55, at 495.

[68] E.g., Waldemar A. Solf, "A Response to Telford Taylor's 'Nuremberg and Vietnam: An American Tragedy,'" *Akron Law Review* 5 (1972): 43–67; reprinted in Joseph Goldstein, Burke Marshall, and Jack Schwartz, *The My Lai Massacre and Its Cover-up: Beyond the Reach of the Law?* (New York: Free Press, 1976), 15, n.7.

[69] E.g., *U.S. News & World Report* (19 April 1971), at 20; and Joseph W. Bishop Jr., *Justice under Fire: A Study of Military Law* (New York: Charter House, 1974), 291.

Table 4.2 **Sentencing of Marines Convicted of the Murder/Manslaughter of Vietnamese Noncombatants, 1965–1971**

Individual	*Sentence at Trial, in yrs*	*Sentence approved by CA*	*Sentence Approved by NCMR*	*Action by USCMA*	*Sentence After parole (P) or clemency (C), in yrs*	*Confinem't Actually Served*
M. McGee	10	10	7	App. denied	C: 6 yrs, 6 mo	6 yrs, 6 mo.
F.C. Schultz	Life	Life	25	Affirmed	C: 6	6 yrs
T.L. Wilson	5	5	5	App. denied	C: denied	5 yrs
S.J. Luczko	Life	Life	3	App. denied	?	unavailable
C. Keenan	Life	25	5	App. denied	C: 2 yrs, 9 mo	2 yrs, ½ mo.
J.H. Boyd	4	4	4	App. denied	C: denied	3 yrs, ½ mo.
J.D. Potter	Life	Life	Life	App. denied	C: 12	12 yrs, 1mo.
R.L. Vogel	50	35	10	?	C: 8	9 yrs, ½ mo.
C. Ferguson	Life	35	5	App. denied	C: 2 yrs, 5 mo	2 yrs, 10 mo.
E.P. Boltik	30	30	Dis. insane	n/a	n/a	n/a
Two Two	10	5	5	No petition	C: 4	3 yrs, 7½ mo
Wilkerson	Life	30	30	App. denied	C: 3	2 yrs, ½ mo.
Hamilton	Life	Life	Life	App. denied	C: 9	8 yrs, 9 mo.
R.E. Wilson	Life	20	20	App. denied	C: 7 yrs, 1 mo	7 yrs, 1 mo.
D.R. Allen	Life	20	20	App. denied	C: 7	2 yrs, 11 mo.
J. Belknap	2	2	2	App. denied	C: denied	1yr, 3 mo.
Licciardo	2	2	2	?	C: denied	1 yr, 4 mo.

(continued)

Table 4.2 **Continued**

Individual	*Sentence at Trial, in yrs*	*Sentence approved by CA*	*Sentence Approved by NCMR*	*Action by USCMA*	*Sentence After parole (P) or clemency (C), in yrs*	*Confinem't Actually Served*
J. Maushart	2	2	2	App. denied	?	1 yr, 4 mo.
S.D. Crider	Life	Life	3	App. denied	?	3 yrs, 8½ mo
R.J. Reese	Life	30	3	App. denied	?	2 yrs, 4 mo.
D.W. Parr	4	1 yr, 3 mo.	8 mo.	No petition	C: denied	7 mo. +
F. Sikorski	Life	30	15	10 years	P: 3	3 yrs.
M. Stamats	Life	40	15	App. denied	P: 3 9/12	3 yrs, 8 mo.
S.G. Green	5	1	1	App. denied	C: denied	8 ½ mo.
M. Schwarz	Life	1	1	No petition	C: denied	9 ½ mo.
J.H. Jones	20	20	Dismissed	n/a	n/a	n/a
R.T. Taylor	Life	25	25	App. denied	C: 19	7 yrs, 8 mo.

Sentence at trial = the sentence imposed by the Marine Corps general court-martial in Vietnam that heard the case.

Sentence approved by CA = the sentence approved by the officer who initiated the court-martial (the Convening Authority, or CA) and who, with his senior judge advocate's advice, first reviewed the trial and sentence. CAs have the authority to reduce a court-martial sentence but cannot increase punishment.

Sentence approved by NCMR = the sentence approved after legal review of case by (for sailors and marines) the Navy-Marine Corps Court of Criminal Appeals, in Washington. Lawyer counsel represents accused throughout this review.

Action by USCMA = the action taken following another, de novo, appellate review by US Court of Military Appeals, the 3-civilian judge highest military appellate court. (Now the 5-judge Court of Appeals for the Armed Forces.)

Sentence after review by clemency and/ or parole boards = sentence reductions awarded upon the periodic, statutory reviews conducted by civilian boards.

Confinement actually served = determined by the author's physical review of surviving Naval Clemency and Parole Board records.

Dis. Insane = case dismissed when the prisoner was found to be legally insane.

? = instances in which records are incomplete, missing, or not made available.

Marine court-martial statistics are representative examples that, because of their lesser number, are more accessible than Army records, which are scattered among various major Army commands. Marine Corps records of confinement actually served are maintained by the Navy Clemency and Parole Board. The periods of time served is available in all but one of the twenty-seven Marine cases. (Portions of the following sentencing table appear in Lewy's *America in Vietnam*.[70])

Even without knowing the specifics of particular cases, this sentencing table (Table 4.2) reveals a disparity of sentences, from two years to life, each sentence for the offenses of murder or manslaughter. The dissimilarities raise questions regarding the legitimacy not of the court-martial process, but of the clemency and parole system, which is regulated by federal law. As in the civilian justice system, acquittals and unequal sentences are not unique in similar, even related, cases. Such disparate sentences are documented in numerous studies.[71] Posttrial clemency actions, on the other hand, are individual and unique. Rather than leveling sentence differences, the clemency process "makes disparity in time served as great as the discrepancies in time imposed."[72]

The Geneva Conventions speak of "effective penal sanctions."[73] How effective were the punishments for US war crimes in Vietnam? An answer is suggested by examining the prosecution of Marines for the homicide of Vietnamese noncombatants shown in the foregoing sentencing table. No other law of war offense is traceable in sufficient numbers to yield meaningful comparisons.

In several of the cases shown in the sentencing table there were multiple victims or associated crimes, such as aggravated assault or rape. Do the punishments imposed at trial reflect the seriousness of the offenses, or were they "wrist slaps"? In the 27 cases shown, along with their attendant punishments, such as dishonorable discharges, reductions in grade, and loss of pay and allowances, the sentences imposed at trial included, in fifteen cases, confinement for life; three cases included confinement for 20, 30, and 50 years. Only in seven of the twenty-seven cases was the confinement imposed less than 10 years. These are quite substantial sentences.

Trial-level sentences do not tell the whole story, however. In both civilian and military practice, sentences are often mitigated at the appellate level. After military appellate-level mitigation, also shown in the sentencing table, the

[70] Lewy, *America in Vietnam*, supra note 47, at table 10–15. 458.

[71] Roger Hood and Richard Sparks, *Key Issues in Criminology* (New York: McGraw-Hill, 1970), 141–156, e.g., cites six such studies from the United States and England. Barbara Hudson, *Justice through Punishment: A Critique of the "Justice" Model of Corrections* (New York: Palgrave-Macmillan, 1987), 43–48, notes another six.

[72] Hudson, *Justice through Punishment*, p. 46.

[73] 1949 Geneva Conventions common Article 49/50/129/146.

27 sentences were confinement for life in two cases; 30 years confinement in another; 20 to 30 years in five others; 10 to 20 years in three others; 5 to 10 in five others; less than 5 years confinement in ten cases; and two convictions set aside, one by reason of procedural error, the other for insanity.[74] Although sentences were significantly lessened in many of the cases, the range still remained generally high.

Case comparisons are suspect, but that range of *mitigated* court-martial sentence is comparable to or higher than *trial-level* sentences in American civilian jurisdictions. For example, in the first half of 1970, the year in which several of the 27 Marines were tried, 132 homicide convictions in, for example, Pennsylvania state courts, resulted in sentences ranging from probation (in 37 cases!), to confinement for life (in 3 cases). Other Pennsylvania sentences for homicide were confinement for 1 year (in 45 cases), 2 years (18 cases), 3 to 4 years (14 cases), 5 years (7 cases), 6 or more years (7 cases), and one sentence to death.[75] Granted, "homicide" is an umbrella term that includes acts less serious than murder, but the mitigated Marine Corps war crime sentences, imposed under active service conditions in a combat zone, compared to Pennsylvania trial court sentences, still cover a similar, or higher, span of confinement. (There is no practical means of determining what sentence reductions may have resulted from further appellate action in the Pennsylvania civilian cases.)

In US Federal District Courts (as opposed to Pennsylvania *state* courts) in 1973, the first year such statistics were compiled, sentences for all of the twenty-five convicted first- and second-degree murderers ranged from probation (in two cases), to confinement for 3 to 5 years (three cases), to 5 years and over—the breakdown is no more specific—in twenty cases.[76] These federal trial court sentences, like the state trial court sentences, are no more harsh than the *mitigated* sentences imposed in Marine cases.

How do the court-martial sentences for murdering Vietnamese noncombatants compare with court-martial sentences imposed in the same period on military personnel for murdering fellow-American soldiers? In five such convictions for premeditated murder, sentences to confinement for life resulted. Those sentences were reduced on appeal to 30 years in one case, 15 years in another. (In two other cases the life sentences were set aside for new sentence or trial

[74] Lewy, *America in Vietnam* 458, supra note 47, at table 10–15, 458.

[75] Franklin E. Zimring, Joel Eigen, and Sheila O'Malley, "Punishing Homicide in Philadelphia: Perspectives on the Death Penalty," *Chicago Law Review* 43 (Winter, 1976): 227–234, see table VI. The table's percentages have been translated into discrete numbers, here.

[76] Michael J. Hindelang et al., eds., *Sourcebook of Criminal Justice Statistics* (Washington, DC: US Department of Justice, 1973), table 5.38. The rudimentary breakdown lists seven punishment categories: 1 year and under; 1–3 years; 3–5 years; 5 years and over; probation; fine; and "other."

proceedings.)[77] In other words, there was no appreciable difference in court-martial sentences whether the victims were American or Vietnamese.

Acquittals can be as revealing as sentences imposed, since acquittals may indicate the reluctance of a court to convict, let alone sentence, an accused. Sixteen Marines, or 37 percent of those tried for murdering Vietnamese noncombatants, were acquitted or had their charges judicially dismissed.[78] In US Federal District Courts in 1969, to select a random year during the Vietnam conflict, 33 percent of the civilian homicide cases that went to trial resulted in acquittal or dismissal,[79] a rate essentially the same as Marine Corps courts-martial throughout the war for the same offense.

After sentence reductions and appeals are completed, clemency and parole become possibilities. The Supreme Court held in a Vietnam-era decision, *Parker v. Levy*, that "the military establishment is subject to the control of the civilian Commander in Chief and the civilian departmental heads under him, and its function is to carry out the policies made by those civilian superiors."[80] Among those civilian-made policies is the court-martial clemency and parole program, provided for in federal law,[81] case law,[82] and military regulations.[83] Federal law allows the service secretaries to "provide a system of parole for offenders who are confined in military correctional facilities"[84] and directs the secretaries to establish a system for remission or suspension of the unexecuted part of sentences of selected offenders.[85]

Each armed service's clemency and parole boards typically consist of five members. The chairperson is a civilian experienced in corrections, with knowledge of military personnel policies. The four other board members are senior military officers, at least one of whom must be a judge advocate.[86]

[77] Respectively, *U.S. v. Thomas*, 41 CMR 828 (NCMR, 1970); *U.S. v. Brandy*, 40 CMR 674 (ACMR, 1969); *U.S. v. Walker*, 41 CMR 632 (ACMR, 1969); *U.S. v. Newsome*, 42 CMR 695 (ACMR, 1970); and *U.S. v. Jones*, 44 CMR 818 (ACMR, 1969).

[78] Letter, Brigadier General John R. DeBarr, general court-martial military judge in Vietnam, to Prof. Gunter Lewy (9 March 1976), on file with author. Actual acquittal rates were not recorded.

[79] *Statistical Abstract of the United States 1970* (Washington: US Department of Commerce, 1970), table 236 at 153.

[80] *Parker, Warden, et al. v. Levy*, 417 U.S. 733, 751 (1974).

[81] 10 U.S.C., §§ 952, Parole; 953, Remission or suspension of sentence; and 871, Execution of sentence; suspension of sentence.

[82] E.g., *Sima v. United States*, 96 F. Supp. 932 (Ct. Cl., 1951), pertaining to the clemency authority of the secretary and under secretary of the Navy.

[83] UCMJ, Art. 74, Remission and suspension; and Army Regulation 27-10, "Military Justice," Section V, Post-trial, which is a typical service implementing order.

[84] 10 U.S.C., § 952, Parole.

[85] 10 U.S.C., § 953, Remission or suspension of sentence.

[86] US Army Regulation 15-130, Army Clemency and Parole Board, para. 2–3.

Military prisoners are eligible for clemency (as opposed to parole) after serving specified periods of their confinement. For example, if the prisoner's sentence to confinement is ten to twenty years, clemency consideration will be no later than two years from the date confinement began. Clemency reconsideration will be annually thereafter. If the sentence is from twenty to thirty years, clemency consideration will be no later than three years into the prisoner's confinement. Thirty years or more, no later than five years.[87] When "exceptional circumstances exist or for other good cause,"[88] however, a board may consider a prisoner serving a sentence of *any length* for clemency *any time* prior to completing his sentence. In other words, despite pages of specific guidelines, the board has an essentially free hand to act in any case at any time.

Generally speaking, a prisoner is eligible for parole (as opposed to clemency) consideration after serving one-third of his period of confinement. But, as in clemency regulations, the board "may waive any parole eligibility requirement."[89] Standards for consideration for both clemency and parole span factors one might anticipate, from combat service to prior criminality; from the protection of society to deterrence. Given such broad authority it is not surprising that clemency and parole actions injected substantial reductions in many Vietnam War crime convictions—even with military officers on each board.

Court-martial sentences for Vietnam-era war crimes were substantial, even heavy, when compared to sentences imposed in civilian courts. Nor were there discernible differences in court-martial sentences for the murder of Americans and those imposed for Vietnamese victims. Thus, it is fair to say that Vietnam-era military courts fully executed their responsibilities in light of the "effective sentencing" envisioned by the Geneva Conventions. Once military sentences were reviewed in the calm of the United States, and clemency exercised by clemency and parole panels, sentences were often cut significantly. By 1970, the war had become unpopular and military confinement facilities were overflowing. The pressures to grant clemency were significant. But the military courts' results, before clemency was considered, remain notable.

Vietnam was not the first instance of civilian reductions in court-martial sentences, of course. Congress first provided for court-martial review by civilian authorities in 1786, when they revised the Articles of War following a commander's execution of three soldiers without benefit of trial.[90] President Abraham Lincoln frequently reduced the penalties imposed by military tribunals.[91] After

87 Ibid., para. 3.1.d.

88 Ibid., para. 3.1.d.(10).

89 Ibid., para. 3.1.e.

90 William Winthrop, *Military Law and Precedents* (Washington, DC: GPO, 1920), 972.

91 Jonathan Lurie, *Arming Military Justice*, vol. 1 (Princeton, NJ: Princeton University Press, 1992), 32, fn. 35.

World War I, 28,000 courts-martial were reviewed by special clemency boards and hundreds of sentences modified or disapproved entirely.[92] Even so, given the seriousness with which Vietnam courts-martial evidently viewed war crimes, the actual time served was sometimes akin to lenient-appearing civilian cases that bring outraged letters to the editor.

Trial-level sentence reductions in military cases are, however, significantly different from those made in domestic cases. In military practice, the senior officer empowered to initiate a court-martial is the convening authority (the "CA"). The Vietnam-era UCMJ required the CA to review the verbatim record of each trial he ordered convened. (There were no women CAs in Vietnam and virtually none anywhere in the military.) The CA was empowered to reduce, or set aside entirely, sentences and findings of guilt. A CA may in no way increase punishments,[93] but he is first in a line of individuals who can award clemency. But, unlike clemency bodies, CAs often personally know the convicted soldier or Marine, as well as receiving recommendations from the convicted man's immediate commanders. At the court-martial level, at least, military clemency decisions are not made on the cold record but on the advice of fellow-soldiers or Marines who eat, sleep, and live with the convicted individual, often for months, sometimes in the crucible of combat.

The "M. Schwarz" case in the sentencing table, above, illustrates the unique nature of military trial-level clemency. Private Michael Schwarz was an amazingly poor Marine, with a record of three courts-martial and several nonjudicial punishments before arriving in Vietnam. In February 1970, in the hamlet of Son Thang-4, Schwarz and four other Marines, with pointblank small arms fire, murdered sixteen civilian women and children, including babies. There was no apparent reason for the murders, and none was offered at trial. Four of the five were charged with premeditated murder and were court-martialed. The fifth was flipped to testify against the others. Schwarz was convicted and sentenced to confinement for life. Another of the four, "S. G. Green" in the sentencing table, was convicted of fewer counts and, with a compelling personal background, sentenced to a surprising mere five years. The other two, including the decorated patrol leader who forcefully ordered his subordinates to fire on the victims, were acquitted. The CA, a two-star general, was a hard Texan schooled in philosophy. He was greatly troubled by the acquittal of the patrol leader who had driven the killings and who, at trial, enjoyed the pro bono services of four experienced civilian defense lawyers and three Marine judge advocates, juxtaposed with the convictions of Schwarz and Green. The CA's "dilemma was that

92 Ibid., 83, fn. 41.

93 *Manual for Courts-Martial, United States 1969*, rev. ed. (Washington, DC: GPO, 1969), Art. 88.

some who participated in Son Thang's slaughter were paying no price at all. 'He really disdained these persons . . . [but] he still wanted to see justice done, equity preserved, without excusing them for their actions' "[94] His solution? For both Schwarz and Green he reduced their periods of confinement to one year, essentially time served. Their loss of all pay and allowances and dishonorable discharges remained in force.

The CA's clemency was the outcome of a troubling case, the results of which, acquittal of the principle actor and a hammer for two lesser actors, was morally unjust but legally unobjectionable. In his limited power to balance the equities, the CA could not attack the acquittals, so he mitigated the convictions. One may argue that freeing guilty men because other apparently guilty men walked was in itself inequitable, but the CAs clemency was the result of an effort to achieve fairness as he saw it. In the sentencing table, however, the reader only sees a life sentence reduced to one year.

Ignorantia Legis Non Excusat

Mistakes were made. In Vietnam, US tactics such as the strategic hamlet program, free fire zones, the Phoenix program, and body counts, in addition to individual war crimes committed by soldiers and Marines, tarnish the record of American involvement in Vietnam, as well as diminishing the nation's adherence to the Geneva Conventions.

In 1962, the US and South Vietnamese governments were concerned about increasing enemy support among the South's populace. "To stop those advances, the two governments introduced the Strategic Hamlet Program, the idea of which was to move South Vietnamese farmers into new villages that were surrounded by walls and patrolled by the military."[95] Tone deaf to the moral and legal implications of the program, General Westmoreland wrote, "So sympathetic were some of the people to the VC that the only way to establish control short of constant combat operations among the people was to remove the people and destroy the village. That done, operations to find the enemy could be conducted without fear of civilian casualties."[96] Under the relocation program, South Vietnamese farmers were forcibly removed from the villages where they had lived their entire lives and where their ancestors were entombed, bringing

[94] Gary Solis, *Son Thang: An American War Crime* (Annapolis, MD: Naval Institute Press, 1997), 275.

[95] Robert Coram, *Brute: The Life of Victor Krulak, U.S. Marine* (New York: Little Brown, 2010), 270.

[96] Westmoreland, *A Soldier Reports*, supra, note 2, at 152.

only what they could carry, to distant sterile government-built "hamlets" of plywood and corrugated tin roofing. The Strategic Hamlet Program's resettlement centers "became instruments of control rather than pacification. The peasants resented having to leave their homes and gardens and being herded into fortified stockades."[97]

The Strategic Hamlet Program also disregarded Article 49 of Geneva Convention IV, Relative to the Protection of Civilian Persons: "Individual or mass forcible transfers . . . are prohibited, regardless of their motive." Earlier, the ICRC had written of such transfers, "There is doubtless no need to give an account here of the painful recollections called forth by the 'deportations' of the Second World War. . . . [T]he prohibition . . . is intended to forbid such hateful practices for all time. . . . [T]he prohibition is absolute and allows no exceptions."[98]

The transfer of civilians from contested areas to strategic hamlets allowed the establishment of free fire zones. "Once such a zone was established, anyone remaining in the area was considered an enemy combatant and was subject to attack by aircraft or artillery without prior approval by the Vietnamese government or higher [US] headquarters."[99] Any individual observed in a free fire zone was automatically considered an enemy and could be targeted. But "free-fire zones cannot be reconciled with binding IHL [International Humanitarian Law] obligations . . . [and do] not relieve the attacker of the duty to distinguish between civilians and combatants."[100] It is a foremost principle in warfare is that combatants must distinguish between civilians and combatants and target only the latter. Vietnamese civilians exiled to strategic hamlets soon resented their treatment more than they feared the Vietcong (VC) and returned to their villages. Often, however, their villages had by then been designated free fire zones. Civilian casualties inevitably resulted.

The Phoenix program was part of the 1968 US/South Vietnamese Accelerated Pacification Program. Initially sponsored by the Central Intelligence Agency (CIA), the covert program was designed to identify, capture, or kill VC infrastructure (VCI) members in rural areas. Well intended as the program was, allegations of torture and summary executions were soon raised.[101] "The charge that Phoenix was an assassination program arose because reported results always included a considerable number listed as killed. . . . Most of those neutralized

[97] Lewy, *America in Vietnam*, supra, note 47, at 25.

[98] Jean Pictet, ed., *Commentary, IV Geneva Convention* (Geneva: ICRC, 1958), 278–279.

[99] Spector, *After Tet*, supra, note 51, at 198.

[100] James G. Stewart, "The UN Commission of Inquiry on Lebanon: A Legal Appraisal," *Journal of International Criminal Justice* 5, no. 5 (November 2007), 1039, 1047–1048.

[101] Nils Melzer, *Targeted Killing in International Law* (Oxford: Oxford University Press, 2008), 412: "Sober assessments show that US commando units operating under the so-called 'Phoenix' program in Vietnam 'often killed as many VCI as they captured.' "

were low-level members of the VCI playing relatively unimportant roles."[102] Nevertheless, Phoenix was confirmed in postwar North Vietnamese interviews to have been an effective anti-VCI program. But, subverted by corrupt South Vietnamese participation and unwilling to reveal the extent of its operations, Phoenix became a media target and antiwar rallying point that, to this day, is perceived as an American violation of the law of war.[103] The strategic effectiveness of the Phoenix program has been drowned out by antiwar criticism, deserved or not.

No American policy in the Vietnam conflict was as perniciously contrary to the American military ethos, more greatly harmed perceptions of US military efforts, or engendered more war crimes at the small unit level, as "body count." General Westmoreland wrote:

> Statistics were, admittedly, an imperfect gauge of progress, yet in the absence of conventional front lines, how else to measure it? . . . How else, too, to judge whether we were meeting the essentially statistical goals that Washington officials had set . . . ? The most controversial of the statistics was the number of enemy killed, which was based on tally in the field and known as "body count." I abhorred the term. . . . Yet the term was already so firmly established in the lexicon of the war by the time I arrived that there seemed little point in trying to change it. It had been introduced in the early 1960s to appease the American press whose members were questioning the validity of casualty reports. . . . I directed several detailed studies which determined as well as anybody could that the count probably erred on the side of caution.[104]

Subsequent reports document that commanders from lieutenant to general inflated body count as a means to satisfy civilian and military superiors, or as a route to favored follow-on assignments, combat awards, and promotion. In 1974, General Douglas Kinnard surveyed 173 fellow general officers who served in Vietnam as to inflated body counts. Eighty-one of the generals (61 percent) responded that body counts were "often inflated."[105] In 1991, General Norman Schwarzkopf said, "Body count was a big lie. Okay, I was forced to participate in that lie. Many times, people would call me up on the radio after a battle and say, What was your body count?' I'd say, 'I don't know what the body

[102] Lewy, *America in Vietnam*, supra, note 47, at 281.

[103] Dale Andradé, *Ashes to Ashes* (Lexington MA: Lexington Books, 1990), favorably reviews the Phoenix program.

[104] Westmoreland, *A Soldier Reports*, supra, note 2, at 273.

[105] Lewy, *America in Vietnam*, supra, note 47, at 81.

count was.' They'd say, 'Well, make one up. We have to report a body count.' So, eventually, just to get them off your back, you'd say, 'Okay, the body count was 250.' "[106] (Which part of General Schwarzkopf's account is the "forced to participate" part?)

The law of war issue is obvious. "The pressure for a large number of kills might lead to the inclination to include civilians in the count of 'enemy dead,' and perhaps weaken whatever restraints may have existed against killing unarmed civilians."[107] In fact, the body count mentality loosened moral restraints and *unquestionably* led to civilian deaths. Lieutenant Calley (granted, not the most reliable source) reports that, prior to My Lai, "Medina [Calley's company commander] said, 'What is the body count?' . . . I would say to Medina, 'Three,' Medina would tell the Colonel, 'Six.' He would double it. But anything went in a body count: the buffalos, cows, the Vietnamese, and I have always wondered, *Who gives a flying——?*"[108]

Conclusion

Vietnam was a window through which we can examine America's and the military's commitment to the law of war and the Geneva Conventions. Did the nation honor those commitments? Did the nation's military make every reasonable effort to prevent our armed forces from committing grave breaches of the Conventions? When war crimes were discovered, did the military act to impose personal criminal liability? Were the punishments imposed on the convicted significant and proportional to the offenses charged? Or were we a nation of hypocrites and international law offenders? Individuals are likely to read the data, limited as it is and, like blind men describing an elephant, reach differing conclusions.

Most war crimes, by their nature surreptitious and hidden, are never discovered. Objective data regarding discovered battlefield offenses is largely nonexistent. The difficulty of sifting unlawful violence in a sea of lawful carnage is evident. When battlefield courts-martial resulted in conviction, were the sentences appropriate? Appropriate by what standard? Appropriate compared to what? Appropriate in whose eyes?

The fact that not all war crimes resulted in a trial does not indicate a disregard of the Conventions. Lenient sentences, or seemingly too-generous

[106] UPI, "General Admits Vietnam Body Counts Were Lies," *Detroit News* (11 March 1991), 6.

[107] Spector, *After Tet*, supra, note 51, at 221.

[108] John Sack, *Lieutenant Calley: His Own Story* (New York: Viking Press, 1971), 118. Italics and ellipses in original.

clemency, hardly suggest the armed forces were law of war scofflaws. Was General Westmoreland a war criminal, along with World War II Japanese General Yamashita, who was convicted and hanged by a military commission for failure to control his troops? Or did Westmoreland take all reasonable steps a commander could take to prevent war crimes, and did he direct the prosecution of offenders when they were discovered? Was General David Petraeus a war criminal for the war crimes perpetrated by troops under his command in Iraq and Afghanistan? Of course not.

It is no challenge for critics to focus on some aspect of the war crime continuum, from undiscovered criminality, to a decision to not charge, to a trial acquittal, to questionable clemency, and cry "foul," particularly when the military itself provided evidence of its too frequent failure to effectively deal with criminality. But the crimes of an individual *civilian* do not indicate his employer's organization is criminal. The offenses of an individual soldier similarly do not render the Army lawless; the crimes of a platoon of twenty-five soldiers do not implicate the institution as a whole.

Questions of America honoring the Conventions reach higher than the misdeeds of individual combatants and their trials, of course. What of questionable, even unlawful national policies and wartime strategies that were executed in South Vietnam? A similar question might be asked of today's conflicts. Such questions dog every armed conflict.

Two million six hundred forty-four thousand American servicemen and women served in South Vietnam, virtually all of them with courage and honor. Their service gives perspective to the miniscule number, relatively speaking, of law of war offenders, appalling as some offenders' actions were. The nation's, and the military's, observance of the Geneva Conventions and the laws of war were genuine commitments, if sometimes imperfectly carried out.

5

Geneva Convention Compliance in Iraq and Afghanistan

ELIZABETH GRIMM ARSENAULT

What difference—if any—have the Geneva Conventions made in US behavior leading up to and during the wars in Iraq and Afghanistan? How do the laws of war matter in the fight against nonstate actors who not only ignore the law, but make every effort to publicize their noncompliance? For more than fifteen years, the United States and its allies have wrestled with how to apply the laws of war to the conflicts against Al Qaeda, the Taliban, and—more recently—the Islamic State in Iraq and Syria (ISIS). Domestic and international debates have occurred concurrent to these policy debates about what techniques can and should be used in this struggle. This chapter seeks to add to this dialogue about the role and efficacy of international law and to determine how to reconcile the treatment of combatants and civilians with beliefs in justice, the universality of human rights, and achieving US mission objectives in Iraq and Afghanistan.

From Counterterrorism to Counterinsurgency

US compliance with the Geneva Conventions in Iraq and Afghanistan appeared to vary with the particular subject matter and battle space. In military operations during these wars, the United States was more effective at avoiding the intentional targeting of civilians than at avoiding military endeavors that knowingly placed civilians at risk or destroyed civilian infrastructure. Legal specialists assessed the legality of virtually every proposed target to monitor adherence to norms governing aerial bombardment. Legal specialists also, however, flagrantly overlooked Common Article 3's minimum prescription that all captured individuals—insurgents and terrorists included—have the right to be treated humanely at all times. What explains this variation?

From the photographs of Abu Ghraib to the story of the civilian atrocities in Haditha at the hands of US Marines, compliance with the international laws protecting civilians and belligerents often seemed coincidental—rather than elemental—to the military mission. Yet, remarkably, US authorities carried out a course correction to comply more stringently with both the letter and the spirit of the Conventions regarding noncombatant and combatant treatment. This course correction can be explained through examining the shift in mission objectives: When the United States approached Iraq and Afghanistan as purely counterterror operations, the goal was to disrupt the enemy; however, with a shift to a population-centric counterinsurgency mission, noncompliance with the Geneva Conventions equated to mission failure. Rather than a strict focus on eliminating the enemy, US counterinsurgency forces also sought to ensure the safety and security of the civilian population. In this way, protecting civilians and treating prisoners humanely were not coincidental aspects of the military operations, but were the objective of the military operations. The shift from counterterrorism to counterinsurgency increased US sensitivity to civilian casualties and the operational consequences of prisoner abuse. Civilian deaths, civilian injuries, and civilian property damage lessened the likelihood that progovernment forces would prevail because they provided fodder for antigovernment elements' rhetoric and hurt local support for US and International Security Assistance Force (ISAF) troops. Similarly, prisoner abuse decreased the legitimacy of progovernment forces and supported the narrative, fundraising, and recruitment of the insurgents. The tactical considerations of counterinsurgency—employing restraint to avoid creating more insurgents—rendered humane treatment the goal of the military missions. Compliance with the Geneva Conventions, avoiding excessive force, and treating captured individuals humanely challenged al-Qaeda's narrative.

The military conflict in Afghanistan following the attacks of 9/11 and the 2003 conflict in Iraq initially were defined as counterterror operations against al-Qaeda's global jihadist network, a network that sought to expel Western forces and influence from Islamic society and restore an Islamic caliphate ruled by sharia law. In this "global war on terror," the administration crafted military operations with the intent of disrupting al-Qaeda and the Taliban, their operations, and their fundraising.

Counterterror operations generally seek to dismantle the group itself and its supporters and to render the operating environment around the group more hostile to the group's interests, making it harder for the group to recruit, train, distribute propaganda, move freely, and collect intelligence. The 2003 National Strategy for Combating Terrorism put forward four steps in the US mission against al-Qaeda and its allies: defeat, deny, diminish, and defend.[1] The first

[1] *National Strategy for Combating Terrorism*, Executive Office of the President, February 2003, http://www.state.gov/documents/organization/60172.pdf.

step, defeat terrorists and their organizations, involves a whole-government approach to target their political, economic, and physical sources of power. It involves relying on a range of intelligence-collection capabilities to pinpoint terrorist locations of training, fundraising, communications, and safe havens. The second component of the strategy requires the denial of safe haven, support, and sponsorship to terrorists. In this step, if states are unwilling to change their policies of support for terror groups, the United States, "in cooperation with friends and allies, or if necessary, acting independently, will take appropriate steps to convince them to change their policies."[2] This step is predicated on the fact that the terrorist organizations that have posed the greatest threat over the longest period of time all share one characteristic unrelated to their size, ideology, or goals: they possessed a safe haven.[3] Severing state support for the terrorist group inhibits its ability to coordinate, plan, and execute violent attacks. The third step in the strategy involves diminishing the conditions such as poverty, political or judicial vacuums, or failing or failed states that terrorists seek to capitalize on.[4] The fourth step addresses the defense of US citizens at home and abroad through improved coordination and cooperation among federal, state, and local agencies committed to law enforcement and defense.[5] This 2003 strategy—issued one month prior to the beginning of the Iraq War—does not generally focus on the foreign civilian population. With the exception of step three, which seeks to redress the causes that may have given rise to terrorism in the first place, this is a strategy focused on kinetic activity against a terrorist opponent. This was the strategy that guided initial US counterterror operations in Iraq.

In contrast, the "hearts and minds" approach to counterinsurgency strategy adopted by the United States in 2006 almost exclusively focused on the population. This approach began from the premise that political and military actions could not be separated. According to David Galula, a French scholar and practitioner associated with this strategy, the counterinsurgent must develop a military approach to locate and remove the insurgents as well as a political approach to pinpoint the supporters, enhance the legitimacy of the government, and build

[2] Ibid., 17.

[3] Daniel Byman, "Denying Terrorist Safe Havens: Homeland Security Efforts to Counter Threats from Pakistan, Yemen and Somalia," Testimony before the Subcommittee on Oversight, Investigations and Management of the Committee on Homeland Security, United States House of Representatives, 112th Cong., 3 June 2011, http://www.brookings.edu/research/testimony/2011/06/03-terrorism-byman; Robert D. Lamb, "Ungoverned Areas and Threats from Safe Havens," US Department of Defense, Office of the Under Secretary of Defense for Policy, 2008, http://www.cissm.umd.edu/papers/files/ugashreportfinal.pdf.

[4] *National Strategy*, 22.

[5] Ibid., 24–25.

or rebuild the institutions of the state.[6] Winning the credibility of the people is the mission of this counterinsurgency strategy, and the credibility of the people cannot be won with excessive force, arbitrary detention, or indiscriminant violence.[7] Counterinsurgents want the population to choose to support them over the terrorist or insurgent—thus the political actions all seek to make the people safer in order to convince them to choose the counterinsurgents. Galula argues that in these struggles, some small percentage of the population will always support the counterinsurgent, some small percentage of the population will always support the insurgent, and the vast majority of the population will actually be neutral. The goal of counterinsurgency operations should be to force the neutral majority to make a decision to support the counterinsurgent.[8]

When the United States shifted from a purely counterterrorism approach to a strategy that embraced the hearts-and-minds goals of counterinsurgency, compliance with the Geneva Conventions became central. The self-imposed limitations on US behavior met both counterinsurgency goals and international humanitarian standards. The following sections examine the arc of US compliance with both the Fourth Geneva Convention and the Third Geneva Convention. Each section begins first with an assessment of operations in Afghanistan and then Iraq before addressing how the United States corrected its course following the adoption of a counterinsurgency posture. Achieving perfection in the treatment of prisoners of war (POWs) and civilians is not possible, but with the shift to counterinsurgency methods, the United States improved its compliance with international humanitarian law.

Compliance with the Fourth Geneva Convention and Additional Protocol I

Avoiding civilian casualties has been a goal of US operations in both Iraq and Afghanistan, though compliance with the Conventions increased with the shift in strategies. US military leaders and civilian policymakers repeatedly stressed the importance of minimizing civilian casualties both leading up to and during the US engagements in Iraq and Afghanistan. Speaking about the US-led conflict in Afghanistan, General Tommy Franks stated, "I can't imagine there's been a conflict in history where there has been less collateral damage, less unintended

[6] David Galula, *Counterinsurgency Warfare: Theory and Practice* (Westport, CT: Praeger Security International, 1964).

[7] Ibid., 52.

[8] Ibid., 53.

consequences."[9] One of the findings from Wikileaks in 2008 was the revelation of detailed guidelines in Iraq to protect civilians.[10] Prior to the invasion of Iraq in 2003, the US Department of Defense (DoD) hosted reporters at a briefing to outline US military targeting and procedures to minimize casualties to noncombatants and prevent collateral damage. Officials made a point of drawing sharp distinctions between the mandates of international law, which distinguish between combatants and noncombatants and state that civilians must be protected, and the actions of Saddam Hussein. The briefing stated,

> He [Saddam Hussein] deliberately constructs mosques near military facilities, uses schools, hospitals, orphanages and cultural treasures to shield military forces, thereby exposing helpless men, women and children to danger. These are not tactics of war, they're crimes of war. Deploying human shields is not a military strategy, it's murder, it's a violation of the laws of armed conflict and a crime against humanity, and will be treated as such.[11]

In highlighting Saddam's violations of the laws of war, the United States thus acknowledged these laws' application in occupied Iraq, and further defined this position in a March 2004 memorandum to the president titled "'Protected Person' Status in Occupied Iraq under the Fourth Geneva Convention," which opens, "The Geneva Convention Relative to the Protection of Civilian Persons in Time of War (IV) governs the United States occupation of Iraq."[12]

Assessing the actual extent of civilian causalities in Iraq and Afghanistan and drawing conclusions about the level of Geneva Convention compliance, however, has been problematic for a variety of reasons. Unfortunately, due to the nature of armed conflict, a number of civilians will necessarily perish, even if a state strictly adheres to the laws of war. In addition, estimating the number of civilian dead is complicated by incomplete public records, different counting methodologies, the challenges of disaggregating combatants from noncombatants, and the dangers of independent reporting from the affected areas.[13]

[9] P. W. Singer, "How Many Lives Is This War Worth?" *Los Angeles Times*, 27 March 2003.

[10] W. Arkin, "Iraq Rules Need More Airing," *Washington Post*, 4 February 2008.

[11] "Department of Defense Background Briefing on Targeting," 5 March 2003.

[12] Jack L. Goldsmith III, "'Protected Person' Status in Occupied Iraq under the Fourth Geneva Convention," Office of Legal Counsel, 18 March 2004, http://nsarchive.gwu.edu/torturingdemocracy/documents/20040318.pdf.

[13] This chapter does not focus explicitly on the question of civilian causalities from drone strikes. While this question constitutes an important debate in both policy and scholarship, in-depth examination is outside of the scope of this piece. Many of the same challenges apply to assessing the civilian causalities from drones, particularly in Pakistan; however, that question is not examined here. Other

Afghanistan: Assessing Civilian Casualties

Following the attacks of September 11, 2001 against the World Trade Center and the Pentagon, the Bush administration took immediate action to condemn the perpetrators and the attacks. On September 18, 2001 Congress authorized military action against the "nations, organizations, or persons" that "authorized, committed, or aided the terrorist attacks."[14] In addition to this authorization, the UN Security Council also condemned the attacks, adopting two resolutions in September 2001: Resolution 1368, which signaled that the attacks constituted a threat to peace, and Resolution 1373, which sought to prevent the organization, movement, and fundraising activities of terrorist groups. On October 7, 2001, Operation Enduring Freedom commenced an aerial bombing campaign against the Taliban and al-Qaeda in Afghanistan. Twenty-seven coalition countries with forces in Afghanistan deployed more than 14,000 troops in support of the war on terror. Capitalizing on initial successes, Coalition forces and the Northern Alliance captured significant territory in northern Afghanistan in the early fall and eventually assumed control of Kabul in November 2001 after the Taliban withdrew from the capital. After these immediate successes, the United States largely turned over responsibility for Afghanistan to ISAF, and the operation became an economy of force mission for the US military. As a result—and due to the exigencies of Operation Iraqi Freedom (OIF)—casualty reporting of Afghan citizens did not begin till 2007.[15]

Despite the claim by former Secretary of Defense Donald Rumsfeld that, "We don't do body counts on other people,"[16] the DoD does occasionally provide Afghan civilian casualty data in its reports.[17] In addition, there have been many systematic attempts made to approximate the extent of civilian suffering from pro-Government and insurgent violence in Afghanistan. Foremost among these sources is the United Nations Assistance Mission to Afghanistan (UNAMA), which semiannually reports casualty data of Afghan civilians. In 2015, UNAMA reported 11,002 civilian casualties—7,457 injured and 3,545 killed—resulting from both anti-Government and pro-Government forces, the highest number since beginning its data collection in 2009. This civilian casualty rate reflects

works have examined the extent to which drones represent a discriminant tool that allows for precise, inexpensive, and timely targeting versus the extent to which they challenge state sovereignty and support terrorist recruitment. Daniel Byman, "Why Drones Work," *Foreign Affairs* 92 (July/August 2013); Audrey Kurth Cronin, "Why Drones Fail," *Foreign Affairs* 92 (July/August 2013).

14 "Authorization for Use of Military Force," Public Law 107-40 [S. J. RES. 23] (2001).

15 S. G. Chesser, "Afghanistan Casualties: Military Forces and Civilians," (Washington, DC, Congressional Research Service, 2012).

16 "Transcript: Donald Rumsfeld on 'FOX News Sunday'," *Fox News*, 2 November 2003, http://www.foxnews.com/story/0,2933,101956,00.html.

17 Chesser, "Afghanistan Casualties."

a 4 percent decrease in civilian deaths but 9 percent increase in injuries compared to 2014, the deadliest year for civilians on record.[18] The midyear UNAMA report for 2016 brought the total number of civilian casualties from 1 January 2009 to 30 June 2016 to 63,934, reflecting 40,993 civilians injured and 22,941 killed.[19] Though the various estimates of civilian casualties are often contested, the Congressional Research Service further aggregates data from a variety of sources to gauge the casualties sustained during OEF; its most recent report, published in 2012, presents slightly more conservative estimates than those presented by UNAMA, but corroborates the same trends.[20]

What accounts for this extent of civilian death? The dynamics have changed with evolving strategy: Civilian casualties after 2009 have increasingly resulted from improvised explosive devices (IEDs), a tactic borrowed from insurgents in Iraq; suicide attacks by antigovernment elements; and more frequent ground engagements; while air strikes have decreased as a major cause. These changing dynamics are the result of the evolution in strategy from counterterrorism to counterinsurgency. The greater emphasis on ground operations has naturally led to a relative increase in casualties in that arena, while the focus on avoiding casualties has led to greater discrimination in air strikes. Both sides are culpable: Though antigovernment forces are consistently responsible for the vast majority of civilian deaths, significant civilian suffering has occurred as a result of drone and other air attacks by progovernment forces. The transfer of responsibility from withdrawing Coalition forces to Afghan forces, in keeping with the goals of counterinsurgency, can account for the renewed surge in casualties in 2014 and 2015.[21] UNAMA attributes 17 percent of the 2015 civilian casualties to progovernment forces, but of that 17 percent, only 2 percent to international military forces (and the remaining 14 percent to Afghan national security forces and 1 percent to progovernment armed groups).[22]

Iraq: Assessing Civilian Casualties

The trend lines for civilian suffering in Afghanistan dramatically differ from those in Iraq, where civilian deaths declined after 2007, the height of the sectarian conflict. Later civilian casualty counts were complicated by the ISIS-related violence

[18] *Afghanistan Annual Report 2015: Protection of Civilians in Armed Conflict* (Kabul, Afghanistan: United Nations Assistance Mission in Afghanistan, 2016): 1.

[19] *Afghanistan Midyear Report 2016: Protection of Civilians in Armed Conflict* (Kabul, Afghanistan: United Nations Assistance Mission in Afghanistan, 2016): 1.

[20] Chesser, "Afghanistan Casualties."

[21] *Afghanistan Annual Report 2014: Protection of Civilians in Armed Conflict* (Kabul, Afghanistan: United Nations Assistance Mission in Afghanistan, 2015): 11.

[22] *Afghanistan Annual Report 2015*, 3.

and the spillover effects of the Syrian Civil War. In March 2003, OIF commenced, with the fall of Baghdad occurring one month later. In May 2003, President Bush declared an end to major combat operations, and the US-led coalition created the Coalition Provisional Authority as a transitional government in Iraq. Many decisions made at this time—including the de-Baathification of the oil industry, government, education, and other major elements of Iraq's political, economic, and cultural infrastructure—had important long-term consequences on US military outcomes. During the postconflict reconstruction, both Sunni and Shi'a insurgent groups took up arms against the Coalition forces and sought to terrorize and eventually seize control of embryonic Iraqi security services. Civilians were caught in the crossfire of this violence, which took the form of brutal urban guerrilla assaults, including IED attacks, convoy attacks, suicide attacks, and firefights outside of police stations, targeting and deterring new recruits.

In the immediate aftermath of the US invasion, a paucity of data existed on the extent of civilian casualties. Few government or nongovernmental sources tracked the civilian suffering. Subsequently, however, the US government, through the DoD, several Iraqi ministries, and the United Nations began to track these trends. In addition, several nongovernmental organizations—such as the Iraq Body Count (IBC), the Associated Press, the Brookings Institution, the Iraq Coalition Casualty Count, and Iraq Family Health Survey—also provide estimates for civilian casualty figures; these estimates were also confounded in later years by the growing violence incited by ISIS. Gaps and inconsistencies, unfortunately, plague all these estimates. Due to the challenges of estimating these totals and the problems of competing methodologies, the Congressional Research Service compiles government—US and Iraqi—and nongovernmental data from a variety of sources to gauge the casualties sustained in OIF.[23] These various estimates, measuring by different metrics and over different lengths of time, range from 48,796 civilian casualties (as estimated by the Iraq Coalition Casualty Count between March 2005 and October 2010) to 112,625 (as estimated by the Brookings *Iraq Index* between May 2003 and April 2010) to over 1,000,000 (as estimated by Opinion Business Research from March 2003 to September 2007).[24] With such disparate estimates, it is difficult to accurately attribute these casualties to a particular force or tactic.

Iraq Body Count has compiled thousands of reports from diverse sources to track civilian casualties over the course of combat in Iraq. Except for a slight rise in 2007, coinciding with the surge, casualties from the US-led Coalition forces in Iraq (excluding Iraqi state forces) decreased annually from the very first year of

[23] H. Fischer, "Iraq Casualties: U.S. Military Forces and Iraqi Civilians, Police, and Security Forces" (Washington, DC: Congressional Research Service, 2011).

[24] Ibid., 9.

the invasion, even as total casualties rose significantly between 2005 and 2007.[25] According to IBC, the US-led coalition has been responsible for 13 percent of all civilian deaths between 2003 and 2011, totaling 15,141. The data shows that civilians are killed most frequently by gunfire, then explosives such as IEDs or suicide attacks, and least commonly by air attacks, which again declined significantly after 2003. Use of explosives and air attacks by Coalition forces as a cause of civilian casualties decreased after 2003, while casualties due to Coalition gunfire increased from 2003 to 2004, declined slightly in 2005, and then stayed relatively stable through 2007 before declining again.[26] These trends, like those seen in Afghanistan, indicate that US-led forces exercised increasing discrimination in using large-scale aerial or bombing attacks, while engaging in more conflict on the ground.

Civilian Protections

Despite the high numbers of civilian casualties over the last decade in Iraq and Afghanistan, the US military attempted to comply with the Additional Protocol I of the Geneva Conventions governing civilian treatment and the principles of discrimination and proportionality. Additional Protocol I was meant to strengthen the protection of victims of international armed conflicts and place limits on the way wars are fought.[27] The United States did not sign or ratify Additional Protocols I or II in 1977, but it has recognized the most rules of Protocol I as customary law. In 2011, the State Department reaffirmed the US government's support for the fundamental guarantees of humane treatment laid out in Additional Protocol II and Article 75 of Additional Protocol I.[28] US authorities claim to fulfill the discrimination rules of Protocol I to ensure civilian protection by vetting target lists with legal specialists, restricting rules of engagement to minimize civilian casualties, and formally estimating collateral damage prior to strikes.

Target Lists

One of the measures by which the US military has protected civilians in the engagements in Iraq and Afghanistan was by determining targeting lists that are

[25] "Iraqi Deaths from Violence 2003–2011," *Iraq Body Count*, 3 January 2012, https://www.iraqbodycount.org/analysis/numbers/2011/.

[26] Ibid.

[27] "The Geneva Conventions of 1949 and Their Additional Protocols," *ICRC*, 29 October 2010, https://www.icrc.org/eng/war-and-law/treaties-customary-law/geneva-conventions/overview-geneva-conventions.htm.

[28] H. H. Koh, "U.S. Reaffirms Its Deep and Abiding Commitment to International Humanitarian Law at ICRC Conference," US Mission to the UN, 28 November 2011, https://geneva.usmission.gov/2011/11/28/icrc-conference/.

vetted by Judge Advocates General (JAG) Corps attorneys. Similar to previous engagements in the Persian Gulf War and in Kosovo, JAGs provide advice to the combatant commanders on all aspects of the laws of war. In particular, they provide assessments on the legal aspects of a proposed mission, objective, and the prosecution of that target.[29] In OIF, legal analysis regarding the laws of war was provided to commanders prior to commencing bombing to ensure that key infrastructure—irrigation canals, pipelines, public utilities—and facilities such as schools and hospitals were avoided.[30] Vetting the target lists allowed the JAGs to ensure that the violence employed was discriminatory and that civilian death and property damage were minimized. In addition to the legal analysis provided, members of the intelligence community provided imagery data about targets and trajectories to commanders in order to reduce the potential harm to civilian populations.[31] This intelligence identified medical facilities and civilian infrastructure facilities, which were included on the "no strike" list for OIF. In addition, the US Joint Forces Joint Fires and Targeting Handbook explicitly provided guidance on munitions usage and restrictions, restricted targets, and a no-strike list. Items on the no-strike list specifically included civilians protected under the laws of war as well as civilian institutions, such as embassies of noncombatant states, cultural sites, religious establishments, hospitals, and schools.[32]

Collateral Damage Estimates

In addition to the legal and intelligence review of planned targets, the United States used a formal process for collateral damage estimation for all preplanned strikes. According to Chairman of the Joint Chiefs of Staff Instruction 3160.01 (2009), commanders must weigh the risk of civilian casualties against military necessity through a collateral damage estimate methodology that relies on a computer software package. This methodology required that commanders assess proportionality and discrimination within the framework of the military decision-making process by taking into account the destructive capability of the potential weapons to be employed, the method of employment, the nature of the target, the location of the target with respect to civilian property, and the

[29] D. Kurle, "Lawyers Provide Operational Advice to Commanders," US Air Force, 12 March 2010, http://www.af.mil/News/Features/Display/tabid/273/Article/143010/lawyers-provide-operational-advice-to-commanders.aspx.

[30] Major D. Saumer, "During International Military Operations, the U.S. Army JAG Corps Weighs All the Evidence before an Enemy Target Can Be Selected" 2011, http://www.goarmy.com/jag/milestone-cases/international-military-operations.html.

[31] *Support to Iraqi Freedom*, Annual Report 2003, Central Intelligence Agency, 25 April 2007, https://www.cia.gov/library/reports/archived-reports-1/Ann_Rpt_2003/iraq.html.

[32] *Joint Fires and Targeting Handbook* (Norfolk, VA: US Joint Forces Command, 2007).

presence of civilians (both within the target and surrounding area).[33] Other computer software tools, such as FAST-CD v1.0 Joint Warfare Analysis Center, further allowed targeteers to predict the fragmentation patterns based on the weapon employed, angle, and fuse timing.[34]

Where Are the Existing Gaps?

Despite relying on all of the measures listed above to protect civilians in conflict, US efforts to fully protect civilians in Iraq and Afghanistan were often lacking primarily due to reliance on close air support and the inability to effectively deploy critical weapons systems that would limit civilian casualties. In addition, the use of precision-guided weapons with global positioning systems and drone strikes were intended to increase accuracy and minimize collateral damage, but has unintentionally resulted in hundreds of civilian deaths.

Close Air Support

As the insurgencies gained strength in both countries, airpower allowed the US military to minimize its ground presence. In particular, the reliance on close air support (CAS) to damage and destroy targets allowed US and coalition forces to deploy substantially fewer troops on the ground than typically would be required for stability operations and population-centric counterinsurgency. In 2007, CAS operations sharply increased in both theaters, due to the impact of the surge in Iraq and the increased operational tempo of the Taliban in Afghanistan. In this time period, US and coalition forces exercised restraint, as evidenced by the total number of CAS sorties compared with the number of sorties in which munitions were deployed.[35] Yet, this reliance on CAS significantly impacted the rate of civilian casualties. According to Human Rights Watch, in 2006, 116 civilian casualties in Afghanistan were attributed to 13 US and NATO airstrikes; in 2007, 321 civilians were killed in 22 airstrikes; and in the first seven months of 2008, 119 civilians were killed in 12 air strikes.[36] These figures do not include, however, the 2008 incident in which an AC-130 gunship attacked a target at night that was believed to be a meeting of Taliban insurgent leaders, but later

[33] *No Strike and Collateral Damage Estimation Methodology*, Joint Chiefs of Staff Manual 3160.01 (Washington, DC: US Joint Chiefs of Staff, 2009).

[34] A. T. Wilson, *Building the Beast: Proposals to Improve USAF Targeting Training* (Maxwell Air Force Base, AL: Air Command and Staff College, 2006).

[35] A. H. Cordesman, *U.S. Airpower in Iraq and Afghanistan: 2004–2007* (Washington, DC: Center for Strategic and International Studies, 2007).

[36] *Troops in Contact: Airstrikes and Civilian Deaths in Afghanistan*, 8 September 2008, http://www.hrw.org/reports/2008/09/08/troops-contact-0#_Toc208224420.

reporting revealed was in actuality a wedding party in Kandahar.[37] The strike is believed to have killed at least 40 civilians and wounded 28 more. Nor do the figures include the 2009 CAS incident in the western province of Farah, which caused rioting and uproar in Afghanistan. The target of the Farah air strikes was a building used by Taliban insurgents. The seven-hour sustained bombardment by B-1 aircraft included seven 500-pound satellite-guided bombs and two 2,000-pound satellite-guided bombs.[38] US officials claimed between 20 and 30 Afghan civilians died in the incident,[39] yet the Afghan government claimed 140 civilians died as a result of these air strikes.[40]

With the surge in Afghanistan in 2009 came an increase in the number of casualties attributed to ground engagements, and a relative decline in the prevalence of casualties from airstrikes. In 2008, airstrikes by progovernment forces accounted for 26 percent of all civilian casualties, and for 67 percent of all casualties attributed to progovernment forces. In 2009, aerial attacks accounted for 61 percent of all progovernment-inflicted casualties; 39 percent in 2010; 46 percent in 2011; 35 percent in 2012; 19 percent in 2013; 11 percent in 2014; and 16 percent in 2015. Casualties from aerial attacks are comparatively easy to track and for which to allocate blame because only progovernment forces have this tactic available to them (first only international forces, and later Afghan forces as well). With the exception of 2011, casualties by aerial attacks fell steadily from 631 in 2009 to 159 in 2014, before rising again to 296 in 2015 as Afghan forces began planning autonomous aerial operations. As a whole, this data shows decreased casualties as a result of the increased discrimination dictated by the transition to counterinsurgency in Afghanistan.

Civilians have also unfortunately suffered both directly from cluster munitions and indirectly from unexploded ordnance. According to the 2010 Cluster Munition Monitor, nearly 13,000 cluster munitions, which contain approximately 1.8 to 2 million submunitions, were used by the United States and the UK during the major combat period in Iraq.[41]

Inability to Deploy Innovative Weapons Systems

Despite an interest in deploying nonlethal weapons to Iraq and Afghanistan to promote military objectives while minimizing casualties, property damage, or

[37] A. W. Wafa and J. F. Burns, "U.S. Airstrike Reported to Hit Afghan Wedding," *New York Times*, 6 November 2008.

[38] E. Bumiller and E. Schmitt, "Joint Chiefs Chairman Criticizes Afghan Air Strikes," *New York Times*, 19 May 2009.

[39] J. Garamone, "Report Points to Irregularities in Farah Air Strike Incident," 8 June 2009, http://www.centcom.mil/news/news-article/report-points-to-irregularities-in-farah-air-strike-incident.

[40] M. Tran, "U.S. Military Admits Errors in Air Strikes That Killed Scores of Afghan Civilians," *The Guardian*, 3 June 2009.

[41] *Cluster Munition Monitor 2010*, Mines Action Canada, October 2010.

infrastructure destruction, few of these weapons have been used in the field. Though the US military invested $120 million in nonlethal weapons in 2010, many of these weapons were not being relied on tactically.[42] A decision was made not to deploy the nonlethal Active Denial System—a directed energy weapon in which microwaves create a burning sensation—in Iraq following concerns about the public perception of a microwave energy weapon.[43] The Active Denial System was deployed in Afghanistan in order to assist with crowd dispersal,[44] but was almost immediately withdrawn from that theater.[45]

Course Corrections

Due to the costly errors of CAS, the civilian deaths and suffering from unexploded ordnance, and the inability of the US military to rely on new weapons systems to minimize civilian impact, the US military corrected its course to provide new training, doctrine, and practice so that Geneva compliance aligned with counterinsurgency goals.

The Farah air strikes prompted a May 2009 meeting between Afghan President Hamid Karzai and the American ambassador to Afghanistan, Lieutenant General Karl Eikenberry. Against the backdrop of the civilian causalities caused by US CAS, Ambassador Eikenberry pledged that the United States would work "tirelessly" to find ways to reduce the price paid by civilians.[46] After the release of the investigation into the Farah strikes, the military took immediate efforts to put this verbal pledge into doctrine and practice.

In recognition of the effect of the civilian deaths from CAS operations to the overall goals of the counterinsurgency, General Stanley McChrystal issued a new tactical directive in July 2009. Cognizant of the fact that in a population-centric insurgency, the goal is to win the support of the people and enhance the legitimacy of the government, this directive explicitly stated that leaders at all levels must "scrutinize and limit the use of force like CAS" against locations with substantial civilian populations. It stated that, "Commanders must weigh the gain of using CAS against the cost of civilian causalities, which in the long run make mission success more difficult and turn the Afghan people against us."[47]

[42] T. McMillan, "Blinding Lasers Replace Guns for Peacekeeping," *Bloomberg*, 27 July 2011.

[43] S. Weinberger, "No Pain Ray Weapon for Iraq," *Wired*, 30 August 2007, http://www.wired.com/dangerroom/2007/08/no-pain-ray-for/.

[44] D. Cairns, "US Army Heat Ray Gun in Afghanistan," *BBC*, 15 July 2010, http://www.bbc.co.uk/newsbeat/10646540.

[45] "U.S. Withdraws 'Pain Ray' from Afghan War Zone," *Daily Mail*, 28 July 2010, http://www.dailymail.co.uk/news/article-1297361/US-withdraws-pain-ray-Afghan-war-zone.html#ixzz0uiZgM7Uf.

[46] C. Gall, "A Vow to Cut Afghan Civilian Deaths," *New York Times*, 20 May 2009.

[47] S. McChrystal, "Tactical Directive. ISAF," Kabul, Afghanistan, 2009.

Complying with the Fourth Geneva Convention and Additional Protocol I and minimizing civilian casualties became a cornerstone of McChrystal's philosophy about how to win in Afghanistan. Prior to being confirmed as the Commander of US Forces and ISAF in Afghanistan, General McChrystal testified before the US Senate Armed Services Committee in June 2009 and affirmed the central role of protecting civilians in a counterinsurgency. He stated:

> How we conduct operations is vital to success. This is a critical point. It may be "the" critical point. This is a struggle for the support of the Afghan people. Our willingness to operate in ways that minimize casualties or damage, even when doing so makes our task more difficult, is essential to our credibility. I cannot overstate my commitment to the importance of this concept.[48]

General McChrystal also issued counterinsurgency training guidance for US and ISAF forces in Afghanistan. This guidance strongly emphasized that the "people are the prize" and that "protecting the Afghan people is the mission."[49]

Following the release of McChrystal's directive that placed the protection of civilians as mission critical, many soldiers balked at these new tightened rules of engagement. In the *Rolling Stone* article that eventually prompted McChrystal's ouster, one Special Forces officer stated, "His [McChrystal's] rules of engagement put soldiers' lives in even greater danger. Every real soldier will tell you the same thing."[50] Despite the backlash, the restraints imposed by McChrystal did cause a decrease in insurgent attacks. In a paper released by the nonprofit National Bureau of Economic Research, the findings indicated that civilian casualties are associated with an increase in attacks by Afghan militants, including the Taliban.[51] Under General David Petraeus's leadership as well, the rules of engagement further tightened, linking a disciplined use of force to mission success. His August 2010 directive, recently declassified, banned air strikes and artillery fire when it could not be determined who was on the ground. He sought to limit civilian deaths at checkpoints and during night raids. Most importantly, Petraeus emphasized,

> Fight hard *and* fight with discipline. Hunt the enemy aggressively, but use only the firepower needed to win a fight. We can't win without

[48] *Hearing to Consider the Nominations of Admiral James G. Stavridis; Lieutenant General Douglas M. Fraser; and Lieutenant General Stanley A. McChrystal* (Washington, DC: US Senate Committee on Armed Services, 2009).

[49] S. McChrystal, "COMISAF/USFOR—A Counterinsurgency (COIN) Training Guidance," Kabul, Afghanistan, 2009.

[50] M. Hastings, "The Runaway General," *Rolling Stone*, 1108/1109 (2010).

[51] L. N. Condra, J. H. Felter, et al., "The Effect of Civilian Casualties in Afghanistan and Iraq," Working Paper 16152, National Bureau of Economic Research, 2010.

> fighting, but we also cannot kill or capture our way to victory. Moreover, if we kill civilians or damage their property in the course of our operations, we will create more enemies than our operations eliminate. That's exactly what the Taliban want. Don't fall into their trap. We must continue our efforts to reduce civilian casualties to an absolute minimum. [Emphasis in original.][52]

In this way, compliance with the Fourth Geneva Convention, Additional Protocol I, and protecting civilians was framed as in the best interests of the United States to defeat the insurgency and promote the legitimacy of the Afghan government. The policy led to a decrease of civilian deaths at the hands of the US military in Afghanistan, despite an increased level of violence overall due to insurgent attacks. Indeed, although the number of progovernment forces in Afghanistan grew by 107,000 in 2010, the number of casualties attributed to these forces by UNAMA dropped by 21 percent from the previous year, highlighting the intense focus on preserving civilian lives.[53]

In addition, in order to minimize the danger to civilians of cluster munitions, the DoD issued a new policy on this type of weapon in 2008, While deeming them legitimate weapons, the policy stated nevertheless that all cluster munitions stocks that exceed operational requirements would be removed.[54] This policy was the culmination of a year-long DoD review of cluster munitions and their impact on civilians. President Barack Obama subsequently signed legislation in 2009 to ban most kinds of cluster bomb exports by the United States.[55]

Whereas US civilian and military leaders stressed the importance of protecting civilians from the beginning of both conflicts in the war on terror, different determinations were initially made with regard to the Third Geneva Convention governing POW treatment. The next section examines the compliance decisions and actions with regard to the humane treatment of captured combatants.

Compliance with the Third Geneva Convention

Due to the nature of the war on terror, a war against nonstate actors rather than traditional state opponents, the Bush administration at first determined that neither Al Qaeda nor the Taliban should receive Geneva Convention protections as

[52] David Petraeus, "COMISAF's Counterinsurgency Guidance," Kabul, Afghanistan, 2010.

[53] *Afghanistan Annual Report . . . 2010*, iv.

[54] R. M. Gates, "DoD Policy on Cluster Munitions and Unintended Harm to Civilians," Washington, DC: Department of Defense, 2008.

[55] "US: Cluster Bomb Exports Banned," 12 March 2009, http://www.hrw.org/news/2009/03/12/us-cluster-bomb-exports-banned.

POWs. In the case of captured members of Al Qaeda, the administration determined that because the group was not—and could not be—a signatory to the Conventions, its members were not eligible to receive Geneva rights. Whereas the Taliban could reasonably be considered to be representatives of Afghanistan, a signatory to the Conventions, the Bush administration determined that its members relinquished any rights they might have been afforded by failing to meet the Geneva standards for combatants: possessing a responsible command structure; affixing a distinctive sign recognizable at a distance; carrying arms openly; and obeying the laws and customs of war.[56] Some members of Al Qaeda and the Taliban were denied even the minimum protections outlined in Common Article 3 during the early years of the military engagements. In addition, many influential actors in the Bush administration opposed these Geneva standards, deeming them outdated, outmoded, and ineffective in confronting the realities of a war against a nonstate actor.[57]

Interestingly, in 2001 US military authorities initially assumed their forces would comply with the Third Geneva Convention in Afghanistan. According to the Schlesinger Report, the Commander of US Central Command (CENTCOM) issued an order on 17 October 2001 stating that the Geneva Conventions would be applied according to the letter of the law. As specified by this order,

> Belligerents would be screened to determine whether or not they were entitled to prisoner of war status. If an individual was entitled to prisoner of war status, the protections of Geneva Convention III would apply. If armed forces personnel were in doubt as to a detained individual's status, Geneva Convention III rights would be accorded to the detainee until a Geneva Convention III Article 5 tribunal made a definitive status determination.[58]

This order is consistent with standard practice according to international law, which states when POW status is in doubt, captured fighters shall benefit from Geneva protections until a determination is made about their status.[59]

[56] John C. Yoo, "Application of Treaties and Laws to Al Qaeda and Taliban Detainees," in *The Torture Papers: The Road to Abu Ghraib*, ed. Karen J. Greenberg and Joshua L. Dratel (New York: Cambridge University Press, 2005), 38–79.

[57] Alberto R. Gonzales, "Decision Re Application of the Geneva Convention on Prisoners of War to the Conflict with al-Qaeda and the Taliban," in Greenberg and Dratel, *The Torture Papers*, 118–121.

[58] James R. Schlesinger, *Final Report of the Independent Panel to Review DoD Detention Operations* (Arlington, VA: Office of the Secretary of Defense, 24 August 2004), https://www.ciaonet.org/catalog/14651, 80.

[59] Charles J. Dunlap Jr., "International Law and Terrorism: Some 'Qs & As' for Operators," *The Army Lawyer*, November 2002, http://people.duke.edu/~pfeaver/dunlapterrorism.pdf.

At the same time, policymakers in Washington assessed that defeating al-Qaeda required new ways of thinking. One day after the CENTCOM order stating that the Geneva Conventions would apply, Vice President Dick Cheney stated:

> I spent four years at the Pentagon working with some of the finest men and women I have ever met. More people died there on September 11 than we lost in combat in the Gulf War. When you think of that attack and of the merciless horror inflicted at the World Trade Center, no punishment for the terrorist seems too harsh.[60]

This belief was supported by a series of legal memos that, taken together, examined the applicability of international law to the conflicts faced and examined the extent of the president's executive powers in wartime. The Office of Legal Counsel (OLC) then issued two opinions to the White House about the definition of torture under the Convention Against Torture (CAT) as embodied in the US federal antitorture statute. These two memos, known as the "Bybee Memos," were sent on 1 August 2002 and were written by then-Deputy Assistant Attorney General John C. Yoo, although they were signed by Jay Bybee, then-Assistant Attorney General for the OLC.[61] The first Bybee memo provided an analysis of the conduct allowed under the US federal antitorture statute. The memo concluded that "acts may be cruel, inhumane, or degrading, but still not produce the pain and suffering of the requisite intensity to fall within Section 2340A's proscription against torture."[62] In the case of mental suffering, acts qualify as torture if they result in "significant psychological harm of significant duration, e.g., lasting for months or even years."[63] In the case of physical suffering, acts constitute torture if they are "equivalent in intensity to the pain accompanying serious physical injury, such as organ failure, impairment of bodily function, or even death."[64] As David Cole asks:

> What, by the way, is the level of pain associated with death? Surely it is fundamentally unknowable, as we cannot ask dead people how they

[60] Dick Cheney, "Remarks at the 56th Annual Alfred E. Smith Memorial Foundation Dinner," Waldorf-Astoria Hotel, New York, 18 October 2001, http://georgewbush-whitehouse.archives.gov/vicepresident/news-speeches/speeches/vp20011018.html.

[61] "A Guide to the Memos on Torture." *New York Times*, 25 June 2004.

[62] Jay Bybee, "Standards of Conduct for Interrogation under 18 U.S.C. §§ 2340-2340a," in Greenberg and Dratel, *The Torture Papers*, 172.

[63] Ibid.

[64] Ibid. Individuals within the broader CIA community disagree with the characterization of techniques like waterboarding as torture. Former director Robert James Woolsey has claimed

> would rate their pain on a scale of one to ten. Moreover, general observation would tell us that some people die in terrible pain, while others seem to die at peace, almost painlessly.[65]

The second Bybee memo analyzed the legality of classified interrogation techniques requested by the CIA. This 18-page memo was addressed to John Rizzo, acting general counsel of the CIA, and examined the federal prohibitions against torture for a specific case: the interrogation of Zayn al-Abidin Muhammad Husayn (Abu Zubaydah), a suspected senior al-Qaeda leader captured in Pakistan in March 2002 who turned out not even to be a member of al-Qaeda.[66]

The memo analyzed ten techniques the CIA wanted to apply to Zubaydah—"attention grasp, walling, facial hold, facial slap (insult slap), cramped confinement, wall standing, stress positions, sleep deprivation, insects placed in a confinement box, and the waterboard"—and concluded that these methods, used either separately, or as a course of increasing pressure, would not violate the US federal antitorture statute.[67] It concluded with the assessment that Agency personnel, in interrogating Zubaydah using the above ten methods, would neither cause severe pain and suffering nor intend to do so.[68] A recently released CIA memo from February 2002 regarding "POW's and Questioning," though largely still redacted, acknowledges that a detainee granted POW status (and thus covered by the Geneva Convention) leaves interrogators "few alternatives to simply asking questions," but the author shortly thereafter questions how to circumvent this reality: "then the optic becomes how legally defensible is a particular act that probably violates the convention, but ultimately saves lives."[69] Whether CIA torture saved any lives is doubtful.

waterboarding is "not as permanently damaging as other forms of torture" such as "pulling out fingernails." In 2002, the CIA lawyer Jonathan Fredman said torture "is basically subject to perception," in a meeting at Guantánamo Bay, implying that techniques such as waterboarding would not constitute torture if executed correctly. He said, "If the detainee dies, you're doing it wrong." "Former CIA Directors Defend Waterboarding, Rectal Rehydration," *RT International*, 12 December 2014, https://www.rt.com/usa/214031-cia-directors-waterboarding-torture/; Joby Warrick, "CIA Played Larger Role in Advising Pentagon," *Washington Post*, 18 June 2008.

[65] D. Cole, "The Taint of Torture: The Roles of Law and Policy in Our Descent to the Dark Side," *Houston Law Review* 49 (2012): 60.

[66] "Central Intelligence Agency, Office of Inspector General Special Review: Counterterrorism Detention and Interrogation Activities," Appendix B, Central Intelligence Agency, Office of Inspector General, 7 May 2004, http://www2.gwu.edu/~nsarchiv/torture_archive/20040507.pdf.

[67] Jay Bybee, "Memorandum for John Rizzo, Acting General Counsel of the Central Intelligence Agency: Interrogation of Al Qaeda Operative," Department of Justice, 1 August 2002, http://www.washingtonpost.com/wp-srv/nation/pdf/OfficeofLegalCounsel_Aug2Memo_041609.pdf.

[68] "Central Intelligence Agency, Office of Inspector General Special Review," 20.

[69] "POW's and Questioning," Central Intelligence Agency, 1 February 2002, released 13 June 2016, https://www.cia.gov/library/readingroom/document/6552082.

Equally extraordinary was the DoD's analysis of new interrogation techniques to apply to captured fighters. Rumsfeld approved eighteen new techniques for use at the Guantánamo Bay detention facility, documented by an approval memo dated 2 December 2002.[70] The need for information from the detainees was perceived to be imminent. As General Myers, then-Chairman of the Joint Chiefs of Staff said, "There was a sense of urgency that in my forty years of military experience hadn't existed in other contingencies."[71] The development of the techniques approved by Rumsfeld began with a memo from General Michael Dunlavey, the Commander of Joint Task Force 170 (JTF-170) in Guantánamo Bay, to the head of US Southern Command requesting approval for additional, harsh interrogation techniques. The techniques approved and subsequently used on detainees included: removal of clothing, 20-hour interrogations, poking and pushing, and stress positions.[72] It was an extraordinary response to a perceived extraordinary necessity and likely violated international law.

Taken together, the legal memos interpreted US obligations under the Geneva Conventions and the CAT as being secondary to the president's national security obligations to the state.

Press accounts, witness statements, and photographic evidence began to surface that the US government was subjecting detainees to treatment that violated the Third Geneva Convention, customary international law, and US domestic law against torture. One month after the US Army reported that seventeen soldiers had been removed from duty for mistreating Iraqi soldiers, CBS's *60 Minutes II* broadcast the details of the story in April 2004. The CBS segment detailed accounts of physical, psychological, and sexual abuse of individuals held at Abu Ghraib prison in Iraq at the hands of the 372nd Military Police Company of the US Army. The photographs shown during the *60 Minutes* segment graphically portrayed US soldiers humiliating and abusing Iraqi prisoners. The now iconic images—an Iraqi detainee draped in a poncho and hood standing with electrical wires attached to his hands on top of a box, a pyramid of naked detainees, and detainees crawling on the dirty floor at the ends of leashes—stunned many domestic and international observers. Further allegations of torture by the journalist Seymour M. Hersh in *The New Yorker* and revelations of the existence of "black site" covert prisons by *Washington Post* reporters Dana Priest and Barton Gellman prompted questions about the future applicability of international

[70] "Memoranda: Counter-Resistance Techniques," Department of Defense, 2002, http://nsarchive.gwu.edu/NSAEBB/NSAEBB127/02.12.02.pdf.

[71] Philippe Sands, *Torture Team: Rumsfeld's Memo and the Betrayal of American Values* (New York, NY: Palgrave Macmillan, 2008), 88.

[72] "Memoranda: Counter-Resistance Techniques," n.p.

humanitarian law, America's historical commitment to human rights principles, and, ultimately US identity.

In response, the Supreme Court examined the legality of some of the legal directives issued during the conflicts in Afghanistan and Iraq. Among many notable cases, *Hamdan v. Rumsfeld*, 548 U.S. 557 (2006), specifically examined the applicability of Common Article 3 and held that the conflict with al-Qaeda and Taliban constituted a conflict "not of an international character." The Court ruled that Hamdan's trial by military commission was unlawful because it proceeded without the determination by a competent tribunal that he was not a POW. The Court further held that Common Article 3 of the Geneva Conventions was applicable to the al-Qaeda and Taliban prisoners held at Guantánamo Bay, despite the fact that the combatants were nonstate actors. In response to this ruling by the Court, the DoD consequently revised its directive on POWs and detainees, stating that, "All persons subject to this Directive shall observe the requirements of the law of war, and shall apply, without regard to a detainee's legal status, at a minimum the standards articulated in Common Article 3 to the Geneva Conventions of 1949."[73]

The DoD also began several official inquiries to determine the standard of treatment provided to detainees while in US custody and to ascertain the political and military motivations that drove DoD behavior regarding detainee treatment. Taken together, the reports—including the Jacoby Report,[74] the Formica Report,[75] Taguba Report,[76] the Schlesinger Report,[77] the Fay-Jones Report,[78] and the Mikolashek Report,[79] recognized that violations of the Geneva Conventions occurred during the war on terror, yet the reports differ in the causes of this abuse, ranging from doctrinal confusion, to poor education and training, to failures of leadership.

In light of these internal inquiries and intense domestic and international scrutiny about US detainee operations, several leadership changes were enacted

[73] *Department of Defense Detainee Program*, DoD Directive 2310.01E (2006).

[74] C. H. Jacoby, *CFC-A AO Detainee Operations Report of Inspection* (Washington, DC: Department of Defense, 2004).

[75] R. P. Formica, *Article 15-6 Investigation of CJSOTF-AP and 5th SF Group Detention Operations* (Washington, DC: Department of Defense, 2004).

[76] Antonio Taguba, *Taguba Report: AR15-6 Investigation of the 800th Military Police Brigade*, U.S. Department of Defense, May 2004, released 19 October 2004, https://fas.org/irp/agency/dod/taguba.pdf.

[77] Schlesinger, *Final Report*.

[78] George R. Fay and Anthony R. Jones, *AR 15-6 Investigation of the Abu Ghraib Detention Facility and the 205th Military Intelligence Brigade: Fay/Jones Report*, Department of Defense, 23 August 2004, released 10 December 2012, http://s3.amazonaws.com/corpwatch.org/downloads/FayReport.pdf.

[79] P. T. Mikolashek, *Detainee Operations Inspection* (Washington, DC: Department of the Army, 2004).

at Abu Ghraib. General Janis Karpinski was immediately removed from command and her successor, General Geoffrey Miller, was subsequently removed after reports surfaced of harsh treatment under his command at Guantánamo. Eventually, detainee operations were led by Army Major General John Gardner. Cognizant of the stain of Abu Ghraib and the mistrust that the abuse fostered of Americans, Gardner sought to address the allegations of abuse at the hands of Iraqi jailers.[80] He also created a more nuanced categorization system for the detainees, based on their disciplinary record, level of military training, explanations for detention, interactions with others, and activity with any vigilante sharia courts inside the prison.[81] To prevent radicalization inside the prisons, Gardner advocated frequent and abrupt prisoner relocation and filling empty hours of detention with activity, civics classes, and vocational training.[82] In addition, following the abuses at Abu Ghraib, a new detention facility called Camp Bucca was constructed in southern Iraq near the Kuwaiti border.

Gardner's successor, Marine Corps Major General Douglas Stone, continued these efforts to improve detainee quality of life and minimize the possibility of prison radicalization. In April 2007, Stone took over Task Force 134 and assumed responsibility for detainee operations in Iraq. The number of detainees held by the United States during this time swelled as a result of the surge, from 13,000 in early 2006 to its peak of 25,000 in late 2007.[83] Stone—consistent with the counterinsurgency doctrine both espoused and employed by General Petraeus—sought to "win in the battlefield of the brain" by encouraging detainees to read and interpret the Koran themselves.[84] Under Stone, the classes, vocational training, and Islamic discussion continued, as well as pay-for-work programs in order to prepare detainees to reenter Iraqi society and contribute to the reconstruction.[85] In addition, detainees under Stone were allowed to remit their salaries to their families. Review panels were established to evaluate detentions and to determine when prisoners might be ready for release, and prisoners were provided access to good medical care. These efforts at deradicalization and preparations for reintegration mirror attempts made in domestic prison systems to modify behavior in the long-term. Stone also sought to change the public perception—both US and Iraqi—of detainee operations by actively working on strategic communication. He participated in a bloggers'

[80] E. Schmitt and T. Shanker, "U.S., Citing Abuse in Iraqi Prisons, Holds Detainees," *New York Times*, 25 December 2005.

[81] C. Benard, E. O'Connell, et al., *The Battle behind the Wire: U.S. Prisoner and Detainee Operations from World War II to Iraq* (Santa Monica: RAND Corporation. 2011).

[82] Ibid.

[83] Ibid.

[84] "Detainees Chief Sees Koran as Key Ally," *Financial Times*, 16 July 2007.

[85] S. L. Quigley, "Lessons Learned at Abu Ghraib Drive Current Detainee Policies," 2 June 2008, http://www.defense.gov/news/newsarticle.aspx?id=50081.

roundtable in 2007, in which he directly answered questions about detainee policies and practices,[86] as well as press visits and interviews with Al-Iraqiya, Al Arabiya TV, Al Jazeera English, and Baghdad Satellite TV.[87] Stone's course corrections provide a positive model that can be expanded on in any future occupations.

Detainee operations in Afghanistan have received significantly less publicity than in Iraq. Following the US-led invasion of Afghanistan in October 2001, captured detainees were held at Bagram Theater Internment Facility (BTIF), located approximately forty miles north of Kabul. Similar to Guantánamo, debates surfaced about the rights of detainees, as many of them were held without access to legal representation and only rudimentary reviews of their classification as "enemy combatants."[88] Interestingly, national and international debate centered around the fate of around 250 detainees at Guantánamo, whereas the number of detainees held in Afghanistan was often more than double: BTIF normally housed between 400 to 600 detainees.

In 2009, President Obama conducted a wide-ranging review of Afghan operations, policies, and requirements, including those for detainee treatment. Following this review of detainee policy—and incorporating lessons learned from detainee treatment of the tens of thousands of prisoners in Iraq—the detainees in Afghanistan were moved to a new facility on the Bagram Air Base with a larger capacity. The new facility included review boards, which allow the prisoners to question and challenge their internment, comprising three US military officials advised by a military lawyer.[89] Under increasing pressure for Afghan autonomy over the detainment system, coalition forces began transferring detainees to Afghan prisons in the following years, though suspended the transfers in January 2013 amid reports of human rights abuses in said prisons.[90] The US closed the Bagram detention center, its last in Afghanistan, in December 2014 as part of the Bilateral Security Agreement signed by the United States and Afghanistan three months prior. Upon its closing, all remaining prisoners were transferred to Afghan custody.[91]

[86] "Department of Defense Bloggers Roundtable with Major General Douglas Stone," Department of Defense, 18 September 2007, http://www.defenselink.mil/dodcmsshare/BloggerAssets/2007-09/091807Stone_transcript.pdf

[87] Benard, O'Connell, et al., "The Battle behind the Wire."

[88] T. Golden and E. Schmitt, "A Growing Afghan Prison Rivals Bleak Guantánamo," *New York Times*, 26 February 2006.

[89] A. J. Rubin, "U.S. Readies New Facility for Afghan Detainees," *New York Times*, 16 November 2009.

[90] Rod Nordland and Thom Shanker, "U.S. Military Stops Sending Detainees to Some Afghan Prisons on Rights Fears," *New York Times*, 16 January 2013.

[91] Sudarsan Raghavan, "Last U.S. Detention Site Closes in Afghanistan to Sever Another Link to Post-9/11 Interrogations," *Washington Post*, 11 December 2014.

In addition, per a directive issued by former Secretary of Defense Robert Gates in June 2009, General Stanley McChrystal completed an overall assessment of the situation in Afghanistan against the backdrop of the rising insurgency and diminishing government legitimacy. McChrystal's classified report was leaked to the media and a subsequent redacted report was released by the administration. This assessment recommended a shift in strategy from offensive military operations to a comprehensive population-centric counterinsurgency, of which detainee operations were a critical component.[92] In the assessment, General McChrystal argued that the conditions in prisons and weak judicial system in Afghanistan were directly fostering the insurgency and created the possibility of turning detention operations into a strategic liability for US and ISAF forces. In this assessment, McChrystal claimed that, "There are more insurgents per square foot in corrections facilities than anywhere else in Afghanistan. Unchecked, Taliban/al-Qaeda leaders patiently coordinate and plan, unconcerned with interference from prison personnel or the military."[93] The US unit charged with detainee operations in Afghanistan, Task Force Guardian, faced tremendous challenges in the smooth functioning of detainee operations. One of them was the controversial 96-hour rule, created by NATO forces in 2005, which stipulated that detainees can only be held for 96 hours, at which point the Coalition forces are either forced to release them or turn them over to Afghan authorities.[94] In March 2010, General Petraeus told the Senate Armed Services Committee that US troops could hold detainees for up to fourteen days, rather than four days, before either releasing or transferring them over to the Afghan government.[95]

Conclusion

The question of how to promote compliance with international humanitarian law is not simply a military concern: it is a matter of identity and leadership for the United States. The central importance of respecting the laws of war in

[92] S. McChrystal, "United States Force-Afghanistan (USFOR-A), Initial Assessment of the Commander of the NATO International Security Assistance Forces-Afghanistan (COMISAF)" (Kabul, Afghanistan: International Security Assistance Forces-Afghanistan, 2009).

[93] J. Boone, "US to Tackle Breeding Ground for Insurgents in Afghan Jails," *The Guardian*, 14 October 2009.

[94] A. Boudreau and S. Zamost, "U.S. Reviewing Afghanistan Detainee Policy," *CNN*, 18 February 2010, http://articles.cnn.com/2010-02-18/world/afghanistan.detainees_1_nato-troops-afghan-authorities-afghan-government?_s=PM:WORLD.

[95] A. Boudreau and S. Zamost, "U.S. to End 96-Hour Rule for Afghan Detainees," *CNN*, 17 March 2010, http://articles.cnn.com/2010-03-17/world/afghanistan.nato.detainees_1_detainees-afghan-authorities-afghan-government?_s=PM:WORLD.

US culture dates back to the US Revolutionary War. During the Civil War, the Union issued the Lieber Code, a set of instructions ensuring that field commanders properly treated captured soldiers as POWs, rather than common criminals. In the intervening years, norms outlining appropriate standards of POW treatment and the necessity of minimizing harm to civilians in war have been integrated into US military law—assimilated into military doctrine and included in actors' belief structures—through extensive training and education. As a result, protecting prisoners and civilians have become important components of US military identity and the identity of the United States writ large. Many of the decisions made during US counterterror operations in Iraq and Afghanistan not only called into question US identity but also unintentionally undermined its reputation, foreign policy goals, and the strength of its alliances.

Yet, in both Iraq and Afghanistan, the US military corrected its course and shifted its military strategy from counterterrorism to counterinsurgency. As the Army's Counterinsurgency Manual (FM 3-24) states, in order to gain the popular support it needed to confront insurgent threats, the United States needed an unequivocal message that it was committed to upholding the law and basic principles of human rights. In order to "clear, hold, and build" in Iraq and Afghanistan, the United States needed to be seen again as a defender of human rights. Thus, complying with the Geneva Conventions by treating captured belligerents humanely and protecting civilians was not an afterthought of the mission: it was the mission. By adapting practice to comply with the Conventions, the people became the prize in the war on terror.

6

The French Army and the Geneva Conventions during the Algerian War of Independence and After

RAPHAËLLE BRANCHE

By the mid-1950s, France had experienced a dramatic change in its role in the world. The second biggest colonial empire in the world, it rapidly became a middle power, whose new interests had to focus on the Western side of the planet and more specifically on the soon-to-be-born European Community. After a protracted war in Asia, France lost its territories there, namely Indochina. Two years later, in 1956, the Tunisian and Moroccan protectorates were granted independence. The future of the African colonies was redrawn in a new set of relationships with France, soon to be considered as mere diplomatic relations.

The "War without a Name"

Algeria stood apart. It was not technically part of the empire but part of France itself. Made a colony for settlers, Algeria was divided into French departments. On the eve of the war, the population of European descent (and the native Jews) amounted to one million, whereas native Algerians were around eight million. Algeria was actually not France, and the country faced many ambiguities. Not the least of them was the status of the native population: Although they were considered to be French (exclusive of any other nationality), they were not granted the same rights as other French people. Designated as "French Muslims," the native people of Algeria were reduced to a collective identity framed by religion. Islam became therefore an almost intrinsic native quality (especially after all native Jews had been declared French citizens by the Cremieux Decret in 1870). On this basis, the native people of Algeria, les "indigenes," that is, natives from Muslim background, were required to obey special regulations known as "le code de l'indigénat." This code was quite similar to regulations addressing the subaltern situation in any colonial territory.

After World War I, nationalism flourished in Algeria. A tiny minority in the metropole at first, the more radical of the Algerian nationalists gained influence in the 1930s in Algeria itself. Their claim for independence met the claims for cultural empowerment following religious and Arabic lines that the Association of the Oulemas defended and managed to spread throughout the country. This convergence forced the French authorities to implement political reforms in order to give the natives more political rights, although still far from the one-man-one-vote system.

Yet, in this context, the majority of the Algerian nationalists chose to act on a legal basis: They remained committed to tactics inspired by the French workers' movement and rejected the use of violence. Only a small minority favored armed struggle. These men founded the National Liberation Front (FLN), which was brought into being with a series of attacks during the night of 31 October 1954. For seven and half years, the French would have to face these guerrilla fighters fighting for an independent Algeria. They would have to face them in the countryside as well as in the cities, where, as of the autumn of 1956, the FLN resorted to blind terrorist attacks. In the first years of what they called "events in Algeria," the French authorities could but witness the rapid spread of the nationalist involvement. By the end of 1956, Algeria was in flames and France had to call for all its conscripts to be sent there. In this war without a name—as it was later dubbed—the issue of the Geneva Conventions was revealing. It had to be considered first from an official point of view and then on the ground (were the Geneva Conventions known and respected?). Since the end of the war, attention to the French Army's behavior has waxed and waned in public debate, but discussion of the legacy of the Algerian War has produced real changes in France's understanding of its obligations during wartime. The last section of this chapter reviews briefly the development of international humanitarian law in France up to the present.

Relevance of the Geneva Conventions

The specific situation of Algeria made it easier for the French authorities not to recognize a state of war. They acknowledged only an internal affair and wanted other countries to stay out of it.[1] The armed forces were just "maintaining order"

[1] They adopted the same position toward South Africa: They agreed to condemn apartheid on a moral basis but refused to do more as apartheid was considered an internal aspect of South Africa's

in a French territory. What about the Geneva Conventions in this context? Although France signed the treaties and ratified them in 1951, it was very reluctant to consider that they were relevant to the situation it was facing in Algeria. And yet, the Geneva Conventions were applicable to the situation. If not a war, it was at least a noninternational armed conflict. The International Committee of the Red Cross (ICRC) tried to convince the French authorities to let the Swiss delegates do their job. They partly succeeded.

At the very beginning of the war, the head of the French Government was a liberal, well regarded for having negotiated the end of the war in Indochina. Pierre Mendès-France entangled the ICRC within very strict limits, since its delegates were ordered to concern themselves with one matter only: the conditions under which prisoners were detained. But they were forbidden to call them prisoners under the Third Convention. And, for almost the entire war, officials were very careful not to let anybody talk about the Geneva Conventions.[2]

France found herself in a paradoxical situation indeed. The so-called events taking place in Algeria warranted the treatment of prisoners, under the Third Convention, as prisoners taken in armed conflict. Yet, the Third Convention was not officially recognized. Hence, it was still deemed permissible to turn a blind eye. Moreover, these same "events" were not supposed to justify the application of the First Convention to those wounded on the battlefield, or the Fourth to civilian populations!

France's reluctance was not limited to the Geneva Conventions. Let us take the European Convention on Human Rights. France was a signatory of the 1950 Convention. The great French lawyer, René Cassin, was the vice-chairman of the UN Commission on Human Rights from 1946 to 1955 and then chairman from 1955 to 1957.[3] He was also a member of the European Court of Human Rights and later its president, the Court itself was based in Strasbourg, a French city. Yet, France constantly refused to ratify the European Convention on Human

sovereignty so to speak. Cf. Instructions to the French delegation at the 25th session of the UN human rights commission, February–March 1959. Cassin Archives, Centre Historique des Archives Nationales (CHAN), Paris.

[2] On the Algerian missions of the ICRC, see Raphaëlle Branche, "Entre droit humanitaire et intérêts politiques: Les missions algériennes du CICR," *La Revue Historique* 609 (1999): 101–125; Fabian Klose, "'Source of Embarrassment': Human Rights, State of Emergency, and the Wars of Decolonization," in *Human Rights in the Twentieth Century*, ed. Stefan-Ludwig Hoffmann (Cambridge, UK: Cambridge University Press, 2011), pp. 237–257; Fabian Klose, *Menschenrechte im Schatten kolonialer Gewalt. Die Dekolonisierungskriege in Kenia und Algerien 1945–1962* (Munich: De Gruyter Oldenbourg Verlag, 2009); English version: Fabian Klose, *Human Rights in the Shadow of Colonial Violence: The Wars of Independence in Kenya and Algeria*, trans. Donna Geyer (Philadelphia: University of Pennsylvania Press, 2013).

[3] Again vice-chairman in 1959.

Rights. The situation faced by the French in Algeria was not the only reason (there was also a problem regarding the French law on confessional schools), but it did hamper the ratification.

Torture and the Status of Prisoners

This reluctance has to do with the Algerian situation. The war France was waging in Algeria led its armed forces to numerous violations of the Conventions and, more broadly, of human rights. To put it briefly, there was extensive use of torture within the ranks of the French army. Torture was a central means to win the war and not collateral damage, committed by some ill-disciplined soldiers. Summary executions were not rare, and arbitrary internment in camps was a common practice. Indeed, French officers assumed they had to use terror to win a war on terror.

Yet, as the war deepened, the situation of some prisoners on the ground improved. They were not considered prisoners of war (POWs) but simply "outlaws" or "rebels" under arrest.[4] There was a real concern about denomination, as many instructions show: even an armed combatant taken on the battlefield was not supposed to be called a POW. Nevertheless, after the use of torture was made public during the repression that took place in Algiers in 1957, France had to gain credence to its will to strongly affirm the rule of law in Algeria. By the end of 1957, the head of the army in Algeria, General Salan, issued a note stating that "rebels taken prisoner while combating and who did not take part in any odious action such as banditry or terrorism" should be taken care of in a way "as close as possible as the way in which prisoners of war are taken care of by civilized countries."[5] Following this new vision of the enemy as a combatant, the military authorities created what they called "military internment centers" meant to house "rebels captured while armed" in March 1958. The vocabulary was carefully chosen and the centers were dubbed military internment camps and not camps for military inmates (*centres militaires d'internés*, CMIs).

General Salan made it very clear: the inmates "should not be considered prisoners of war. The Geneva conventions did not apply to them." The search for intelligence was still "authorized."[6] And yet, though it was claimed that the Third

[4] See Raphaëlle Branche, "The French in Algeria: Can There Be Prisoners of War in a 'Domestic' Operation?" in *Prisoners in War*, ed. Sibylle Scheipers (Oxford, Oxford University Press, 2010), pp. 173–186.

[5] Note by General Salan, 24 November 1957, 1H 3799/2, Service Historique de la Défense (SHD), Vincennes.

[6] Note on the CMI, 19 March 1958, 1H1100/1 (SHD).

Convention did not apply to the detainees in these camps, their creation was a slight acknowledgment of the prisoners' specificity. The prisoners captured while armed were put in separate camps and, finally, they were granted some recognition as soldiers. The four missions organized by the ICRC after the creation of the CMIs noticed this improvement in their reports. Notably, the prisoners detained in the CMIs were spared from judicial repression: they did not have to face a trial—which could still mean, at that time, being sentenced to death and executed.

International Law and the Algerian Bid for Legitimacy

From the beginning of the war, the Algerian nationalists opposing France decided to publicize French violations of the Geneva Conventions. Yet they did it according to a specific agenda that revealed how political this claim for the Geneva Conventions to be respected was. The first years of the war, the internecine violence between nationalists was strong: The FLN, who decided to launch the armed struggle, opposed the old party led by Messali Hadj and renamed Algerian National Movement (MNA). More used to legal arguments and prone to act according to traditional political means of contestation, the MNA knew how to build legal arguments and to oppose France on this field. The movement was therefore the first to use such accusations against France. The FLN took it over once the struggle for power over the MNA was over in Algeria.

At first, the Algerian nationalists emphasized the topic of genocide. The first Algerian nationalist leader, Messali Hadj denounced the "Inhumanity and crime against the Algerian civilian population."[7] It claimed that the repression was "assuming a genocidal character."

> The most infamous police tortures are meted out, while mass searches are carried out by day and night; mass imprisonments of Algerian patriots affiliated with the National Algerian Movement, fill jails in France and in Algeria. Speedy justice, sentences to hundreds of years in prison, or to punishment by death for those found guilty of holding an offensive opinion. An unprecedented terror thus prevails. What is even more

[7] "The black paper on French repression in Algeria," written by the MNA and sent to the American government (20 September 1955), CAB/12/93 Archives Nationales d'Outre-Mer (ANOM), Aix-en-Provence.

> immoral is that the authorities have taken recourse to the Hitlerite methods of collective repression which includes Women, Children and the aged.[8]

Messali was targeting the United Nations and the North Atlantic Treaty Organization (NATO), the biggest French allies: He argued about the promises of World War II, when Algerian people helped the French and the Allies to win the war. He insisted on the concept of self-determination that the Atlantic Charter promoted. The Geneva Conventions were not yet on the agenda.

Later, the United Nations became a battleground for the FLN as well.[9] From 1957 onward, the FLN insisted on putting the Algerian issue on the UN General Assembly's agenda. On the one hand, it publicized the situation of the Algerian civilians. It dwelled on a few significant cases involving torture and suspicious death under custody. The situation of the civilians was also a great opportunity for the FLN to talk about genocide and concentration camps. Indeed the French strategy of gathering the population of the most dangerous zones in camps, leading to at least two million people in these resettlement camps, gave the FLN massive arguments against the French.

On the other hand, some French soldiers taken prisoner by the National Liberation Army were used: Their liberations were overpublicized, aiming at increasing the FLN's international audience and respectability. By April 1960, the Provisional Government for the Algerian Republic (GPRA) went one step further by publicly stating that it ratified the Geneva Conventions. The ICRC had regularly failed in obtaining guarantees that the prisoners taken by the Algerian nationalists be well treated; it failed even in obtaining a list of them. In May 1958, it had sent a memorandum to both parties in order to get some improvement for the prisoners but had never received an official answer. By March 1959, a summary of the Geneva Conventions had been tailored for the GPRA and sent to it. But the GPRA had its own agenda and the ICRC had to admit it. In June 1960, the ICRC reacted by acknowledging the fact[10] and kept trying to obtain lists of detainees from the GPRA.

[8] Memorandum on recent bloody events in Algeria, submitted by Messali Hadj, president of the Algerian National Movement (MNA) to the Secretary General of the United Nations (5 September 1955), CAB/12/93 (ANOM).

[9] Cf. Matthew Connelly, *A Diplomatic Revolution: Algeria's Fight for Independence and the Origins of the Post–Cold War Era* (Oxford: Oxford University Press, 2002).

[10] PV of the deliberations, présidence du conseil of the ICRC, 23 June 1960, 210/008/2 (ICRC, Geneva).

The main goal for the GPRA had nothing to do with the observance of the Geneva Conventions or the prisoners. In fact, two French prisoners were sentenced to death and executed the following summer. The decree stating GPRA's adhesion was part of a vast international plan built by the nationalists in order to act as a State. By adopting a position reserved for a state, the GPRA intended to affirm its own legitimacy as the representative of all the Algerians and Algeria's protostatehood. It was also a means of stressing France's persistent denial regarding the relevance of the Geneva Conventions in the war.

The Prospect of Peace and the Improvement of Prisoners' Conditions

Actually, the situation was really changing and negotiations on their way regarding the future of Algeria. Strikingly, as the negotiations' process between France and the GPRA improved, the treatment of the military prisoners did improve. Paradoxically, it was the prospect of peace between the two parties that rendered it necessary to depict the events in terms of war, of opposing "sides" and "enemy" soldiers. Only with such an officially designated enemy could peace be concluded.

With this perspective the POWs could expect an actual improvement of their situation. Following General de Gaulle's speech on self-determination in September 1959, the officers in charge of some camps were reminded to take the Geneva Conventions into account, if not to strictly comply with them, by the military commission visiting the camps, the Commission d'Inspection des Centres de Détention Administrative (CICDA). In April 1961, new rules were issued for the CMIs. The head of the CICDA considered them to be "largely inspired by the Geneva conventions." He made it very clear for his civil correspondent in Algiers: "the CMI are in fact POWs camps that were not given this name in order to avoid acknowledging de facto the FLN as a belligerent."[11] Indeed, as the war came close to an end, the enemy, originally considered a "rebel" against the state, was transformed into an enemy that was both external and legitimate.

Let us not forget, however, that throughout the war and despite being the vast majority of the victims, civilians were granted no protection at all. This leads me to my next point: the issue of the Geneva Conventions on the ground.

[11] Note from General de Saint Martin, head of the CICDA, to the head of civil affaires by the délégué général in Algiers, 21 November 1961, 1H 1100/4 (SHD).

The Geneva Conventions in Practice

Were the French soldiers and their officers aware of the Conventions? Did they have any room to maneuver just to comply with them if they wanted to?

The French army was a conscript army. Military service was thereby compulsory, and every French man had to enlist. The war in Algeria was the first one to be waged with this army (the war in Indochina was restricted to professional soldiers) since the defeat France had suffered in 1940. Although Algerian nationalism was a rising tide at least from the 1930s onward, the uprising came as a surprise and the French army was not really prepared to deal with it. The men sent to Algeria were roughly trained and, in some years, they did not even receive their training before reaching Algeria. International rules were mentioned as much as French law, but nothing specific was given to them about these rules. The notion of "laws of war" was indeed vaguely mentioned.[12]

On the ground, it appears that law was, generally, perceived as a brake. As France was not officially waging a war, for example, every death had to be declared to the gendarmerie, which was supposed to investigate the causes of the death! This absurd situation led the military to try to emancipate themselves from the law, perceived as only coercive. As the war went on, they succeeded in getting more freedom from the government and laws were passed according to the necessities they were stressing.

Moreover law and justice were part of the repression imposed on Algerian nationalists. They were considered as outlaws and rebels and therefore charged for murders, for criminal associations, and so on. Justice and law were on the French side. Yet, some officers wanted the course of justice to be more repressive, to act more rapidly and to sentence to death many more people. Summary justice is part of this view. These same officers did not think they had to comply with any rules, except the rules of war that they were, indeed, setting up. These men were dominant in the French army in Algeria at least from 1957 to the beginning of 1960. These were the worst years of the war as far as violations of laws are concerned.

But what if someone wished to comply with the Conventions and to respect the civilian population or some prisoner? The Geneva Conventions were not helpful. Indeed, the basic rules of war were to respect the civilians and the prisoners, and every French soldier knew them, every French officer as well. To respect a civilian or a prisoner was easy as soon as you had your leader agreeing.

[12] On the status of the acts of violence committed by the French soldiers, see my PhD thesis, "L'armée et la torture pendant la guerre d'Algérie: Les soldats, leurs chefs et les violences illégales" (IEP de Paris, 2000). Later published: *La torture et l'armée pendant la guerre d'Algérie, 1954–1962* (Paris: Gallimard, 2001; Arabic version: Algiers: M'doukal, 2011).

And the most important leader for the rank-and-file soldier was the sergeant, then the lieutenant or the captain—no higher level was helpful, as it was too far from where the "real war" was being waged.

The useful concepts were not legal ones but the concepts of morality and honor. The respect due to prisoners, for example, was linked to the "French rules of humanity."[13]

The main responsibility fell to the junior officers. This is always the situation in a war: junior officers are the ones dealing with fear, anger, and brutality. But it is even more the case in a war such as the French Algerian war, when the higher ranks failed to provide a behavior guide strongly and effectively tied to disciplinary measures. The orders from above were vague, resembling much more wishful thinking than orders. For example, it was not until the end of 1959 that the ministry of defense, Pierre Guillaumat, issued an explicit order forbidding specific kinds of torture, namely, "coercive methods such as waterboarding, electricity or hoist."[14] Guillaumat insisted that the order be transmitted down to the lowest hierarchical level. Yet there is no evidence that this was successfully accomplished. On the contrary, his follower, Pierre Messmer, issued the same kind of interdiction in July 1960, and General Crepin, follower of General Challe, waited almost six months before transmitting it to his subordinates, forbidding them "arbitrary treatment while arresting people," "brutality while searching," "unworthy treatment during interrogation," and "discrimination while controlling" with a vocabulary of the usual euphemisms, giving the individual soldier responsibility to decide what was to be considered "worthy" or not.[15]

As a result, a rank-and-file soldier, or even a junior officer, wishing to comply with the Geneva Conventions, must have felt, sometimes, very lonely.

It should be added that the 1933 general disciplinary code was still in use. It commanded the subordinate to obey any order. Moreover, contrary to nowadays, it was not easy to send information abroad. Censorship still existed, and soldiers were afraid of it. They felt at the mercy of heir officers, and some of them were said to have feared for their lives: Ultimately, the same officer sending people to torture could send you, one day or another, on some dangerous mission.[16]

[13] Outside combat, the French rules of humanity continue to apply. Here is the statement of the interministerial circular of 1 July 1955.

[14] Letter from the Ministry of Defense to General Challe, the head of the Army in Algeria, 23 December 1959, Private Archives (Instruction from Pierre Messmer to General Crépin, 18 July 1960, 1H 3617/1, SHD).

[15] Letter from General Crépin to the officers in charge of the regional commands of Algeria, 30 November 1960, 1H 1261/5 (SHD).

[16] On this aspect, see chapter 5, "The Soldiers and Their Chiefs (to order, to refuse or to obey, to cover-up and be covered)" in Branche, *La torture*.

The Broader Political Context

These internal tensions the soldiers were facing were linked to external tensions: tensions existing between the goals assigned to the French army in Algeria, namely, to win the population's support and to extract the FLN from this population. The soldiers were asked to wage counter-guerrilla warfare, but they were also meant to help with schools, with medicine, with road building, and so forth. They were, in some cases, involved in investigations as policemen would be but without the same legal restrictions. Most of all, they had a political part to play, since they had to take up the challenge of the nationalists claiming that France had not improved the Algerians' lives and was not respecting the Algerian collective identity. It was, indeed, an impossible task, especially once the FLN had grown in strength and managed to take political control of the vast majority of the Algerian people, in one way or another.

This impossible challenge led the French army to a dead end. The political end was not the one the army was fighting for on the ground. The dead end was expressed by a moral vocabulary, both within the military ranks and outside the army. The army was facing a "moral crisis," and, as some newspapers put it, so was the whole nation.

This crisis was also a crisis between the army and the nation. Acting outside the constraints of the law, some officers were prone to behave as if they were the political leaders, as if they knew better since they knew from the battleground what was supposed to be really going on. First in 1958, then in 1961, some senior officers tried to impose their views on the government. They succeeded once, in 1958. By threatening the government and declaring Algeria under the order of several "Comités de Salut Public" all over the territory and even in Corsica, the military succeeded in having the Président de la République call for another man to be the head of the government. Pierre Pflimlin had to resign, and Charles de Gaulle was called back to power. He managed to gain the confidence of enough people not only to calm down the military in Algeria but also to bury the Fourth Republic. Although the Fifth Republic was not the danger to public liberties some were afraid of, the regime gave De Gaulle free rein to solve the Algerian problem. Thus, at the origin of these huge changes in France's political system was the defiance expressed by some officers in Algiers. This definitely led to a need to reconsider the relationship between the army and the nation. In April 1961, four of the most prestigious French officers, two of them formers heads of the army in Algeria (General Salan and General Challe), tried to replay the May 1958 coup. They failed dramatically, notably because they could not gain enough support from the military. Yet, lots of officers chose to resign after the war and shared a sense of betrayal about politics and De Gaulle in particular. After 1962, the French army had to build a new identity.

Legacies of the Algerian War for Human Rights and Humanitarian Law

Lessons had to be learned from the Algerian war. If we consider the numerous changes within the French army since 1962, what about the Geneva Conventions? Are they better taught? Better known?

The Algerian war undoubtedly hampered the French steps toward the recognition of any international framework regarding human rights. Thus, quite rapidly after the end of the war, the imprescriptibility of crimes against humanity was added to the French penal code (1964). In 1966, the general rules of discipline changed and mentioned the necessity to respect the laws of war and the international conventions.

The 1972, the General Military Statute insisted on each level's responsibility: the responsibility of the lowest ranks should not deprive the higher ranks of their own responsibility.[17] The 1975 new Code de Discipline Générale did the same. And the new commander in chief,[18] General Jean Lagarde, issued ten directives aimed at the individuals within the army. The international conventions are mentioned, as are the laws of war. The soldiers have to obey, but they should not be ordered into an action violating these laws and conventions.[19]

Another article was added to the Règlement de Discipline Générale in 1982. Military personnel are told to behave humanely with people out of action (once the combat is over). They are forbidden to use any means causing pain or useless damage, compromising other people's dignity or integrity (be they sick persons, wounded, prisoners, or civilians). The sanitary staff were ordered to refuse any kind of participation, even a passive one, to "cruel, inhumane or degrading treatments."[20]

Thus, as far as the general instructions to the French army are concerned, the Algerian war was quite far away by the end of the 1970s. Nevertheless, when we look closer at the Geneva Conventions, the French position was not so progressive.

[17] Article 15 du statut général des militaires de 1972.

[18] Chef d'Etat Major de l'armée de terre.

[19] "Les militaires doivent obéissance aux ordres de leurs supérieurs et sont responsables de l'exécution des missions qui leur sont confiées. Toutefois, il ne peut leur être ordonné et ils ne peuvent accomplir des actes qui sont contraires aux lois, aux coutumes de la guerre et aux conventions internationales ou qui constituent des crimes ou des délits notamment contre la sûreté et l'intégrité de l'État. La responsabilité propre des subordonnés ne dégage les supérieurs d'aucune de leurs responsabilités." Extrait de la loi N° 72-662 du 13 juillet 1972 portant statut général des militaires, BOC:SC, p. 784; BOEM 300*, 332 et 651.

[20] Extrait de l'instruction N° 52000/DEF/C/5 du 10 décembre 1979 portant application du règlement de discipline générale dans les armées (art. 9), BOC, p.4749; BOEM 130, 144, 150 et 300*.

The second Additional Protocol had to wait until 1984 to be ratified, and France was particularly slow in ratifying the first one. It was only ratified in 2001 and with restrictions.[21] The first Additional Protocol made it very clear that a struggle involving people fighting against a colonial domination was assimilated to an international armed conflict. This would have been repellent to France in the 1950s or even at the beginning of the 1960s. But times were changing, and so did the stumbling block: the nuclear weapons issue took the place of the colonial issue. Indeed, France refused to ratify it for more than twenty years, arguing that, although they were not supposed to deal with nuclear weapons, the new regulations might compromise France's legitimate right to self-defense.[22]

Ethics and the Individual

What about today? Quite rapidly, the conscript army came to an end. What was supposed to be a gentle process was indeed a rupture in 1996. French military men are now professional. How is this new army dealing with the Geneva Conventions and, if any, the memory of the Algerian war?

The French army is insisting very much on its new moral foundations. The basic document issued in 1999 is titled "Foundations and Principles" and it makes it very clear that ethics are not a question of disciplinary rules but rather a question of individual fulfillment. Therefore this document is said to be a "guide for thought and action." The Algerian war is very lightly remembered as "decolonization conflicts that had, sometimes, shattered convictions."

Particularly striking are the promotion of the individual and the notion of ethics. These two features reveal a change in the way authority is envisaged. Authority needs to be distinguished from authoritarianism and obedience does not have to be blind. The leader has to be aware of his soldiers' identities and to respect them, especially when they disagree with specific orders regarding the ethics.

The strength of the army is said to stem from the collective military unit (be it a platoon, a company, or a regiment). But this collective unit is not supposed to crush people but rather to gain from them, from their specificities uniting for the *better*. The document gave the soldiers extracts from the Declaration of the

[21] Law passed in January 2001. Actual ratification in October. LOI no 2001-79 du 30 janvier 2001 autorisant l'adhésion au protocole additionnel aux conventions de Genève du 12 août 1949 relatif à la protection des victimes des conflits armés internationaux (protocole I) (ensemble deux annexes) (1).

[22] On the French arguments, see Henri Meyrowitz, "La France et les protocoles additionnels aux conventions de Genève," *Politique Etrangère* 45, no. 4 (1980): 949–66.

Rights of Man and of the Citizen, the Universal Declaration of Human Rights, and the 1949 Geneva Conventions to help them think and act. No extract from the Additional Protocols is given.

Two years later, in 2001, a light eleven-point "Code of Soldier's Behavior" was given to every soldier in the army. Point 4: Orders have to be obeyed provided that they do not contravene the laws of war and the international conventions. The soldiers are told to be proud of their flag and its motto "Honor and Motherland." On the one hand, honor stems from ancient times and chivalric values. They are explicitly mentioned in some other texts, and medieval knights are supposed to epitomize military virtues, totally disconnected—needless to say—from any political context. On the other hand, Motherland is connected deeply with the French Republic and, what is even trickier, with universal values. Indeed the Declaration of the Rights of Man and of the Citizen is presented as French (which it is, of course) and universal. Therefore nothing universal is unknown to French people. To be a patriot, to serve one's country, is to be a citizen of the world and a person of virtue, even respecting the international conventions.[23]

The Algerian experience may appear as a very old story, from a very remote past, and yet, it may not be so far away.[24] The colonial empire is dead, but the tasks French soldiers were facing in its last big country (i.e., Algeria) are still there. The multifaceted war waged in Algeria has a lot in common with the operations the French army is facing today. To guard crops, to help mothers with their children, to watch building construction or checkpoints: so many actions that the French experienced in Algeria. It is still worth learning the lessons of it.

[23] In 2005 a new text stated, "Any subordinate can refuse to carry out illegal orders."

[24] In the context of the war against terror, I was asked to address the issue of torture against terrorism. See Raphaëlle Branche, "The French State Faced with the Algerian Nationalists (1954–1962): A War against Terrorism?" in *Democracies at War against Terrorism*, ed. Samy Cohen (New York: Palgrave Macmillan, 2008), pp. 59–76; and "Torture of Terrorists? Use of Torture in a 'War against Terrorism': Justifications, Methods and Effects: The Case of France in Algeria, 1954–1962," *International Review of the Red Cross* 89, no. 3 (November 2007).

7

Russia, Chechnya, and the Geneva Conventions, 1994–2006

Norms and the Problem of Internalization

MARK KRAMER

This chapter discusses Russia's position vis-à-vis the four Geneva Conventions of 1949 and the two Additional Protocols of 1977 and the implications for the two wars fought by Russian troops against separatist guerrillas in Chechnya in 1994–2006.[1] The chapter begins by tracing the Soviet Union's policies toward the Conventions and Additional Protocols and the effects (or lack thereof) of these documents on Soviet military operations both abroad and at home from the late 1940s through the early 1990s. The experience with the Conventions and Additional Protocols during the Soviet era has helped to shape the policies of the Russian Federation, which, as the legal successor state to the USSR, inherited the Soviet government's obligations under international treaties and agreements. The chapter highlights the changes and continuities in post-Soviet Russia's position and then uses the recent Russian-Chechen wars as a case study.

The chapter sheds light not only on Russia's policies in Chechnya but also on recent scholarly literature regarding international norms and state behavior. A norm in international relations can be defined as a shared conception of the appropriate way to behave or the appropriate stance to take on a particular issue.[2] Over time, as a norm grows more prevalent, actors in the system come to

[1] For the full texts of these documents and related materials, see the booklet put out by the International Committee of the Red Cross, *1949 Conventions and Additional Protocols, and Their Commentaries* (Geneva: ICRC, 2007). For a useful discussion of the genesis of the Geneva Conventions and Additional Protocols, see Geoffrey Best, *War and Law since 1945* (Oxford: Clarendon Press, 1994), esp. chs. 5 and 6.

[2] For other deontological definitions, see Martha Finnemore and Kathryn Sikkink, "International Norm Dynamics and Political Change," *International Organization* 52, no. 4 (Autumn 1998): 891; Henning Boekle, Volker Rittberger, and Wolfgang Wagner, "Normen und Außenpolitik: Konstrukt

expect that other actors will comply with it. The growing acceptance of a norm does not preclude the establishment of mechanisms to monitor and, if necessary, enforce compliance with it, but, at least in principle, a norm could eventually become self-enforcing or nearly so.[3] Scholars who analyze international norms have sought to explain how norms emerge and spread, how they come to be accepted and internalized, and why individuals and states comply (or fail to comply) with them.[4] The focus here is on the last of these topics—compliance (or noncompliance) with norms relating to international humanitarian law (IHL) and human rights. A key aspect of this topic is the process of internalization. Although political leaders and military personnel might comply with a norm even when they have not internalized it—perhaps out of fear of punishment or of public disgrace—the likelihood of compliance will almost certainly be greater when internalization has occurred.

The case of Russia's wars in Chechnya illustrates why compliance with international humanitarian norms becomes much more problematic when internalization has not occurred. The brutality of Russia's military operations in Chechnya from 1994 to 2006 stemmed not so much from a lack of awareness of these norms as from a lack of willingness to comply with them, regardless of the country's supposed commitment to uphold them. Policymakers in Moscow may have pledged their acceptance of humanitarian principles by signing and ratifying international treaties, but when faced with the exigencies of armed conflict they simply ignored their commitments and gave the Russian army and internal security forces a free hand. Even during the height of military operations in the two Chechen wars, when Russia deployed up to 100,000 regular army forces to fight, the Russian government argued that the combat did not amount to an "armed conflict" and was instead merely an "internal disturbance" not covered by the Geneva Conventions. Russian military and security force commanders, for their part, were in many instances aware of the basic norms of IHL, but they had no desire or incentive to abide by them. The case of Russia's wars and counterinsurgency operations in Chechnya thus underscores what can happen when internalization at all levels of political and military power is nonexistent and

ivistische Außenpolitiktheorie," Working Paper No. 34 (Tübingen: Institut für Politikwissenschaft, 1999), p. 5; and Thomas Risse and Kathryn Sikkink, "The Socialization of International Human Rights Norms into Domestic Practices: An Introduction," in *The Power of Human Rights: International Norms and Domestic Change*, ed. Thomas Risse, Stephen C. Ropp, and Kathryn Sikkink (New York: Cambridge University Press, 1999), p. 2.

[3] For interesting case studies of international norms for which enforcement mechanisms are deemphasized or omitted, see Dinah Shelton, ed., *Commitment and Compliance: The Role of Non-Binding Norms in the International Legal System* (New York: Oxford University Press, 2000).

[4] See, for example, Jeffrey T. Checkel, "Why Comply? Social Learning and European Identity Change," *International Organization* 55, no. 3 (Summer 2001): 553–588.

when other factors that might induce compliance (e.g., supranational enforcement bodies) are also absent.

The chapter draws on Russian government documents (both published and unpublished), analyses by Russian experts on international law, the training manuals and guidelines used by Russian Defense Ministry and Internal Affairs Ministry (MVD) officers, other materials from the main military and MVD academies, unpublished information regarding the rules of engagement given to Russian federal commanders and servicemen in Chechnya,[5] and 107 interviews with senior Russian military and MVD officers, Russian servicemen who have been deployed in Chechnya, Russian international law specialists, representatives of nongovernmental organizations (NGOs), Russian government officials, and ordinary Chechen civilians.

The Soviet Legacy

Because the Russian Federation is the successor state to the Soviet Union under international law, and because the Russian Defense Ministry and Russian MVD inherited the bulk of the Soviet Defense Ministry and Soviet MVD, Russian policy toward the Geneva Conventions and Additional Protocols has been influenced by the Soviet Union's experience. Hence, a brief overview of Soviet policy is essential here.

Signing, Ratifying, and Incorporating the Conventions

The Soviet Union signed the four Geneva Conventions (though with reservations regarding Conventions III and IV) in December 1949 and ratified them in April 1954.[6] From 1974 to 1977, Soviet officials played an active role in the Geneva Conference on the Reaffirmation and Development of International Humanitarian Law Applicable in Armed Conflicts, which ended in June 1977 with agreement on two Additional Protocols to the Geneva Conventions.

[5] I tried to obtain information about the rules of engagement given to the security forces that are under the jurisdiction of the pro-Moscow Chechen government, but I was repeatedly told that the Chechen security commanders are allowed to act at their own discretion and that guidelines for them are mostly informal.

[6] "Ukaz Prezidiuma Verkhovnogo soveta SSSR ot 17 aprelya 1954 g.," in *Sbornik zakonov SSSR i ukazov Prezidiuma Verkhovnogo soveta SSSR, 1938–1975*, 4 vols., ed. M. I. Yumashev, A. V. Kaliteevskaya, and R. N. Vladimirtsev (Moscow: Izvestiya Sovetov deputatov trudyashchikhsya SSSR, 1975), vol. 2, pp. 249–250.

These two protocols, one dealing with "international armed conflicts" and the other with "non-international armed conflicts" (i.e., civil wars), were supposed to broaden "the 1949 Geneva Convention protection of victims of war" by taking account of "changes in the nature of armed conflicts in the past quarter century."[7] From the Soviet perspective, this expansion of coverage was a welcome step in giving a privileged status to anti-Western guerrilla movements in the Third World.[8] The Soviet government signed the two Additional Protocols in December 1977 but did not end up ratifying them until September 1989, shortly after Soviet troops completed their withdrawal from Afghanistan.

Conventions I and II were incorporated into the legal guidelines for Soviet military commanders and servicemen in February 1958, when the Soviet defense minister, Marshal Rodion Malinovskii, issued Directive No. 20, titled "Instructions for the Adoption within the Armed Forces of the USSR of the Geneva Conventions of 12 August 1949 on the Amelioration of the Condition of the Wounded and Sick in Armies in the Field and of Individuals Shipwrecked at Sea."[9] The Soviet legislature followed up in December 1958 by including provisions (Articles 32 and 33) relating to Conventions I and II in the amended Law on Criminal Responsibility for Crimes against the State.[10] Until February 1990, however, Conventions III and IV (regarding treatment of prisoners of war [POWs] and protection of the civilian population) and the two Additional Protocols were left out of the Soviet Defense Ministry's legal guidelines. On 19–20 January 1990, Soviet military and internal security forces undertook a large-scale incursion into Soviet Azerbaijan and quickly crushed the Azerbaijani Popular Front—an operation that, unlike crackdowns elsewhere in the USSR over the previous few years, did not provoke controversy or criticism in Moscow.

[7] Michael Bothe, Karl Josef Petsch, and Waldemar A. Solf, *New Rules for Victims of Armed Conflicts: Commentary on the Two 1977 Protocols Additional to the Geneva Conventions of 1949* (The Hague: Nijhoff, 1982), pp. 16–17.

[8] I. P. Blishchenko, *Osvobodivshiesya strany i mezhdunarodnoe pravo* (Moscow: Mezhdunarodnye otnosheniya, 1988). Blishchenko, a prominent specialist on international law, was a member of the Soviet delegation at the 1974–1977 Geneva Conference.

[9] "Prikaz Ministra oborony SSSR ot 5 fevralya 1958 goda No. 20: Instruktisya po primeneniyu v vooruzhenykh silakh Soyuza SSR Zhenevskikh konventsii ot 12 avgusta 1949 g. ob uluchshenii uchasti ranenykh, bol'nykh v deistvuyushchikh armiyakh i lits, poterpevshikh korablekrushenie na more," in *Spravochnik po zakonodatel'stvu dlya ofitserov Sovetskoi Armii i Voenno-Morskogo Flota*, ed. B. S. Popov and L. G. Ivashov (Moscow: Voenizdat, 1988), pp. 432–436.

[10] "Zakon ob ugolovnoi otvetsvennosti za prestupleniya protiv gosudarstvennoi vlasti," in *Spravochnik ofitsera po sovetskomu zakonodatel'stvu*, ed. I. F. Pobezhimov and B. A. Viktorov (Moscow: Voenizdat, 1966), p. 309.

A few weeks later, with the fighting in Azerbaijan over, Soviet Defense Minister Dmitrii Yazov signed Directive No. 75, "On the Proclamation of the Geneva Conventions regarding the Protection of Victims of War."[11]

The issuance of this directive marked the first time that legal guidelines for the Soviet armed forces took at least nominal account of the full range of IHL (*mezhdunarodnoe gumanitarnoe pravo* in Russian). Yazov's signature of the directive was preceded by a contentious debate within the Soviet High Command and Soviet Defense Council.[12] A number of influential generals, such as Vladislav Achalov (the commander of Soviet Airborne Forces) and Valentin Varennikov (the commander-in-chief of Soviet Ground Forces), spoke strongly against the directive. Yazov himself was initially skeptical of it, citing the "unfounded criticism and malicious hostility" that supposedly were already being directed against the armed forces for their role in cracking down on political and nationalist unrest in the Caucasus and elsewhere. Some of the proponents of the directive cited the atrocities perpetrated by Afghan guerrillas against Soviet POWs during the 1979–1989 war as a reason for emphasizing Convention III and the Additional Protocols. Other supporters argued that the directive would give a boost to the "new political thinking" espoused by Mikhail Gorbachev, who headed both the Communist Party of the Soviet Union (CPSU) and the Soviet Defense Council. Ultimately, Yazov acquiesced in the decision by the Soviet Council of Ministers (at the behest of Gorbachev, who had just assumed the new post of Soviet president while remaining party leader) to authorize promulgation of the directive.

Soviet Military Interventions Abroad: The Geneva Conventions in Practice

Even though the four Geneva Conventions and two Additional Protocols were not formally incorporated into Soviet military guidance until 1990, this did not mean that Soviet troops invariably acted with unrestrained brutality in earlier years. On five occasions after 1949, Soviet soldiers openly took part in military operations abroad—in East Germany in June 1953, in Hungary in October–November 1956, in Czechoslovakia in August 1968, at a number of disputed sites along the border with China from March to September 1969, and in Afghanistan

[11] "Prikaz Ministra oborony SSSR ot 16 fevralya 1990 goda No. 75 'Ob ob'yavlenii Zhenevskikh konventsii o zashchite zhertv voiny ot 12 avgusta 1949 g. i Dopolnitel'nykh protokolov k nim,'" 16 February 1990, Moscow, published text with Conventions and Additional Protocols appended.

[12] A partly typed, partly handwritten summary of this debate, compiled by Mikhail Gorbachev's chief foreign policy advisor, Anatolii Chernyaev, from discussions with Gorbachev and Marshal Sergei Akhromeev (the former chief of the Soviet General Staff who at this time was a personal military advisor to Gorbachev), is stored in Arkhiv Gorbachev-Fonda, Fond 2, Dokument 3411.

from December 1979 to February 1989. (Soviet military pilots also surreptitiously engaged in aerial combat during the Korean War and conflicts in the Middle East, but their participation in those instances was not openly acknowledged until many years later.) In the five cases of openly acknowledged operations abroad, the USSR's record of compliance with the Geneva Conventions was mixed.

East Germany, 1953

In June 1953 the Soviet Union had not yet ratified the Geneva Conventions and was only eight years away from the end of a devastating war in which Soviet and German troops had clashed with unremitting ferocity. The Soviet occupation of eastern Germany from 1945 on had been extraordinarily harsh. Nonetheless, when seventeen Soviet tank and mechanized divisions, supplemented by artillery, communications, and logistics regiments and battalions, were deployed on 17 June 1953 to quell a vast uprising in East Germany, they behaved with surprising decorum, relying mainly on intimidation rather than the direct use of force. The limited fighting that took place was almost all over within a day. A top-secret US intelligence report at the time noted, "the Soviet troops [in putting down the rebellion] demonstrated a remarkable discipline, restraint, and cool-headedness, which came as a surprise to all, foremost to the East Germans."[13] Whether this restraint would have continued if large-scale violent resistance had erupted and been sustained for many weeks in numerous East German cities is, of course, a different matter.

Hungary, 1956

The Soviet Union's initial intervention in Hungary on 23 October 1956 involved only a limited number of Soviet troops, but the introduction of even this small contingent of Soviet forces into Budapest merely fueled the rebellion and converted it from a mass protest against the Stalinist regime in Hungary into an anti-Soviet (as well as anti-Stalinist) uprising aimed at breaking Hungary away from the USSR. On 27 October, the Hungarian Red Cross, whose headquarters and vehicles had been largely destroyed by Soviet gunfire and bombardment, urged the International Committee of the Red Cross (ICRC) to undertake an

[13] "Briefing Paper on Recent Developments in East Germany and Implications for U.S. Policy" (Secret/Security Information), 25 September 1953, Foreign Service Despatch [*sic*] from U.S. High Commissioner in Germany/Berlin (HICOG/BE) to U.S. Department of State, in U.S. National Archives II, Record Group 59, 762B.00/9-2253, p. 15.

emergency relief operation and to "ensure that the provisions of the Fourth Geneva Convention for the protection of the civilian population are strictly respected."[14] The ICRC made a preliminary delivery of relief supplies via the Hungarian Red Cross on 29 October, but Soviet commanders prevented the ICRC from bringing in additional supplies by air two days later. The ICRC managed to deliver food and other materials by ground on 1 November, but from then until 11 November the Soviet Union blocked any further ICRC deliveries by either air or ground. Starting on 31 October, the ICRC repeatedly broadcast an appeal on shortwave radio exhorting "all concerned" to abide by "several fundamental principles contained in the Geneva Conventions."[15] On 4 November, at the urging of the Hungarian Red Cross, the ICRC issued a further appeal calling on all "commanders and combatants in Hungary" to allow the ICRC to evacuate and care for all the wounded "in accordance with the provisions of Article 15 of the Fourth Geneva Convention."[16] Soviet commanders brushed aside this plea as they continued with a much larger invasion of Hungary, using more than 100,000 Soviet soldiers. The crackdown on the Hungarian rebels was brutal and caused great destruction and bloodshed among civilians. By the time the fighting diminished on 9 November, more than 2,500 Hungarian civilians were dead, and more than 19,000 were wounded.[17]

Afterward, the Soviet Union did permit the ICRC to resume relief operations in Hungary, which lasted from 11 November 1956 until 25 June 1957, despite occasional disruptions and harassment. Nonetheless, overall the invasion of Hungary was notable mostly for the Soviet Union's failure to comply with key provisions of the Geneva Conventions. Subsequent investigations by international legal organizations and by a United Nations (UN) special committee on the crisis concluded that Soviet forces in Hungary had been culpable of "flagrant violations" of the Geneva Conventions, including "shooting indiscriminately" at civilians and unarmed fighters who were trying to surrender as well as "many cases of shooting at ambulances, Red Cross vehicles, and the doctors and nurses in those vehicles."[18] Soviet officials dismissed these accusations out of hand and refused to respond on a point-by-point basis when the UN General Assembly

[14] International Committee of the Red Cross (ICRC), *Report on the Relief Action in Hungary, October 1956–June 1957* (Geneva: ICRC, 1957), pp. 5, 7.

[15] ICRC, *Report on the Relief Action in Hungary*, p. 7.

[16] ICRC, *Report on the Relief Action in Hungary*, p. 8.

[17] "Néhány statisztikai adat a forradalomról," in *A vidék forradalma 1956*, ed. Attila Szakolczai and László Varga (Budapest: 1956-os Intézet, 2004), pp. 371–372.

[18] United Nations, *Report of the Special Committee on the Problem of Hungary*, General Assembly Official Records, 11th Session, New York, 1957, esp. the section titled "Hostilities," pp. 230–232. See also International Commission of Jurists, *Hungarian Situation in the Light of the Geneva Convention of 1949* (The Hague: ICJ, December 1956).

convened a special emergency session on 4–10 November 1956 to discuss the situation in Hungary. Under Soviet pressure, the matter was eventually removed from the United Nations' agenda altogether.

Czechoslovakia, 1968

The more than 400,000 Soviet and allied troops who invaded and occupied Czechoslovakia in August and September 1968 did not encounter any violent resistance. As a result, civilian casualties were very limited (though 104 people did die and 335 were seriously injured through accidents or when putting up nonviolent resistance during the invasion and initial weeks of occupation).[19] Western governments and international legal experts accused the Soviet Union of having violated the UN Charter and other international agreements restricting the use of force, but they did not allege that Soviet troops had violated the Geneva Conventions. Even if such charges *had* been voiced, Soviet leaders staunchly rejected the notion that the entry of Soviet troops into Czechoslovakia was counter to international law. With the promulgation of the so-called Brezhnev Doctrine (a Western, not Soviet, term referring to a set of authoritative Soviet statements justifying the invasion), the Soviet Union embraced the notion that the "laws of class struggle" take legal precedence over "abstract concepts of sovereignty."[20] Elaborating on this notion, Soviet theorists began distinguishing between "bourgeois" and "class-based" versions of international law. They argued that the intervention of Soviet and East European troops, far from transgressing the principles of respect for sovereignty and noninterference, had actually buttressed them by "defending Czechoslovakia's independence and sovereignty *as a socialist state*" against "the counterrevolutionary forces that would like to deprive it of this sovereignty."[21] The "bourgeois" concepts of independence and sovereignty, according to this argument, were invalid because they lacked "class content" and because the norms of international law were meaningful only within "the general context of class struggle." The Brezhnev Doctrine did not refer specifically to the Geneva Conventions, because it dealt primarily with resort to armed force (*ius ad bellum*) rather than the conduct of war itself

[19] "Oběti srpna žalují: Z duverne zprávy pro pět nejvyšších představitelů Československého podzimu 1968," *Občanský deník* (Prague), 24 July 1990, p. 3 (Part 1), 26 July 1990, p. 3 (Part 2), 31 July 1990, p. 3 (Part 3), 2 August 1990, p. 3 (Part 4), 4 August 1990, p. 3 (Part 5), and 7 August 1990, p. 3 (Part 6).

[20] S. Kovalev, "Suverenitet i internatsional'nye obyazannosti sotsialisticheskikh stran," *Pravda* (Moscow), 26 September 1968, p. 4. See also "Zashchita sotsializma—vysshii internatsional'nyi dolg," *Pravda* (Moscow), 22 August 1968, pp. 2–3.

[21] A. Sovetov, "Sovremennyi etap bor'by mezhdu sotsializmom i imperializmom," *Mezhdunarodnaya zhizn'* (Moscow), No. 11 (November 1968), p. 7 (emphasis added).

(*ius in bello*) or military occupation, the matters treated by the Hague and Geneva Conventions. But it had far-reaching implications for how Soviet leaders might subsequently construe their obligations under the Conventions.

The Sino-Soviet Border Conflict, 1969

The border conflict that erupted between Chinese and Soviet garrisons on a disputed island (known as Damanskii to the Soviet side and Zhenbao to the Chinese) in the Ussuri River in early March 1969 was preceded by several weeks of skirmishes that caused injuries to a few soldiers on both sides but no damage to civilians living on the island. The major battle that flared up on 2 March resulted in the deaths of some fifty Soviet soldiers, including the commander of the Soviet garrison. Newly available documents from China and Russia make clear that the Chinese forces instigated these clashes at the behest of the Chinese Communist Party (CCP) leader Mao Zedong and that Soviet political leaders and military commanders were caught off-guard.[22] Another round of deadly clashes on the island, involving heavy artillery, main battle tanks, and other armored combat vehicles, ensued in mid-March, causing many dozens of casualties. After these initial hostilities, Soviet officials alleged that Chinese soldiers were deliberately surrounding themselves with civilian farmers and livestock when advancing on Soviet positions—a charge that, if true, would have pointed to a clear violation of the Geneva Conventions. (There is, however, little evidence that Chinese troops did deliberately use such tactics.) Low-level skirmishes continued throughout the spring and summer, and on 13 August a group of more than three hundred heavily armed Soviet soldiers confronted and destroyed a squadron of thirty Chinese troops in the Chinese border zone along China's Tielieketi region in Xinjiang. Although Xinjiang was sparsely populated, the intense fighting and risk of wider hostilities posed a constant threat to civilian settlements. Neither side, however, took any steps to prevent collateral damage from the conflict. In late August the Chinese authorities began evacuating civilians from Xinjiang and other border areas and ordered local CCP organizations and ordinary citizens to be prepared for a major Soviet attack. On 11 September, as fears loomed in Beijing that the Soviet Union might launch a preventive nuclear strike against

[22] For useful accounts, see Major-General Vitalii Bubenin, *Krovavyi sneg Damanskogo: Sobytiya, 1966–1969* (Moscow: Kuchkovo pole, 2004), esp. pp. 150–187; Yang Kuisong, "The Sino-Soviet Border Clash of 1969: From Zhenbao Island to Sino-American Rapprochement," *Cold War History* 1, no. 1 (February 2001): 21–52; Lyle J. Goldstein, "Return to Zhenbao Island: Who Started Shooting and Why It Mattered," *China Quarterly*, no. 168 (December 2001): 985–997; and Thomas W. Robinson, "The Sino-Soviet Border Conflict," in *Diplomacy of Power: Soviet Armed Forces as a Political Instrument*, ed. Stephen S. Kaplan (Washington, DC: Brookings Institution Press, 1981), pp. 265–313, esp. 273–282, 295–301.

China, Soviet Premier Aleksei Kosgyin and Chinese Premier Zhou Enlai held emergency talks at the Beijing airport that helped to defuse the prospect of all-out war but did not eliminate severe tensions and fears of renewed fighting.[23] No further clashes actually transpired, but all evidence suggests that concern about danger to Chinese civilians in the border regions played no role in the USSR's (or China's) decision to refrain from further combat.

The War in Afghanistan, 1979–1989

The nine years of warfare that followed the Soviet invasion of Afghanistan in December 1979 were marked by unrestrained violence and destruction. Immense suffering was inflicted on Afghan civilians. The guerrillas resisting the Soviet occupation routinely committed atrocities during the war, but Soviet forces were responsible for the overwhelming share of the bloodshed and misery endured by the civilian population. Western governments, NGOs, UN special envoys, and international legal experts repeatedly accused the Soviet Union of gross violations of the Geneva Conventions and international human rights agreements, but Soviet leaders dismissed these allegations and blocked efforts by NGOs, UN commissions, and other international bodies to conduct more in-depth investigations.[24] Even during the Gorbachev era, the Soviet government did not formally respond to charges that Soviet troops in Afghanistan had been culpable of systematic violations of the Geneva Conventions.

Internal Use of Force: A Role for the Geneva Conventions?

Within the USSR, Soviet military and internal security forces were employed after World War II in at least one contingency that undoubtedly could have been regarded as an "armed conflict not of an international character" and thereby covered not only by Common Article 3 of the Geneva Conventions but also by Additional Protocol II (after 1977). The counterinsurgency operations conducted by Soviet state security and military forces against armed

[23] G. V. Kireev, *Rossiya-Kitai: Neizvestnye stranitsy pogranichnykh peregovorov* (Moscow: ROSSPEN, 2006), pp. 94–107; and Zhong gong zhong yang wen xian yan jiu shi bian, *Zhou Enlai nian pu, 1949–1976*, 3 vols. (Beijing: Zhong gong zhong yang wen xian chu ban she, 1997), vol. 3, pp. 1082–1084. See also the two sets of firsthand recollections of the longtime Soviet envoy in China, Aleksei Elizavetin, in "Peregovory A. N. Kosygina i Chzhou Enlaya v Pekinskom aeroportu," *Problemy Dal'nego vostoka* (Moscow), No. 1 (January–February 1993): 36–63, esp. 54–62, and in "Trudnye gody v Kitae," in *Diplomaty vspominayut: Mir glazami veteranov diplomaticheskoi sluzhby*, ed. P. P. Petrik (Moscow: Nauchnaya kniga, 1997), pp. 357–377, esp. 368–373.

[24] Marcus J. Dolder, "International Standards of Protection versus the Effects of Two Decades of War on the Afghan People," *Refugee Survey Quarterly* 19, no. 2 (2000): 128–131.

resistance groups in western Ukraine, western Belarus, and the three Baltic states (Lithuania, Latvia, Estonia) from the mid-1940s through the mid-1950s were on a much larger scale than some internal conflicts in later years in which Common Article 3 and Additional Protocol II were deemed applicable. In all these regions, particularly western Ukraine and Lithuania, Soviet troops resorted to systematic torture (especially prior to Joseph Stalin's death in March 1953), mass reprisals, and indiscriminate violence and destruction of villages and other residential areas.[25] Tens of thousands of civilians (as well as thousands of insurgents) were killed, and vast numbers suffered injuries, torture, and other abuse. Not until the mid-1950s were the insurgent groups annihilated once and for all.

Deployments of Soviet military and state security forces for domestic crackdowns after Stalin's death were of a much smaller magnitude. Even though Soviet troops behaved brutally on some occasions—in Georgia in March 1956, Novocherkassk in June 1962, and Georgia in April 1989, among other instances—these abuses did not come within the purview of Common Article 3 of the conventions or Article 1 of Additional Protocol II, both of which specifically do "not apply to internal disturbances and tensions."[26] The largest number of casualties occurred during a Soviet army incursion into Azerbaijan in January 1990, when at least 140 civilians were killed and more than 720 were wounded.[27] Yet even that operation, which was intended to crush the Azerbaijani Popular Front, would probably not have qualified as the sort of noninternational armed conflict envisaged in Common Article 3 or in Additional Protocol II. That said, if the Soviet Union had lasted for several more years (or longer), Common Article 3 and Additional Protocol II might eventually have become relevant. As concerns mounted in official circles in Moscow at the end of the 1980s and early 1990s that Soviet troops might soon have to be used against large-scale separatist movements (especially in the Caucasus) or other rebellious groups, the prospect

[25] Yuri Zhukov, "Examining the Authoritarian Model of Counter-insurgency: The Soviet Campaign against the Ukrainian Insurgent Army," *Small Wars and Insurgencies* 18, no. 3 (September 2007): 439–466.

[26] On the instances of "mass disturbances" and subsequent crackdowns in the USSR from 1953 on, see V. A. Kozlov, *Massovye besporyadki v SSSR pri Khrushcheve i Brezhneve, 1953-nachalo 1980-kh* (Novosibirsk: Sibir'skii khronograf, 1999). Kozlov, the deputy director of the State Archive of the Russian Federation, had full access to documents on this topic (including some documents that are off-limits to scholars), but his book focuses almost entirely on the 1950s and early 1960s and offers only a superficial discussion of later years.

[27] For data on casualties, see the section on the Soviet Union in US Department of State, *Country Reports on Human Rights Practices, 1990* (Washington, DC: US Government Printing Office, February 1991), p. 521. The figure of "at least 140" dead comes from a highly classified CIA analysis of the operation, "USSR: Prospects for an Insurgency in Azerbaijan," in CIA, *A Compendium of Recent Insurgency Analyses*, GI 90-10043 (Secret), August 1990, p. 5. Limited portions of this study were declassified in 1999 and made available via the CIA's online reading room (www.foia.cia.gov).

of an internal armed conflict that would fall within the scope of Common Article 3 and Additional Protocol II seemed distinctly plausible. Hence, Yazov's signature of Directive No. 75 was not an insignificant or purely symbolic act. The behind-the-scenes debate that preceded the directive indicated that Soviet military and security commanders were worried about "having [their] hands tied" during future domestic contingencies.

The Shift into the Post-Soviet Era

As noted earlier, the government of the Russian Federation inherited the Soviet Union's obligations under the Geneva Conventions and Additional Protocols. The main guidelines on IHL compiled by the Russian Defense Ministry affirm that the Russian Federation, as the legal successor to the Soviet Union, is a participant in nearly all protocols of IHL. Thus, the norms and principles of the law of armed conflicts are obligatory for all categories of service personnel to fulfill when undertaking combat operations and when carrying out peacekeeping missions. Consequently, every serviceman must know them.[28]

Paragraph 4 of Article 15 of the Russian Constitution states: "The universally recognized norms of international law and the international treaties and agreements of the Russian Federation shall be a component part of [the country's] legal system. If an international treaty or agreement of the Russian Federation fixes rules other than those envisaged by law, the rules of the international agreement shall be applied."[29] In principle, this formulation establishes the Geneva Conventions and Additional Protocols as Russian law.

By the time the Russian constitution was adopted in December 1993, the Russian government had taken significant steps toward integrating the Geneva Conventions and Additional Protocols into the new, post-Soviet polity. In 1992 the ICRC was allowed (indeed encouraged) to open a branch in Moscow, something that had never been permitted during the Soviet era. In the spring of 1993, the ICRC also opened a regional office in the North Caucasus, headquartered in Nal'chik (the capital of Kabardino-Balkaria), which during both of the Chechen wars was responsible for "running a major humanitarian operation comprising both protection and assistance programs for the vulnerable populations affected by the conflict in Chechnya" and for "the promotion of [IHL]."[30]

[28] Russian Ministry of Defense, *Normy mezhdunarodnogo gumanitarnogo prava pri vedenii boevykh deistvii*, Moscow, June 2009.

[29] "Konstitutsiya Rossiiskoi Federatsii, prinyata vsenarodnym golosovaniem 12 dekabrya 1993 goda," in *Zakonodatel'nye akty Rossiiskoi Federatsii* (Moscow: Yuridicheskaya literatura, 2008), vol. 2, p. 71.

[30] ICRC, *ICRC Annual Report 2009* (Geneva: ICRC, May 2010), p. 283.

The Wars in Chechnya

The legal steps adopted by the Russian government in 1992–1993 were important, but they had no effect on Russia's conduct in either of the wars it fought in Chechnya after the breakup of the Soviet Union—the first lasting from December 1994 to August 1996 and the second lasting from October 1999 through late 2006. At the start of the first war, the Russian authorities ordered the armed forces to "use all means at the state's disposal . . . to ensure state security, legality, civil rights and liberties, and the protection of public order; to combat crime; and to disarm all illegal armed formations" in Chechnya and adjacent areas of the North Caucasus. But during that war and again in the second war, the Russian government consistently argued that the violence was not a sustained insurgency and did not rise to the level of a "non-international armed conflict" covered by Common Article 3 and Additional Protocol II. Official rejection of the Geneva Conventions' relevance was reflected in the conduct of the war, which entailed widespread atrocities against combatants and civilians alike.

Denying the Conventions' Applicability

The government's argument for the irrelevance of the Geneva Conventions came under legal challenge in 1995 from two groups of deputies in the Russian parliament who contended that the Russian government was violating its international legal obligations by failing to apply the Geneva Conventions to the situation in Chechnya. Apparently, this was "the first time a national court [had] been called upon to scrutinize compliance by a state's armed forces with international rules concerning the protection of civilians and the conduct of hostilities during an armed conflict."[31] On 31 July 1995 the Russian Constitutional Court issued a mixed ruling.[32] On the one hand, the court ruled that the war came within the scope of Additional Protocol II and that Russian federal forces had violated the terms of the protocol. On the other hand, the court stipulated that the Russian government and armed forces had not been obliged to comply with Additional Protocol II because the protocol had not been duly incorporated into the Russian legal system. Although the Russian government did not accept that IHL was applicable to the war, the ruling overall gave the government precisely

[31] Paola Gaeta, "The Armed Conflict in Chechnya before the Russian Constitutional Court," *European Journal of International Law* 7, no. 4 (1996): 564.

[32] "Postanovlenie Konstitutsionnogo Suda Rossiiskoi Federatsii," 31 July 1995, in *Sobranie zakonodatel'stva Rossiiskoi Federatsii*, no. 33 (1995), Art. 3424.

what it wanted: de facto authorization for federal forces in Chechnya to continue disregarding the Geneva Conventions and related documents.[33]

The Constitutional Court did not explain why it believed that the war fell within the scope of Additional Protocol II, nor did it explain why it did not invoke other IHL obligations that are self-executing and would not have to be implemented through legislation. Under Article 15 of the Russian Constitution, these obligations should have been binding on Russian federal forces, but the court made no mention of them. Nor has the court clarified the matter in subsequent years, allowing the impact of the July 1995 ruling to stand. Although the Russian Supreme Court issued a regulation in October 2003 that calls on lower courts to apply principles of international law, the Supreme Court itself has routinely ignored this regulation in subsequent cases brought before it, including those pertaining to atrocities by federal forces in Chechnya.[34]

The Russian government, for its part, has never deviated from the position it staked out in 1995, namely, that counterinsurgency operations in Chechnya do not fall within the scope of the Geneva Conventions or Additional Protocols or other IHL agreements. Standard Russian textbooks on IHL and the laws of war, especially those used in military academies and schools, do not cover Chechnya, except to note that the Geneva Conventions and other IHL documents do not pertain to Chechnya.[35] Russian military academies cover the Geneva Conventions and other IHL documents, but the curriculum on these topics specifically excludes any discussion of the "internal disturbances" in Chechnya. Instead, the IHL training is intended mainly for Russian commanders and troops assigned to international peacekeeping missions.[36] US officers who have worked with Russian peacekeeping units in the Balkans attest that the

[33] In the first fifteen years after the court's ruling, no legislative modifications needed to implement Additional Protocol II were even considered, much less adopted. See Bakhtiar Tuzmukhamedov, "Kak voevat' po pravilam?" *Nezavisimaya gazeta* (Moscow), 15 February 2010, p. 11.

[34] "Postanovlenie Plenuma Verkhovnogo Suda Rossiiskoi Federatsii ot 10 oktyabrya 2003 goda: O primenenii sudami obshchei yurisdiktsii obshchepriznannykh printsipov i norm mezhdunarodnogo prava i mezhdunarodnykh dogovorov Rossiiskoi Federatsii," in *Postanovleniya Plenuma Verkhovnogo Suda Rossiiskoi Federatsii*, vol. 43, item 5. On the court's subsequent activities, see Anton Burkov, "Russia and the European Court of Human Rights: Reform of the Court and of Russian Judicial Practice?" CEPS Commentary, Centre for European Policy Studies, May 2010.

[35] See, for example, Colonel V. A. Yablotskii, *Mezhdunarodnoe gumanitarnoe pravo v bloke gumnitarnykh distsiplin: Uchebnoe posobie dlya vuzov sukhoputnykh voisk* (Kazan': Institut gosudarstva i prava, 2005), p. 115.

[36] "Obshchestvenno-gosudarstvennaya podgotovka: Zakony voiny—v zakonakh," *Soldat Otechestva* (Moscow), 10 June 2000, p. 6, along with other articles published under the rubric "Mezhdunarodnoe zakonodatel'stvo o pravovom polozhenii uchastnikov boevykh deistvii v mirotvorcheskikh operatsii."

Russian forces have generally been well versed in the Geneva Conventions and are usually given copies of relevant IHL materials.[37]

The situation with Russian soldiers sent to Chechnya from 1994 through 2007 was entirely different. Because the Russian government's official position during both wars was that the fighting in Chechnya was not covered by IHL, troops from the Russian army and the Russian MVD deployed in Chechnya were not given any training in the Geneva Conventions and were regularly given assignments that contravened basic principles of IHL (and even Russian domestic law). Many of the commanding officers from the Russian army who were stationed in Chechnya were aware of the Geneva Conventions, and some commanders understood the provisions thoroughly, but none of them felt under any obligation to comply with the conventions or associated documents. A colonel serving with the 42nd Motorized Rifle Division observed in July 2006 that "these sorts of international agreements [the Geneva Conventions] do not apply here, not at all. We're dealing with terrorists. It's out of the question. This is a counterterrorist operation."[38]

Troops from the Russian MVD—the agency that officially oversaw all operations in Chechnya from September 2003 to April 2009—were given no training at all in the Geneva Conventions or other IHL documents. Neither the main academy of the MVD (Moskovskaya Akademiya MVD) in Moscow nor any of the ministry's regional schools and academies cover IHL, and the standard textbooks used at the academies refer only to Russian domestic law, not to the Geneva Conventions or Additional Protocols. A whole chapter of the main textbook focuses on the Federal Law on Combating Terrorism (passed originally in 1998 and periodically amended since then), but it does not link it in any way to IHL. When asked in late 2007 why the MVD has never offered any training in the Geneva Conventions to its soldiers before sending them to Chechnya, an MVD lieutenant colonel who had been in Chechnya on three different tours seemed puzzled by the question. "We are in charge of a counterterrorist operation; this is not an international war." When he was then asked specifically about Common Article 3 and Additional Protocol II and whether the fighting in Chechnya at any point would have qualified as an "armed conflict not of an international character," he replied negatively: "This is not a civil war. It is not a civil war. In a civil war you have two competing centers of power. We are fighting isolated bands of terrorists, not a civil war."[39]

[37] Interview with Brigadier General (ret.) Kevin Ryan, former US military liaison with Russian peacekeeping units in the Balkans, in Cambridge, Massachusetts, 25 March 2009.

[38] Author's interview with Colonel Gennadii Sleznyak in Gudermes, Chechnya, 28 July 2006.

[39] Author's interview.

These frequent characterizations of the Chechen wars as "counterterrorist operations" outside the auspices of IHL rather than as "armed conflicts" were in line with official policy. In response to ICRC queries in late 1994 and early 1995, the Russian government formally notified the international body that it did "not regard the current operation as coming under the auspices" of IHL because it was "only a limited operation to cope with an internal disorder and to combat terrorists." That position remained unchanged throughout the first war, and essentially the same position was adopted at the start of the second war.[40] The Russian authorities did acknowledge in early 2000 that the "counterterrorist operation" in the second war had begun with a "military phase," but they expressly denied that this meant the operation should be governed by IHL. The Russian Defense Ministry, which was in charge of the "counterterrorist operation" during the first year-and-a-half (before yielding command to the Federal Security Service), consistently stuck by its finding that the fighting in Chechnya was no more than an "internal disturbance" unaffected by IHL.[41]

During both wars, Russian human rights activists and a few Russian international legal specialists disputed the Russian government's position. In June 2000, for example, a professor of law at the Russian Academy of Military Sciences, Captain Vladimir Galitskii, argued that "the events in Chechnya [during both wars] should be classified as an internal armed conflict, in the course of which it is obligatory to adopt Article 3, common to all four Geneva Conventions from 12 August 1949, and Protocol II from 8 June 1977 in its entirety."[42] This view, however, made no headway within the Russian government or military establishment. Galitskii complained, "Unfortunately, many in Russian state, political, and military circles do not always correctly understand the essence of the laws of armed conflict." Whether because of a lack of "correct understanding" or for other reasons, the Russian government rejected Galitskii's position and felt under no obligation in Chechnya to comply with the provisions of the Geneva Conventions.

[40] Valeriya Sycheva, "Rossiyu obvinili v narushenii Zhenevskoi konventsii," *Segodnya* (Moscow), 10 November 1999, p. 1.

[41] Sergei Batyushkin, "K mandatu—S pochteniem: Mezhdunarodnoe voennoe pravo, znat' i soblyudat'," *Armeiskii sbornik* (Moscow), no. 6 (June 2003): 14–17.

[42] Vladimir Galitskii, "Voina v pravovom vakuume: Zakony—ne pomekha, a pomoshch' v bor'be s 'vnutrennim vragom,'" *Nezavisimoe voennoe obozrenie*, No. 21 (16 June 2000), cited in Matthew Evangelista, *The Chechen Wars: Will Russia Go the Way of the Soviet Union?* (Washington, DC: Brookings Institution Press, 2002), pp. 141–142.

Consequences and Lack of Accountability

Throughout the two wars, atrocities were committed by both sides at the expense of civilians.[43] Russian troops engaged in systematic abuses of noncombatants, including torture, rape, forced disappearances, mass roundups (*zachistki*), kidnapping, and summary executions. Far from seeking to rectify these abuses, commanding officers frequently condoned them or at least turned a blind eye. The Chechen guerrillas, for their part, often used civilians as human shields and resorted to grisly revenge attacks against suspected collaborators. Both the Russian troops and the Chechen guerrillas also engaged in kidnapping for ransom.

During the first Russian-Chechen war, the abuses committed by Russian forces were often ignored but occasionally did provoke a public outcry. Reports broadcast by the independent NTV station that were highly critical of official policy helped to focus public sentiment in Russia against the conflict. During the second war, President Vladimir Putin reimposed state control of television (not least NTV) and ensured that all coverage was compatible with official aims. When Russian news programs during the second war referred to Chechnya, they dwelt solely on the invidious deeds of Chechen "bandits" and "terrorists." No atrocities by Russian federal forces were ever mentioned. Instead, television stations broadcast dramatic series featuring the heroic exploits of Russian troops in Chechnya and the reconstruction undertaken first by Ahmad Kadyrov and then by his son, Ramzan. Although the Russian press was less subject to state interference, the large majority of Russian citizens received all or most of their information about Chechnya from television. Most of the time, the subject was kept off the air entirely.

Moreover, even print journalists in Russia who tried to cover the abuses committed by Russian troops in Chechnya came under great pressure from the government, which closed down several newspapers that it deemed "unacceptably hostile" for reporting on such abuses. The government also orchestrated the beating or intimidation of outspoken reporters who reported candidly on the situation in Chechnya. Among the victims were Andrei Babitskii and Anna Politkovskaya, who was assassinated in late 2006. Russian officials often physically prevented "undesirable" journalists (including Babitskii and Politkovskaya) from traveling to Chechnya. Even if the government did not restrict access,

[43] The literature on this topic is enormous, including dozens of thorough reports by Memorial, Human Rights Watch, Amnesty International, the International Refuges Council, and many other organizations. For vivid on-scene accounts, see Anna Politkovskaya's books about Chechnya, including: *A Small Corner of Hell: Dispatches from Chechnya*, trans. Alexander Burry and Tatiana Tulchinsky (Chicago: University of Chicago Press, 2003); and *A Russian Diary: A Journalist's Final Account of Life, Corruption, and Death in Putin's Russia*, trans. Arch Tait (New York: Random House, 2007).

reporters were aware that a visit to Chechnya would place them in constant danger from rebel forces and criminal gangs. As a result, newspaper coverage often relied solely on information provided by federal commanders, who never mentioned anything that would be construed as a violation of the Geneva Conventions. All of these factors enabled the Russian government to mold public perceptions of the conflict.

Another reason for the lack of any accountability in Russia for the failure to comply with the Geneva Conventions was Putin's success in undermining opposition parties and political competition in Russia. During the first Russian-Chechen war, some of the strongest criticism of Russian atrocities came from opposition party leaders in the Russian parliament and from Yeltsin's rivals in the 1996 presidential election. During the second war, by contrast, Putin brought the parliament under his control and used his high popularity ratings and leverage with the media (especially television) to eviscerate the two parties that embraced Western-style liberal democracy. He also increasingly marginalized all other political organizations that posed even the slightest challenge to his own power or challenged the conduct of the Chechen war. The result was that the continuing bloodshed in Chechnya almost never came onto the political agenda. Only one of Putin's rivals in the 2004 Russian presidential campaign, Ivan Rybkin, dared to raise the issue at all, and he was quickly forced to drop it after coming under vehement attack from Putin's spokesmen and aides.[44] A few members of the Russian parliament (mostly from the Union of Right Forces and from Yabloko) occasionally raised pointed questions about the conduct of the war and the abuses committed by Russian forces, but no parliamentary committee ever held hearings on the conflict. Nor was any parliamentary or independent commission set up to examine the conduct of the war.

In the absence of genuine political debate about the role of IHL in the Russian-Chechen war, a grassroots movement to hold the authorities responsible for violations of the Geneva Conventions was a nonstarter. Some Russian and international NGOs, such as Memorial, Human Rights Watch, and Amnesty International, published many critical reports about the rampant torture, killing, and other abuses perpetrated by both sides in Chechnya, but these reports were consistently ignored by the Russian government, which felt under no obligation to punish war crimes and abuses committed during the second war. On the few rare occasions when Russian soldiers were prosecuted for having committed serious crimes in Chechnya, they were charged solely under domestic law. Despite the Russian Supreme Court's regulation of October 2003, not a single

[44] See Jonathan Steele, "I was kidnapped, Says Putin Election Rival," *The Guardian*, 13 February 2004.

prosecution was brought that made even a passing reference to the Geneva Conventions or other IHL provisions. In practical terms, then, the Russian government's effort to exclude Chechnya from the purview of IHL proved highly successful during both wars.

Prospects

Russia's failure to abide by the central provisions of IHL during the wars in Chechnya foreshadows what might happen if large-scale fighting flares up again in the North Caucasus—a scenario that seems distinctly plausible in light of the ongoing instability in Ingushetia and Dagestan (both of which have become havens for former Chechen fighters, who also might seek to resume guerrilla warfare in Chechnya). Concern about Russia's adherence to the Geneva Conventions in international armed conflicts is also warranted, given Russian interference in and annexation of the Crimean region of Ukraine and the involvement of Russian military forces elsewhere in the country. Russia's military involvement in the conflict in Syria has raised additional concerns about the country's adherence to the law, with well-documented attacks against civilian objects, including hospitals and groups of fleeing refugees, and indiscriminate bombing of population centers. Many of the practices echo the worst abuses of the wars in Chechnya.

The only bright spot in the picture regards not the Geneva Conventions but the European Convention on Human Rights (ECHR). As of August 2016, the European Court of Human Rights (ECtHR) "has delivered more than 250 judgments finding violations of the Convention in connection with the armed conflict in the Chechen Republic of the Russian Federation. About 60% of the applications concern enforced disappearances; other issues include killing and injuries to civilians, destruction of homes and property, indiscriminate use of force, use of landmines, illegal detention, torture and inhuman conditions of detention."[45] The court held the Russian government and security forces accountable for such extrajudicial killings, torture, and forced disappearances. In numerous cases, the ECtHR also ruled that Russia, by withholding key documents and other material evidence, had failed to live up to its obligation as a member of the European Council to "provide all necessary facilities" to the court to assist consideration of a case. The Russian government has repeatedly criticized the court and alleged

[45] European Court of Human Rights, *Fact Sheet—Armed Conflicts*, August 2016, http://echr.coe.int/Documents/FS_Armed_conflicts_ENG.pdf; Freek van der Vet, "Seeking Life, Finding Justice: Russian NGO Litigation and Chechen Disappearances before the European Court of Human Rights," *Human Rights Review* 13, no. 3 (September 2012), 303–325.

that it is biased, but the rulings clearly have been embarrassing for the Russian authorities, and indeed the Russian government has consistently provided the designated compensation to the plaintiffs. Although these cases were treated as transgressions of human rights law (specifically the ECHR) rather than of IHL, the line between the two was blurred in this instance, as elsewhere.[46] All of the abuses occurred that during the 1999–2006 war could therefore just as easily fall under the Geneva Conventions.

Heartening though the role of the ECtHR in these cases may be, the results do not seem likely to foster greater compliance on the part of the Russian government with the basic norms of IHL. In July 2008 the president of the Federation of Human Rights, Souhayr Belhassen, argued, "Today the European Court of Human Rights is the only hope Chechen victims and their families have for justice. Russia has an obligation to comply with the European Court rulings by carrying out meaningful investigations. But none of the investigations it has opened since the rulings has been credible, nor has the government addressed the underlying causes of the abuses."[47] Tanya Lokshina of the Russian branch of Human Rights Watch similarly noted that the Russian government "has not meaningfully implemented the core of the [ECtHR's] rulings: It has not taken sufficient steps to ensure effective investigations, hold perpetrators accountable, or prevent similar violations from recurring in the future."[48]

Short of greater high-level and public "demand" in Russia for compliance with the Geneva Conventions and Additional Protocols, the Russian army and security forces are unlikely to abide by IHL in future conflicts in the North Caucasus. Moreover, given concerns that Russia's actions vis-à-vis Ukraine starting in February 2014 violate even more central provisions of international law—such as the UN Charter's prohibition on the use of armed force except in self-defense—Russia's compliance with the laws of war will remain in doubt. Regarding internalization of Geneva norms, the Russian case must be judged a failure.

[46] William Abresch, "A Human Rights Law of Internal Armed Conflict: The European Court of Human Rights in Chechnya," *European Journal of International Law* 16, no. 4 (2005): 741–767.

[47] Human Rights Watch, "Chechnya: European Court Last Hope for Victims," 9 June 2008, http://www.hrw.org/news/2008/06/08/chechnya-european-court-last-hope-victims.

[48] "Doklad Tat'yany Lokshinoi, issledovatelya Kh'yuman Raits Votch po Rossii," 19 May 2010, report prepared for meeting with Russian President Dmitrii Medvedev and various Russian human rights activists who work in the North Caucasus.

8

The Application of International Humanitarian Law by the Israel Defense Forces

A Legal and Organizational Analysis

AMICHAI COHEN AND EYAL BEN-ARI

Introduction

Nina Tannenwald contends that the laws of war are one of the few bulwarks, however fragile, against the unrestrained violence of states.[1] Her argument centers on the tension between the uses of organized state violence and the discourses and practices restraining them. Indeed, the very expertise of the military (along with other security forces) as bearer of the legitimate (if sometimes contested) use of organized violence has always been subject to a host of limiting factors.[2] Armed conflict is not conducted in a social vacuum but is an intensely social activity that will severely affect the conduct of war and the formation and running of military establishments. The culture, social values, beliefs and ideology prevalent within a society will determine both tactics and strategy in war;

[1] Nina Tannenwald, "Introduction: Assessing the Effects and Effectiveness of the Geneva Conventions," in this volume.

[2] Eyal Ben-Ari, "Between Violence and Restraint: Human Rights, Humanitarian Consequences and the Israeli Military in the Al-Aqsa Intifada," in *The Moral Dimension of Asymmetrical Warfare: Counter-Terrorism, Democratic Values and Military Ethics*, ed. Ted van Baarda and Desirée Verweij (Amsterdam: Martinus Nijhoff, 2009); Bernard Boene, "How Unique Should the Military Be? A Review of Representative Literature and Outline of Synthetic Formulation," *European Journal of Sociology* 31, no. 1 (1990): 3–59.

those who can or cannot join the military; what tasks and functions they will carry out and what ends are pursued in war.[3]

A number of important interrelated processes restraining military action have developed over the past two decades. From our perspective the most important is the emergence of what may be called a global human rights regime: comprising networks of governmental, intergovernmental, and civil society groups that work by circulating information, forcing transparency, putting pressure on specific states, and very often mobilizing protest through electronic means. This human rights regime has become increasingly entrenched "at a global level in international declarations, conventions, and agreements that are negotiated, implemented and monitored by national, international and transnational institutions."[4] As Merry explains, this development is part of a longer move taking place over the past fifty years: transnational organizations and innumerable non-governmental organizations (NGOs) have created a new legal order through transnational processes of information gathering, conferences and discussions under the auspices of the UN and regional bodies, and so forth. Conventions, treaties, and implementation systems are created by international teams, then ratified by states, which assume responsibility for enforcing them, with some monitoring by a global body. Even though the human rights system lacks the sanctioning power of state law, its expansion and elaboration creates new discursive legal space within the global arena.[5]

A central implication of the expansion of the global human rights regime has been the increasing intrusion of judicial considerations into various sectors of societies including the military. Thus in many of the armed forces of the industrial democracies, there is an increasing "juridification" of the military sphere.[6]

In this chapter then, we analyze how the increasing juridification of the military and specifically the demands to apply international humanitarian law (IHL) have impacted the Israel Defense Forces (IDF). Indeed, Israel is a fitting case for the study of the implementation of IHL, because Israel is a liberal democracy marked by political institution, courts, and a free media that allow

[3] James Dingley, "War, The Military, and Sociology," in *Eight Essays in Contemporary War Essays*, ed. Magnus Christiansson (Stockholm: Military Academy Karlberg Acta Politica II, 2007), pp. 193–226, at p. 196.

[4] Jane K. Cowan, Marie-Benedicte Dembour, and Richard A. Wilson, "Introduction," in *Culture and Rights: Anthropological Perspectives*, ed. Jane K. Cowan, Marie-Benedicte Dembour, and Richard A. Wilson (Cambridge: Cambridge University Press, 2001), pp. 1–16, at p. 12.

[5] Sally Engle Merry, "Changing Rights, Changing Culture," in Cowan, Dembour, and Wilson, *Culture and Rights: Anthropological Perspectives*, pp. 31–55, at p. 35.

[6] Gerry R. Rubin, "United Kingdom Military Law: Autonomy, Civilianization, Juridification," *Modern Law Review* 65 (2002): 36–57.

relatively free access to decision-makers and decision-making processes. Yet the prolonged occupation of the territories coupled with constant armed conflicts allow a sophisticated assessment of Israel's relationship with IHL and its development over time. As in other countries, the past decades have seen the relatively autonomous sphere of the military increasingly come under judicial overview. In Israel this has meant the adjudication of the civilian courts in such matters as the official formulation inscribed on the graves of soldiers, cases of sexual harassment brought against officers, or violations of environmental laws.

From our perspective, juridification has also involved the IDF's compliance with IHL and other legal frameworks. In order to analyze this compliance our discussion is structured in four sections: First we offer a general multilevel and multidimensional model of military compliance; second an analysis of the external role of IHL in Israel, describing the law and the institutions external to the military that are involved in applying it; third a description of the role of the operational legal advisors in the IDF that deal mainly with operational command; and fourth, a discussion of the ceremonies intended to promote compliance with IHL involving soldiers and junior officers.

A note on methodology: This article is based on work carried out by the two authors, who have been involved in research regarding the legal and organizational aspects of military actions in Israel. The second author carried out interviews with four Israeli academic experts in IHL, four interviews with members of NGOs, and numerous interviews with troops and commanders related to the Second Intifada.[7] In addition, we have had numerous off-the-record conversations with members of the IDF's Military Advocate General (MAG) and reviewed a plethora of newspaper articles, reports of NGOs, and secondary material.

Compliance and the Israel Defense Forces: A Descriptive Model

The compliance of Israel (indeed of any nation) with IHL cannot be viewed as a question to which a simple answer can be given. First, there is the question of metrics—how does one measure compliance? Because there is no simple binary answer to this question except in extreme cases, the answer necessarily involves a spectrum along which different norms achieve different degrees of compliance on different levels of decisions and actions. Concretely, we view compliance as

[7] Eyal Ben-Ari, Zev Lehrer, Uzi Ben-Shalom, and Ariel Vainer, *Rethinking Contemporary Warfare: A Sociological View of the Al-Aqsa Intifada* (Albany: State University of New York Press, 2010).

Table 8.1 **Levels of Decision-Making**

Tactical: soldiers, junior officers	Operational: Mid–high level officers	Policy: Supreme Military and Civilian Command

arranged along an axis, from lower levels involving tactical decisions of specific soldiers or junior officers, through operational decisions of mid- to upper-level military commanders, ending with policy decisions of the supreme command and the civilian masters of the military (Table 8.1). At each level, the sources of and solutions to noncompliance are different.

High-Level Command and Civilian Decision-Makers

There are many reasons why high-level military and civilian political leadership give orders that violate IHL. Compliance or noncompliance at this level is not an issue of knowledge, but of politics. For various reasons, the analysis of which is outside the scope of this research, political leaders make informed decisions to violate IHL, just as they may decide to violate other norms of international or domestic law.[8] Hence, at this level compliance with IHL is based on the pressure formal and informal institutions, movements, or organizations apply to decision-makers. Hence both domestic and international institutions have recently directed their attention toward reviewing *military policies* for their conformity with IHL. This is done mainly through applying law and legal institutions. We call it "law as power," because law is used here as creating counterpressure to other forms of power.

Soldiers and Low-Level Officers

Sources of noncompliance at the low level of soldiers and officers derive from several sources. First, at this level most soldiers do not speak about compliance with IHL. They speak about their interaction with the enemy on a day-to-day basis and their fear of terrorist attacks directed at them; they are influenced by factors such as the orders of their immediate commanders and the culture of

[8] Jack L. Goldsmith and Eric A. Posner, *The Limits of International Law* (Oxford: Oxford University Press, 2005).

Table 8.2 **Sources of Noncompliance**

	Soldiers	*Mid- to High-Level Officers*	*Supreme Military and Civilian Command*
Sources of noncompliance	personal interest, peer pressure, unit culture	intrinsic military problem, tunnel vision, immediate military interest	state interest, political preferences

the specific unit within which they serve. Hence, noncompliance at this level should be seen not as resulting from intentional noncompliance with IHL, but as a reflection of unit culture or norms of control that may promote disrespect for adversaries' life and possessions and from the personal views of soldiers that may derive from political backgrounds.

Mid-Level Officers and Operational Command

A more complex case is the case of mid-level and operational command officers. Here, we would expect the officers to have some knowledge of IHL and an understanding of the strategic effects of this law. Yet, reasons for noncompliance with IHL here are not due to an informed decision not to respect IHL, but rather because of institutional motivations: the need to win, the incentives to make the operation successful. Because this is an institutional problem, it can be dealt with through institutional means.

At each level different factors play a role, and each of the categories results in a different level of compliance (Table 8.2). This chapter proceeds in the following way: It first describes the different factors and actors affecting compliance with IHL, and following that tries to determine how each factor affects compliance at each level.

The Civic Legal Front—The Status of International Law in Israeli Law

The formal status of international law in domestic Israeli law has remained unchanged since Israel became an independent state in 1948. Basically, Israel follows the rules of the British legal tradition, which differentiates between treaty (or conventional) international law and customary international law. Israel has adopted a dualistic system with respect to the adoption of international treaty (or conventional) law: While the formal authority to ratify international law resides with the Israeli government, treaty ratification does not turn the international obligation into domestic law. International obligations are not enforceable in domestic courts unless and until the relevant treaty has been formally "incorporated," usually by the enactment of domestic legislation expressly accepting the international obligation into domestic law. In other words, there exists a "double barrier" to the enforcement of international law: Not only does international law require ratification by the Israeli government but also it must be internalized by the Parliament—the Knesset.

Customary international law, by contrast, possesses a much stronger status in domestic Israeli law. By definition, it obligates Israel on the international plane. More to the point, it automatically becomes part of domestic Israeli law, without requiring further action by any Israeli institution. Hence, customary international law is enforced by domestic courts without need for any action by the Knesset.[9]

The Geneva Conventions in Israeli Law

Since 1951 Israel has been a party to the Geneva conventions of 1949, which are therefore binding on the country. However, Israel is not party to the Additional Protocols to the Geneva Convention of 1977. Hence, obligations included in the protocols are binding only as far as they are considered customary international law. Moreover, even formally, the question of Israel's adherence to the Geneva Conventions, IHL, and laws of armed conflict in general is very complicated.

First, Israel has not incorporated the Geneva Conventions, that is, there is no specific Israeli law enacting them into domestic legislation. Contrary to common practice in many Western democracies, Israel possesses no "War Crimes Act." Likewise, the Geneva Conventions were not incorporated per se into the Military Justice Act (though naturally many of the norms appearing in this statute are parallel to the ones enumerated in the Geneva Conventions. As explained, Israeli dualistic doctrine required *incorporation* (enactment of the international treaty by domestic legislation) as a condition for judicial application of international treaty law—a problem not existing with regard to any international norms considered *customary international law* (automatically considered part of Israeli domestic legal system). With regard to IHL—the Hague regulations (1907) were considered customary international law.

Second, there is one instance in which Israel has constantly confronted the question of its obligation to international law and that is the application of the

[9] For descriptions and explanations of the Israeli system see David Kretzmer, *The Occupation of Justice: The Supreme Court of Israel and the Occupied Territories* (Albany: SUNY Press, 2002).

laws of occupation included in the Hague regulations (1907) and the Fourth Geneva Conventions (GC IV). Since June 1967, when it first occupied the territories, Israel has publicly claimed that the territories should not be considered occupied according to international law, since they never had any legitimate sovereign: Jordan (in the West Bank) and Egypt (in the Gaza strip) were not considered by most nations to be the legitimate sovereigns of the territories they controlled. Hence, Israel's claim was that the territories were "administered" by Israel.

As a result, Israel accepted the applicability to them of the Hague regulations of 1907, but has denied the applicability of the laws of occupation included in the GC IV. The formal explanation for this seemingly bizarre legal position lies in the different semantic definitions of "occupation" in article 2 of the GC IV, and article 42 of the Hague regulations. One of us has previously suggested that the real explanation lies in the different norms included in these two treaties. Those specified in the Hague regulations seemed to be much more in line with what Israel actually thought it should be doing in the territories.[10] Even so, on several occasions Israel has declared that although it does not view itself as bound by the GC IV regarding the occupied territories, it nevertheless will act in accordance with all "humanitarian" provisions of this treaty. It is not exactly clear what this declaration is intended to exclude, since the Geneva Conventions deal only in humanitarian provisions. These declarations were intended to denote that Israel does not accept any limit on the establishment of settlements, which appear to be forbidden by article 49 of GC IV.

Application of the Geneva Conventions by the Israeli Supreme Court

The Israeli Supreme Court has been central in applying the Geneva Conventions to the occupied territories. Almost immediately after the end of the 1967 war, the Court, sitting as the High Court of Justice, declared that it had authority to adjudicate appeals against actions of military authorities in the territories. These cases were brought with the implicit, and sometimes explicit, support of state lawyers who were looking for ways to reign in the military. During the course of over four decades of occupation, the Supreme Court has dealt with tens of thousands of cases relating to the territories, many of which were based on the international law of occupation. Until 2000, the court followed the lead of the government and based its decisions on the principles of the Hague regulations. This move was based on two arguments: First, that the position of the Israeli government is that the GC IV is not applicable, and second, that the GC IV was not

[10] Amichai Cohen, "Administering the Territories," *Israel Law Review* 37 (2005): 24–71.

incorporated into Israeli law. The Hague regulations, however, were considered customary international law and hence applicable in court. Moreover, during the first stage of occupation, until 1979, and even until 1999, the court usually approved IDF operations in the territories, even when examined against international norms included in the Geneva Conventions and the Hague Regulations. These decisions were heavily criticized, and an important commentator concluded, "In its decision relating to the Occupied Territories the court has rationalized virtually all controversial actions of the Israeli Authorities, especially those most problematic under principles of International Humanitarian Law."[11]

From 2000 a significant change occurred in the attitude of the Israeli Supreme Court. First, the court has expanded its jurisprudence to include application of the GC IV. In recent cases, the Court even based some decisions on the First Additional Protocol to the Geneva Conventions (which Israel, like the United States, is not party to), justifying its action on the grounds that some of the norms in this protocol are considered customary international law. The court never explained this change of heart. However, government lawyers seemed to support this move, and the claim that the GC IV is not customary international law became more and more improbable as the years passed and with the universal accession to this treaty.

Even more important, since 2000 several decisions have declared military *policies* void on the grounds that they are incompatible with IHL. One example is the cluster of Rafah decisions (declaring that the IDF should allow humanitarian aid into the Gaza strip even during the course of an ongoing military operation); a second is the targeted killing decision (allowing the use of targeted killing only if certain strict conditions are fulfilled) (H.C.J. 769/02); a third is the separation barrier decisions (redrawing the alignment of the separation barrier in many places due to IHL and human rights considerations) (H.C.J. 2056/04); and fourth is the neighbor policy decision (declaring illegal the IDF's use of neighbors and relatives to help in arresting wanted suspects in the territories) (H.C.J. 3799/02).[12]

While these decisions were mostly about applying the international law of occupation, since 2000 Israel has been involved in an armed conflict with the Palestinians, and the court has declared this clash to be subject to the international law of armed conflict, or IHL. In effect this assertion implies that it is an armed conflict, international or noninternational, between the parties, and in several cases the court applied the entire gamut of IHL. Actually, the Israeli Supreme Court may be the only judicial body in the world that has demonstrated a willingness to enforce IHL on the army *ex ante*, that is, before an action is taken, or

[11] Kretzmer, *The Occupation of Justice*, p. 197.

[12] Amichai Cohen, "The Supreme Court and the Arab Israeli Conflict: An International Law Perspective," *Kiryat Hamishpat* [*Ono Academic College Law Journal*] 6 (2006): 263–332 [in Hebrew].

even while a military operation is in progress.[13] This point does not imply that the court necessarily intervenes in every military operation, since nonintervention is still the norm. What can be said, however, is that the "shadow" of possible judicial intervention lies over almost every military operation undertaken, thus causing the IDF to constantly take IHL into account (a point we presently return to).

It should be noted that this judicial review is, by nature, limited and almost arbitrary, because the court is a reactive institution and is only involved in cases brought to it by applicants. Furthermore, judges are not impartial arbitrators in these cases but are part of Israeli society. Thus their decisions are inevitably affected by their perception of Israel as being a country subject to terror attacks and needing to protect itself against an especially vicious enemy. In addition, the Israeli Supreme Court has only rarely dealt with the application of IHL in the sense that criminal activities have taken place (that is, after the fact). We return to this point later.

Traditional scholarship has viewed the application of IHL by the Supreme Court mainly at the policy level. Though its decisions have certainly made a difference to national policies there are recurring, sometimes justified criticisms voiced in this regard. First, specific decisions have been criticized for their adherence to IHL. For example, the Court's decisions about the separation barrier have been viewed by the International Court of Justice as an incorrect interpretation of IHL. Similarly, the decisions of the Court approving measures Israel enforced with regard to the Gaza strip since 2006 has been forcefully criticized as an incorrect application of IHL.

Until a central authoritative institution is created in regard to international law, the question of whether the Supreme Court correctly applies IHL remains open. To our mind, the more important criticism of this method of application by the Court is that it is somewhat arbitrary and it cannot plausibly claim to be involved in each policy. Even though the Israeli Court is the most intrusive of any other domestic court with regard to the application of IHL, some institutional limitations still preclude it from dealing with all questions. Thus, the court consistently refused to deal with the issue of the settlements, branding it a political question. Similarly, the court sometimes refused to intervene when specific

[13] The Israeli Supreme Court sitting as the High Court of Justice is perhaps the most flexible court in the world in terms of accepting appeals. It actually has no "standing" limitation, and it very rarely uses such avoidance doctrines such as "political question" or "foreign affairs." Furthermore, access to the Israeli Supreme Court in appeals coming from the territories is even easier. The unique situation in the Palestinian-Israeli conflict, taking place very close to Israel's populated centers, the enormous number of NGOs dispersed all over the territories, the flexibility of the High Court of Justice, which allows almost direct access to Supreme Court justices around the clock, all amount to possibilities almost incomprehensible in other Western democracies.

operational decisions were taken, which seemed to the court to be within the sphere of expertise of the military.

The Israeli Supreme Court is not the only external institution acting in this area that includes an ever-growing network of NGOs and human rights organizations. These organizations, many of which are part of an international network or supported by international funding, have a distinct impact on the way international law is implemented in Israel. First, many of them work through petitions to the Israeli Supreme Court to change Israeli practices. Second, because they are part of an international network, they are able to garner international support and apply international pressure. One recent phenomenon has been the use of international fact-finding missions. The most famous is the United Nations Fact Finding Mission on the Gaza Conflict (the Goldstone Commission). In its report, released in September 2009, the commission severely criticized several of the policies of the IDF in Operation Cast Lead in the Gaza strip (December 2008–January 2009). When international criticism against Israeli military actions were raised with regard to the Flotilla incident of May 2010, Israel was quick to form its own special commission of inquiry, in order to fend off probable international pressure (the Turkle commission).

It is difficult to estimate the impact and effectiveness of these international pressures. Doubtless, some of the most egregious policies used in the past by Israel have been abandoned. Yet other harsh measures have been adopted and there is no assurance that the overall situation has not become worse. In addition, in an effort to counter the pressure applied by NGOs, some members of the Israeli political establishment, including the Knesset, have begun a campaign against them. In any case, these developments support our major contentions that these pressures are regarded by the Israeli government as part of the cost-benefit analysis of the interests involved.

The International Law Department of the Military Advocate General

The IDF has developed several institutional means for enforcing the rules of IHL in military activities. Especially noteworthy is DABLA, the Hebrew acronym for the International Law Division that is part of the MAG of the IDF. It is involved in advising military authorities on all matters of international law. An academic expert in IHL with some familiarity with the unit recounted its rapid growth: While twenty years ago the unit comprised about two to three people, it now has about twenty members. All of our commentators, moreover, mentioned that these officers were of an excellent quality (some have gone back to academia to do their PhDs or to join the ranks of universities as adjunct professors). In addition, during times of intense conflict—as in Operation Cast Lead[14]—reservists are also mobilized to help the regular officers. Currently the reservist unit of DABLA numbers approximately thirty lawyers. In relative terms this development makes DABLA the fastest-growing unit of the IDF, a fact that is especially remarkable given that overall the IDF has downsized and is indicative of the importance of judicial advice on IHL for the military.

The School for Military Law—another part of the MAG—is responsible for disseminating information about international law to the fighting units. The School is responsible for instructing only officers, which means that the members of the lower ranks do not usually receive any courses in IHL. Within the school, officers are taught the IDF's rules of military conduct, and carry with them "cards" on which those rules are printed. The basic military officers' course includes some fundamental training on IHL—an hour and half of classroom learning, and a further computer simulation that lasts for about another half a day. The most advanced course of IHL in the IDF involves officers trained to be battalion and brigade commanders, who receive a twenty-eight-hour course on IHL. There is very little training in the units after these initial courses.

Note, however, that a conscious decision was made not to provide these soldiers with instruction respecting the contents of the Geneva Conventions in basic officer training. While we have no official explanation of this move, as we shall see, there is an institutional logic in this move, to introduce IHL with its complex standards only to high-level commanders.

The unit of Legal Advisors in the Territories constitutes a special contingent that operates according to rules and regulations that are supposed to be commensurate with the international law of occupation. Its legal advisors are responsible for presenting to commanders the limits of military occupation based on this law. But by far the most important of these units for the day-to-day operation of fighting forces is DABLA, and consequently we take a closer look at it.

As the unit responsible for advising the military on aspects of international laws, and especially the laws of armed conflicts, during the past decade or so, DABLA has developed a system, called Legal Operational Counsel, whereby its representatives constitute part of every planning and decision-making process for operations. Like the legal counseling offered commanders around the world, this system implies that every operation undertaken by the IDF must include an assessment of IHL and endorsement by a DABLA representative.[15] Advice is provided on issues such as rules of engagement, the destruction of houses next

[14] *Yediot Aharanot*, 19 January 2009.

[15] *Haaretz*, 1 March 2001.

to outposts and roads, or temporary incursions into areas under Palestinian sovereignty.[16] However, the MAG now makes a distinction between legal advice given at the planning level (down to division level) and at execution, where the commanders are in the "heat" of battle.[17]

The impetus for integrating DABLA representatives in discussions of operational plans was, according to a retired colonel and former head of the unit, the change that occurred at the beginning of the Second Intifada. During this period, military actions in the territories moved from being centered on policing to much more intense forms related to low-intensity conflict. In addition, during that period international norms began to change and plans to establish the International Criminal Court were laid down. As he tells it:

> The commanders hear this and say, there is a court that I can find myself in. Where is my lawyer? It becomes natural for the military system to place a lawyer where he has not been before.[18]

Later actions of Israeli human rights movements such as Gush Shalom or Yesh Gevul demonstrate that the expectations of commanders were realistic, since these groups have systematically gathered evidence of war crimes and through transnational contacts led the opening of various investigations into IDF actions.[19] Several Israeli officers were prosecuted in different countries, and several have literally escaped being arrested in Western countries by sheer luck. In addition, there have been threats to arrest and indict former Chief of Staff Yaalon in New Zealand and former officer in command of the Southern Command Almog in Britain. This constant risk is definitely internalized by Israeli officers and legal advisors, and is constantly cited as a major impetus for the implementation of IHL, and adherence to it.

According to Riesner, the most dramatic change occurred when the military began to seek legal advice in regard to the assassination of Palestinians. As he recounts:

> In the first discussions of targeted preventions [*sikul memookad*] there was a very strange feeling. The officers didn't understand why lawyers were sitting in the room, what are they doing there. I would go there

[16] *Kol Hair*, 4 May 2001.

[17] *Haaretz*, 19 February 2009.

[18] *Haaretz*, 22 January 2009.

[19] Deena R. Hurwitz, "Universal Jurisdiction and the Dilemmas of International Criminal Justice: The Sabra and Shatila Case in Belgium," in *Human Rights Advocacy Stories*, ed. Hurwitz et al. (New York: Foundation Press, 2009), p. 267.

> myself; I was senior enough so that no one would tell me to leave. So it's like an enema, you have to do it with a lot of Vaseline and you have to give them the feeling that we have not come to take their place. With time interesting things happened, they learned to recognize all of the considerations and would repeat our mantras so often that we felt that we were redundant. We advised them so that they could make decisions without us.[20]

When asked if he had ever expressed complete opposition to the military's proposal, Reisner answered:

> There was a case when I told a senior officer: from this point and beyond it is illegal, and if you do that there is a high chance that I will have to open up a case against you. We cannot allow you to do this and he did not do it. The usual idea was that the lawyer sets out the boundaries. He clarifies to the commander what the red lines are and that beyond them he should not act and that all that happens beyond those lines is his responsibility. Because we are the military's lawyers, where it is gray [areas] we will try to defend.

More recently, especially in Operation Cast Lead (the IDF operation in the Gaza strip, January 2009), a DABLA representative was attached to every unit down to the divisional level and staffed their positions 24 hours a day. The aim of this move according to representatives of the MAG,

> was to link to the military from inside during planning and formulation [of plans]. When you create a bank of targets, when you plan a strike ahead of time there is time for legal advice but there are no lawyers at the level of running operations combat (*nihul hakerav*). When the pilot has three seconds to decide if he has to move the missile from the target because he has seen civilians, he doesn't have time for legal consultation. This decision he takes by himself.[21]

Although formally DABLA representatives possess only an advisory capacity, they claimed in interviews and public presentations that in Operation Cast Lead the IDF never took any action against their advice.

[20] *Haaretz*, 22 January 2009.

[21] *Yediot Aharonot*, 19 January 2009.

The Limitations of DABLA

The DABLA confronts a number of problems. First, within the IDF, DABLA representatives are considered the last word on international law. Most of their decisions and opinions are secret, and hence there exists very little external review of the substantive content of their decisions. For example, on several occasions during Operation Cast Lead the IDF claimed to have followed DABLA advice—as in bombing a graduation ceremony of Hamas police officers in Gaza, and targeting Hamas government institutions not connected to military actions such as the ministries of Education or the Interior—although it appears that its actions were at the very least questionable under IHL.

Second, DABLA officers are not specialists in international law. Most are young graduates of law faculties in Israeli institutions who usually receive training in a system allowing high school graduates to defer their compulsory military service until after acquiring a profession of military importance as medicine, engineering, or law. Under this system, upon graduating, military professionals are assigned to units in which they make use of their skills. This point means that all the graduates entering the MAG know about IHL is what they have been taught in Israeli law schools, which actually does not amount to much, since most Israeli law students take a basic introductory course in international law but only very few take an advanced course on IHL, and even fewer involve themselves with any advanced academic work in this subject. There is no rule by which DABLA, considered the most prestigious of MAG units, will accept only those who did advanced work in IHL. Even more striking is how DABLA recruits reservists to man advisory positions in wartime. One reservist we spoke to declared that he knew nothing about public international law before joining DABLA (he did not even take the relevant course at law school). As a result, most DABLA attorneys acquire the legal knowledge that they require while serving within the military, and this situation necessarily encourages them to follow earlier opinions voiced within the organization. While some DABLA officers undertake advanced degrees in IHL during later stages of their service, this work is done only after they have spent many years in DABLA, and have already become part of its institutional culture.

Third, as a number of observers told us, below the divisional level the IDF has encountered legal difficulties in regard to such issues as cover fire, booby-trapped houses, or destroying buildings. Since DABLA representatives are not involved in the operational decisions of small units, it is widely acknowledged that actions at such levels may contradict IHL or what DABLA representatives would have advised. As one longtime member of a human rights group told us, sometimes there is a disconnect between commanders (say at the brigade level) who are often very committed to professional conduct and the levels underneath them. This situation is exacerbated both by the boredom of the troops (with long hours, weeks on end on "ordinary" patrolling roadblock duty) and by the autonomy given lower levels in the IDF. One example was the use of "cluster bombs" in heavily populated areas, a decision taken by a lower-level commander in the field and then overruled once DABLA advisors became aware of it.

Fourth is an inherent limitation in the use of IHL because it is quite an ambiguous set of norms constantly criticized as vague or ill-fitting for contemporary conflicts.[22] Because of its ambiguity, and the tendency of the Israeli Supreme Court to intervene in military decisions as described above, there is always a chance that DABLA advice will be reviewed by that Court. This phenomenon poses a dilemma for DABLA. Because the legal source of their advice is ambiguous, it would be difficult for them to support a very restrictive approach vis-à-vis the IDF. Yet a more liberal approach (i.e., allowing the army to act in certain ways using a more flexible interpretation of IHL) might lead to the Israeli Supreme Court overturning DABLA's legal opinion, thus harming their legitimacy in the eyes of the commanders. These dilemmas might cause several possible results—all of them problematic for DABLA: One might simply be DABLA's exclusion from the decision loop by superiors, since there is no assurance that their opinion would be accepted by the court. Another possible result might be turning DABLA into a collection of "yes-men," whose only function is to justify the actions of the authorities. Another possibility is that military lawyers become overly anxious and prohibitive, fearing the result in court at every stage of the trial.

The Institutional Context of DABLA Activities: Role Strain

The organizational model of DABLA reflects these challenges. Like military physicians, military lawyers belong, at once, to two professional communities. In the insightful words of Moshe Hirsch,[23] a professor of law, they suffer from what sociologists call role strain: attempting to meet two sometimes divergent sets of expectations, since they (simultaneously) want to belong to the IHL community and belong to the military. Yet fear of military superiors is usually not the governing consideration for these individuals, because, more importantly, they seem to morally assimilate the military world view (as do individuals in any large organization). To be sure, they genuinely see themselves as marking limits and boundaries for military commanders, but over the years they become increasingly identified with the interests of the state and the IDF. They are gatekeepers

[22] David Kaye, "Complexity in Law of War," in *Developments in International Law: The Progress of International Organization*, ed. Russell A. Miller and Rebecca M. Bratspies (Leiden: Martinus Nijhoff, 2008).

[23] Personal communication.

but also see themselves as allowing the military to win. Since brigade and divisional commanders need their advice, they find themselves under tremendous pressure that is even more severe during times of intense conflict. These are the reasons they create interpretations favorable to the military.

There is an important element of perception here. In the eyes of many commanders, DABLA officers are independent lawyers who restrain military action. As an astute academic with experience with IHL, told us, MAG for their part see themselves as the agents of the law in the IDF and not as apologists for the IDF (like representatives of the Ministry of Foreign Affairs who explain policy). Organizationally however, they are different from lawyers belonging to the State Attorney's office, who are institutionally very independent. Thus for example, while the latter have indicted prime ministers, a president, and ministers, not one brigade commander has been indicted since the first Intifada.

Limiters and Enablers

Accordingly, lawyers in DABLA are both enablers and limiters of military action. This is evident in the statement of the MAG, Brigadier General Mandelblit:

> The laws of war are intended to order and limit, but not to prevent, the killing and destruction which are part of the reality of war. The lawyers of the MAG work to aid the IDF fight within the limits of this regime.[24]

An unnamed officer from the MAG echoed these words, "Our aim is not to shackle the military, but to give it tools so that it can win in a legal manner."[25] Along these lines, in Operation Cast Lead in Gaza, DABLA lawyers mitigated military action suggesting that families whose residences were to be bombed be notified ahead of time by SMS or phone.[26] Some criticism was voiced at this practice, which seems to have been successful in the Second Lebanon War, because in Gaza the families had nowhere to escape to. But as a number of experts from academia noted, by transmitting a constant message that commanders must restrain their forces, DABLA did have at least a modicum of influence. In reply to criticism about DABLA being too permissive, Reisner argued, looking back at his stint during the early 2000s:

> We defended [in the courts] all the policies that were on the edge—the neighbor policy, destruction of houses, expulsion, targeted

[24] *Haaretz*, 1 January 2009.
[25] *Haaretz*, 1 January 2009.
[26] *Haaretz*, 22 January 2009.

> assassinations. We defended all of the magic solutions for the fight against terror. In this respect DABLA is a restraining body but it is not a body that stops action. If the military comes and says "Here is a magic solution, is it within the area that is allowed?" I would say "I am prepared to try and defend it, but am not sure that I will succeed." In the white areas I will allow action, in black areas I will forbid but in the gray area I will participate in the dilemma. I don't stop in the gray.[27]

According to *Haaretz* (22 January 2009), the relatively weak standing of DABLA representatives in the Southern Command improved somewhat during Operation Cast Lead. At the beginning of the attack the impression created was that the forces in the field were taking too much liberty in destroying houses and uprooting trees. These actions contradicted the directive in the legal appendix to the order given to the commanders and troops. The legal appendix outlined the principles of international law, clarified what are war crimes and demanded to investigate any case in which there was a suspicion that such crimes had been committed. This appendix directed the commanders to be especially careful in the use of cluster bombs, weapons containing phosphorus, or antipersonnel mines. It stated, "Before use of these weapons there is a need to obtain a detailed opinion from MAG/DABLA."[28] More specifically it stated, "Where there in an operational alternative that will answer the military's need by limiting the range of damage to property that is not involved it should be chosen." Yet DABLA representatives obtained the impression that some commanders did not understand that they were under internal IDF review and thus applied pressure to create rules for the destruction of houses or uprooting trees. In other cases DABLA lawyers expressed concern at the delay of the forces in evacuating wounded Palestinians. As Haaretz concluded, "in terms of results their position did not always influence the forces in the field."[29]

But the wider problem is that legal advice may sometimes suspend commanders' moral judgment and be seen as authorizing certain actions.[30] When a legal consultant says that an action is "OK, but problematic" the military often sees this as a green light for action. This kind of problem, in turn, may be compounded by differences between units. At the operational level the brigade and battalion commanders have tremendous influence: In Operation Cast Lead there were almost no complaints about the Paratroopers brigade, but some were

[27] *Haaretz*, 22 January 2009.

[28] *Haaretz*, 22 January 2009.

[29] *Haaretz*, 22 January 2009.

[30] Yuval Shany, personal communication; Yishai Ber, public comment, 6 February 2010, Tel Aviv University.

voiced against the Givati and to an extent the Golani brigades. In addition, during the second author's research on the Second Intifada, soldiers explained that strict military prison terms for soldiers who had humiliated Palestinians led to a marked change of attitude among the rest of a unit's troops.

To conclude this section, the MAG and especially DABLA are a conduit of IHL into the military but also a body that justifies or sanctions military action. They are professional experts that bring to the IDF a specialized expertise forming a source of authority for action. In the institutional sense, they are best seen as "agents of compliance." Their role is to internalize international law into the decision-making process of the IDF.

In the Field: Perspectives from the Frontlines

Criticism of DABLA usually focuses on the higher level of decision-making, whereas it seems that a lot of the effects of DABLA are actually on the tactical levels. In strategic decisions it is quite clear that many of the opinions of DABLA are supportive of the positions of the military, or at least try to find a way to accommodate the requirements of the IDF. Yet, focusing only on these cases misses a major influence of DABLA, lawyers at those levels in which they did not allow specific action to take place or targets to be bombed. It is on the tactical echelons that the effect of "operational" legal advice is the greatest, when commanders' decisions are actually reviewed by lawyers. It is to this dimension of the relations between IHL and military force that we now turn.

From the perspective of commanders of the combat arms, and especially the ground forces, laws pertaining to war and combat exist as an undifferentiated set of rules and restrictions. In fact we would argue that many commanders cannot, and do not, differentiate between IHL, applications of domestic law, or other international laws of war. For the vast majority of these individuals the Geneva Conventions belong to a broad and indiscriminate category of "international laws." They are uninterested in the finer legal distinctions involved. Part of the reason for this situation is related to the actual legal situation in which a mix of various legal systems and laws apply in the territories. But both in their day-to-day activities and in times of crisis what is (naturally) of interest to commanders is the impact of legal restrictions on specific actions rather than the legal status of the Jewish settlements or structural exploitations created by the occupation.

Yet the perceived environment of international law does have an impact on the actions of the IDF. Desiree Verweij,[31] an expert in military ethics, suggests that part of the restraint on military action results from an internalization by

[31] Personal communication.

the military of the "gaze" of other—the media, social movements, and NGOs, for instance. It is for this reason that there is now widespread talk about how the armed forces of the industrial democracies operate "under the shadow" of judicial proceedings. But by Verweij's suggestions, we understand more than a simple model of external influences on soldiers' morality and action. This "gaze" of (various) others is first internalized in the rhetoric of such armed forces as the IDF use; second, it is adopted into the organizational structures and practices by which they operate; and third, it begins at times to fit soldiers' and officers' self-image as military professionals and as human beings.[32] Colonomos argues[33] that it would be wrong to see the move to greater restraints as a simple reaction on the part of military and state leaders to external pressures. Rather normative leadership may derive from within the armed forces through the work of lawyers, consultants, ethicists, and commanders. All of these practices must fit the professional "self-concept" of commanders and soldiers as valuing human life and as perpetrating violence in a restrained manner that fits wider public attitudes to such actions. The IDF seminars on "human dignity," legal counsel to brigade commanders, or inspections to improve effective action do have concrete effects. Our point, then, is that the emphasis on legal restrictions is not simply limited to either rhetoric or concrete operational applications. Rather, many soldiers and most officers act in ways that they perceive to be proper and professional in safeguarding these considerations.

The following excerpts are intended to give a flavor of the kinds of considerations that come to bear on military action at the tactical level. During the Second Intifada, one of authors had a conversation with a commander of an infantry company. We were discussing the use of snipers when he said,

> The weight of the decision, of your discretion. Sometimes one shot can create a lot of harm; the place where it hit. It could be that there are ten girls around him so that it's better not to shoot so that no girl will get hit. . . . Because this is a game of scoring points and so that it won't be written in the newspaper that the IDF killed two terrorists and that as a result two girls were killed, it's very important.[34]

[32] Erella Grassianni, "Morality and Normalcy in A-Symmetrical Conflict: Distancing, Denial and Moral Numbing among Israeli Conscripts in Everyday Practices of Occupation," doctoral dissertation, Amsterdam, The Free University, 2009.

[33] Ariel Colonomos, "Tying the Gordian Knot: Targeted Killings and the Ethics of Prevention," paper presented at a conference on "The Moral Dimension of Asymmetrical Warfare," organized by The Netherlands Defence Academy, Amsterdam, October 2006.

[34] Personal communication.

The commander of an infantry brigade, Givati, whose soldiers operated for two weeks in Operation Cast Lead, told *Haaretz* that in his opinion IDF did not use excessive fire:

> I won't send ten soldiers to a house that we suspect of being booby-trapped so that they will explode, before I have created the conditions that will assure their safety. . . . In Operation "Hot Winter" that took place in March 2008 in Jabeliya [a refugee camp in the Gaza strip] I lost two soldiers who were shot by armed people who came out of one of the houses. We understood that in confronting the enemy one has to create advantageous conditions for putting in our forces and that is the way we acted.[35]

When asked about the high number of civilian casualties in the same operation, the commander of Paratrooper Brigade said his soldiers made a huge effort to ensure that civilians were not harmed.

> I am not ashamed and not afraid. I can depend on the state [of Israel] and hope that it will be able to defend the officers it sent. All that we did was according to the international law of armed conflict. I said to the soldiers: "Even if a terrorist shot at you, the minute he puts his gun down you don't shoot him." According to international law, every civilian installation that has the enemy in it, even a hospital, it is allowed to attack. You have to remember that with all of the destruction, the damage and the casualties, we still did not use our maximal power. I was restrained and I restrained. In the First Lebanon War they brought along 155 [mm] artillery pieces and shot at the top floors of buildings to clean them. This was not done here. Soldiers entered high buildings to clean them up themselves. Think about how many soldiers are in the stairways of such a building. What kind of disaster could happen if, god forbid, such a structure falls down.[36]

These excerpts underscore the mix of professional conduct and the application of international laws of war to specific acts at base of the reasoning of these commanders.

[35] *Haaretz*, 19 January 2009.

[36] *Haaretz*, 23 January 2009.

Violations: Rituals of Rationality, Individuation, and Purification

At the end of the day, many violations happen at the lower tactical levels. Some are violations of direct orders while others result from their ambiguity. What happens when violations occur and are discovered by senior commanders directly or through the reports of the media or human rights groups? To begin with, the policy for initiating legal proceedings against violators has changed over the past decades. During the First Intifada, the policy was to investigate every Palestinian death,[37] but shortly after the Second Intifada began the IDF revised its guidelines to probe only cases in which civilians were suspected of being harmed without justification. For example, between 2000 and 2007 the IDF indicted just 10 percent of soldiers suspected of criminal offenses against Palestinians, and Yesh Din [lit. "There is Law"], an Israeli human rights group, reported that these figures raise questions about Israel's willingness to prosecute its troops.[38] When prosecution does take place, it can be expressed either in internal disciplinary hearings within units or in courts-martial.

There are two further mechanisms for dealing with violations within the Israeli military.

Coherent Procedures, Rites of Rationality

The first is an extension of the same logic of rationality used in regard to military action in general and precision warfare in particular. Put bluntly, deviations from accurate fire are often treated as "unfortunate accidents" or "classification errors" that can be rectified by means of organizational learning.[39] Take an explanation for five Palestinian children killed by an accidental explosion of an Israeli remote control bomb. A senior officer tells a journalist, "There has to be an assessment about whether the lessons of the past have been learned. . . . [The IDF has a duty] to perfect and focus its schemes so that harming innocent civilians is prevented."[40] Or, take the following reasoning in which representatives of the Israeli Air Force warn against expecting zero collateral damage:

> All it would take is for a missile to veer off-course by a few meters because of a technical malfunction and civilians would be killed. And

[37] Amnon Strasnov, *Justice under Fire: The Judicial System in the Intifada* (Tel-Aviv: Yediot Aharonot, 1994) [in Hebrew].

[38] *Jerusalem Post*, 19 December 2007.

[39] Ben-Ari et al., *Rethinking Contemporary Warfare.*

[40] *Maariv*, 25 November 2001.

> another thing: When tensions escalate, such as under massive Qassam fire from the Gaza Strip, the IDF is more active and also takes more risks, leading to more civilian casualties among the Palestinians.[41]

This logic-of-action leads to a series of what may be termed "rituals of rationality"—a gamut of activities in and around safety and minimizing collateral damage—that include briefings and debriefings, formulating and changing rules of engagement, creating "review boards," writing new training manuals, and elaborating new guidelines.[42] These actions are examples of how organizational structures and practices are created in order to address external expectations deriving from global environments.

Personalizing Mistakes, the Military, and Human Rights

The second mechanism centers on personalizing violations rather than attributing them to organizational or structural factors. Personalization is encased within a specific view of the relations between legal rights, organizational responsibility, and military action. First, in much of the professional military literature legal restrictions are most often connected to rules of engagement. Within this professional literature one finds very little discussion about people's right to a home, livelihood, or health.[43] Actions are usually compartmentalized: When talked about, the actions of the military are most often linked to the concrete physical violation of people's bodies (killing, wounding) or humiliation by concrete individuals. This compartmentalization is related not only to the interests of the IDF but to wider assumptions at base of legal discourse: The culture of human rights. "is individualistic in conception; it addresses suffering through a legal/technical, rather than an ethical, framework."[44]

Indeed, in contemporary societies such as Israel, responses to violations have centered largely on the formal machinery developed for protecting human rights, which assumes that the individual is responsible for his or her actions. This largely ignores the possibility that the cause of violations may be found within the social, economic, and political structures that define the current codes. The emphasis on the individual, in turn, fits with the bureaucratic and judicial logic

[41] *Haaretz*, 30 December 2007.

[42] For an example, see James Ron, "Savage Restraint: Israel, Palestine and the Dialectics of Repression" *Social Problems* 47, no. 4 (2000): 445–472, at p. 462.

[43] Physicians for Human Rights, *A Legacy of Injustice: A Critique of Israeli Approaches to the Right of Health of Palestinians in the Occupied Territories* (December 2002), http://reliefweb.int/report/israel/opt-legacy-injustice-critique-israeli-approaches-right-health-palestinians-occupied.

[44] Cowan et al., *Culture and Rights*, p. 12.

of the military both by focusing on the responsibility and accountability of persons and by being limited to the perpetration of direct physical violence or humiliation instigated by specific soldiers. Accordingly, when senior commanders in IDF encounter the use of "undue" physical force they most often allocate responsibility to the individual soldiers who carried it out and take appropriate disciplinary action (overwhelmingly within the military).

Rites of Purification

This is the background to the high-publicity courts-martial in regard to particularly blatant violations of rules. Sociologically, these are akin to ritual acts of degradation (of individual soldiers) and purification (of the military) that signal to the IDF's environment that violations are taken seriously. A few short examples may suffice. In 2007 Ground Arm Command (GOC) Southern Command Yoav Galant decided to dismiss an infantry officer, whose troops wounded a 14-year-old Palestinian girl while employing the banned "neighbor policy," in which Palestinian civilians are ordered to assist troops in arresting wanted militants.[45] Similarly, the IDF's military prosecutor indicted an officer involved in the shooting of a Palestinian civilian in the West Bank. The officer, a lieutenant, and five of his men commandeered a local taxi, drove through the town of Dahariya and shot an unarmed Palestinian who aroused their suspicion. The officer acted on his own initiative in violation of military orders, and left the wounded man on the ground without treating him, the investigation found.[46] Furthermore, Chief of Staff Gabi Ashkenazi later decided that the lessons of this incident would be taught in all IDF commanders' training courses.

In another case, a brigade commander was filmed ordering one of his soldiers to shoot a handcuffed demonstrator. The officer claimed that he meant that the soldier would not actually shoot the demonstrator, but only frighten him, and the soldier misunderstood the order. The MAG decided at first to prosecute the officer for "conduct unbecoming a soldier," a relatively light offense. In what was termed an almost unprecedented decision of the Israeli Supreme Court, the court ordered the MAG to prosecute the officer for a more serious offense.[47]

An explanation favored by the IDF is that such cases are irregularities or aberrations. For instance, an officer who served in the territories said to one of us, "The cases that were exposed were done so only in a few cases in which the

[45] *Haaretz*, 6 August 2007.

[46] *Haaretz*, 23 August 2007.

[47] Israeli Supreme Court 2009: HCJ 7195/08 Abu Rachma v. Brigadier General Avichai Mandelblit, Military Advocate General, decision of 1 July 2009, http://elyon1.court.gov.il/files_eng/08/950/071/r09/08071950.r09.htm.

Palestinians complained about it to the IDF or when an officer passes somewhere and sees that something is wrong." More significantly, the IDF spokesman replied in response to media queries about violence against Palestinians that "the cases described are *not known* in the IDF as a [regular] phenomenon (emphasis added)."[48] And according to him,

> For a time, there were a number of cases in which Palestinians were delayed in roadblocks for a few hours. The process of checking identity cards and permits to pass is the factor that [explains this situation]. . . . [T]he IDF denounces such cases. When soldiers are caught acting like that they are court-martialed strictly. According to him, from the beginning of the Intifada eight investigations were begun by the military police in cases of delay of Palestinians in roadblocks or violent incidents at roadblocks.[49]

By defining various phenomena as irregularities and denouncing them, the IDF as an organization individualizes illegal and unjustifiable actions by attributing them to a few nonprofessional soldiers, the proverbial "few rotten apples," and in this way cleanses itself. To sum up then in regard to violations: this is a case not of ritual compliance but rather ritual purification.

Conclusions

In this chapter we have dealt with the effects of IHL on the IDF. We differentiated between three levels of effects that are summarized in the following table (Table 8.3).

The main effect at the policy level entails the role of the GC IV in Israeli law. In this respect we follow Ron, who argues in a comparative vein, that the influence of international human rights norms is likely to be stronger among those states such as Israel that are dependent on international flows of aid, trade, and legitimacy.[50] In this sense we suggest that the influence of IHL should be seen as part of the ways in which the IDF, like similar militaries, is increasingly transparent to external monitoring bodies whether they be formal or informal, or governmental or nongovernmental. In the case of Israel, this kind of international

[48] *Haaretz*, 23 July 2001.

[49] *Haaretz*, 23 July 2001.

[50] James Ron, *Frontiers and Ghettos: State Violence in Serbia and Israel* (Berkeley: University of California Press, 2003), pp. xiii, 6.

Table 8.3 **Sources of Noncompliance, Solutions, and Mechanisms of Success**

	Soldiers and Junior Officers	*Mid- to High-Level Officers*	*Supreme Military and Civilian Leadership*
Sources of noncompliance	Personal interest, peer pressure, unit culture	Intrinsic military problem, tunnel vision, immediate military interest	State interest, political preferences
Solutions	Education, rites, court martial	Strong legal advice	Strong external control—High court of Justice, international pressure
Success	Ceremonies (law as culture)	Compliance agents (law as an institution)	Cost-benefit analysis (law as power)

pressure is combined with domestic criticism that may be launched by political groups, social movements, or various media. As Ignatieff underscores:

> Those who equate the violence inflicted by Israel with that inflicted by Palestinian suicide bombers ignore real differences in institutional accountability in the two cases. In Israel, allegations of torture, house demolitions, illegal detention, and unjustified force have all ended up before the Israeli Supreme Court, and in a significant number of instances the conduct has been censured and stopped. This is not to claim that legal oversight is always effective, or to acquit Israeli forces of blame when crimes are committed. But it is to argue that all agents of force in a democratic state, like Israel, lie under the burden of justification, and the possibility of review and censure, that are entirely absent on the other side.[51]

The context within which the IDF operates is important because it is related to the manner by which the armed forces "manage" their relations with their organizational environments to assure support, legitimacy, and the continued allocation of resources. It in this sense that the influence of IHL and public debates and discussions about this influence should be seen: through them the

[51] Michael Ignatieff, *The Warrior's Honor: Ethnic War and the Modern Conscience* (London: Chatto and Windus, 1998), p. 110.

IDF transmits certain messages to, and manages the expectation of, its environments (and the self-image of commanders and troops as military professionals). To be sure, the global discourses of international law themselves wane according to historical circumstances such as the September 11 attacks against the United States, when practices that were previously seen as unacceptable came to be perceived as legitimate.

The institutional accountability of the IDF should, however, be also understood as related to the internal dynamics of this military establishment. As we showed, the IDF is marked by more than symbolic or "ritual" compliance to IHL. The various representatives of the MAG in actual decision-making processes demonstrate that legal considerations go beyond "mere" incorporation into military manuals and military education to the actual actions of Israel's military forces. We have, however, shown that there are places where the ritualistic mechanisms such as degradation and purification are part of the relations between the IDF and its environment.

9

Noncompliance with the Geneva Conventions in the Wars of Yugoslav Secession

R. CRAIG NATION

Introduction

Organized violence on the territory of the former Yugoslavia between 1991 and 2002 claimed over 100,000 lives, resulted in the forced displacement of more than three million citizens, and left a legacy of physical destruction and psychological devastation.[1] Unfolding against the background of the end of Cold War bipolarity, the Balkan wars sounded a discordant counterpoint to efforts to construct a more harmonious European order, and became a preoccupation for the instances concerned with restoring regional stability. Few conflicts have been more intensively scrutinized by outside observers. It is not an exaggeration to claim that the Yugoslav wars have "impinged on global consciousness" as much if not more than any other contemporary armed conflict. As an "archetypal

[1] The conclusions expressed in this study are based on a perusal of the large professional literature devoted to the Yugoslav wars of the 1990s; research in archival sources; the records of the International Criminal Tribunal for Former Yugoslavia; and conversations and interviews with scholars, journalists, political and military leaders, combatants, and civilian representatives of the former Yugoslav republics. The anonymity of all sources is carefully respected. My own interpretation of the war is presented in R. Craig Nation, *War in the Balkans 1991–2002* (Honolulu: University Press of the Pacific, 2004). The present study makes no attempt to cast judgment on issues of responsibility—it makes do with the presumption that all parties to the conflict were to some extent guilty, albeit to different degrees, of violations of the laws and customs of war, and seeks to explain the reasons why. A grant from the International Research and Exchange Board helped support fieldwork in conjunction with the project.

paradigm" of "a new type of organized violence," they exert a disproportionate influence on the ways in which we understand and react to modern warfare.[2]

The Balkan conflict provided numerous examples of the legal and ethical challenges inherent in modern war—state failure and its destabilizing consequences, the lack of restraint in poorly controlled civil conflicts with a powerful ethnic or cultural component, systematic violence against noncombatants elevated to the status of a military strategy, the primacy of identity politics as opposed to more classic geopolitical goals, use of terror as a means of shaping the operational environment, and the dilemmas of great power intervention and the responsibility to protect in cases defined by strategic ambiguity. With a ratio of civilian to military casualties in the area of 3 to 1 (the ratio is disputed and difficult to determine), and a long litany of atrocities on record, the conflict posed the challenges of realizing the modern war convention's imperative to respect the status of noncombatants, encourage military restraint, and ensure compliance to basic civilizational norms and humanitarian standards, with particular starkness.

Numerous episodes during the series of conflicts constitute egregious examples of war crimes. In the spring and summer of 1992, Serb paramilitary forces, abetted by regular units of the Yugoslav People's Army (Jugoslovenska Narodna Armija—JNA) pursued a purposeful campaign of ethnic cleansing in the Drina river valley and eastern Bosnia, killing the residents of occupied communities at random and forcing thousands into flight.[3] On 16 April 1993, forces representing the self-styled Croat Community of Herceg-Bosnia perpetrated a deliberate massacre of the inhabitants of the predominantly Muslim village of Ahmići in western Bosnia's Lašva Valley, burning the village to the ground and dynamiting the minaret of the central mosque.[4] In the early period of the siege of Sarajevo

[2] The thesis is developed in Mary Kaldor, *New Wars and Old Wars*, 2nd ed. (Stanford: Stanford University Press, 2007), p. 33, and Rupert Smith, *The Utility of Force: The Art of War in the Modern World* (London: Allen Lane, 2005). During 1995 and 1996 Lieutenant General Rupert Smith commanded United Nations (UN) forces in Sarajevo.

[3] Smail Čekić, *The Aggression in Bosnia and Genocide against the Bosnians, 1991–1993* (Sarajevo: Ljilian, 1994); Hans Trotter, et al., *"Ethnische Sauberungen" in der nordostbosnischen Stadt Zvornik von April bis Juni 1992* (Vienna: Ludwig Baltzman Institute for Human Rights, 1994); and Nijaz Mašić, *Istina o Bratunacu: Agresija, genocide, i oslobodilačka borba 1992–1995* (Tuzla: Opština Bratuncu sa Privreminim Sjedištem u Tuzli, 1996). The expulsion of populations on ethnic grounds has been defined by the ICTFY as a "Joint Criminal Enterprise" with political motivation.

[4] US Central Intelligence Agency analysts refer to the episode as the "Guernica of the Bosnian Conflict," Central Intelligence Agency, Office of Russian and European Analysis, *Balkan Battlegrounds: A Military History of the Yugoslav Conflict, 1900–1995*, 2 vols. (Washington, DC: Central Intelligence Agency, May 2002), vol. 1, p. 130. In numerous rulings, the International Criminal Tribunal for Former Yugoslavia has described these events as crimes against humanity. The political leader of the Croat Community in Central Bosnia, Dario Kordić, was sentenced by the court on four counts of crimes against humanity to a twenty-five-year prison term. Tihomir Blaškić, operational

in 1992 and 1993, Muslim militia leaders abducted and murdered by decapitation dozens of Serbs, throwing their bodies into a natural crevice known as the Kazani pit.[5] The Army of the Republic of Bosnia and Herzegovina expelled thousands of Croats from the Bugojno region in 1993 and 1994.[6] After the fall of Srebrenica to the Army of the Serb Republic in July 1995, more than 8,000 prisoners were massacred and 25,000 residents (women, children, and the elderly) forcefully expelled while a Dutch UN peacekeeping battalion looked on helplessly.[7] The case of Srebrenica was extraordinary, but the litany of violations

commander in the area, was originally sentenced to a forty-five-year term, reduced on appeal to nine years. United Nations, International Tribunal for the Prosecution of Persons Responsible for Serious Violations of International Humanitarian Law Committed in the Territory of Former Yugoslavia since 1991, Case No. IT-95-14/2-T, 26 February 2002, and Case IT-95-14-T, 3 March 2000. Miroslav Brado, a member of the Croatian Defense Council (HVO) 4th Military Police Battalion antiterrorist unit, was sentenced to twenty years' imprisonment after pleading guilty to participation in the Ahmići attacks.

[5] With the war still underway, the Bosnian government tried and convicted 14 Muslim soldiers in association with these atrocities (most received light sentences). The Muslim militia leader Mušan Topalović (Caco), leader of the self-styled 10th Mountain Brigade considered responsible for overseeing the killings, was murdered in October 1993. An effort to exhume bodies from the pit was initiated but abandoned after twenty-nine had been removed. Observers indicated that the pits contained "many more." Chris Hedges, "Postscript to Sarajevo's Anguish: Muslim Killings of Serbs Detailed," *New York Times*, 12 November 1997.

[6] The Appellate Chamber of the Court of Bosnia and Herzegovina sentenced the Bosnians Senad Dautović to seven and Nisvet Gasal and Musajb Kukavica to four years each for crimes committed against Croatians in Bugojno in 1993 and 1994. The verdict remains contested. For a Croat perspective, see H. Rovčanin, "Bugojno—udruženi zločnački pothvat: Zločine nad Hrvatima u Bugojnu," *Dnevni list*, 23 November 2011.

[7] Jan Honig and Norbert Both, *Srebrenica: Record of a War Crime* (New York: Penguin Books, 1997); and David Rohde, *Endgame: The Betrayal and Fall of Srebrenica, Europe's Worst Massacre since World War II* (New York: Farrar, Straus and Giroux, 1997). The official Dutch report on the episode, which encompasses more than seven thousand pages including documentation, is particularly detailed. J. C. H. Blom et al., *Srebrenica: Reconstruction, Background, Consequences and Analysis of the Fall of a Safe Area* (Amsterdam: Nederlands Instituut voor Oorlogsdocumentie, April 2002). In its judgment in the case of Radislav Krstić, the commander of the Drina Corps of the Bosnian Serb Army, the ICFY ruled that the Srebrenica massacre constituted an act of genocide. Krstić was originally convicted on the charge of genocide, and sentenced to forty-five years in prison, but an Appeals Court later revised the charge to "aiding and abetting" genocide, with the sentence reduced to thirty-five years. See United Nations, International Criminal Tribunal for Former Yugoslavia, Case Information Sheet-Radislav Krstić, Srebrebica-Drina Corps, Case IT-98-33. In March 2016 the Bosnian Serb political leader Radovan Karadžić was convicted of genocide for involvement in the Srebrenica massacre and sentenced to forty years imprisonment. Karadžić was tried on two counts of genocide, one addressing violations in Bosnian municipalities and the other the case of Srebrenica. He was acquitted on the first count. He was also found guilty on five counts of crimes against humanity (persecution, extermination, murder, deportation, and inhumane acts) and four counts of violation of the laws and customs of war (murder, terror, unlawful attacks on civilians, and hostage-taking). The commander of Bosnian Serb armed forces General Ratko Mladić is currently on trial, accused of a

does not document isolated events. A war aim for nearly all contending parties was to secure control over contested territory, leading to the phenomenon of "ethnic cleansing" (*etničko čišćenje*), characterized by the use of force and terrorist violence to drive out rival communities.[8] The bloody consequences, dramatically displayed in the global media, posed an ethical challenge that would have consequences. The Yugoslav wars also gave rise to the International Criminal Tribunal for Former Yugoslavia (ICTY), an experiment in the use of juridical means under UN auspices to impose the principle of responsibility in cases of war crimes and massive human rights violations.[9]

Socialist Yugoslavia and International Humanitarian Law

The Socialist Federal Republic of Yugoslavia (SFRY) ratified the Geneva Conventions on 21 April 1950, and subsequently the 1977 Additional Protocols. The SFRY was a party to all major universal human rights instruments, including the United Nations Convention against Torture, the Universal Declaration of Human Rights, and the International Covenant on Civil and Political Rights.

During the first phase of the violent disintegration of the SFRY, Belgrade, as the capital of the newly constituted Federal Republic of Yugoslavia (FRY) claimed the status of legal successor. The request was refused, and the FRY was required to reapply for admission to the United Nations as a new state. On 27 April 1992 Belgrade proclaimed the FRY's succession to the obligations of the SFRY pertaining to the Geneva Conventions.

similar list of violations. See United Nations, International Tribunal for the Prosecution of Persons Responsible for Serious Violations of International Humanitarian Law Committed in the Territory of the Former Yugoslavia since 1991, Case IT-95-5/18-T.

[8] Drazen Petrovic, "Ethnic Cleansing—An Attempt at a Methodology," *European Journal of International Law* 5, no. 4 (1998); and William A. Schabas, "Ethnic Cleansing and Genocide: Similarities and Differences," *European Yearbook of Minority Issues* 3, no. 1 (2003). The issue remains highly charged. See Svetozar Livada, *Etničko Čišćenje: Ozakonjeni zločin stoljeća* (Zagreb: Prosvjeta, 1997), and the recent catalog of expulsions of Serbs, "Etničko Čišćenje Srba u Federatsiji BiH: Rezultati popisa," *Magazin*, 4 July 2016.

[9] The formal name of the organization is the International Tribunal for the Prosecution of Persons Responsible for Serious Violations of International Humanitarian Law in the Territory of Former Yugoslavia since 1991. Resolution 827 of the UN Security Council, passed on 25 May 1993, granted the Tribunal jurisdiction over four cluster areas of criminal behavior: grave breaches of the Geneva Conventions; violations of the laws and customs of war; genocide; and crimes against humanity. See Richard Ashby Wilson, "Judging History: The Historical Record of the International Criminal Tribunal for Former Yugoslavia," *Human Rights Quarterly* 27, no. 3 (2005): 908–942.

In a sequence of regional wars between 1991 and 1999, the SFRY split into six new independent states (the status of a seventh entity, the Republic of Kosovo, remains under dispute).[10] All of the successor states ratified the Geneva Conventions and Additional Protocols: Slovenia on 26 March 1992; Croatia on 11 May 1992; Bosnia and Herzegovina on 31 December 1992; the Republic of Macedonia on 1 September 1993; and Montenegro on 2 August 2006. All of the state actors involved in the Yugoslav wars were therefore parties to the Geneva Conventions and professed respect for the principles, norms, legal strictures, and conventions embodied in Geneva law. In fact, the breakaway republics whose secession sparked armed conflict on their territory (Slovenia, Croatia, and Bosnia and Herzegovina) pushed through ratification as soon as possible. This was in part an effort to reinforce claims to sovereignty, and in part to establish the moral high ground and use adherence as a point of appeal in order to resist military assaults that in some cases included significant violations of international humanitarian law.

The Yugoslav People's Army was a professional military force with a mature system of military training and education.[11] Information concerning the Geneva Conventions was incorporated in training manuals. Officers were familiarized with the law of war and armed conflict and foundations of military ethics (the first course in officer training programs), and were held responsible for inculcating legal and ethical principles and standards among the soldiers under their command. These principles were discussed in a sophisticated professional literature. The origins of the JNA as a partisan force waging irregular warfare to resist German and Italian occupation (and later charged with confronting a possible invasion by the Soviet Union) made Yugoslav officers particularly sensitive to the JNA's character as a people's army as reflected in institutional tradition and official mission statements. The JNA systematically propagated the national ideology of *bratstva i jedinstvo* (brotherhood and unity) or comity between the various communities that made up multinational Yugoslavia. It viewed itself, and was widely viewed as, an embodiment of the Yugoslav national idea.

Yugoslav official historians called special attention to the war crimes committed by occupation forces and local collaborators in Yugoslavia during World War II, including the *subjugation* of Yugoslavia (its extinction as a subject of international law), deliberate bombing of the civilian population, and mistreatment

[10] The Republic of Kosovo declared independence from Serbia on 17 February 2008. To date (August 2016) 113 countries have recognized its independence. Kosovo has become a member of the International Monetary Fund and World Bank, but has not yet applied for admission to the United Nations, or adhered to the Geneva Conventions.

[11] Zvezdan Marković, *Jugoslovenska Ljudska Armada* (Ljubljana: Založba Defensor, 2007).

of prisoners of war including violations of the Hague rules and the Geneva Convention of 1929, discrimination against diplomatic and consular officers, economic plunder, the looting of civilian goods, the forcible resettlement of people, and genocide.[12] These violations were expounded in basic education and popular culture, particularly the widely viewed films depicting partisan operations in Yugoslavia during the war.[13]

Yugoslav national defense policy was based on universal male conscription and called for the maintenance of a standing reserve force. Territorial Defense Forces paralleled the standing army on the regional level. Over 50 percent of the JNA was permanently stationed in Bosnia and Herzegovina, which was organized as a territorial sanctuary from which resistance could be sustained in the event of invasion. As an institution the JNA was strongly supportive of Titoist orthodoxy and usually stood foursquare against movements for democratic reform.[14]

The JNA broke apart during 1991–1992, together with the SFRY.[15] It was replaced by a number of spin-off armies and armed formations representing new or aspiring nation-states seeking to secure control of contested territory, impose secession from the Yugoslav Federation, or avoid incorporation as minority communities within other consolidating state entities. These included the Slovene Defense Forces; the Yugoslav Armed Forces (Vojska Jugoslavie—VJ); the Serb Army of the Krajina; the Army of the Serb Republic (Vojska Republike Srpske—VRS); the Croatian Army (Hrvatska Vojska—HV); the Army of Bosnia and Herzegovina (Armija Bosne i Hercegovine—ABH); the Montenegrin Army; and the Macedonian Army. A significant number of paramilitary and irregular forces also took the field, including various Serb militias (the Kapitan Dragan Militia, the White Eagles of Vojislav Šešelj, the Tigers of Željko Ražnatović [Arkan]; and the Serb Scorpions—participants in the Srebrenica massacre); the Croatian Defense Forces (Hrvatska Odbrambene Snaga—HOS) associated with Dobroslav Paraga's Croatian Party of Rights (Hrvatska Stranka Prava—HSP); the Muslim militia of besieged Sarajevo including the Wolves of Jusuf Prazina (Juka); the Bihać militia of Fikret Abdić; the Kosovo Liberation Army; the National Liberation Army of Macedonia, and many others. The Yugoslav wars were characterized by military improvisation, with hastily assembled or

[12] Vladimir Dedijer, *Istorija Jugoslavije* (Belgrade: Prosveta, 2007).

[13] Such films were produced on a regular basis from the 1950s through the 1980s, and were quite popular. Veljko Bulajić's *Kozara* (1962) is a good example.

[14] Marinko Ogorec, *Vojna sila bivše Jugoslavije* (Rijeka: Otokar Keršovani, 2001).

[15] Dragan Vukšić, *JNA i raspad SFR Jugoslavije: Od čuvara do grobara svoje države* (Stara Pazova: Tekomgraf, 2006); and Davor Marijan, *Slom Titove Armije: JNA i raspad Jugoslavije 1987–1992* (Zagreb: Hrvatski Institut za Povijest, 2008).

radically transformed military organizations assuming strategic responsibilities for which they were often unprepared.

The recognition of secessionist entities by the international community also transformed the Yugoslav conflict into what Ingrid Detter has called an *internationalized war*, defined as "wars which started as internal conflicts but which, as new States emerge, become wars on the world scene in the sphere of international law."[16] The acknowledged dismemberment of Yugoslavia thus had important legal consequences. Once the independence of the breakaway republics was recognized, the wars of Yugoslav secession could be classified as interstate contests, bringing them within the purview of grave breaches and the violations of the laws and customs of war developed in Protocol I of the Geneva Conventions (responsibility for crimes against humanity and genocide also applies to non-international armed conflicts). In general, the anarchic breakup of socialist Yugoslavia, fragmentation of the JNA, and emergence of contending spin-off forces are among the Yugoslav wars' most salient features.

Yugoslavia was a developed European state that enjoyed relative material prosperity, high educational standards, and a rich and varied cultural foundation. How to account for the horrifying violence that accompanied its anarchic disintegration? What factors worked to subvert the standards of military professionalism and decency that JNA officers, and Yugoslav citizens soldiers, had been taught to understand and trained to respect? Why were the Geneva rules to which Yugoslavia and its successor states had pledged allegiance, and the discourse of civilization with which they are linked, so ineffective in preventing purposeful violence against civilians, violations of the law of war, and massive atrocities? Part of the answer to these difficult questions derives from the nature of armed conflict itself; part from the specific characteristics of the wars of Yugoslav secession; and part from the context of contemporary "new wars," which the Yugoslav conflict exemplified.

Sources of Noncompliance: The Failed State Syndrome

The breakup of the Yugoslav Federation was not inevitable. There was always a strong current of opinion in all Yugoslav republics and regions supporting the creation of a recast or renewed federation. The agent of disintegration was not

[16] Ingrid Detter, *The Law of War*, 2nd ed. (Cambridge: Cambridge University Press, 2002), p. 14. The Trial Chamber of the ICTY ruled on the legal classification of the war in Bosnia and Herzegovina, designating it as an "international armed conflict through 1992" with the Federal Republic of Yugoslavia as a belligerent.

popular will, but rather ethnic entrepreneurs who sought to leverage integral nationalism as a source of political legitimacy. The disintegration of the Yugoslav state was for this group of leaders an *intended* consequence, and they were ready to embrace hate narratives and strategies of violence as a means to mobilize followers, impose discipline, and drive relations with neighboring republics beyond the point of no return. Yugoslavia was willfully transformed into a failed state.[17] Purposeful violations of ethical standards became an integral part of strategies of disassociation, the first goal of which was to make continued cohabitation between Yugoslavia's various ethnic communities impossible. As a consequence, both administrative controls and normative constraints concerning political violence were subverted.

The Yugoslav state was unwilling and unable to respond effectively to the disintegrative forces that welled from within. The task was further complicated when secessionist movements found sources of external support.[18] Max Weber famously described the state's ability to assert "a monopoly on the legitimate use of physical force within its border," as a basic condition of sovereignty.[19] In the Yugoslav case, a crisis of centralized leadership and the emergence of spin-off armies and armed militias with international backing created necessary preconditions for a breakdown of respect for international conventions and norms concerning war and armed conflict.

The Yugoslav federal state made several apparent attempts to use armed force to break the momentum of secessionist movements and reassert centralized control, directed against the secessionist republics of Slovenia and Croatia in the summers of 1990 and 1991. Absent political will, the attempts failed. By this point the "Yugoslav" leadership in Belgrade had been usurped by Slobodan Milošević and the Serbian nationalist movement with which he had become associated. As a result, the campaign into Slovenia was not pursued wholeheartedly. Milošević had long before communicated to his Slovene counterpart Milan Kučan a disinclination to resist Slovenia's withdrawal from the Yugoslav

[17] V. P. Gagnon Jr., *The Myth of Ethnic War* (Ithaca, NY: Cornell University Press, 2004).

[18] The most dramatic and disastrous manifestation of such support was German backing for Slovene and Croatian independence. See Hanns W. Maull, "Germany in the Yugoslav Crisis," *Survival* 37, no. 4 (Winter 1995–1996): 99–130. This support had an important cultural foundation. In the words of Johann Reisműller, the influential Balkan correspondent of the *Frankfurter Allgemeine Zeitung*, the source of the problem was "the Serbian leadership with its oriental understanding of justice and governance" and the existence inside Yugoslavia of "two entirely foreign cultures and civilizations." Cited from Johann Georg Reissműller, *Der Krieg vor unserer Haustűr: Hintergrűnde der kroatischen Tragődie* (Stuttgart: Deutsche Verlags-Anstalt, 1992), pp. 10, 81.

[19] Max Weber, *Politik als Beruf* (Berlin: Duncker & Humboldt, 1958).

Federation.[20] The JNA moved on Zagreb in the summer of 1991, but could not achieve its operational goals. Ethnic mobilization and declining morale was weakening its ranks, and both political commitment and material resources were not up to the task. Armored thrusts toward Zagreb were delayed as a result of Croat resistance during the siege of Vukovar (April–November 1991). The city fell after a series of costly assaults, but the advance on Zagreb was not renewed. At this point Milošević's goal was not to reunite Yugoslavia by force, but to secure control over areas with significant Serb populations.[21] Rather than a prelude to national restoration, the campaign became a preview of the vile forms of conduct that national disassociation would make space for. When the town of Vukovar finally fell to Yugoslav forces on 18 November 1991, hundreds of soldiers and civilians were massacred and at least 30,000 Croat civilians deported from the town and its surrounding area.[22]

[20] Janez Drnovšek, *Moja resnica* (Ljubljana: Mladinska knjiga, 1996), p. 209. According to the memoir of Borisav Jović, *Poslednji dani RFRJ: Izvodi iz dnevnika*, 2nd ed. (Belgrade: Narodna Biblioteka Srbije, 1996), vol. 1, p. 65, on 30 June 1991 the JNA presented an operational plan to use armed force to reverse Slovene separatism, which was turned down by Belgrade. These machinations were not widely known. Individuals who served in leadership positions with the Slovene resistance, in conversation with the author, remarked that the possibility of a Yugoslav offensive that would crush their movement was a significant personal and political concern.

[21] The Serb commander Života Panić later claimed to have urged an advance against Zagreb on the political leadership, but in vain. See his remarks in Marco Ventura, "Jugoslavia, un omicidio perfetto," in *La Guerra dei dieci anni—Jugoslavia 1991–2001: I fatti, I personaggi, le ragioni dei conflitti*, ed. Alessandro Marzo Magno (Milan: Il Saggiatore, 2001), p. 123. The Yugoslav Defense Minister states in a memoir that the original plan called for the conquest of Zagreb and restoration of the republic's territorial integrity. Velijko Kadijević, *Moje videjenje raspada: Vojska bez države* (Belgrade: Politika, 1993), pp. 134–136.

[22] The ICTY indicted seven individuals for their role in the Vukovar massacres, including Slobodan Milošević, who died in custody before his case could be resolved. The local commander of Serb forces, Mile Mrkšić, was sentenced to twenty years incarceration on charges of murder, torture, and cruel treatment for his role in the events. United Nations, International Tribunal for the Prosecution of Persons Responsible for Serious Violations of International Humanitarian Law Committed in the Territory of Former Yugoslavia since 1991, Case No. IT-95-13/1-T, 27 September 2007. Following the fall of the city the Serbian media speculated on the consequences of what was perceived as a major defeat for the political leadership in Zagreb. See "Hrvatska posle Vukovara," *Vreme*, no. 2134, 22 November 1991, pp. 10–16. In fact the major victim was the JNA. In the year that followed, its officer corps was systematically purged of officers of Yugoslav orientation. The army was renamed the Yugoslav Armed Forces (*Vojska Jugoslavije*-VJ) and transformed into an instrument for the pursuit of the hegemonic policies of Belgrade. The unfortunate legacy of the battle for Vukovar lives on. In September 2013, a riotous mob in the city destroyed bilingual signs (Croatian and Serbian) placed on government offices in accordance with the Croatian constitution (35 percent of the city's population today is Serbian). "Nastavljeni protesti u Vukovara," *Vesti*, 9 September 2013.

Sources of Noncompliance: Professional Military Education and Training

Training and education in the law of war within the JNA was pursued professionally but left much to be desired. To some extent this was due to inadequacies common to many military organizations, where formal instruction in these areas is seen to conflict with the overarching cult of the warrior. It was also due to factors distinct to Yugoslav and political and strategic culture. Conversations with JNA veterans reveal a tendency to conflate training in the law of war with indoctrination in Yugoslav communist ideology. Yugoslav citizens and soldiers were taught that they enjoyed a superior form of political and social order and served a state that could not, by definition, wage aggressive war with illicit means. But communist ideology also propagated merciless struggle against "enemies of the revolution," an orientation that could be applied to different kinds of "enemies" under changed circumstances.[23] As was the case elsewhere in the communist world, the contradictions inherent in Yugoslavia's official ideology encouraged cynicism. One former conscript, who had gone on to achieve prominence as a publicist, recalled how as a young soldier he was disciplined by loss of leave for questioning the army's failure to respond to manifestations of Croatian nationalism in the Dalmatian city were his unit was based. His position was correct, he was told by a superior officer, but it was politically problematic to undertake such actions and there were "some questions that could not be asked." What was true on the micro level also applied at higher levels. Against the background of Yugoslavia's disintegration, the once revered slogan *brotherhood and unity* would come to be mocked as yet another shallow manifestation of communist propaganda. The collapse of European communism from 1989 onward seems to have shattered whatever residual force official Yugoslav ideology might have possessed, including the civilizing assertions embedded within it.

Military training procedures were often of limited effectiveness. Typically, veterans recall instruction in the law of war and injunctions concerning respectful treatment of noncombatants as having been superficial and presented in a pro forma and noncompelling manner. When asked to describe some of the principles imparted in the instruction, former soldiers and officers often respond in a confused ("what is he asking?") or dismissive ("Oh yes, we had to learn all of that") manner. The law of war was imparted through a legalist prism that assumed unquestioned respect for accepted standards of conduct on the part of the command authority—an assumption that would not be borne out during

[23] Oleg V. Valetskii, *Iugoslavskaia voina: 1991–1995 gody* (Moscow: Izdatel'stvo "Kraft+", 2011), p. 357.

Yugoslavia's civil wars and that clashed with the widespread popular image of warfare as essentially unconstrained. The foundation for instruction remained the primacy of discipline within the chain of command including the admonition that failure to carry out orders to the letter would result in serious consequences. Very little if any attention was devoted to circumstances where soldiers would be obliged to listen to the dictates of personal conscience and contemplate the need to question or disobey orders to carry out illegal or unethical actions.[24] It would be unfair, however, to single out the JNA for special censure in this regard. Standards of compliance seem to have been internalized by both conscripted soldiers and officers to a normal and acceptable degree. It was the breakup of the JNA, the delegitimization of the moral and ethical context of Yugoslav communism, and the emergence of new armed formations without the time, or some cases the inclination, to develop effective instruction in war law and military ethics, that defined the context within which the wars of Yugoslav secession would be fought.

Sources of Noncompliance: Exclusionary Nationalism

Yugoslavia's disintegration was paralleled by the delegitimization of the ideology and value-structure that sustained it. This left a vacuum that a variety of uncompromising integral nationalisms were quick to fill. The wars of Yugoslav secession were defined by the political representatives of all belligerents as wars of national survival. As servants of new or aspiring national states, military officers were subjected to political direction that demanded harshness and systematically sought to demonize the enemy and portray it as hostile, barbaric, and unworthy of respect. From the outset, state failure, military fragmentation, and a state of crisis in which emerging polities confronted an imminent threat of armed aggression combined to create the perception of a state of emergency where normal rules did not apply.

When the JNA shattered its traditional values, institutional ethos, strategic direction, and very raison d'être were also destroyed. These are attributes that a military organization cannot reconstitute overnight. The spin-off armies came into being in extraordinary circumstances, on a foundation of ideologies of national intolerance where the dictates of war and what was perceived as military necessity tended to dominate. During the first phase of combat operations,

[24] Mark J. Osiel, *Obeying Orders: Atrocity, Military Discipline and the Law of War* (New Brunswick: Transaction Publishers, 2002).

with military forces being assembled chaotically and under duress, and with the Yugoslav military tradition effectively discarded, little or no legal or ethical training was provided despite declaratory compliance with Geneva rules on the part of the new political entities that the armed forces represented or sought to defend. Only in the postwar period would a substantive tradition of legal training be recreated in the new national armies of the Yugoslav successor states, and then in most cases according to Western and NATO guidelines rather than Yugoslav national traditions.[25] Among the Yugoslav successor states professional military education continues to struggle with the legacy of the wars of secession. In war colleges and military training institutions there is powerful resistance to drawing lessons learned that reflect critically on military performance in service of the nation during what are usually regarded as wars of self-defense and national independence.

The spin-off armies that emerged from the JNA were in most cases built on Yugoslav Territorial Defense components organized on the republican level. The quality of training within these units in socialist Yugoslavia varied from republic to republic. Slovene veterans consistently assert that one of the reasons the ten-day Slovene-Yugoslav war produced so few violations, and no indictments by the ICTY, was the uniquely high level of training that Slovene territorial defense formations enjoyed.[26] As a general rule, however, territorial defense units were trained to a lower standard than regular army units. They are commonly described as arenas within which local prejudices were reinforced, and where ethnic friction in multinational Yugoslavia was aggravated rather than transcended. The degree to which territorial defense forces internalized instruction in the law of war and military ethics was clearly inadequate in many cases. These lacunae carried over into the spin-off armies with former Yugoslav territorial defense components as their foundation.

[25] R. Craig Nation, "NATO in the Balkans: A Force for Stability?" *Southeastern Europe* 35, no. 1 (2010).

[26] Albin Mikulić, *Defending Democratic Slovenia 1991* (Ljubljana: Republic of Slovenia Ministry of Defense, 2006), describes the events of the ten-day war from a Slovene perspective. The Slovene war nonetheless gave rise to questionable episodes that provided a hint of the way in which the violent breakup of Yugoslavia would proceed. Slovene defiance was a carefully planned act of armed secession. With a ten-to-one advantage in the number of effectives on the ground, Slovene forces seized control of border-crossing stations and brought the Yugoslav Army casernes on Slovenian territory under siege, denying supply of food and water. The Slovenes commandeered trucks to serve as barricades at crossings and eight international drivers, who refused to abandon their vehicles, died when the barricades were attacked by Yugoslav aviation. On 27 June two unarmed Gazelle helicopters carrying bread shipments were shot down by the Slovene air force over Ljubljana. The Slovene commander of this operation told the author that he had received orders from the highest political authorities to allow no violations of Ljubljana airspace under any circumstances.

The argument that the Yugoslav Federation, in both its interwar and Titoist variants, was a bad idea from the start has a long pedigree. The conviction that the inevitable friction between the diverse peoples that constituted the federation was bound to explode, as it did during World War II and again in the 1990s, and that "ancient hatreds" for a despised Other was a fundamental source of the brutalities associated with the Yugoslav wars of secession is widespread.[27] It has been an influential argument in US policy circles since the publication of Robert Kaplan's *Balkan Ghosts* in 1993, widely read as a primer on the tradition of Balkan violence.[28] In fact, Tito's Yugoslavia had been remarkably successful in promoting economic growth, re-creating a shared political space after the terrible bloodletting of the world war, promoting a shared civic identity, and enhancing the country's international standing. Today the Tito years are widely viewed within the Yugoslav successor states, not least by those who never experienced them, as halcyon days of harmony, stability, and prosperity.[29] The critical role in promoting Yugoslavia's implosion was played by militant minorities who, against the background of a structural crisis combining economic decline with the political disorientation occasioned by the delegitimization of European communism, used the emotional appeal of exclusionary nationalism to secure power, win the passive allegiance of a critical mass of the citizenry, and unleash transformed military organizations and brutalized militias in an assault against the very concept of a multinational state. The ruthlessness with which the wars were waged grew out of systematically propagated hate narratives and the perceived need to create facts on the ground that would legitimate the radical appeal of an intolerant nationalism that under normal circumstances Yugoslav citizens might not have been predisposed to tolerate or accept.

[27] See the influential study by Ivo Banac, *The National Question in Yugoslavia: Origins, History, Politics* (Ithaca, NY: Cornell University Press, 1984). In the words of Philip Boulanger, *La Bosnie-Herzégovine: Une geopolitique de la de déchirure* (Paris: Éditions Karthala, 2002), p. 32, "the first Yugoslavia did nothing more than to impose, from above, a common structure upon peoples with histories, cultures, and collective memories that were radically different. The Yugoslav idea may be viewed as an ill-considered attempt to found a small empire in the face of great empires."

[28] Robert Kaplan, *Balkan Ghosts: A Journey through History* (New York: St. Martin's Press, 1993). An aide to President William Clinton famously (though anonymously) remarked that the book (built on Rebecca West's much greater *Black Lamb, Grey Falcon*) was influential in shaping the chief executive's thinking about the war.

[29] Nicole Lindstrom, "Yugonostalgia: Restorative and Reflective Nostalgia in Former Yugoslavia," *East Central Europe/L'Europe du Centre Est/Eine wissenschaftliche Zeitung* 32, no. 1 (January 2006), pp. 231–242. As a frequent visitor to the Yugoslav successor states, when I note to acquaintances that I was resident in Yugoslavia from 1977 to 1979, I am regularly told, by young and old, how fortunate I am to have been present during that "golden age."

Sources of Noncompliance: Desertion and Emigration

The disintegration of Yugoslavia provoked widespread desertion from the JNA, as citizen soldiers with primary allegiance to separatist republics simply walked away. More than two decades later, soldiers who opted for this course of action continue to defend their choice with pride. The majority of deserters, however, found ways to flee abroad. Many of the soldiers most sensitized to the destructive character of the ideologies of national intolerance driving the war toward extremes, and who might have been most likely to raise objections to improper conduct and abuses of power, were as a result removed from the ranks, and from society at large. The dynamic of emigration also weakened the military potential of the successor states, made their leaderships more dependent on unreliable and ill-disciplined irregular forces to accomplish military tasks, and made the pursuit of decision on the battlefield more elusive. Particularly in the case of Milošević's Serbia, with its proactive role in promoting conflict, the outbreak of fighting provoked the permanent emigration of an entire generation of Serbian youth. Serbian sources estimate that between 1991 and 1999 no fewer than 300,000 young people fled the country.[30] This was a form of political protest as well as draft resistance—émigrés generally describe their primary motive as allegiance to the Yugoslav idea and protest against primitive nationalism. Revealingly, the Serbian authorities viewed conscientious objection as a mortal threat. Gangs of hooligans were called on to intimidate public demonstrations of protest, and oppositionists often found themselves arrested, conscripted, and sent to the front.

Sources of Noncompliance: The Role of Irregular Forces

Many of the Yugoslav wars' most egregious violations were committed by irregular and paramilitary forces, including the armed wings of various political factions, private militias led by charismatic political entrepreneurs or warlords, foreign mercenary contingents (Mujahedeen, Russian, Italian, Greek), renegade police elements abetted by local armed civilians, and armed criminal bands.[31]

[30] Askold Krushelnycky, "Yugoslavia: UN Seeks Refugee Status for Serbian Deserters," *Radio Free Europe/Radio Liberty*, 9 November 1999.

[31] The role of criminal formations, sometimes acting in concert with organs of state power, was an important and sometimes underappreciated aspect of the Yugoslav conflict. It is a recurrent feature

Such formations were employed by responsible political authorities to accomplish "dirty work" that could be construed as offensive to honor, disintegrative of morale, illegal, or potentially damaging to the reputation of an aspiring nation-state. The UN Commission of Experts on the Former Yugoslavia counted forty-five such organizations active in Bosnia and Herzegovina alone.[32] In the early stages of the conflict a majority of combatants in the field did not wear distinctive uniforms, emblems, or insignias of rank. Chains of command were blurred, often intentionally, in order to obscure from where military initiatives were emerging, to conceal responsibility and establish claims of plausible deniability. In an environment characterized by the breakdown of traditional sources of authority, locally recruited militias sometimes acted with nearly complete autonomy in limited areas. The result was interaction between a confusing array of combatant forces operating within competing command structures, or outside the control of any formal structure—a situation where traditional sources of military restraint had reduced relevance.

The tasks performed by irregular forces included classic military functions such as close combat and urban operations, but also, as described in the ICTY statutes, acts of murder, extermination, enslavement, deportation, mass imprisonment, torture, and rape. The Serbian ethnic cleansing campaign in eastern Bosnia during 1992 was spearheaded by paramilitary formations.[33] Provocative incidents set the stage for the occupation of towns and villages accompanied by random killing. Commonly such actions included collaboration between regular and irregular forces. A typical pattern would begin with a heavy artillery bombardment of a targeted village, followed by an infantry assault clearing the way for paramilitary units to go door-to-door killing and terrorizing local residents. A round-up of non-Serbs, and their incarceration in hastily constructed detention centers, would follow. Under the direction of local police officers and paramilitaries, these camps became incubators for abuse. Survivors describe apparently willful violations including beatings, rape, inadequate nutrition, and vile humiliations such as coercing prisoners to consume their own excrement. Fighters with Paraga's HOS militia, which played an important role during the siege of Vukovar in 1991, adopted the black-shirted uniform and "Ready for the Homeland" (*Za Dom Spremni*) slogan of the genocidal Independent State

of contemporary "new wars." See Francesco Strazzari, *Notte balcanica: Guerre, crimine, stati falliti alle soglie d'europa* (Bologna: Il Mulino, 2008).

[32] United Nations Security Council, *Commission of Experts on the Former Yugoslavia Final Report*, S/1994/674-27 May 1994, Part III, Section A, "The Military Structure of the Warring Factions and the Strategies and Tactics They Employ."

[33] James Gow, *The Serbian Project and Its Adversaries: A Strategy of War Crimes* (Montreal: McGill-Queens University Press, 2003).

of Croatia during World War II. Muslim guerrillas built up from the criminal underworld and only loosely linked to the Bosnian chain of command carried out savage attacks against Serb civilians in Sarajevo and central Bosnia.[34] The training (normally nominal and focused entirely on tactical procedures) that these formations received was often imbued with an aggressive cult of violence for its own sake, intolerant nationalist extremism, sadism, and racial prejudice. Their business was politically sanctioned violence built on competing discourses of ethnic resentment, victimization, and dehumanization. The rationalization of brutality was represented as an alternative to the soft humanitarianism of the modern war convention, an assertion of will based on the ethos of *Blut und Boden*, and a necessary means to achieve the strategic goal of territorial consolidation. The paramilitary formations prepared and presented themselves as a conscious negation of the premises of international humanitarian law.

The systematic rape of female detainees was a particularly disturbing manifestation of such conduct. The number of rape victims during the course of the war has been estimated as high as 30,000, but it is difficult to arrive at a reliable figure.[35] Mass rapes carried out in Serb detention centers or in homes set apart to house women during the war in Croatia, if not organized then at least condoned by local commanders, have earned special notoriety, but all belligerent forces were to some extent involved in such activity. The ICTY set a precedent by characterizing the rape of Bosnian Serb women carried out at the Čelebići detention center in Konjić on the Neretva River in central Bosnia, coadministered during 1992 by the Bosnian Muslims and Croats, as acts of torture, grave breaches of the Geneva Conventions, and a violation of the laws and customs of war, and condemning three of the camp commanders to sentences ranging from seven to twenty years.[36] Sexual predation has always been a part of warfare, but the dehumanization of despised Others that grew from the context of ethnic mobilization in former Yugoslavia, and lack of imposed restraint within overlapping command hierarchies, seems to have encouraged the phenomenon.[37]

[34] Xahier Agirre Aranburo, *Yugoslavia y las Ejércitos: La Legitimad Militar en Tiempo de Genocido* (Madrid: Los Libros de la Catarata, 1997).

[35] Franke Wilmer, *The Social Construction of Man, the State and War: Identity, Conflict, and Violence in the Former Yugoslavia* (New York: Routledge, 2002), p. 60.

[36] United Nations, International Criminal Tribunal for Former Yugoslavia, CC/PUI/364-E, Celebici Case: The Judgement of the Trial Chamber, 16 November 1998.

[37] The author participated in interviews with rape victims during the Yugoslav conflict. Victims, seeking to assert their dignity in the face of unspeakable violations, were characteristically reticent to discuss the violations at length or to speculate about the motives of their assailants. The testimony was nonetheless overwhelming. It is an important foundation for what Nicola Henry calls "the preservation of post-conflict collective memory and the recognition of rape as a serious human rights violation." Nicola Henry, *War and Rape: Law, Memory and Justice* (New York: Routledge, 2011), p. 130.

In the war's first phase paramilitary formations sometimes acted with a degree of autonomy. Their provocations had the effect of upping the ante in localized disputes and pushing reluctant political leaders toward confrontation. In general, however, and increasingly as new national armies became more consolidated, their actions became more closely coordinated with political authorities and assisted by regular forces in service of consistent strategic goals. Partisans of strategies of violence used irregular forces to create facts on the ground and pressure more cautious and traditional leaders to buy in to their priorities.

Despite or because of the close ties between irregular formations and the new national entities that they purported to serve, the regular armed forces failed to restrain them from committing grave breaches of the Geneva Conventions and violations of war law. In the minds of responsible military professionals, irregular units were generally viewed as unreliable and lacking in discipline, distasteful rowdies and bullies situated outside the purview of the chain of command. During the course of the war, regular armies sought to tighten discipline and restrain misconduct within their own ranks—on this level, respect for the Geneva rules never disappeared. In some cases authorities sought to eliminate paramilitaries by incorporating them into regular army formations. In others, politically inconvenient or discredited paramilitary forces were forcefully dissolved and their leaders unceremoniously detained or murdered. The majority of Serbian militias were eventually subordinated to the national command. In 1992 Croatia took steps to break the HOS militia, including the arrest of its founder Paraga and the assassination of military commander Blaž Kraljević and eight members of his staff.[38] The Bosnian government turned against the Muslim militias that had been instrumental in the early defense of Sarajevo once their services were no longer considered essential. On 26 October 1993 the militias were disbanded and their most prominent leader Mušan Topalović (Caco) was murdered, possibly to eliminate a potentially inconvenient witness.[39] When they were active in the field, however, the paramilitaries were by and large permitted to develop and apply their own, normally abusive, tactical precepts. State failure ensured that much of the violence in the Yugoslav wars would be localized, outside of clear lines of command responsibility, in a domain of social relations and interactions

[38] Following Kraljević's assassination the HOS militia was disbanded. During the trial of Martin Naletilić and Vinko Martinović before the ICTY prosecutors argued that Kraljević was killed on the orders of the Croatian Democratic Community (HDZ), which opposed his uncompromising radicalism. United Nations, International Criminal Tribunal for Former Yugoslavia, Naletilić and Martinović, "Tuta i Štela," (IT-98-34), 31 March 2003. See also "Je li Tuta platio atentatorima po pet tisuću maraca," *Vjesnik*, 13 May 2003.

[39] Senad Pecianin and Vildana Selim Begovic, "The Exclusive Truth about the Crimes of 'Caco'," *The Centre for Peace in the Balkans*, 1 June 2000.

within which the structural constraints of International Humanitarian Law simply did not apply.

Violations of the law of war were not the exclusive prerogative of irregular forces and it would be incorrect to assume that the majority of these formations were ever entirely out of control. In most cases they remained subordinate to and an integral part of the designs of new national entities that tolerated or encouraged abuses in the service of strategic goals.[40] Some of the most serious violations were spearheaded by Special Forces and Interior Ministry contingents attached to regular armies, with specialized training and an institutional ethic intended to prepare them to operate in the shadows and if need be in contravention of military convention. Serbian Special Forces carried out an oversight function during ethnic cleansing campaigns in Bosnia and Herzegovina, Bosnian Serb Special Forces and the Serb Scorpion militia conducted the horrendous massacres at Srebrenica, and units under the direction of the Serbian Ministry of Internal Affairs coordinated ethnic cleansing operations in Kosovo during 1999. Regular forces were also implicated in war crimes, but more selectively and as the exception rather than the rule. The Bosnian Serb bombardment of Sarajevo and Croat bombardment of besieged Mostar were primarily the work of regular army units. So was Croatia's Operation Storm during 1955, which included the forceful expulsion of nearly all the Serb population of the Kninska Krajina including numerous cases of murder and terrorism, and ranks as the worst single incident of ethnic cleansing during the entire series of Yugoslav wars.[41]

[40] According to one insider account, Serbian paramilitaries "were all organized with the consent of Milošević's secret police and armed, commanded and controlled by its officers." Miloš Vasić, "The Yugoslav Army and the Post-Yugoslav Armies," in *Yugoslavia and After: A Study in Fragmentation, Despair and Rebirth*, ed. David A. Dyker and Ivan Vejvoda (London: Longman, 1996), p. 134. Roksanda Ninčić et al., "Drina bez Čuprije," *Vreme*, 21 October 1991, p. 20, documents the allegation. The connection is confirmed by interviews with Serbian veterans. For James Gow, *The Serbian Project and Its Adversaries*, p. 2, "the committing of war crimes was the essence of Serbian strategy in the war."

[41] Davor Marijan, *Oluja* (Zagreb: Hrvatski Memorijalno-Dokumentacijski Centar Domovinskog Rata, 2007), presents Operation Storm from a sympathetic perspective typical of postconflict national narratives. Giacomo Scotti, *Croazia, Operazione Tempesta* (Rome: Gamberetti Editrice, 1996), is harshly critical of the goals and conduct of the operation. Croatian General Ante Gotovina was convicted, together with two other defendants, by the ICTY on 15 April 2011, charged with participating in a "joint criminal enterprise" in conjunction with Operation Storm (other conspirators named included deceased Croatian president Franjo Tudjman, Minister of Defense Gojko Šušak, and Chiefs of Staff Janko Bobetko and Zvonimir Červenko) including acts of deportation and forcible transfer, plunder, and destruction. United Nations, International Criminal Tribunal for Former Yugoslavia, Judgement Summary for Gotovina et al., The Hague, 15 April 2011. On 16 November 2012 the Appeals Panel of the ICTY presided over by Theodor Meron by a three-to-two vote reversed the verdict and declared Gotovina not guilty.

Nonetheless, the degree of involvement of paramilitary units and Special Forces in the most egregious instances of grave breaches of the Geneva Conventions stands out. Military professionalism can and should be an important source of constraint in war, and of compliance with the laws and customs of armed conflict. The fragmentation of the military function that took place against the background of Yugoslavia's political collapse gave rise to irregular formations many of whose members were adolescents, subjected to charismatic but often amateurish leadership, imbued with an ethos of exclusionary nationalism and racism, caught up in cults of machismo and domination (often absorbed from the Rambo culture of the modern mass entertainment media), bent on personal gain, without scruples and ready to be manipulated for political ends. The majority of these factions were animated by an *animus furandi* that scorned traditional values and perpetrated an ethic that "would not sign up to the Geneva Conventions even if asked."[42] The emergence of such factions was an important source of noncompliance with Geneva law throughout the entire series of armed confrontations in former Yugoslavia from 1991 to 1999.

Sources of Noncompliance: Operational Context

The operational environment within which the Yugoslav wars were waged also contributed to a weakening of respect for war law. The goal of all belligerent factions was to secure control over contested areas in order to defend the territorial integrity of new national states, or to carve out and annex regions that had been purged to eliminate minority populations. Hence the phenomenon of ethnic cleansing (defined by the UN Commission of Experts as "rendering an area ethnically homogenous by using force or intimidation to remove persons from given groups from an area" and specifically designated as "contrary to international law") whereby military control became synonymous with terrorist assaults on local populations intended to provoke mass flight.[43]

Alexander Downes's study of violence against noncombatants in warfare identifies the goal of territorial conquest as one of two primary factors contributing to an increase in civilian casualties. The logic of indiscriminate mass killing emerges from an attempt "to implement racial or nationalist ideologies calling for the ethnic, national, or religious purification" of disputed territories and to "resolve military or political conflicts between ethnic groups over the control of territory," and tends to be manifested as "a tactic of early rather than later

[42] Christopher Coker, *Ethics in War in the 21st Century* (Abington: Routledge, 2008), p. 5.

[43] United Nations Security Council, *Commission of Experts on the Former Yugoslavia Final Report*, S/1994/674-27 May 1994, Part II Section B, "Ethnic Cleansing."

resort."[44] The observation could serve as a description of the course of events in former Yugoslavia as well as an account of causation. In any case, as an explanation for purposeful victimization of noncombatants and disregard for the modern war convention in the wars of Yugoslav secession it is apt.

None of the parties to the Yugoslav wars possessed sufficient force structure to maintain extended fronts or execute large-scale operational maneuver. Strategies of annihilation were beyond their reach. All of the spin-off armies were plagued by an insufficiency of trained and motivated infantry forces. The Serb and Croat sides in particular compensated with a resort to artillery barrages to clear disputed terrain, with disastrous consequences for civilian populations. After the first chaotic months of fighting, when Serb forces possessed a limited operational advantage and used it to secure control over large swaths of territory in Croatia and Bosnia and Herzegovina, all engaged armies were forced to fragment their forces and make do with the pursuit of modest tactical advances. Only external intervention was able to break up consequent logjams. The Yugoslav wars did not include large-scale set-piece battles between industrial armies with uniformed soldiery representing states in a formal state of belligerency—the circumstances for which the Geneva Conventions were originally devised.

Besiegement played an important role in the wars. Though besiegement has been an integral part of warfare from the origins of the institution, it can be argued that sieges may now be classified as illegal in contemporary land warfare.[45] However, this contestable assertion had no discernible effect on the conduct of military operations during the Yugoslav wars. The protracted partial siege of Sarajevo became an international cause célèbre, but it was not a unique case. Many of the dynamics of the Sarajevo encirclement were also present during the Croat siege of east Mostar between May 1993 and January 1994, best known because of the destruction by targeted artillery fire on 9 November 1993 of the 16th-century Old Bridge (*Stari Most*), considered by some as a symbol of the city's historical Muslim identity.[46]

[44] Alexander B. Downes, *Targeting Civilians in War* (Ithaca: Cornell University Press, 2008), pp. 5, 10.

[45] Detter, *The Law of War*, p. 314.

[46] Jadranko Prlić (who presided during the war over the Croatian entity of Herceg-Bosna's defense force, the Croatian Defense Council) was sentenced to a twenty-five-year prison term in 2013 by the ICTY for engaging in a "joint criminal enterprise" (said to include President Franjo Tudjman, Defense Minister Gojko Šušak, General Janko Bobetko, and Mate Boban et al.) to ethnically cleanse Bosnian Muslims. The indictment included a reference to the willful and wanton destruction of the *Stari Most*, judged not justified by military necessity and interpreted as a violation of the laws and customs of war. United Nations, International Criminal Tribunal for the Former Yugoslavia, Judgement Summary for Jadranko Prlić and Others, The Hague, 29 May 2013.

The siege of Sarajevo (April 1992–February 1996) was carefully planned. In January 1992, with the war in Croatia winding down and Yugoslavia in an advancing state of disintegration, the JNA reinforced its Sarajevo garrison, constructed a series of new roads opening access to the surrounding mountains, and brought in nearly seven hundred artillery pieces to ring the city. On 2 May 1992, following the Bosnian declaration of independence, the Serbs launched a major attack into the city, but achieved only limited gains. Thereafter, and for years to come, the city was subjected to daily rounds of bombardment by mortar fire, and systematic sniper fire. Local offensives were launched on occasion to tighten control over access routes by seizing strategic terrain covering mountain passes leading into the Sarajevo basin, but there were no further attempts to seize the city itself by storm. Though defended by a military garrison, Sarajevo had ceased to be a prize of war—it was in effect being held hostage to serve as a bargaining chip in an eventual round of negotiations.

In retrospect, the Serb strategy appears disastrously flawed. The human and material toll of the bombardment (more than 10,000 killed, 85 percent of whom were civilians including over 1,300 children, another 50,000 wounded, 60 percent of the city's buildings damaged, the destruction of important cultural monuments and institutions such as the famous National Library or *Večnica*) brought great discredit on the Serb cause. The fate of the city attracted a tremendous amount of international attention, inspired by a profound moral indignation.[47]

To some extent the standard narrative of events, built on the themes of victimization, martyrdom, and genocide, obscured a more complex reality. Sarajevo was never defenseless. It maintained an intimidating perimeter defense, and the defending forces conducted counterstrikes, including sniping and shelling, against Serb positions and Serb suburbs outside the ring of encirclement. A significant part of the Serb population of encircled Sarajevo (which fell from 13 percent to 5 percent of the city's population between 1991 and 1994) was subjected to ethnic cleansing. Bosnian Serbs of military age were exposed to

[47] In June 1992 the French president François Mitterrand made a surprise visit to the city and succeeded in opening access to Butmir airport. Thereafter the city was graced by a long list of celebrity visits. Christiane Amanpour broadcast repeatedly from Sarajevo. The French pundit Bernard-Henri Levy was one of the first prominent Western intellectuals to pay his regards, and went on to produce two films and a book devoted to the Bosnian war. Joan Baez staged a public concert in the city during 1993, and in August of that year Susan Sontag directed a performance of Beckett's *Waiting for Godot*, an ironic comment on international intervention *manqué*, by candlelight, in a Sarajevo school. In June 1994 Zuban Mehta conducted a performance of Mozart's *Requiem* in the ruins of the *Večnica*. The Archbishop of Paris, Cardinal Jean-Marie Lustiger, an Auschwitz survivor as a child, used a Christmas visit in 1993 to draw parallels with the Holocaust. The British actress Vanessa Redgrave, Spanish novelist Juan Goytisolo, French filmmaker Jean-Luc Godard, Irish pop singer Bono, and many others made the Sarajevo odyssey.

forced conscription on pain of confiscation of property. The Bosnian government refused to allow the city's population to evacuate under international auspices, for fear that depopulation would weaken their claim to the area in a negotiated end game. There are also persistent arguments that the Bosnian leadership resorted to "black propaganda" by conducting artillery strikes against their own population, presuming they would be blamed on the Serb party and increase pressures for international intervention.[48]

Control of the city was not vital to the Bosnian Serbs' military goals. Much of the territorial foundation for a Serb Republic within the confines of Bosnia and Herzegovina, including the city of Banja Luka as a potential capital, fell into Serb hands during the first months of the war. Maintaining the siege absorbed manpower that the Serb party could have used to effect elsewhere.[49] To some extent the siege seems to have been pursued in contravention of strategic logic, as an act of spite or malice (*iz inata*), of racial distain, and of defiance toward the Bosnian government and its many international supporters. These were goals that embraced the logic of attacks against civilians and encouraged disregard for international norms. Susan Woodward has suggested that the Serb faction sought to efface multinational Sarajevo because it "stood as a mockery to national exclusiveness."[50] The Bosnian Serb leader Momčilo Krajišnik seemed to confirm this judgment in a 1994 interview, asserting, "the significance of Sarajevo for our struggle is immense. Here it is being demonstrated that there is no future for any kind of unitary state."[51] In a study of what he calls the "politics of urban

[48] This is particularly the case with the two bombardments of the Markale market in central Sarajevo of 5 February and 28 August 1995, which together resulted in the deaths of 105 people and the wounding of 234 others, and became major international incidents. For an explication of the case against the Bosnian leadership see "Serby ne prichastny k vzryvu na Saraevskom rynke," *Russkaia liniia*, 9 July 2007. Whatever the technical justification for these accusations, Serb shelling of the city over several years was entirely consistent with such horrendous outcomes. On 5 December 2003 the Bosnian Serb general Stanislav Galić was convicted by the ICTY of responsibility for supervising the shelling and sniping of Sarajevo, including the attacks on the Markale market, and sentenced to 20 years imprisonment on charges of crimes against humanity and unlawfully inflicting terror on civilians. On 30 November 2006 the ICTY Appeals Chamber extended the sentence to life imprisonment. United Nations, International Tribunal for the Prosecution of Persons Responsible for Serious Violations of International Humanitarian Law in the Territory of Former Yugoslavia since 1991, Case No. IT-98—29-A, 30 November 2006.

[49] Jovan Divjak, a Bosnian Serb serving as deputy commander for the Army of Bosnia and Herzegovina, estimates that the Bosnian Serbs assigned 29,000 effectives to the siege of Sarajevo to cover sixty-four kilometers of front—too small a force to seize and hold an area where the Serb advantage in mechanized forces would be neutralized by terrain, but a drain on resources that could have been moved to other theaters of war. Cited by Zlatko Dizdarević, "Bosnia Erzegovina 1991–1993," in Magno, *La Guerra del dieci anni*, pp. 173–174.

[50] Susan L. Woodward, *Balkan Tragedy: Chaos and Dissolution after the Cold War* (Washington, DC: The Brookings Institution Press, 1995), p. 235.

[51] Cited from "Ljudi i vreme, Momčilo Krajišnik," *Vreme*, 28 November 1994, p. 55.

destruction," Martin Coward uses the example of Sarajevo as one of several case studies illustrating the purposeful destruction of the shared space and heterogeneity represented by urban centers as a strategy on the part of exclusionary regimes aiming at the forceful imposition of a homogeneous national culture.[52] These reflections touch on a profound source of noncompliance with Geneva rules in contemporary armed conflicts. The mentality that produced the protracted siege of Sarajevo was foreign to the idiom of warfare to which the Geneva Conventions are addressed.

Sources of Noncompliance: Revenge and Atrocity

Hugo Grotius wrote that "an infallible rule of action, which is written in the hearts of all men," required them to refuse to participate in "atrocious cruelty."[53] War law presumes that soldiers of sound mind can discern when they are ordered to engage in actions that violate common-sense rules of decency and are therefore manifestly illegal. The unmistakable immorality of atrocities such as the murder of noncombatants, execution of prisoners, rape, pillage, and torture should place them beyond the pale, consigned to the realm of depravity rather than acceptable military conduct.

Honor and self-respect can be powerful motivators, but they may also be displaced by blind rage provoked by perceived violations committed against "one's own" by a dehumanized enemy. Moreover, soldiers operate within hierarchical command structures that make obedience the most fundamental of obligations. They are subject to the normal human tendency to defer to authority figures even when required to engage in actions that offend the conscience.[54] Controlling such tendencies and avoiding egregious violations is part of the burden of command. To a significant extent, then, the breakdown of respect for Geneva rules during the Yugoslav wars can be attributed to failures of leadership.

At the highest level, the manipulative resort, by former communist leaders once pledged to the ideals of Titoism, to strategies of violence to discredit and dismantle the Yugoslav Federation created an ethical climate propitious to atrocity. Exclusionary nationalism became the cement for the aspiring separatist regimes, including the manipulation of historical memory in service of national hatred. Prior to the crisis of the Yugoslav state at the end of the 1980s, ethnic rivalry was a muted theme in national life. In the Yugoslav case the revival of

[52] Martin Coward, *Urbicide: The Politics of Urban Destruction* (New York: Routledge, 2008).

[53] Hugo Grotius, *The Rights of War and Peace* (Indianapolis: Liberty Fund, 2005).

[54] Stanley Miligram, *Obedience to Authority: An Experimental View* (New York: Harper & Row, 1974).

long buried resentments derived from the genocide of World War II became a particular source of animosity. The entire paraphernalia of ethnic nationalism banned under Tito was brought back with a vengeance. Dehumanization of the enemy became a standard technique for building esprit de corps among combatants. Officers and leaders frequently voiced racially or culturally degrading comments about real or prospective rivals in the course of their interactions with both soldiers and citizens, as well as in civil society.[55] Intimidating social pressure was generated to repress opposition to the prevailing war fever, creating a climate of fear that has left powerful traces to this day, where candid discussions concerning the wars must still be conducted with discretion and people are willing to "open up" only in an environment of trust. When fighting erupted, state-controlled media launched propaganda campaigns intended to provoke hatred and fear. Ethnic solidarity became a factor encouraging ruthlessness. The pornography of violence—attention devoted to atrocities purportedly committed by the enemy—served to prime the pump of vengefulness.[56] Both victims and victimizers shared the same emotional ground. Writing from besieged Sarajevo, the respected journalist Zlatko Dizdarević saw fit to denounce the besiegers as a "subhuman horde" and "nocturnal beasts."[57]

Individual combatants reacted to such pressures in diverse ways. Some opted for *agonized obedience*, regretting the assignments but rationalizing behavior on the basis of the assumption, common to all soldiering, that there was no way out. Others chose *emotional distancing* by adopting an equally common fatalism that ceded moral authority to national leaders and the military chain of command. Still others, a small but destructive minority, embraced the dictates of *aggression and cruelty*, including classic manifestations of sadism such as rape, humiliation, mutilation of the bodies of the fallen, and murder, all intended to reinforce domination over the despised Other.[58] Commanders were sometimes instructed to carry out such actions. On occasion they opted to resist, and on

[55] Particularly striking is the televised interview accorded by the Bosnian Serb commander Ratko Mladić to the BBC on 2 July 1993, where, relaxed and effusive, he opines in a racially offensive manner about the habits of Bosnian Muslims. Extracts from the interview appear in the BBC documentary *The Death of Yugoslavia*.

[56] The Serbian widow of a Yugoslav diplomat from Croatia, with homes in Split and Belgrade, recounts viewing a newscast in the autumn of 1991 on Belgrade television including graphic images of mutilated cadavers, described as Serb victims of *Ustaša* terror. Upon returning to Split, she viewed the identical images on Croatian television with the cadavers described as Croat victims of *Chetnik* terror. The targeted use of the pornography of violence was widespread.

[57] Zlatko Dizdarević, *Sarajevo: A War Journal* (New York: Fromm International, 1993), pp. 20, 29 and 83.

[58] David L. Perry, *Partly Cloudy: Ethics in War, Espionage, Covert Action, and Interrogation* (Lanham, MD: Scarecrow Press, 2009), pp. 71–90.

occasion not, thereby surrendering the capacity to impose restraint. The climate of reprisal and revenge that the purposeful commission of atrocities promoted shattered the honor of the combatant, the assumption of respect between practitioners of the profession of arms that is a foundation for all military ethics, undermined the logic of deterrence through proportional response, and ensured that the Yugoslav wars would be fought out in an emotional environment where the fragile injunctions of the war convention would have reduced relevance.

Hugo Slim notes that "most of the killing of civilians in the world today is done by a relatively small proportion of violent professionals . . . conventional military forces; armed groups; militias; terrorist units; suicide bombers; and criminal gangs."[59] With the exception of terrorists, all of the above-mentioned "violent professionals" perpetrated war crimes during the wars of Yugoslav secession. As in most contemporary "new wars," the imposition of suffering on noncombatants (murder, torture, sexual violence and rape, arbitrary confinement, forced resettlement, the imposition of humiliation and emotional trauma) unfolded in the nontraditional operational context of "war among the people" (to use Rupert Smith's phrase) where distinct kinds of military cultures interacted and the "absolutist and legalistic attitude to discussion of civilian suffering" that characterizes Geneva law became less relevant.[60] The special challenge of constraining armed conflict in this kind of environment draws attention to potential flaws or inadequacies in the existing war convention.

Sources of Noncompliance: Misdirected Legal Oversight

The ICTY, created on 25 May 1993 by the UN Security Council on the basis of Chapter 1 of the UN Charter, became an ambitious attempt to use the Yugoslav wars as a context for expanding the oversight of the international community in regard to international humanitarian law. The wars in Bosnia and Herzegovina from 1992 to 1995, and in Kosovo in 1999, were the first conflicts in history fought in the presence of an international tribunal considered competent to judge crimes committed and empowered to indict, judge, and impose penalties on those determined to be responsible for violations of war law.

In its own estimation, the ICTY strengthened the rule of law and its legacy will have a powerful deterrent effect on future would-be violators, forced

[59] Hugo Slim, *Killing Civilians: Method, Madness, and Morality in War* (New York: Columbia University Press, 2008), p. 214.

[60] Ibid., p. 260.

to think more carefully about the potential consequences of their actions. In 2004, the tribunal published a list of five achievements that it claimed to have accomplished:

- "Spearheading the shift from impunity to accountability" in view of the classic reluctance of national tribunals to take on this kind of responsibility.
- "Establishing the facts" on the basis of extensive evidence gathering.
- "Bringing justice to thousands and giving them a voice," particularly through the testimony of witnesses in public forums.
- "Accomplishments in International Law," including judgments on critical legal concepts in the domain of war law that had not been ruled on since the Nuremberg trials.
- "Strengthening the rule of law" by promoting international standards in war crimes prosecution.[61]

The ICTY was also a stimulus to the creation of a permanent international tribunal, the International Criminal Court (ICC), competent to judge individuals for the crimes of genocide, crimes against humanity, war crimes, and crimes of aggression.[62] International humanitarian law, it is argued, has become more robust and effective as a result.

Did legal oversight impose meaningful incentives to comply with Geneva law during the wars of Yugoslav secession? Unfortunately the ICTY has been and remains a contested institution whose work can be evaluated in different ways. With the arrest of Goran Hadžić on 20 July 2011 the Tribunal completed its trial register, and in 2013 a so-called International Residual Mechanism for Criminal Tribunals formally replaced it, charged with overseeing all remaining work. In 2016 the important trial of Ratko Mladić was still underway, in addition to several appeal processes. The ICTY has convicted more than 160 individuals, ranging from common soldiers to general officers, prime ministers, and a head of state (Slobodan Milošević). However, the Tribunal's final judgments are being imposed more than twenty years after the violations in question were committed. This is an inordinately long period of time—the old saw that justice deferred is justice denied is to some extent relevant.

Expressions of remorse before the Tribunal on the part of those sentenced have been nearly nonexistent. The typical response has been an unapologetic assertion that no crimes were committed coupled with scornful dismissal of the

[61] United Nations, International Criminal Tribunal for the Former Yugoslavia, *The Tribunal's Accomplishments in Justice and Law*, 2004.

[62] William A. Schabas, *An Introduction to the International Criminal Court*, 2nd ed. (Cambridge: Cambridge University Press, 2004).

institution's legitimacy. Public reactions to sentencing have been muted at best, and in some cases aggressively hostile. Informal discussions with Serbs and Montenegrins concerning the detainment of the longtime fugitives Karadžić and Mladić elicit the typical response that this is "ancient history—we want to forget these awful wars and look forward." The sentencing of Croat General Ante Gotovina in April 2011 to twenty-four years imprisonment for his role in the ethnic cleansing of the Kninska Krajina designated as Operation Storm (*Oluja*) sparked large demonstrations of protest in Zagreb. In an opinion poll undertaken in the summer of 2011, Croats designated Gotovina as the second most important Croat of the 20th century (after Franjo Tudjman!).[63] Upon returning to Croatia in 2013 after his sentence was overturned by the ICTY Appeals Chamber, Gotovina was greeted as a hero and received at the presidential palace. Today, billboards bearing his image and lauding his work may be seen all over the country. Operation Storm is commemorated annually with a victory celebration in Croatia, while in Serbia it is memorialized as a Day of Mourning.[64] In Bosnia and Herzegovina the work of the Tribunal is often compared to or elided with the intrusive role of other international instances in the affairs of the Republic and the perpetuation of "ethnic oligarchies" and political malfunction with which that role is associated. In general, opinion polls demonstrate a failure on the part of the ICTY to achieve general acceptance and legitimacy among affected populations.[65]

The ICTY took years to establish and was not yet fully operational when the war in Bosnia and Herzegovina was brought to an end. It has no power to arrest and it was only with the Dayton Accord of November 1995 that signatories were mandated to "cooperate" with its work. The first targets for indictment were perpetrators on the lower end of chains of command, not those responsible on the strategic or political level. The Tribunal was originally created on the initiative of the international community and justified as a mechanism that could punish those responsible for egregious war crimes, thereby establishing a foundation for reconciliation in a postwar environment.[66] However its external origins, dependence on international donors (led by the United States) for funding, reliance on international professional standards for legal accountability that do not always take into account the specific circumstances of the Yugoslav wars and

[63] "Tuđman najzaslužniji državu kakvu imamo, osvojio 62% glasova," *Večernji list*, 23 June 2011.

[64] Sven Milekic, "Croatia Prepares to Celebrate 'Operation Storm' Victory," *Transitional Balkan Justice*, 4 August 2016.

[65] The Scholars Initiative,' Research Group 10, Vojin Dimitrijević and Julie Mertus, *The Hague Tribunal (ICTY)* (West Lafayette, IN: Institute for Historical Justice and Reconciliation, January 2005).

[66] Theodor Meron, "The Case for Trials in Yugoslavia," *Foreign Affairs* 72, no. 3 (1993): 122–135.

the perceptions of affected populations, and limited authority reduced its ability to accomplish those ends. The Tribunal's procedures, including the issuance of secret indictments, entrapment of suspects, force feeding of an incarcerated indictee engaged in a hunger strike (Vojislav Šešelj), alleged censorship of information on political grounds, and more recently reversal of verdicts apparently based on a redefinition of standards imposed by great power sponsors have been widely criticized from a variety of perspectives.[67] Former lead prosecutor Carla Del Ponte has gone on record criticizing many aspects of the Tribunal's track record on professional grounds, including lack of cooperation from international sponsors and politically motivated favoritism.[68] Del Ponte's former advisor and spokesperson Florence Hartmann has published a scathing indictment of the Tribunal's inner workings, including accusations of deference to the major Western powers' political priorities at the cost of the pursuit of justice.[69]

It is difficult to work through contrasting assessments of the ICTY and to arrive at a definitive assessment of its accomplishments. The Tribunal represents an important step forward in the field of international justice, and has made meaningful contributions to the development of international humanitarian law. The denial of impunity is an important premise that must be respected and cultivated. However, in the Yugoslav case it is not possible to demonstrate a strong correlation between threat of punishment and reluctance or refusal to engage in war crimes on the part of actors and instances caught up in what was perceived as a life and death struggle. Punishment after the fact is warranted, but its deterrent effect must be questioned. The lack of *effective* legal oversight may therefore be reckoned as yet another source of noncompliance with war law in the wars of former Yugoslavia.

Caveats are also required when evaluating the Tribunal's contributions to a process of reconciliation. It was established as an impartial instance, and cannot convincingly be accused of unfairness, but there has clearly been a gap between intention and effect. In the Balkan region a perception of bias is widespread and has reduced the Tribunal's ability to contribute in a meaningful way to a dynamic of reconciliation. The work of the ICTY has precluded the establishment of some kind of Truth and Reconciliation process on the South African model, potentially a more promising approach to the challenge of postconflict peace

[67] R. Craig Nation, "The Balkan Wars and the International War Convention," in *Reflections on the Balkan Wars: Ten Years after the Break-Up of Yugoslavia*, ed. Jeffrey S. Morton and R. Craig Nation (New York: Palgrave Macmillan, 2004), pp. 147–164.

[68] Carla Del Ponte, *La caccia: Io e i criminali di Guerra* (Milan: Feltrinelli, 2008).

[69] Florence Hartmann, *Paix et châtiment: Les guerres secrets de la politique et de la justice internationale* (Paris: Flammarion, 2007). Hartmann was herself indicted by the Tribunal, convicted of disclosing confidential evidence relevant to the decision to acquit Serbia of direct responsibility for the Srebrenica massacre, and sentenced to pay a 7,000-Euro fine.

building. No moral reckoning of the sources of the war has been undertaken, nor is it part of the mandate or competency of a legal tribunal to move in that direction.[70] The sensitivities of what should be the Tribunal's most important constituency, the peoples of former Yugoslavia, have been neglected. Indeed, the work of the Tribunal might be said to demonstrate the inevitable limitations of a narrowly focused punitive and judicial approach to the challenge of reestablishing peace and justice in the wake of large-scale armed confrontations.[71]

Conclusions

The Yugoslav wars of secession may be regarded as a typical example of a type of modern warfare that poses special challenges for the war convention. Yugoslav training and professional military education in the law of war and military ethics was adequate for normal circumstances but insufficiently robust to stand up against the special trials of national disintegration, civil war, and ethnic strife inspired by exclusionary nationalism. Commanders and soldiers were aware of Geneva constraints, but co-opted or expelled from positions of responsibility by new political leaders who embraced hate narratives and strategies of violence designed to discredit and dismember the Yugoslav Federation. The process of ethnic mobilization was driven to extremes by the irregular formations and criminal bands that sprang up in the void created by the decline of central authority. Such formations were used to conquer or defend, and purge through ethnic cleansing, disputed territories to be incorporated into emerging national states. The dismemberment of the JNA and the rise of spin-off armies and paramilitaries led to a general weakening of good order and disciple. The manipulation of nationalism for political ends created an emotional ground allowing for the dehumanization of the enemy that encouraged resort to atrocities. Military professionalism served as a partial barrier to misconduct, but in the context of military fragmentation it was difficult to perpetuate and reconstitute. The most intense wave of violations occurred at the onset of the fighting. Lacking compelling national interests in the outcome, reactions by the international community were slow and inadequate. Efforts to impose accountability through the work

[70] These issues are addressed in a growing literature devoted to the theme of *jus post bellum*, or the cultivation of justice as a basis for enduring peace. For an introduction see Carsten Stahn and Jann K. Kleffner, eds., *Jus Post Bellum: Towards a Law of Transition from Conflict to Peace* (The Hague: T.M.C. Asser Press, 2008) and Gary J. Bass, "Jus Post Bellum," *Philosophy and Public Affairs* 52, no. 4 (2004): 384–412.

[71] This thesis is developed in Danilo Zola, *Chi dice umanità: Guerra, diretto e ordine globale* (Turin: Einaudi, 2000).

of the ICTY do not seem to have had a meaningful effect on the behavior of belligerents. The result was a strategic disaster whose consequences are still felt throughout the Balkan region and in Europe as a whole.

How to encourage more consistent compliance with Geneva law in future conflicts of a comparable nature? At a minimum it will be necessary to take account of the gap between the conventional interstate conflicts for which the Conventions were originally devised and the special demands of contemporary new wars, where consolidated sovereign states with clear chains of command are no longer primary actors, ill-disciplined irregular forces play a greater role, and emotionally laden discourses of identity, cultural integrity, and confessional orientation often trump more classic geostrategic goals. The punitive and legalistic dimensions of Geneva law will not become irrelevant, but may need to be balanced by a greater emphasis on conflict prevention, depoliticized international oversight, and strategies of reconciliation.

10

"Be Karbala Miravim!"

Iran, or the Challenges of Internalizing International Humanitarian Law in a Muslim Country

ANICÉE VAN ENGELAND

While the war with Iraq is a distant, yet vivid, memory, its impact on the Islamic Republic of Iran (IRI) was profound—including on the evolution of Iran's approach to international humanitarian law (IHL). Iran still has some important steps to take with regard to the integration of IHL within the domestic legal system. The stakes are high, as Iran has an Islamic legal system and is in constant search for its own legal identity, putting at risk the universality and unity of IHL: While Iran has made efforts to integrate various universal humanitarian instruments such as the Geneva Conventions, the country has taken a stance by "Islamizing" an important part of its legislation after the 1979 revolution, including humanitarian law. The outcome is a sort of hybrid humanitarian legal system, mixing the Geneva Conventions and Islamic humanitarian standards.

Soldiers leaving for the front line during the Iran-Iraq War (1980–1988) used to sing "Be Karbala Miravim," a song evoking the Battle of Karbala in the year 680 (61 in the Islamic calendar) during which the grandson of Prophet Mohammad, Imam Hussain, fought the troops of the Ommeyad and Sunni Caliph Yazid. Imam Hussain's troops were made up of seventy-two men and children, all of whom were killed. This event, very important in Shia Islam, is commemorated every year during Ashura. This is why Iranian soldiers sang, "We are going to Karbala," in honor of Imam Hussain—because they too were leading a jihad against the Sunni oppressor. The fact that both wars entailed Muslims killing fellow Muslims, as well as children, would seem to raise ethical problems for believers, and—for the war of the 1980s—conflicts with the legal regime of the Geneva Conventions.

This chapter considers the extent to which Islamic governance can integrate IHL into its own legal system. It addresses the consequences of the emergence of an Islamic-universal hybrid legal system with regard to the protection of civilians and the conduct of hostilities. The stakes are high since IHL's efficiency and necessity have been questioned several times:[1] The existence of the Iranian hybrid system of law can be perceived as a threat by scholars arguing that international law is at risk of fragmentation due to the variety of domestic and regional approaches to fundamental legal standards.[2] The importance of those stakes is illustrated by the Iran-Iraq War: The process of mixing a universal secular legal system with a religious domestic law occurred at a crucial time when Iran was at war with Iraq, with clear effects on the protection of civilians and the conduct of hostilities.

This chapter pursues an original approach to explain how Iranian humanitarian standards seek conciliation with universal standards in order to uphold protection of civilians and principles of conduct of hostilities. The Iranian understanding of humanitarian standards constitutes an illustration of one possible Islamic approach to humanitarian law,[3] as each Muslim system of governance and school of thought has its own interpretation of humanitarian standards and war ethics. But far from representing a risk of fragmentation or a threat to IHL, the Iranian understanding can be enriching for IHL, if approached in a constructive fashion.

The first part of this chapter looks at the degree of internalization of IHL in Iranian law and the impact of Islamization. The second part examines the Iran-Iraq War as an illustration of the effects of the Islamization of humanitarian law. The third part is devoted to an analysis of the integration of IHL nowadays in army manuals and Iranian law, focusing on the positive changes that have occurred in postconflict Iran. The chapter concludes by looking at prospects for congruence through different attempts to further integration.

[1] For example, the Geneva Conventions were qualified as being "quaint and obsolete" by Alberto Gonzalez in a memorandum: "Memorandum for the President from Alberto R. Gonzales, Decision RE: Application of the Geneva Convention on Prisoners of War to the Conflict with al Qaeda and the Taliban" (25 January 2002) in *The Torture Papers: The Road to Abu Ghraib*, ed. Karen J. Greenberg and Joshua L. Dratel (New York: Cambridge University Press, 2005), 80, pp. 118–121.

[2] Anicée Van Engeland, "Human Rights Strategies to Avoid Fragmentation on International Law as a Threat To peace: The Islamic Republic of Iran as a Case Study," *Interdisciplinary Journal of Human Rights Law* 5, no. 1 (2010–2011): 25–48.

[3] Anicée Van Engeland, "The Differences and Similarities between International Humanitarian Law and Islamic Humanitarian Law: Is there Ground for Reconciliation?" *Journal of Islamic Law and Culture* 10, no. 1 (2008): 89–99; Anicée Van Engeland, "The Challenge of Fragmentation of International Humanitarian Law Regarding the Protection of Civilians—An Islamic Perspective," in *Jihad and the Challenges of International and Domestic Law*, ed. Cherif Bassiouni and Amna Guellali (The Hague: Hague Academic Press, 2010), pp. 139–166.

The Challenge of Integrating International Humanitarian Law into Iranian Law

The internalization of IHL into Iranian law became an issue after the 1979 Islamic revolution: The domestic legal system was brought in line with the new Islamic creed, and the difficulty was to accommodate two sets of law: Islamic Shia law and IHL. Despite having many elements in common, such as protection of civilians or protection of lands, the two legal systems have also some major discrepancies. As a result, the enforcement of IHL has emerged as a challenge for Iran as a Muslim country. This first part seeks to demonstrate the complexity of the Iranian approach to humanitarian law resulting from a hybrid approach.

Geneva Conventions, from the Decline of the Lion to the Rise of the Crescent

The IRI took several steps to Islamize the legal system. The outcome is a hybrid system in which Iranian Islamic law has precedence over IHL. Thus, IHL has not been absorbed by Iranian law: the two legal systems apply side by side. This leads to concrete problems and consequences for the protection of civilians and the respect of the rules in the conduct of hostilities, as illustrated in the second part of this chapter.

Iran signed the Geneva Conventions on 8 December 1949. The Conventions were ratified on 20 February 1957 by the Majles, which was the lower house under the Shah, and the Senate. The Shah's control over all branches of power facilitated the ratification without further discussion. At the time, Iranian law was largely secular, except for family law, so there were no issues of conciliation between IHL and Iranian law. Besides, the ratification of international documents was part of the imperial regime's policy of modernization and secularization of Iran.[4] Part of that strategy of modernization included the isolation of clerics in order to muzzle opposition and to take control over the law to ensure it would remain secular (a strategy that failed in the late seventies, when the Shah had to Islamize large parts of family law to counter the growing power of the clerics). Very few voices were heard against the ratification of the Geneva Conventions or to advocate for an Islamic alternative. The situation changed radically in 1979, when clerics toppled the royal regime. After decades of being sidelined and silenced, clerics changed Iranian law so that it would match Ayatollah Khomeini's approach and would support the principle of *velayat-e*

[4] Jean Pierre Digard Bernard Hourcade and Yann Richard, *L'iran au XXe siècle* (Paris: Fayard, 2007).

faqih, which is still the governance system of the country.[5] Issues of conciliation between the Geneva Conventions and an Islamized Iranian law emerged. Those controversies became a practical issue with the Iraq-Iran War, or "the imposed war," as the Iranians call it.[6]

As an outcome of the radical evolution of post-1979 Iran, the government issued reservations/declarations to the Geneva Conventions on 4 September 1980 and on 12 September 2000. In the 1980 Declaration, the Legal Department of the Ministry of Foreign Affairs of the IRI declared to the Swiss embassy that the government of the IRI would renounce the use of the emblem of the Red Lion and the Red Sun.[7] The Red Lion and Sun Society of Iran had been established in 1922 and admitted by the Red Cross and Red Crescent Societies in 1923.[8] Thus Iran had its own emblem for a long time. After the Islamic revolution, the country adopted the Red Crescent used by other Islamic countries. The decision was officially justified to limit the existence of further emblems that might lead to confusion as to which recognizable emblem the Red Cross movement used. In reality, it was clearly a declaration to the international community that Iran was now an Islamic state, using the crescent as a symbol of Islam. In addition, the lion emblem resembled the imperial regime's symbol; it was therefore a symbol the new regime was keen on replacing with an Islamic emblem. However, in the 2000 Declaration, the Ministry of Foreign Affairs maintained Iran's right of using the Red Lion and Sun emblem again.[9] The Red Lion, it claimed, was the country's coat of arms throughout history and its use was deeply rooted in traditional culture.[10]

The two declarations/reservations to the Geneva Conventions illustrate the new Iranian regime's approach: The change of emblem aimed at demonstrating

[5] *Velayat-e faqih* is the system of governance of the Islamic republic of Iran in which the jurists in Islamic law rule in the absence of the 12th Imam.

[6] The Iranians refer to the Iran-Iraq War as the imposed war (*Jang-e-tahmīlī*) for which Holy Defense (*Defā'-e-moqqaddas*) in the framework of a jihad was allowed. They also called the Iran-Iraq War the "Persian Gulf War" or the "First Gulf War," to distinguish it from the 1991 invasion of Kuwait by Iraq. Iranians considered the Iran-Iraq War to be an imposed war because Iraq invaded Iran, with the support of the majority of the international community, which thought the war could be a way of ending the IRI that they perceived as a threat.

[7] Text Reservation/Declaration, Islamic Republic of Iran, 4 September 1980, Notification made to ICRC on 26 September 1980; see also the *Newsletter of the League of Red Cross Societies* 72, 5 November 1980.

[8] *History of the Iranian Red Crescent Society*, http://www.emdadgar.com/historyen.htm.

[9] Text Reservation/Declaration, Islamic Republic of Iran, 23 July 2000, in Dietrich Schindler and Jiri Toman, *The Laws of Armed Conflicts* (Leiden: Martinus Nijhoff, 1988), p. 576.

[10] Zidane Meriboute, "The Emblems of the 1949 Geneva Conventions: Their Content and Meaning," in *The Yearbook of International Humanitarian Law* (The Hague: TMC Asser, 2000), pp. 258–272.

that Iran had become an Islamic country and that past approaches to humanitarian law were to be changed. Iran did not reject the Geneva Conventions but made it clear that in case of a conflict of laws between the Conventions and Islamic humanitarian law, the latter would supersede the first.[11]

International Law beyond Geneva

While Iran clarified its position with regard to the conflict of norms, it also demonstrated that it wished to be bound internationally by IHL: none of the international conventions were challenged. The IRI has been quite open to criticizing conventions that would not meet Islamic requirements, as illustrated by its refusal to ratify the Convention of the Elimination of Discrimination against Women (CEDAW), despite growing internal demands and international pressure. The argument put forward is that CEDAW contains legal views that cannot be reconciled with Islamic law; the IRI's successive governments have considered the differences between the Iranian Islamic approach to women and international women's rights to be too important to allow a ratification of the document.[12] By contrast, humanitarian documents were not denounced after the change of regime, and some new ones were ratified.

There have been several calls for Iran to ratify Additional Protocol I. The fact that Iran has not yet ratified this document is paradoxical, considering how often it referred to it during the war with Iraq.[13] Since most of the Protocol is now customary international law, ratifying it would be symbolic.

Iran is a party to the Hague Convention on Land Warfare of 1899 but did not become a party to the 1907 Hague Convention dealing with the conduct of hostilities. Iran is bound by the Convention because it is now part of customary international law. Iran signed the Chemical Weapons Convention in 1993 and ratified it in 1997, when the Convention entered into force. Iran was very active during the negotiations for obvious reasons: Iraq used gas and other chemical weapons during the war, with terrible effects for the Iraqi and the Iranian populations.[14] Iran also ratified the 1954 Hague Convention on Protection of Cultural

[11] The UN Iranian representative declared in 1983 that in case of a conflict of law, Islamic Iranian law would override international law: General Assembly of the United Nations, 39th session, 3rd committee, meeting 65, 7 December 1984, A/C.3/39/SR.65.

[12] "CEDAW Rejected in Iran," *Feminist Daily News*, 19 August 2003, http://www.feminist.org/news/newsbyte/uswirestory.asp?id=7996.

[13] Christopher Greenwood, "Customary Law Status of the 1977 Geneva Protocols" in Humanitarian *Law of Armed Conflict: Challenges Ahead: Essays in Honour of Fritz Kalshoven*, ed. A. Delissen and G. T. Tanja (Norwell, MA: Martinus Nijhoff, 2007), pp. 93–114, at p. 100.

[14] Gawdat Bahgat, "Nuclear Proliferation: The Islamic Republic of Iran," *Iranian Studies Journal* 39, no. 3 (2006): 307–327.

Property in the event of armed conflict. It is not a party to the Landmines Convention of Ottawa. It attended the negotiations and the preparatory meetings but as an observer. Indeed Iran keeps a stock of landmines.[15] Sixteen million of them were laid in Iran during the war with Iraq, and many are still buried and unexploded, maiming children and villagers when they are accidentally set off.[16] Rather than join the landmine ban and undertake demining operations, Iran has continued to justify possessing and laying landmines as part of the fight against drug traffickers and human smugglers taking place at the borders with Iraq, Afghanistan, and Pakistan.[17]

The Supremacy of Islamic Law over International Humanitarian Law

The approach to humanitarian law in Iran is unique: One can find the Geneva Conventions' influence but the main framework is Islamic. This weighs heavily on the integration of IHL into Iranian law: Any new bill seeking to implement IHL standards must pass the test of the Guardian Council,[18] which performs the control of constitutionality and "islamicity" of the document. Ratified conventions are constantly adapted, interpreted, or sidelined because of the coexistence of two legal systems, the international one and the Iranian one: for example, Iran executes children under the age of 18 years with full disregard of the International Covenant on Civil and Political Rights it ratified in 1975. The IHL documents also suffered from those "adaptations," as illustrated in what follows, during the Iraq-Iran War.

An Islamic Legal Framework

This alternative legal system constructed by Iran provides an Islamic ethics of war that is perceived to be closer to Iranian identity and needs than IHL is.[19]

[15] "Landmine and Cluster Munition Monitor, Report: Iran," http://www.the-monitor.org/index.php/publications/display?url=lm/2002/iran.html.

[16] US Department of State, *Hidden Killers: The Global Landmine Crisis* (Washington, DC: US Department of State, Bureau of Political-Military Affairs, 1998).

[17] "Landmine and Cluster Munition Monitor, Report: Iran."

[18] The Guardian Council (*hora-ye Negahban-e Qanun-e Assassi*), an institution made up of twelve clerics, is in charge of interpreting the Constitution and checking the constitutionality of every bill (among other tasks).

[19] See, e.g., Sohail H. Hashmi, "Saving and Taking Life in War: Three Modern Muslim Views," *Muslim World* 89, no. 2 (April 1999): 158–180.

This hybrid system, however, creates confusion at the international level and is perceived as a threat to the unity of international law. For example, Iran has its own reasoning on the possession of nuclear weapons, based on Islamic law: It is prohibited (*haram*) to use such a weapon because it targets civilians in an indiscriminate fashion. Meanwhile it would be acceptable (*halal*) to have such a weapon to use it as a deterrent and for leverage in international negotiations. This was made clear in a fatwa issued by the Supreme Leader Khamenei and supported by the clerical establishment.[20] To the extent that the *fatwa* justified Iran's eventual development of a nuclear weapon, it was inconsistent with the country's ratification of the Nuclear Nonproliferation Treaty of 1970, when it committed itself to remain a nonnuclear state. The comprehensive nuclear agreement of 2016 shifted Iran toward international compliance, but tensions remain with the country's interpretation of Islamic law's perspective on nuclear weapons.

Iranian Islamic Law and Kelsen's Pyramid of Norms

To understand better why the internalization of the Geneva Conventions represents a challenge, one has to analyze the main change that occurred with the Islamic Constitution: in Iranian constitutional law, domestic law supersedes international law.[21] The supremacy of national law over international law has been clearly stated by Iran on several occasions: If there is a conflict of law, Islamic Iranian law will take precedence. In 1984, the Iranian ambassador to the United Nations declared:

> The new political order was [. . .] in full accordance and harmony with the deepest moral and religious convictions of the people and therefore was most representative of the traditional, cultural, moral and religious beliefs of Iranian society. It recognized no authority [. . .] apart from Islamic law [. . .] conventions, declarations and resolutions or decisions of international organizations, which were contrary to Islam, had no validity in the Islamic Republic of Iran [. . .] the Universal Declaration of Human Rights, which represented secular understanding of the Judeo-Christian tradition, could not be implemented by Muslims and did not accord with the system of values recognized by

[20] Robert Collier, "Nuclear Weapons Unholy, Iran Says: Islam Forbids Use, Clerics proclaim," *San Francisco Chronicle*, 31 October 2003.

[21] Bita Ghaffari, "Media Role Unique in Promoting International Humanitarian Law," *Iran Daily*, 15 March 2005.

> the Islamic Republic of Iran; his country would therefore not hesitate to violate its provisions.[22]

This does not mean that the Conventions are null in their effects in Iran. One should not exaggerate the impact of this hybrid law in the field: Iran generally complies with the Geneva Conventions because it reflects major Islamic humanitarian standards. Anyone who reads the Islamic religious texts will be struck by the similarities between these Islamic humanitarian principles and IHL: Examples of *siyar*[23] of Islamic law compatible with the Geneva Conventions include this *hadith* that states, "Do not kill an old person, a child, a woman; do not cheat on the booty, do well: God likes the ones who act right."[24] This said, when there is a conflict of laws, Iran is more likely to comply with these religious rules as they reflect the culture of Iran.[25]

The consequences on IHL could be severe, as illustrated by the treatment of prisoners of war (POWs) during the Iran-Iraq War. For example, during the war, the Army of the Guardians of the Islamic Revolution (*Sepah-e Pasadaran*) published a guide on POWs titled "Questions from the Imam on war and jihad." In this guide, Ayatollah Khomeini answered specific questions, including this one: "Can we kill wounded enemies if they cannot be transferred behind the lines and might be recovered by the enemy if they are left behind? Also can we kill a POW if the enemy attacks to retake him?" He responded, "In the name of the Almighty. As long as the enemy maintains a base and sanctuary, the prisoner might again be mobilized against Islam and Moslems. He can be killed."[26]

This is fatwa clearly in violation of Geneva Conventions provisions for taking surrendering prisoners alive and treating POWs well. This is an example of differences that might emerge between IHL and Iranian law. However, these differences are caused by *interpretations* of Islamic legal sources: Indeed, while the *hadith* reported above is part of the positive Islamic legal sources along with the Quran, these sources must be interpreted by human beings to be applied. The process of interpretation by clerics, called *ijtihad,* could potentially be subjective as illustrated by the fatwa on POWs: the interpretation made by Ayatollah

[22] Said Rajaii Khorasani, Iranian ambassador to the United Nations, "Address to the United Nations General Assembly, Thirty-Ninth Session, Third Committee, 65th meeting," 7 December 1984, A/C.3/39/SR.65.

[23] *Siyar* are rules of international law in Islamic law.

[24] *Hadith* quoted in Hamed Sultan, "La conception islamique," *Les dimensions internationales du droit humanitaire* (Paris: Institut Henry-Dunant, Pedone, Unesco, 1986), p. 57.

[25] Interview with Ahmad Ali Noorbala, conducted by Toni Pfanner, Andreas Wigger, and Mostafa Mohaghegh (26 April 2005) *International Review of the Red Cross* 87, no. 858 (June 2005): 1.

[26] *Sepah, Estefsaat Az Hazrate Emam Khomeyni Raje Be Jang Va Jihad* [Guidelines from Imam Khomeini about War and Jihad] (Tehran: Sepah, April 1982).

Khomeini to serve a political and war agenda. Therefore, the commitment to IHL and the Geneva Conventions has been approached differently under the Islamic republic, and universal documents have been accommodated to respect Islamic principles as formulated by clerics in times of war. The issue is to know whether those interpretations reflect Islamic laws of war, an issue that will be addressed in part four of this chapter.

The Iran Islamic Humanitarian Creed at War

Iran's hybrid legislation regulates the laws of war but also sets humanitarian standards. The war between Iraq and Iran provides the best illustration of the two sets of law working together with their attendant successes and failures.

The ideological framework of the IRI explains the resort to jihad theories.[27] Relying on the theories of jihad allowed the late Ayatollah Khomeini to comfort the recently emerged Islamic republic and assert his own power. The basic argument went as follows: Jihad is a necessary instrument to protect Islam (Quran 22:40) and the oppressed (Quran 4:75). A fair war is a defensive war relying on the principle of self-defense (Quran 2:190, 22:39). So, when Islam is threatened, when an Islamic country is under attack or when Muslim people are oppressed, self-defense jihad is legitimate. In the case of the Iran-Iraq War, Iraq, a secular country, attacked and invaded Iran, an Islamic country, oppressing Iranian Muslims. Besides, the regime of Saddam Hussein also oppressed the Shia Muslims in his own country, which justified some of Iran's attacks on Iraqi civilians during the war on the cities.[28] Therefore, self-defense was allowed under Islamic law. In Shia Islam, it is expected the representative of the 12th Imam on earth will declare jihad: in his absence, his representative on earth, Ayatollah Khomeini, declared the defensive jihad against Iraq.[29] Later, when there was pressure from the international community to sign a peace treaty, Iran refused to negotiate, basing its argument on Islamic law: Iraq was still a threat to the country and therefore war was still legitimate.[30] Indeed, according

[27] Ayatollah Khomeini, *Sahifa Ye Nour* (Tehran: Ministry of Culture and Islamic Guidance, 1991), pp. 570–571.

[28] The war on the cities is an episode of the Iran-Iraq War that started in 1985, when troops on the ground were in a stalemate, and Iraq decided to target Iranian cities. Iran retaliated, and civilians were the victims of this exchange of SCUD missiles. The aim of the Iraqi army was to force the IRI to accept defeat and collapse.

[29] Ayatollah Khomeini, *Etela'at*, 10 May 1987.

[30] Ige Dekker and Harry H. G. Post, eds., *The Gulf War of 1980–1988: The Iran-Iraq War in International Legal Perspective* (Dordrecht: Martinus Nijhoff, 1992).

to Iranian Shia interpretation of Islamic law, war shall go on until the threat disappears.[31]

During the war, the IRI developed the doctrine of "the blood overcoming the sword,"[32] by which the sacrifice of the martyrs would summon the strength to confront an enemy who was technologically stronger. This position was supported by a fatwa of Ayatollah Mutahhari, who declared, "a Muslim community equipped with the spirit of jihad is not vulnerable to enemy assaults. Jihad is the reliable shield of God."[33] Iran was also following the basic Islamic principle according to which war has to be waged *fi sabil Allah*, which means in the way of God, respecting Islamic standards of war such as the distinction between civilians and combatants.

The reliance on the *jihadi* creed was also justified by a propaganda still aimed at reinforcing the new system of governance: Iraq's aggression was never recognized as such by the United Nations, creating resentment and justifying the argument that the IRI was isolated on the international scene and was persecuted because of its reliance on Islam. As a result, the war was called "the imposed war": Iranians considered it to be imposed because Iran was attacked and invaded by Iraq, which was seeking to get control over the Gulf.[34] In that regard, domestic law superseded IHL: it helped protect and serve the interests of the IRI better than IHL would have done. It allowed the authorities to demonstrate that Islamic law was self-sufficient and therefore the IRI was self-sufficient. Iran declared international law to be "oppressive and invalid," so that it had a free hand when it came to using Islamic rules of war.[35]

The confusing element is that despite renouncing international law, the Iranian authorities referred to the Geneva Conventions and Additional Protocol I when Iraq attacked commercial Iranian ships in international waters, and again when the shelling by Iraq of Iranian oil wells caused extensive damage to the environment in 1982.[36] The reason for doing so is that Iran never intended to be

[31] Kaiyan Homi Kaikobad, "Ius ad Bellum: Legal Implications of the Iran-Iraq waR," in Dekker and Post, *The Gulf War of 1980–1988*, pp. 51–69.

[32] See Hojjat-ol eslam Seeyd Ali Khameini, 42nd United Nations General Assembly, 22 September 1987, http://www.c-spanvideo.org/program/1206-1. For an analysis, see Steven Ward, "Iran's Challenging Victory Narrative," *Historically Speaking* 10, no. 3 (June 2009): 41–42.

[33] James A. Bill, "Morale vs. Technology: The Power of Iran in the Persian Gulf War," in *The Iran-Iraq War: The Politics of Aggression*, ed. Farhang Rajaee (Gainesville: University Press of Florida, 1993), p. 205.

[34] For a legal analysis of whether or not the attack constituted aggression, see Bahman Bakhtiari, "International Law: Observations and Violations," in Rajaee, *The Iran-Iraq War*, pp. 152–166.

[35] Faraji Moez, *Captivity and Prisoners of War in the Battle of Truth against Falsehood* (Tehran: Ministry of Guidance, 1984).

[36] Rajaee, *The Iran-Iraq War*, pp. 223–224.

sidelined from the international community; it used international law at its convenience, moving between Islamic law and IHL in order to serve the interests of the IRI. This behavior is perhaps most consistent with the realist perspective that Tannenwald outlines in her introduction. At the same time, the war was perceived as a test for the newly established republic, and its leaders seized it an as opportunity to illustrate the strength of using Islam as a governing referent.

The Double Standard Syndrome

There are several reasons for Iran's hybrid approach to humanitarian standards. Other than the ideological/religious factors described above, there is a historical explanation: Iran has a history of mistrust toward the international community. There is a feeling, supported by IRI's propaganda, that the country was and still is victim of a double standard when it comes to the respect of universal human rights.[37] The Carter administration, for example, supported the Shah's administration when it violated human rights by imprisoning political opponents and by repressing public demonstrations in a disproportionate fashion.[38] This is why the late Ayatollah Khomeini denounced the Universal Declaration of Human Rights as a tool for oppression: He made several references to that document to illustrate that it was used by the international community to hinder the development

[37] Mohammed H. Malek and Mark F. Imber, "The Security Council and the Gulf War: A Case of Double Standard," in *International Mediation and the Gulf War*, ed. M. H. Malek (Glasgow: Royston House, 1991), pp. 158–194. An example of this feeling is the request the Iranian officials have made to the international community for war reparations. Since the end of the war with Iraq, there were pressures to have Iraq, Saddam Hussein, and his administration put on trial for gross violations of international law and IHL. Mohsen Baharvand, director of the Foreign Ministry's Legal Department, talked about setting up a special Iraqi tribunal and the rights of victims to reparation. According to him, Hussein and military forces acting under him violated IHL and the Geneva Conventions recurrently. He therefore called for Iran to bring Hussein to justice and to try him for war crimes. The Foreign Ministry and judiciary compiled a bill citing criminal acts committed by Saddam's forces including looting; killing of civilians; raping; forced migration; bombing schools, mosques, and cultural heritage sites; and using banned weapons. Iran did not present the bill to any international organization, because it did not believe it had assurances of a fair trial. See, e.g., Davood Hermidas Bavand, "Iran's War Reparations" *International Studies Journal* 1, no. 4 (Spring 2005): 129; Ali Gholami, "Establishing Iraqi Special Tribunal for Crimes against Humanity and Prosecution of Saddam Hussein," *International Studies Journal* 1, no. 2 (Fall 2004): 137; Hajar Sia-Rostami, "Prosecution of Saddam Hussein and the Position of Islamic Republic of Iran," *International Studies Journal* 1, no. 3 (Winter 2005): 197.

[38] Joshua Muravchik, *The Uncertain Crusade: Jimmy Carter and the Dilemma of Human Rights Policy* (Lanham, MD: Hamilton Press, 1986); Cyrus Vance, *Hard Choices: Critical Years in America's Foreign Policy* (New York: Simon & Schuster, 1983); Zbigniew Brzezinski, *Power and Principle: Memoirs of the National Security Advisor 1977–1981* (New York: Farrar, 1983).

of the Islamic republic of Iran.[39] This propaganda coupled with some events during the war with Iraq had an impact on the enforcement of humanitarian law in Iran.

An illustration of the double standard syndrome is to be found in the aftermath of the Halabja massacre:[40] Iran tried in vain to alert the United Nations about the use of poison gas against civilians by Iraq during the Iran-Iraq War. However, the international community never properly investigated Iraq's violations of humanitarian law.[41] A reason for that lack of in-depth investigation at the time might be that some Western countries were hoping the Iran-Iraq War would bring an end to the Islamic republic and were consequently less open to act on complaints made by Iran.[42] As a result, Iran thought it was clearly demonstrated to all that IHL was only used to undermine the IRI and not to bring states such as Iraq to account for war crimes.

The War with Iraq: The Geneva Conventions Put to the Test

The Iran-Iraq War illustrates the challenges arising under the enforcement of Islamic humanitarian law in concomitance with IHL, with its negative consequences on civilians and the conduct of hostilities. Bellicose interpretations of Islamic law in particular led to violations of IHL. The case also demonstrates the importance of reconciling the Islamic Shia approach of war to IHL.

Total War and the Limits of Internalization

With the outbreak of the Iraq-Iran War, it became clear quite soon that Iran relied on both legal systems, choosing the one that was the most adapted to its

[39] Ruhollah Khomeini, "To Commemorate the First Martyrs of the Revolution," speech, 19 February 1978, in *Islam and Revolution/ Declaration and Writings of Imam Khomeyni*, ed. Hamid Alga (Berkeley: Editions Mizar Press, Contemporary Islamic Thought, Persian Series, 1981), pp. 213–215.

[40] Bahram Mostaghimi and Masoud Taromsari, "Double Standard: The Security Council and the Two Wars," in *Iranian Perspectives on the Iran-Iraq War*, ed. Farhang Rajaee (Gainesville: University Press of Florida, 1997), pp. 62–74.

[41] Patrick E. Tyler, "Officers Say U.S. Aided Iraq in War Despite Use of Gas," *New York Times*, 18 August 2002.

[42] The war between Iraq and Iran and the lack of respect of IHL during that period of time has to be read against its special political backdrop: The Islamic Republic of Iran emerged during the Cold War and relied on the mantra "Neither East, nor West," which clearly challenged the political environment of the time. For many, Iran became a real threat to the balance between the East Bloc and the West Bloc. The IRI built part of its existence on that antagonism.

needs and creed. Since the two sets of laws are somewhat similar, the issue was not the existence of a domestic legal approach to humanitarian law; the problem was with the lack of commitment to respect humanitarian standards, whether Islamic or international.

During the Iran-Iraq War IHL was put to the test: Both sides committed gross violations, such as bombings of civilians, attacks on neutral shipping and on civilian aircraft, and use of chemical weapons.[43] The United Nations issued two resolutions, in 1986 (Resolution 582) and 1987 (Resolution 598) to remind the two warring parties of their obligations under IHL, with little success. The outcome of those violations on both sides was a long armed conflict with a total of victims that is still unknown.

Iraq and Iran declared at the beginning of the conflict that they would respect the two sets of legal standards, but the situation soon deteriorated. It became clear that neither Iraq nor Iran had fully internalized IHL. Iran attacked neutral ships in the Persian Gulf in violation of Article 1 of Hague Convention no XIIII (naval war). Later, Iran violated the Islamic principle of discrimination between civilians and combatants by targeting Iraqi cities. Iran thereby disrespected both sets of law, shedding a new light on its commitment to humanitarian standards, be they international or Islamic.

Iran and Iraq led a total war against each other, without respecting the difference between combatants and civilians. Some have argued that the two governments must have appealed to an Islamic legal tradition that accepts such behavior.[44] Iraq was a secular country at the time so it did not follow an Islamic tradition of war. As far as Iran was concerned, the Shia Islamic tradition clearly forbids the killing of noncombatants. Besides, Iran did not conduct a total war at the beginning:[45] The Iranian government considered it was leading a jihad of self-defense but also acted to protect oppressed Iraqi Muslim populations from the Iraqi government; since Iraqis were considered victims of Saddam Hussein, they had to be spared.[46] This approach changed when Iran realized Iraqis were not rebelling against the unjust rule of Saddam Hussein; besides, Iraq started its bombing campaign on Iranian cities, taking a heavy toll on civilians. It was then that Iran opted for a total war, violating both IHL and Islamic law by targeting civilians. The main issue was not whether to apply IHL or Islamic

[43] United Nations Security Council, Resolution 598, 1987.

[44] Paul Tavernier, "La Guerre du Golfe: Quelques aspects de l'application du droit des conflits armes et du droit humanitaire," in *Nouvel ordre mondial et droits de l'homme: La Guerre du Golfe*, ed. Paul Tavernier (Paris: Editions Publisud, 1993), p. 56.

[45] John Kelsay, *Islam and War: A Study in Comparative Ethics* (Louisville, KY: John Knox Press, 1993), pp. 74–75.

[46] Shahram Chubin and Charles Tripp, *Iran and Iraq at War* (Boulder, CO: Westview, 1988), p. 38.

humanitarian standards but rather the perceived need to adapt to the reality of the war and the change in strategy during one of the bloodiest conflicts of the 20th century.

Even under these circumstances, however, some prominent Iranian figures reminded the authorities of their obligations to respect the distinction between civilians and combatants and the rules for conduct of hostilities under Islamic law. For example, Mehdi Bazargan, a scholar who had served as Iran's first prime minister following the 1979 revolution (he resigned in protest over the takeover of the US embassy), insisted that the Islamic distinction between civilians and combatants be respected by the authorities of the IRI: "According to Islam, it is justifiable retribution only if we, without our own missiles, hit the commanders or senders of the Iraqi missiles rather than hitting civilian areas and killing innocent people and turning their homes and communities into ghost towns and hills of rubble, all in the name of striking military targets."[47] Yet, the Iranian authorities often chose to ignore those Islamic humanitarian standards and guidelines for the conduct of war set forth in the primary Islamic legal sources, the Quran and the *hadith*, to promote more expedient interpretations supporting the war effort.

The Halabja Massacre and Iran's Reliance on International Humanitarian Law

Despite the ongoing violations, Iran often referred to the Geneva Conventions to denounce Iraq, in particular to the mass killings of civilians and the use of new bombs and poison gas.[48] Such instrumental use of the Geneva Conventions is consistent with realist interpretations of Iran's behavior, but the fact that IHL was so ready to hand implies a certain internalization of its norms.

A striking feature of the Iran-Iraq War was the use of poison gas by the Iraqis. Iran did not use chemical weapons, contrary to the propaganda of the Iraqi government and the assertions of the United Nations at the time. A UN official later apologized for not taking into account Iraq's gassing of Iranian civilians, stating, "On one occasion I had to note with deep regret the experts' conclusion that chemical weapons had been used against Iranian civilians in an area adjacent to an urban center lacking any protection against that kind of attack." Those declarations did not sooth an Iran that had been accused of using chemical weapons

[47] Liberation Movement of Iran, *A Warning Concerning the Continuation of the Destructive War* (Houston: Maktab, 1988), p. 14.

[48] Joost Hiltermann, *A Poisonous Affair: America, Iraq and the Gassing of Halabja* (New York: Cambridge University Press, 2007), p. 150.

in Resolution 620 (1988), adopted on 26 August 1988, when actually it was Iraq doing so.[49]

There is some debate over whether or not Iran had access to chemical weapons. It is clear, however, under Islamic rules of war that even if the country had poison gas, it would have been anti-Islamic to use it. Kalshoven believes that Iran simply did not use such weapons because it did not have access to them; otherwise it would have done so. Under Islamic law, however, the use of gas would have been *haram* based on the fact that it targets civilians in a nondiscriminatory and disproportionate fashion. Islamic law prohibits targeting civilians indiscriminately and using weapons that would cause massive and uncontrollable damage. Iran underlined this point in a letter to the United Nations in October 1987: The country would not use poison gas out of respect for "Islamic principles and international law," which discriminate between civilians and combatants.[50] Aside from refraining from using chemical weapons, however, Iran did not consistently follow the norm of discrimination. It bombed Iraqi civilians during the so-called War of the Cities, for example, in response to Iraq's incessant attacks on largely populated areas.

The massacre of Halabja is the event that occasioned most of Iran's appeals to IHL: The Iranian government claimed that genocide took place in the city of Halabja in Iraq.[51] The Kurdish town of Halabja, situated 15 kilometers away from the Iran border, was attacked in March 1988: Iraqi planes launched gas attacks against the Kurdish population as part of the Anfal campaign, which sought to eliminate the Kurds from Iraq. Since the town of Halabja was close to the border, Iranian ambulances, rescue teams, and journalists were the first to arrived after the attack.[52] Iranians rescued survivors, some of whom still live in Iran today.[53] The attack and its level of horror deeply marked the Iranian population, and the authorities used that event to promote Iran as a "humanitarian" nation in contrast to Saddam Hussein's Iraq.[54]

Iran complained in vain to the Security Council about the indiscriminate attacks of Iraq against civilians by bombs and gas attacks.[55] It used the legal

[49] Specialist Report of 14 April 1988 ICJ reports 1986; UN Doc. S/20063 of 25 July 1988 cf the report of 8 May 1987 UN Doc s/18852.

[50] Letter S/19193, 9 October 1987.

[51] Letter S/19892, 19 May 1988.

[52] Andrew Cockburn, "An Inconvenient Truth," *The Nation*, 10 September 2007.

[53] Jean-Jacques Bozonnet, "Treize ans après, le calvaire des Kurdes gazés par Bagdad," *Le Monde*, 28 October 2001; Olivier Piot, "Halabja, vingt ans après," *Le Monde Diplomatique*, http://blog.mondediplo.net/2008-03-20-Halabja-vingt-ans-apres.

[54] Hiltermann, *A Poisonous Affair*, p. 150.

[55] Joost R. Hiltermann, "Outsiders as Enablers," in *Iran, Iraq and the Legacies of War*, ed. L. G. Potter and G. G. Sick (London: Palgrave Macmillan, 2004), pp. 151–156, 157–158.

arsenal at its disposal, and independent external experts were called to testify. The United Nations never condemned Iraq for the use of gas during the war. For the Iranian government, the international toleration of Iraqi violations of humanitarian law in Halabja "eroded the authority of all rules and principles of international law."[56] As a result, Iranian leaders detected "a feeling of acquiescence by the Security Council and indifference of the international community that amounted in their eyes as an encouragement for the ruling regime of Iraq to continue its savage atrocities."[57] Iran subsequently declared, "it is now abundantly clear that the failure of the UN machinery to take the Iraqi regime to task for its genocidal use of chemical weapons in Halabja and other large-scale resorts to chemical warfare against both Iranian and Iraqi targets is at least partially responsible for the continuation and escalation of the criminal behavior shown by Iraqi aggressors."[58] For Iranian authorities, the refusal to take into account the massacre demonstrated that the cards were stacked from the beginning of the war and that IHL was used as a political card among others. Iran then declared, "when political considerations predominate an international organ," and when the Council fails "to discharge its constitutional duties" when gross violations occur, then "the very raison d'être of the organ becomes its immediate victim"[59] and the Council loses its status as an arbiter. The fact that Iran took the Halabja case to the international authorities was part of a show, but it was also genuine: Iranians were the victims of the gas used by the Iraqis, and recognition of the violations of IHL in Halabja would have led to a similar acknowledgment in Iran.

This example of Halabja demonstrates that Iran relied on IHL, unsuccessfully. Yet Iranian officials did not read UN refusal to investigate as a carte blanche to violate humanitarian law or a justification to rely solely on Islamic values. It did, however, erode Iran's trust in international law, further justifying the maintenance of a hybrid system at the expense of international standards.

The Iranian Islamic Approach to Humanitarian Standards: Example of Prisoners of War

An illustration of the violation of international standards is to be found in the treatment of prisoners of war by both sides. In the case of Iran, it provides an example of the problems arising when two sets of laws are applied concomitantly.

[56] Hiltermann, *A Poisonous Affair*.

[57] Letter UN, S/15934, 18 August 1983.

[58] Letter, Iranian representative to the Secretary General in Report of the SG to the Security Council of 26 November 1986, UN doc S/18480; Hiltermann, *A Poisonous Affair*, pp. 151–152.

[59] Hiltermann, *A Poisonous Affair*, p. 152.

Iran and Iraq accused each other of violating the Geneva Conventions with regard to the treatment of POWs.[60] The International Committee of the Red Cross (ICRC) noted summary executions of captive soldiers, abandonment of wounded enemies on the battlefield, and deportation of civilians in POW camps.[61] If Iraq clearly departed from all humanitarian principles, Iran had a strong set of guidelines inspired by Shia interpretations of Islamic law to follow, and, yet, it departed from them to rely on new interpretations that would answer the republic's wartime needs.

The ICRC claimed in 1987 that Iran held 49,285 Iraqis POWs in 15 camps while Iraq held 12,747 Iranian POWs in 10 camps.[62] The monitoring of the situation by the ICRC became increasingly complex as the conflict went on. Soon, the ICRC had almost no access to POWs under the conditions set up by its mandate.[63] From 1987 onward, the ICRC could not visit Iraqi POWs in Iran. The ICRC delegation in Iran had its activities interrupted so often that the organization made a public call in 1983 to the State Members of the Geneva Conventions: it asked them to do whatever possible to encourage Iran's compliance.[64] The ICRC then publicly criticized Iran for not respecting the Geneva Conventions.[65] It was later reported that the IRI was forcing Iraqi prisoners to convert to Shiism or to demonstrate against Saddam Hussein's power.[66]

In 1985, the United Nations mandated a mission to inquire about the situation of POWs and civilian detainees in the Iran-Iraq conflict. The members of the mission visited the two countries in January 1985. They visited POW camps and conducted private interviews.[67] Granting access to the camps did not evidently encourage further respect and internalization of the Geneva Conventions on Iran's part, as an incident in 1985 revealed. In October of that year the Iraqi foreign minister Tariq Aziz claimed that the Iranian military had opened fire on Iraqi prisoners during an ICRC visit.[68] It became clear from reports that a

[60] See report: UNHCR Report, "Treatment of Prisoners of War during the Iraq-Iran War," 16 October 2009.

[61] "Red Cross Criticizes Iran and Iraq," *New York Times*, 12 May 1983.

[62] S. H. Amin, "Iran-Iraq War: Some Legal Issues," in *International Mediation and the Gulf War*, ed. Mohamed H. Malek (Glasgow: Royston House, 1991).

[63] International Committee of the Red Cross (ICRC), *Report of Activities* (Geneva: ICRC, 1980), p. 66 bis.

[64] ICRC, *Report of Activities*.

[65] Yves Sandoz, "Appel du CICR dans le cadre du conflit entre l'Irak et l'Iran," *Annuaire Français de Droit International* 29 (1983): 61–173.

[66] Sandoz, "Appel du CICR."

[67] United Nations, "Situation of Prisoners of War in Iran, Iraq Investigated by Mission," *UN Chronicle*, 1 January 1985.

[68] Letter from Tariq Aziz about the Gorghan Camp, addressed to the Secretary-General (S/16799), 25 October 1985.

dispute arose between two POWs during an ICRC visit and violence spread to the whole camp. Iranian guards at first fired warning shots into the air. Despite the ICRC delegates' efforts to restore order, the detainees rushed to the camp's exit and the guards then opened fire. Order was eventually restored, and three bodies were found.[69] The ICRC seized the opportunity of this incident to lodge a complaint about Iran's compliance with standards for POWs. The organization did not have access to all camps, and private interviews with prisoners were not always ensured. In a public memorandum of 10 February 1984, the ICRC had already complained about the deaths and injuries in POW camps and that "ideological and political pressure, intimidation, systematic 're-education' and attacks on the honor and dignity of the prisoners have remained a constant feature of life in the camps."[70]

Reports of violations of POW rights are in clear contradiction of not only international law but also Islamic law. A *hadith* reports that the Prophet said, "Prisoners are your brothers and companions. It is because of God's compassion that they are in your hands. They are at your mercy, so treat them well as if you were treating yourself, with food, clothes and housing."[71] Besides, forcing POWs to convert to Shia Islam is contradictory to Islam: Islamic humanitarian law protects prisoners' religious beliefs and the Quran clearly states that violence should never be used to convert people (Quran 2:256). Caliph Abu Bakr told his officials that no prisoners should be tied in chains or handcuffed and they shall

[69] Letter from UN Iranian Permanent Representative, Said Rajaie Khorassani, to the Secretary-General, with the ICRC report enclosed, 10 November 1985 (A/39/639-S/16820).

[70] ICRC President Alexander Hay, Statement to the Permanent Representatives in Geneva, 23 November 1985. For the sake of treating the issue in the fairest way possible: Iraq committed violations as well. Iranian prisoners of war in Iraq suffered from bad sanitation facilities and overcrowding. There were alleged secret military camps, which worried the Iranian authorities because they could not keep count of the missing and the dead. There were also rumors that some prisoners of war in camps were actually civilians arrested and deported by the Iraqi soldiers ("POW Dispute May Mar Iran-Iraq Peace," *Sydney Morning Herald*, 9 August 1988). There were also children as young as thirteen years old among the POWs (United Press International, "U.N. Says Iran 'Brainwashing' Iraqi POWs," 2 September 1988). There were reports that biological weapons were tested on Iranian POWs during the 1980s. In January 1998, a journalist confirmed anthrax had been used on Iranian prisoners (UNSC, "UN Security Council: Prisoners of War in Iran and Iraq—The Report of a Mission Dispatched by the Secretary-General," January 1985 [S/16962], 22 February 1985; UNSC, "UN Security Council: Report of the Mission Dispatched by the Secretary-General on the Situation of Prisoners of War in the Islamic Republic of Iran and Iraq," [S/20147], 24 August 1988. A female scientist, Dr. Rihab Taha, the head of Iraq's germ warfare program, confirmed those rumors: January 2003, the Arabic News Website Al-Bawaba/ Associated Press: "Newspaper Report: Iraq Tested Deadly Anthrax on Humans," 18 January 1998.

[71] Quoted in M. K. Erekoussi, "Le Coran et les conventions humanitaires," *Revue Internationale de la Croix Rouge*, 503 (November 1960): 650.

be provided with food (Quran 8:76).[72] They should be provided with clothes and adequate housing.[73] A prisoner cannot be killed, mutilated, or tortured. His dignity should be preserved, as he is a creature of God. Prisoners may be tried if they have committed a major offense against Islam but not for belligerent acts.[74]

According to Islamic tradition, duties toward prisoners are divinely ordained and there is a divine punishment for anyone who would not respect these humanitarian rules. Yet, this tradition did not prevent the issuance of several fatwas that clearly contradicted those Islamic humanitarian values. Therefore the few differences that exist between Islamic humanitarian law as interpreted by the IRI and international law, and which emerged during the war, were mostly caused by interpretations made of Islamic law by authorities. The issue in the 1980s and 1990s was with interpretations of Islamic law and humanitarian law that sought to support the governance system rather than ensure a full internalization of IHL. This limited internalization also affected interpretations of Islamic legal sources.

Despite unresolved issues pertaining to the enforcement of the Geneva Conventions lingering since the Iran-Iraq War, postconflict Iran has made some progress in humanitarian law to further the internalization of IHL and Islamic humanitarian values.

Positive Internalization in Postconflict Society

There are some strong signs of positive integration of IHL, resulting from the work of the authorities and civil society. An example of change has been the organization of a conference on the challenges involved in the respect and implementation of the third Geneva Conventions on the protection of POWs by the National Committee, Payam Azadegan Cultural Institute, and the ICRC in 2010.[75] This event demonstrates a wish to improve Iran's approach and to learn lessons from the Iran-Iraq War. There is some disagreement, however, about the strategy of internalization: While the authorities work on having the two sets of law—IHL and Islamic—working side by side, civil society seeks a congruence of the norms.

[72] Shokry M. el Dakkak, *State's Crimes against Humanity: Genocide, Deportation and Torture from the Perspectives of International and Islamic Laws* (Kuala Lumpur: A.S. Noorden, 2000), 158.

[73] Ayatollah Mohaghegh Damad, "International Humanitarian Law in Islam and Contemporary International Law," in *Islamic Views on Human Rights: Viewpoints of Iranian Scholars*, ed. Husayn Salimi (New Delhi: Kanishka, 2003), pp. 289–293.

[74] Abu Zayd Dabusi, *Kitab Al Asrar* (Amman: Manshurat Wizarat al–Awqaf wa-al-Shuhun wa-al Muqaddasat al-Islamiyah, 2001), p. 148.

[75] ICRC, *Annual Report: Iran, 2010*, http://www.refworld.org/docid/4de6265c1c.html.

International Humanitarian Law and Iranian Military Norms

The internalization of IHL within the legislative body of a country and within the army's judicial code is crucial, since humanitarian law aims at ensuring the protection of civilians and monitors the conduct of hostilities: it is important that parties to a conflict follow the same rules.[76]

Islamicization of the Army

The army was Islamicized through Article 144 of the Constitution and therefore follows Islamic standards regarding war and peace as well as humanitarian rules. Since there are many rules in common between Islamic humanitarian rules and IHL, this could be seen as a minor problem.[77] There are, however, some issues of concern: the Iranian army and the government refer to rules about jihad to define when a war is just and legitimate. They also refer to the Islamic doctrine and philosophy of war and peace in Islam and the conduct of war according to Shari'a principles. In some cases these rules diverge from the expectations of IHL and the Geneva Conventions.

Another concern is that little is known about the integration of the Geneva Conventions into Iranian national and military laws. Iran deploys two parallel land forces, the regular *artesh* (army) and the Army of the Guardians of the Islamic Revolution (*Pasdaran*) that are integrated at the command level. This integration is important with regard to Article 43 of Additional Protocol I, which requires a command structure that "shall enforce compliance with the rules of international law applicable in armed conflict." The command of this dual structure is opaque, and there is little information available about current training of the military and the integration of humanitarian law. Neither the ICRC nor the Iranian National Committee for International Humanitarian Law (INCIHL) has been able to gauge to what extent integration of IHL has taken place, and it is difficult to know exactly what the soldiers are being taught during training. The armed forces never report about humanitarian law training because they consider it a matter of national security.

Even though there are contacts between the army and various IHL organizations, they are not always productive ones, and there is still work to do to ensure that the Geneva Conventions are being internalized in army codes. The INCIHL

[76] Anicée Van Engeland, *Civilian or Combatant? A Challenge for the 21st Century* (New York: Oxford University Press, 2011).

[77] Van Engeland, "The Differences and Similarities between International Humanitarian Law and Islamic Humanitarian Law."

has tried in vain to acquire information about the level of implementation of IHL within the armed forces; it launched a study about "international humanitarian law national implementation in Iran" with the support of the ICRC, but the chief officer of the armed forces halted the program and insisted that there was adequate IHL training in the army. General Oussama Duraj reported, "We train soldiers to ensure that their behavior is in conformity with the IHL principles. And for commanders, the objective is to provide them with a methodology that allows them to approach any situation while making decisions."[78] Soldiers and officers are apparently being trained to respect the Geneva Conventions but are also trained to give the priority to Islamic laws of war. Therefore, the process of internalization within the ranks of the Iranian army is probably limited: The Geneva Conventions rules are integrated as long as they do not contradict Islamic war principles.

The army receives special training in "Principles and Beliefs" with qualified clerical instructors.[79] An example of what is taught includes the following rule based on Quran: "We received pledges from you not to spill each other's blood and not to disperse each other from their country. This means no one has the right the throw people out of their countries and to defend against such actions is a recognized Koranic obligation."[80] Another rule states, "God does not tell you to mistreat armies which are not fighting or show hostility toward you even though they may be infidel and opposed to Islam. On the contrary, if they don't fight you and they don't commit aggression against your country you should treat them justly and kindly."[81] These guidelines are quite general and provide little insight into how humanitarian law principles translate, for example, into rules of engagement, and whether those would conform to the expectations of the Geneva Conventions.

Progress and Changes within the Army

In the wake of the Iran-Iraq War, the Army has allowed the ICRC to play a small role, reflecting a shift that has occurred in the postconflict society; it is also the outcome of a renewed interest in humanitarian law. To sustain this interest, various organizations have sought to increase the level of integration of humanitarian rules into the armed forces. It is against that backdrop that the ICRC reached out again to the military to provide training or information and its invitation was accepted. This new cooperation brings about more transparency and allows for the ICRC to influence the internalization process. However, the dissemination of IHL norms does not happen through the direct teaching of ICRC. Instead,

[78] Ghaffari, "Media Role Unique."
[79] Sepehr Zabih, *The Iranian Military in the Revolution* (London: Routledge, 1988), p. 137.
[80] Ayeh related by Sepehr Zabih, *The Iranian Military*.
[81] Zabih, *The Iranian Military*.

the organization disseminates information, translates major documents, and organizes events (conferences, symposiums, panels) and official meetings. Some army officials have been sent abroad for training, to the ICRC's International Institute of Humanitarian Law in San Remo, Italy.[82] The Iranian Security and Defense Commission, under the authority of the Expediency Discernment Council, supported the contribution of the ICRC to the military. Translated IHL documents have been widely distributed to officials, in particular the ICRC publication *Integrating the Law*.[83] In 2006, the Ministry of Defense and members of the armed forces requested and were provided with IHL training manuals translated into Farsi by the National Committee.[84] The ICRC has posted some of these documents on its website and has begun distributing manuals in Persian around the country to journalists and universities as well as the military.[85]

In 2007, the ICRC reached an agreement with the authorities to provide some training to armed and security forces.[86] The organization submitted a draft for introduction of IHL in military teaching and training programs, together with models of ICRC training programs on the subject. It has also initiated a project to find out to what extent IHL has been integrated into the training of the soldiers.

The Role of Civil Society in Furthering Internalization

While national authorities have taken steps to work on the internalization of IHL, civil society also plays a role. It works on reconciling the two sets of law to improve the enforcement of humanitarian law. The main strategy used to further the knowledge and hopefully the respect of IHL is to use education and training.

The Role of the International Committee of the Red Cross

The ICRC plays a major role in Iran. It works on its regular mandate but focuses also on the task of integrating IHL into Iranian law. The ICRC sent a delegation to the country in 1977, before the Iranian Revolution, and has been going through

[82] ICRC, "The ICRC in the Islamic Republic of Iran," in *ICRC Annual Report 2005* (Geneva: ICRC, 2005).

[83] ICRC, *Integrating the Law* (Geneva: ICRC, 2002).

This booklet draws together the lessons learned by the ICRC over the past few decades and aims to provide authorities and the most senior personnel among arms bearers with an overview of what we have come to call the "integration" process.

[84] ICRC, "The ICRC in the Islamic Republic of Iran," in *ICRC Annual Report 2006* (Geneva: ICRC, 2006).

[85] ICRC, *Integrating the Law*.

[86] ICRC, *Integrating the Law*.

a change of focus of its actions since the end of the Iran-Iraq War. It works on the dissemination of IHL, training, collaboration with the Iranian Red Crescent Society (IRCS), determining the fate of POWs still lost after the war, as well as help with training related to unexploded landmines and treating mine victims.[87] The organization also collaborated with the IRCS after the Bam earthquake, distributing aid and helping in tracing families. It brings help and support to refugees in Iran trying to contact their families through the Red Cross Messages service, which provides the means for family members to communicate during situations of armed conflict or natural disasters. The ICRC has supported the National Committee in its attempts to have the government ratify Additional Protocol I.

The activities of the ICRC have had a real impact on the internalization of IHL in Iran, within the limits imposed by the IRI. It is particularly active in the field of education. It trains the Iranian army but also the public, and has strong ties with the academic world. For example, in 2005 it organized a conference on the role of media in propagating IHL, to which representatives of the Iranian civil society were invited. Mahmoud Boroujerdi, head of the International Center for Dialogue among Civilizations, reminded the attendees that abiding by humanitarian principles was an obligation for all states, but he also highlighted the constraints that the IRI imposes on some of the ICRC's activities. Boroujerdi pointed out, for example, that government's international legal obligation to facilitate ICRC's workers visits to POWs and detainees in international armed conflicts was limited to wartime. During peacetime, the organization is limited in the work it can do for POWs, and has to operate within the framework set by the authorities.[88] This example demonstrates that the government remains sensitive to the issue of Iraqi POWs still detained in Iran, even if the numbers are apparently small, and "Islamic values" can trump the obligations of IHL in the interest of political expediency.[89]

Iran remains a primary focus of the ICRC's program Integrating the Law. It aims to transpose the Geneva legal rules into "concrete mechanisms or measures to ensure compliance." Integration of the rules into military practice "is a continuous process. It must address doctrine, education, training and equipment issues and be backed up by an effective system of sanctions."[90] To reach this aim, the ICRC engages many societal actors in dissemination of the Geneva Conventions, hoping to complete the process of internalization by targeting scholars, students, journalists, officials, and children.

[87] ICRC, "Iran, Islamic Republic of," *Annual Report for 2015*, https://app.icrc.org/files/2015-annual-report/files/2015_ar_iran.pdf.

[88] Ghaffari, "Media Role Unique."

[89] See, e.g., BBC, "Iran Releases Iraqi POWs," 21 January 2002, http://news.bbc.co.uk/1/hi/world/middle_east/1772451.stm.

[90] ICRC, *Integrating the Law*.

The National Committee

The ICRC is supported in its task to internalize universal humanitarian standards into Iranian law by the INCIHL. The decree establishing the Committee (called *Tasvibnameye Heyate Vaziran: Mojaveze Taskihl-e Komitey-e Melli-ye Hoquq-e Bashardoustane djomjourie eslam*) dates to 4 February 1998.[91] The creation of the Committee is the result of a formal request made by Cornelio Sommaruga, then-president of the ICRC, to Ali Akbar Velayeti, Iranian foreign minister.[92]

Part of the Committee's mandate is the dissemination of IHL and the education of civilians and the military, in particular in military colleges and faculties. The Parliament and the government gave this mandate to the Committee. The role of the Committee is also to review the possibility of accessing to Additional Protocol I of the Geneva Conventions. The Secretariat is in charge of preparing a proposition to convince the government. It set up a working group on the compatibility between Iranian law and IHL. In 2007, to commemorate 30th anniversary of the Protocols, Iranian officials attended a roundtable organized by the ICRC in collaboration with local research centers.[93] At this point, Iran's ratification would mainly serve as a symbolic gesture—albeit an important one—since most of Protocol I is now considered customary law. The ongoing dialogue between the ICRC and the Iranian authorities has led to a partnership with the National Committee to establish an IHL reference center to make documents available to the public but especially to the academic community of Iran. The center sponsors a multidisciplinary research group working on the compatibility between Iranian law and IHL in general, with a specific focus on the Geneva Conventions.[94]

Education and Civil Society

The effort to include civil society in disseminating IHL marks a shift in post-conflict Iran. A special Persian edition of the ICRC magazine *al Ansani* (the humanitarian) is published in collaboration with the National Committee. It is distributed to all Red Crescent branches, the media, and academic circles.

[91] There was another decree on 17 May 1999 that officially adopted rules pertaining to the functioning of the Committee, and a further decree H 23001 T/11088 of the Cabinet of Ministers of 11 April 2000 amending some articles of the rules.

[92] The creation of the Committee fell under the mandate of the Iranian Red Crescent Society: Article 1, 3(6) and 9(7) of the Status adopted by Parliament in 1987 explicitly states that the IRCS would be the most competent organ to create the Committee. Article 5 of the IRCS statute states that governmental organs are obliged to cooperate with the IRCS in that respect.

[93] ICRC, "Iran: The 30th Anniversary of Protocols Additional to Geneva Conventions," Tehran, 30 October 2007.

[94] ICRC, "Iran: The 30th Anniversary of Protocols Additional to Geneva Conventions."

Members of the Iranian academic world also work toward the propagation and respect of IHL in Iran. In April 2004, the Graduate Center for International Studies at the University of Tehran and the Program on Humanitarian Policy and Conflict Research at Harvard University organized a conference titled "Interplay between Human Rights and Humanitarian Law: Global and Regional Perspectives."[95] The law and political science departments at the University of Tehran have also concluded an agreement with the ICRC regarding research on children in armed conflicts. And ICRC representatives have visited universities and delivered lectures to professors, researchers, and students.

Several Iranian nongovernmental organizations have collaborated with the ICRC on a pilot project, Exploring Humanitarian Law.[96] Islamic organizations justify their engagement with IHL because they consider it an Islamic duty to maintain peace once a treaty has been signed and to reach out to help Muslims. Like most national branches of the ICRC, the Supreme Council of the IRCS specializes in relief work and humanitarian aid, particularly in response to national disasters. Regarding its relationship with the Iranian government, Dr. Ahmad Ali Noorbala, head of the IRCS, claimed that although the national movement has close and good contacts within the system, it remains faithful first to "the humanitarian principles, values and services of National Red Crescent Society."[97] He added that there were no contradictions between the country's religious values and culture and the mission of the national society. He asserted little difference between Islamic humanitarian values and the rules of IHL.

The ICRC has had more success in penetrating schools and universities than the army, in part thanks to the program Exploring Humanitarian Law and to the support of the National Committee. Indeed, IHL has become an extracurricular topic at school. In addition, university students can benefit from the support of the ICRC during their research on IHL. These efforts represent a bet on future generations, hoping that their familiarity with the Geneva Conventions will contribute to the internalization process.

In addition to disseminating basic principles of humanitarian law, the ICRC has also sought to engage Iranian academic institutions to explore areas of overlap and disagreement between IHL and Islamic law. In November 2006, for example, the Qom Institute of Theology, the Ministry of Foreign Affairs, and

[95] http://www.hpcrresearch.org/partners/university-tehran-center-graduate-international-studies-cgis.

[96] Exploring Humanitarian Law is an international education program for young people between 13 and 18 years of age, to introduce them to the basic rules of IHL.

[97] Interview with Ahmad Ali Noorbala.

the Iranian Red Crescent organized a regional conference on the protection of victims of armed conflict under Islamic law and IHL.[98] A series of humanitarian organizations were present, including Ahl-e Beit World Assembly, the Iranian Foreign Ministry's Institute for Political and International Studies, Imam Sadiq University, the International Center for Islamic Studies, and the Islamic Culture and Communications Organization, among others. The conference and the variety of organizations and scholars present demonstrate the intensity of the debates pertaining to IHL. The fact that so many Iranian research centers and many experts in Islamic law from Iran and other countries participated indicates a high level of interest.

The Iranian authorities use such conferences to highlight what Islam and IHL have in common and to discredit criticism of Islam as warmongering and promote it as a religion of peace (in accordance with Quran 24:55 and 5:127).[99] As Ayatollah Mohsen Araki, the former personal representative of Grand Ayatollah Ali Khamenei and secretary-general of the November 2006 conference, put it, "Considering that Islam is too often misrepresented in the world nowadays, we hope this meeting will open the door to Islam as a source for customary law and humanitarian practice."[100]

One potentially valuable step toward internalization of IHL norms is dissemination at the level of the Iranian judiciary. The ICRC signed agreements with the International Bureau of the Iranian Judiciary to promote the teaching of IHL among judiciary administrative staff. Workshops are organized by the Bureau to promote and disseminate IHL. In 2006, three Iranian judges participated to the 9th South East Asian Teaching Session on IHL and Refugee Law held in New Delhi, India.[101] In addition, the Parliamentary Union of the Organization of Islamic Cooperation (PUOIC) works on raising public awareness of IHL. It requested the ICRC's assistance in preparing model IHL legislation for inclusion in draft resolutions discussed at a PUOIC summit held in Istanbul, Turkey, in April 2005. Prosecutor General Ayatollah Qorbanali Dorri Najafabadi called on the ICRC to strengthen ties with Iran. He declared, "Unconditional allegiance to humanitarian rights is indispensable to modern societies and irrespective of political motivations, all countries should observe human rights." Declarations such as this one demonstrated that the dissemination of the

[98] ICRC, "Iran: Dialogue on Islam and International Humanitarian Law in Qom," Press Release ICRC, 1 December 2006.

[99] Marcel A. Boisard, "The Conduct of Hostilities and the Protection of the Victims of Armed Conflicts in Islam," *Annals of International Studies* 8 (1977): 6.

[100] ICRC, "Iran: Dialogue on Islam."

[101] http://www.refworld.org/pdfid/469378d5c.pdf

Geneva Conventions by humanitarian organizations is efficient. Meanwhile, Iranians continue to refer to religious sources of humanitarian law on the same footing as the Geneva Conventions. Indeed Najafabadi stressed "the role of religion in preventing injustice, terror, violence and criminal acts," since all these actions "are restricted by religious precepts."[102] For Iranian authorities, the two bodies of law exist side by side.

Part of supporting the internalization process also goes through reaching a wider audience by targeting the media. To that end, the ICRC organizes conferences and workshops for journalists, such as the seminar " 'The Mission of Mass Media in Iran: Humanitarian Perspectives and Challenges."[103] The aim of the meeting was to provide training and updates regarding the Geneva Conventions so that journalists would then propagate the knowledge in their articles.

All these efforts aim at propagating the knowledge and understanding of IHL to support a better integration of the norms within the population. These efforts are better documented than the actual internalization of IHL norms within the armed forces. Clearly internalization of secular legal norms alone is not the outcome we can expect in a country such as Iran, with such a strong Islamic identity. A more promising route is to continue to stress the common ground between IHL and Islamic humanitarian standards, ideally via a new hermeneutics of the Shari'a.

Beyond the Clash, a Reconciliation?

Despite the efforts of different international organizations and Iranian civil society, the violations of IHL during the Iran-Iraq War continue to influence our understanding of Iran's compliance with the Geneva Conventions, as do military practices associated with Iran's involvement in the ongoing civil war in Syria. The tension between Islamic law and IHL seem to be at the root of Iran's violations of the laws of war, but as this chapter has maintained, violations were caused by self-serving interpretations of Islamic precepts rather than by Islam itself. Therefore, an important step toward bringing Iran into compliance might be revisiting the Islamic vision of a just war to understand how Iran violated that vision in the past and what can be done in the future to bridge the gap between IHL and Iran's interpretation of Islamic law. This effort should also facilitate the internalization of the Geneva Conventions.

[102] "Calls for Stronger ICRC Ties," *Iran Daily*, 8 March 2007.

[103] Ghaffari, "Media Role Unique."

International Humanitarian Law as a Tool to Transcend Differences?

There is a trend in international law that asserts its universality with little regard for regional or domestic approaches to the law. Yet, those alternative approaches to human rights or humanitarian law are multiple voices that must be heard if one can genuinely speak of "universality." Islamic law provides a reading of humanitarian standards that should not be ignored. Rather than excluding alternative readings, the international community should strive to include them. There should be a conversation or dialogue between the civilizations based on this idea.

The main issue with Islam when it comes to establishing a dialogue is that—as this chapter has stressed—there are multiple interpretations of the rules of war and humanitarian standards. Some might agree with the idea of a conversation to integrate Islamic humanitarian law through necessary compromises, whereas others will insist on a reading of Islam that refuses any compromise. Iran is a country that is open to changing interpretations because of the nature of Shari'a law; it is also a country that offers a range of interpretations, reflecting the diversity of opinions in the country. At one extreme, Abu al Mawdudi claims that Muslims established these humanitarian rules before the Western system came into force; he thus condemns Muslim rulers who have signed and ratified the Geneva Conventions because, he maintains, they have thereby disobeyed God, the Prophet, and Shari'a. "It hurts one's feelings that Muslims are in possession of such a splendid and comprehensive system of law and yet they look forward for guidance to those leaders of the West who could not have dreamed of attaining those heights of truth and justice which was achieved a long time ago."[104] Certainly it is true that Islam boasts a long tradition of political and religious ethics of war and peace.[105] For believers, the inherent nature of Islam as revealed truth makes humanitarian rules divine.[106] Islamic principles have to be respected because God dictated them: it is a matter of faith.[107] When Muslims have to choose between secular and religious rules of warfare, they will go for Islamic rules first. Abandoning Islamic standards of IHL is consequently not a viable option for Iran, as this would deny its Islamic identity. This is why it is essential to find a solution that respects Muslim faith and identity while enforcing IHL.

[104] Abu al Mawdudi, *Human Rights in Islam*, 2nd ed. (Leicester: Islamic Foundation, 1980), p. 43.

[105] Bassam Tibi, "War and Peace in Islam," in *Islamic Political Ethics*, ed. Sohail Hashmi (Princeton: Princeton University Press), p. 177.

[106] Damad, "International Humanitarian Law in Islam," p. 253.

[107] Erekoussi, "Le Coran et les conventions humanitaires," p. 645.

Conciliation between Islamic and International Humanitarian Values

The conciliation model proposed by Professor Abdullahi An Na'im is probably the best in terms of respect for the Islamic identity and promotion of reforms of interpretation of Islamic humanitarian law, since we have to address this double issue when it comes to the internalization of IHL in Iran. According to An Na'im, there can be only one single humanitarian law, and it has to be IHL.[108] This law should, however, reflect all different legal traditions and not have a Eurocentric approach.[109] In particular, a mutual and respectful interaction between Islamic law and international law is required. This interaction between the legal systems should be aimed at maintaining the primacy of international law "as the sole legal framework for international peace and security." His argument is that there is an Islamic law way that is "supportive of the *possibility* of international law." This Islamic law that supports IHL is based on his principle on the new hermeneutics of the Shari'a.[110] The idea rests on supporting a new interpretation of Islamic law that would bridge the differences between the two sets of law.

As An Naim explains, there is no doubt Islamic humanitarian law establishes humanitarian rules during wartime. Reformist Islamic religious ethics insists on presenting Islam as a religion of peace, which, during wartime, respects humanitarian principles.[111] He explains that it is necessary for Islam to have a new look at the world, and there is a need for a renewed and more modern process of interpretation (*ijtihad*) of the Shari'a. Shari'a should be freed from traditional and conservative interpretations.[112] There is therefore the need for liberal *mojtaheds* with modern views whose legal decisions and reasoning take root into reality and take into account the context. They can adapt Islam to IHL, when it needs to be done.[113]

[108] Abdullahi An Naim, "Islamic Law and International Law," presentation at the American Society of Comparative Law and Law and Society Association, Annual Meeting 2004, Atlanta.

[109] Abdullahi An Naim, "Toward an Islamic Hermeneutics for Human Rights" in *Human Rights and Religious Values: an Uneasy Relationship?*, ed. Abdullahi An Naim (Amsterdam: Rodopi ed., 1995); An Na'im, "Islamic Law and International Law."

[110] An Na'im, "Islamic Law and International law," and "Toward an Islamic Hermeneutics for Human Rights."

[111] Abdullahi An Na'im, "Islamic Ambivalence to Political Violence: Islamic Law and International Terrorism," *German Yearbook of International Law* 307 (1988): 31.

[112] Ralph H. Salmi, Cesar Adib Majul, and George K. Tanham, *Islam and Conflict Resolution: Theories and Practices* (Lanham, MD: University Press of America, 1998), p. 108.

[113] Mojtahed Mohamed Shabestari, Muhafa Malikiayn, and Mohsen Kadivar, eds., *Sunnat Va Sekularism: Goftarha-Ye az Abdolkarim Souroush* (Tehran: Hirah Press, 1381/2002).

Is some respect, the task should not be difficult, since original Islamic humanitarian standards and IHL have most rules in common. There are, however, major discrepancies, such as verse 9:5 of the Quran, which encourages the killing of unbelievers. In response to such warmongering parts, the Quran and the *hadith* should be read in accordance with the relevant historical context and by looking at the past to learn lessons. In the case of Iran, for example, not only should Islamic humanitarian law should be perceived as a positive contribution to the history and development of humanitarian law but also it should be revised by clerics to encompass all the lessons learned from the war with Iraq to avoid violations in the future.[114] In that regard, the work done by international organizations and local organizations is crucial: they entertain the memory of past violations and prepare a positive future, taking into account modern and contextualized interpretations of Islam.

This new hermeneutics of Shia Islam is a complicated but important process, as it is respectful of Islamic legal methods and international law at the same time. A new *ijtihad* with a humanitarian view is a way to reconcile the two legal systems.[115] They only need to follow already-existing principles guiding the interpretation of Shari'a when it comes to humanitarian rules.[116] If all the *mojtahedin* keep these rules in mind and their meaning in the universal language, they could interpret Shari'a with a dynamic pacifism. Reforming Islam will be a long process, because there is no single Islam but many Islams.[117] Islamic law is not a local custom because there is no such thing as one interpretation of Islamic law.[118] There is no unique leading figure of authority that has emerged to establish order.

Conclusion

The evolution that took place after the war with Iraq has been crucial for Iran. The authorities have tried to improve the internalization process of IHL, within the framework of Iran's Islamic identity, while civil society has also played a role, supported by the ICRC. Additionally, an important intellectual evolution took

[114] An Na'im, "Islamic Ambivalence," p. 307.

[115] An Na'im, "Islamic Ambivalence," p. 334.

[116] Boisard, "The Conduct of Hostilities," p. 4.

[117] Yvonne Yazbeck Haddad, "Operation Desert Storm and the War of Fatwas," in *Islamic Legal Interpretation and Their Fatwas*, ed. Muhammad Khalid Masud (Cambridge: Harvard University Press, 1996), p. 300.

[118] M. H. Mendeslon, "The Formation of Customary International Law," *Recueil des Cours* 272 (1998): 155.

place whereby many scholars now claim that IHL has been strongly influenced by Islam and is therefore in accordance with Iranian law; there are therefore fewer obstacles to the integration of IHL in Iranian law.[119] Since Iran has demonstrated a will to learn lessons from the war with Iraq, it might be that the differences that still exist between IHL and Islamic law could be bridged via new interpretations of Islam. Congruence between the two sets of law then appears as a realistic possibility for the future.

[119] Statement by Ali Younesi, Deputy Head of the Strategic Research Centre of the Expediency Discernment Council, "Iran: 30th Anniversary of Protocols Additional to the Geneva Conventions," ICRC Press Release, Tehran, 30 October 2007.

11

Private Military and Security Companies

RENÉE DE NEVERS

The private security industry has grown explosively in recent years, due to the United States' heavy reliance on private contractors in Iraq and Afghanistan. The US government has relied on private military and security companies (PMSCs) for a broad range of services in conflict zones over the last decade, including training local security forces, guarding US embassies and bases, intelligence functions in both Iraq and Afghanistan, and supporting US troops in the conflict against the Islamic State in Iraq and Syria (ISIS).[1] Many observers argue that contractors have operated with impunity in these conflict zones, with negative consequences for human rights, for the promotion of the rule of law, and for US efforts to create stability and trust. According to the UN Working Group on Mercenaries, no PMSC or employee has been sanctioned for any human rights violations.[2] Only one private security contractor was prosecuted for actions in Afghanistan, and few working in Iraq were charged with committing crimes there. One of the few cases that was prosecuted involved five employees of Blackwater Worldwide in connection with a 16 September 2007 shooting incident in Baghdad's Nisoor Square, involving a US State Department convoy escorted by Blackwater employees, in which seventeen Iraqi civilians were killed

[1] Sheryl Gay Stolberg and Mark Mazzetti, "Suicide Bombing Puts a Rare Face on CIA's Work," *New York Times*, 6 January 2010; James Risen and Mark Mazzetti, "Blackwater Guards Tied to Secret Raids by CIA," New York Times, 11 December 2009; Marcus Weisgerber, "Back to Iraq: Military Contractors Return in Droves," *Defense One*, 23 February 2016, http://www.defenseone.com/threats/2016/02/back-iraq-us-military-contractors-return-droves/126095/, accessed 4 August 2016.

[2] Jose L. Gomez del Prado, "The Privatization of War: Mercenaries, Private Military and Security Companies," *Global Research*, 9 November 2010, http:/www.globalresearch.ca/, accessed 16 September 2011.

and more were injured.[3] In 2014, five Blackwater employees were charged, and four were convicted of murder, manslaughter, and firearms charges. The four have appealed their convictions.[4]

The PMSC employees are not soldiers, but their activities often place them in conflict zones. Their presence has complicated efforts to ensure the effectiveness of IHL in fluid situations involving state and nonstate actors. This chapter explores how PMSCs fit in the framework of international humanitarian law (IHL), and the broader legal framework governing PMSCs, along with state and international efforts to ensure PMSC compliance with IHL. The Iraq conflict in particular dramatically shaped this industry, and the US experience there shaped our understanding of how IHL applies to PMSCs working with the military. It is important to note, however, that this is a global industry. Companies from many countries are currently operating in conflict zones ranging from Colombia to Sudan. Moreover, PMSCs are likely to emerge in more countries, in light of growing demand and the availability of cheap labor.

I focus on PMSC status under IHL, training of PMSC employees in the laws of war, and the rules of engagement (ROE) under which PMSCs operate. I also examine recent efforts to develop state and international mechanisms both to clarify appropriate PMSC activities and to encourage compliance with IHL and other pertinent legal frameworks.

Background

The PMSCs are "private companies that sell military services."[5] The current corporate model is a relatively recent phenomenon, but the use of private armies has

[3] The fifth guard pled guilty to voluntary manslaughter. Department of Justice, "Four Former Blackwater Employees Found Guilty of Charges in Fatal Nisur Square Shooting in Iraq," 22 October 2014, https://www.justice.gov/opa/pr/four-former-blackwater-employees-found-guilty-charges-fatal-nisur-square-shooting-iraq; Sudarsan Raghavan and Josh White, "Blackwater Guards Fired at Fleeing Cars, Soldiers Say," *Washington Post*, 12 October 2007; Sabrina Tavernise and James Glanz, "Iraqi Report Says Blackwater Guards Fired First," *New York Times*, 19 September 2007.

[4] Eric Tucker, "4 Ex-Blackwater Contractors Appeal Convictions in Shootings," *Military Times*, 2 February 2016, http://www.militarytimes.com/story/military/2016/02/02/4-ex-blackwater-contractors-appeal-convictions-shootings/79684408/, accessed 3 August 2016.

[5] Christopher Kinsey, "Challenging International Law: A Dilemma of Private Security Companies," *Conflict, Security, and Development* 5, no. 3 (December 2005): 270. For extensive discussions of private companies and the range of terms used for them, see: P. W. Singer, *Corporate Warriors: The Rise of the Privatized Military Industry* (Ithaca, NY: Cornell University Press, 2003); Deborah D. Avant, *The Market for Force: The Consequences of Privatizing Security* (Cambridge: Cambridge University Press, 2005).

a long history in war. Mercenaries were particularly common in European wars from the 14th to the 17th centuries, and reliance on these private armed forces only declined with the rise of citizen armies and nation-states.[6] "Mercenary" came to have negative connotations due to colonial powers' reliance on mercenary forces to conduct legally questionable operations when seeking either to establish or to hold on to colonies, and they played a prominent role in decolonization struggles in the mid-20th century.[7] As a result, the Organization of African Unity (OAU, now the African Union, or AU) outlawed mercenarism in 1977, and the UN General Assembly passed the International Convention against the Recruitment, Use, Financing or Training of Mercenaries (Mercenary Convention) in December of 1989.[8]

The PMSCs reject suggestions that they are mercenaries, and the UN Working Group on Mercenaries acknowledges that employees of PMSCs generally cannot be considered mercenaries because they do not fit the definition used in international legal conventions regarding mercenaries. Indeed, Sarah Percy has pointed out that the effort to develop a comprehensive definition of mercenarism resulted in a definition that is virtually unworkable in practice.[9] Some scholars have also argued that the corporate nature of major industry players clearly differs from common understandings of mercenaries and professional soldiers selling their military skills.[10] Yet, this industry's roots lie in the private provision of military force. Some industry leaders found initial employment and growth in programs by major states that outsourced training efforts to help "professionalize" developing world military forces.[11] Other companies formed to fill a long-standing need for protective services independent of military actions, and this need was recognized and filled by former military officers, particularly in the UK.[12] The private provision of military force also emerged as former military

[6] Michael Howard, *War in European History* (Oxford: Oxford University Press, 1976).

[7] Abdel-Fatau Mush and J. 'Kayode Fayemi, eds., *Mercenaries: An African Security Dilemma* (London: Pluto Press, 2000), pp. 16–17.

[8] The texts are at http://www.icrc.org/ihl.nsf/FULL/485 and http://www.un.org/documents/ga/res/44/a44r034.htm, accessed 1 June 2010.

[9] Sarah Percy, "Mercenaries: Strong Norm, Weak Law," *International Organization* 61 (2007): 367–397. For additional discussions of PMSCs and the mercenary conventions, see: Singer, *Corporate Warriors*, pp. 44–48; Sarah Percy, *Regulating the Private Security Industry* (London: Routledge for the International Institute for Strategic Studies, 2006), 14; Anna Leander, "Regulating the Role of Private Military Companies in Shaping Security and Politics," in *From Mercenaries to Market: The Rise and Regulation of Private Military Companies*, ed. Simon Chesterman and Chia Lehnardt (Oxford: Oxford University Press, 2007), pp. 49–64.

[10] Singer, *Corporate Warriors*, pp. 44–48.

[11] Singer, *Corporate Warriors*, pp. 119–135.

[12] Musah and Fayemi, *Mercenaries*, p. 18.

officers—in this case largely South African—recognized that a market existed for professional, capable military forces willing, quite simply, to fight.[13]

In the US context, increased reliance on contractors grew out of a desire to downsize the military after the Cold War in the hope of deriving a "peace dividend" from smaller military forces, and pressures to privatize government functions. More broadly, liberal governance models take for granted the greater efficiency and cost-effectiveness of private companies, and thus contributed to the rapid spread of private defense contracting.[14] Prior to the Iraq War in 2003, the pressure to downsize had already come into conflict with the expanded set of missions that the military was being asked to do, and the gap between capabilities and goals was increasingly filled by contractors.[15] The military has relied on contractors because they free troops for combat tasks, they can provide specialized skills, and they contribute to surge capacity.[16]

The industry's recent growth and visibility is largely due to US reliance on private contractors in Iraq in the 2000s, and the US military continues to rely on contractors in Iraq in its campaign against ISIS.[17] Reliance on a contractor workforce—a broader category than PMSCs—by the US Department of Defense (DOD) has been extensive since the Balkans operations in the 1990s. In both the Balkans and Iraq, contractors made up roughly half of the DOD's workforce, with uniformed personnel making up the remainder. In Afghanistan, the number of contractors, 108,000, made up 62 percent of DOD's workforce in March 2013.[18] The PMSC employees numbered roughly 18,000, in comparison

[13] Executive Outcomes, a company made up primarily of former South African soldiers, was the result, followed by Sandline International. Singer, *Corporate Warriors*, pp. 101–118; David Shearer, *Private Armies and Military Intervention* (London: International Institute for Strategic Studies, 1998); Kevin O'Brien, "Private Military Companies and African Security, 1990–1998," in Musah and Fayemi, *Mercenaries*, pp. 43–75.

[14] Anna Leander, "The Paradoxical Impunity of Private Military Companies: Authority and Limits to Legal Accountability," *Security Dialogue* 41, no. 5 (2010): 467–490; Deborah Avant, Martha Finnemore, and Susan K. Sell, *Who Governs the Globe?* (Cambridge: Cambridge University Press, 2011), ch. 1.

[15] "An Undisciplined Defense: Understanding the $2 Trillion Surge in US Defense Spending," *Project on Defense Alternatives*, Commonwealth Institute, January 2010; Steven L. Schooner, "Why Contractors Fatalities Matter," *Parameters* (Autumn 2009), p. 87. See also Singer, *Corporate Warriors*.

[16] Moshe Schwartz and Jennifer Church, "Department of Defense's Use of Contractors to Support Military Operations: Background, Analysis, and Issues for Congress,", *Congressional Research Service Report R43074*, 17 May 2013, p. 2, https://www.fas.org/sgp/crs/natsec/R43074.pdf, accessed 4 August 2016.

[17] Weisgerber, "Back to Iraq."

[18] Schwartz and Church, "Department of Defense's Use of Contractors," p. 2.

to 65,700 US troops in 2013.[19] In June 2015, 1,800 PMSC employees and 9,060 US troops were in Afghanistan; 90 US citizens working as private security contractors were among the 1,349 contractors supporting 3,550 US troops in Iraq. There may have been additional foreign or host country national PMSCs as well; data on this was not available.[20]

Not only the DOD, but other government agencies, international organizations, and private groups working in Iraq and Afghanistan have long relied on private security companies to protect their employees and projects. In 2010, the ratio of contractor to military personnel was about 1 to 1. But contractors supported the US Agency for International Development (USAID) and the State Department at ratios of 100 to 1 and 18 to 1 respectively.[21] The PMSCs expanded dramatically to meet this increased need for security. Their expanded role in these conflicts meant that PMSC employees also made headlines as the victims of insurgent attacks, most notably the killing and mutilation of four employees of Blackwater USA in Fallujah in March 2004, and in suicide attacks in Afghanistan.[22]

Status

The question of status matters to PMSC employees, because it determines the protections they should be accorded under IHL. Civilians are protected from attack under IHL unless they directly participate in combat. The same is true for

[19] Department of Defense, "Contractor Support of U.S. Operations in the USCENTCOM Area of Responsibility to Include Iraq and Afghanistan," April 2013; Boots on Ground Report, March 2013, cited in Schwartz and Church, "Department of Defense Use of Contractors," p. 2.

[20] Heidi M. Peters, Moshe Schwartz, and Lawrence Kapp, "Department of Defense Contractor and Troop Levels in Iraq and Afghanistan: 2007–2015," CRS Report R44116, 1 December 2015, pp. 1–2, https://www.fas.org/sgp/crs/natsec/R44116.pdf, accessed 4 August 2016.

[21] Commission on Wartime Contracting in Iraq and Afghanistan, *Transforming Wartime Contracting: Controlling Costs, Reducing Risks*, August 2011, pp. 18–20, www.wartimecontracting.gov, accessed September 21, 2011.

[22] It is worth noting that over 1,000 contractors were killed in Iraq between 2003 and mid-2007, and over 7,500 US contractors were injured. Between 2001 and 2009, over 289 contractors were killed in Afghanistan, and 101 contractors were killed there in 2014. Jan Schakowsky, "Schakowsky Uncovers 1,001 Contractor Deaths in Iraq," http://www.house.gov/list/press/il09_schakowsky/pr_contractordeaths_080607.shtml; Walter Pincus, "Contractors in Iraq Have Become U.S. Crutch," *Washington Post*, 20 August 2007; T. Christian Miller, "Contractor Deaths Accelerating in Afghanistan as They Outnumber Soldiers," *ProPublica*, 14 April 2010, http://www.propublica.org/feature/contractor-deaths-accelerating-in-afghanistan-as-they-outnumber-soldiers, accessed 2 June 2010; Micah Zenko, "The New Unknown Soldiers of Afghanistan and Iraq," *Foreign Policy*, 29 May 2015, http://foreignpolicy.com/2015/05/29/the-new-unknown-soldiers-of-afghanistan-and-iraq/, accessed 3 August 2016.

"civilians accompanying the force" (CAFs), a category established to acknowledge that armies employ civilians who may be close to battlefields but remain noncombatants, although they can lawfully be targeted if they are located at clearly military sites. Moreover, like combatants, CAFs are entitled to protection as prisoners of war if they are captured, assuming they have abided by IHL's guidelines.[23]

Although not combatants, PMSCs contracting with the military are generally classified as CAFs. For example, the DOD's 2005 instructions governing contractors defines their status as "civilians accompanying the force" (CAFs).[24] This builds on earlier US policy regarding contractor employees.[25]

Under IHL, PMSCs and their employees cannot be considered lawful combatants. In most cases, PMSC employees are not part of the armed forces of the state they are contracted to support, and their corporations are not militias.[26] Nor do they correspond to the designation of combatant status. First, PMSCs are unlikely to meet IHL's "clear command" criteria for armed groups that may be designated as combatants. Contractor teams tend to be put together for missions based on availability, and are led by "team leaders." They are not distinguished from one another by rank, but by the skills they bring to a particular mission.[27] Moreover, the US Joint Forces Command manual on "armed private security contractors" (APSCs) published in 2010 states, "the principal vehicle for the commander to exercise control [over APSC personnel] is the contract"— not a command structure.[28] Second, particularly when PMSCs rely on local employees, these contractors may be difficult to distinguish from civilians. Third, many contractors are hired as subcontractors to the company that holds the government contract, rather than directly by the government whose combat they may be supporting,[29] and many PMSC employees are "third country nationals," which further erodes the government's command authority over

[23] As the ICRC points out, this applies only to international armed conflicts.

[24] Lindsey Cameron, "International Humanitarian Law and the Regulation of Private Military Companies," Basel Institute on Governance Conference Plenary Paper, 9 February 2007, p. 3. This may be complicated by the nationality of the contractor. Geoffrey S. Corn, "Contractors and the Law," in *Contractors and War: The Transformation of US Expeditionary Operations*, ed. Christopher Kinsey and Malcolm Patterson (Stanford, CA: Stanford University Press, 2012), p. 173.

[25] Michael N. Schmitt, "Humanitarian Law and Direct Participation in Hostilities by Private Contractors or Civilian Employees," *Chicago Journal of International Law* 5, no. 2 (2004): 526–527.

[26] Schmitt, "Humanitarian Law and Direct Participation," p. 523, n53.

[27] Elke Krahmann, "The New Model Soldier and Civil-Military Relations," in *Private Military and Security Companies: Ethics, Policies, and Civil-Military Relations*, ed. Andrew Alexandra, Deane-Peter Baker, and Marina Caparini (London and New York: Routledge, 2008), p. 256.

[28] *Handbook for Armed Private Security Contractors in Contingency Operations* (Suffolk, VA: US Joint Forces Command, 23 February 2010), p. I-3.

[29] Michael E. Guillory, "Civilianizing the Force: Is the United States Crossing the Rubicon?" *Air Force Law Review*, 51 (2001): 140.

them. Subcontracting raises serious questions about which companies can be considered employed by the government and whose employees are thus deserving of CAF status, as opposed to employment by private companies, which are themselves directly employed by the DOD.[30] Fourth, individual contractors are generally hired on the basis of individual short-term contracts. This is appropriate for the companies and their employees, but it suggests that allegiance to a state or a cause is not part of the equation. This stands in sharp contrast to the civilian or professional soldier.

Many PMSCs operating in war zones today are working not for the military, but under contracts with agencies such as the Department of State (DOS), Interior, or CIA, or in the case of the UK, another major employer of PMSCs, the Department for International Development (DFID). This raises questions about whether these contractors can also be considered CAFs. It is likely that only DOD contractors can be considered CAFs, because they are "accompanying" the armed forces and clearly support the military mission, while PMSCs working for other branches of government do not warrant that status. This issue deserves greater clarification by governments, since the examples of Iraq and Afghanistan suggest that PMSCs working for multiple government agencies are likely to be the norm where military operations coincide with reconstruction and development activities.

Status matters, but what PMSCs do is also important, because "direct participation" by civilians in combat erodes their protection against being targeted. It may also make them liable for criminal prosecution if captured. Determining status and what constitutes "direct participation" in conflict is problematic, however, and state actors and the International Committee of the Red Cross (ICRC) do not always agree on how to interpret IHL's guidelines. In 2003, for example, the ICRC initiated a working group effort to clarify what is meant by "direct participation by civilians" in conflicts. Notably, this effort illuminated a disjuncture between the views of state participants and some scholars and those of the ICRC. The ICRC initiated the project hoping to clarify appropriate roles and protections of contractors employed by states in conflict zones, but many state representatives were equally concerned about the guidelines regarding irregular and nonstate armed groups. In the end, the ICRC's final document may have helped clarify what constitutes "direct participation" in hostilities, but it generated significant tensions due to disagreements about the protections accruing to nonstate actors.[31]

[30] In a recent document outlining commander responsibilities over contractors, the Army clarified the military's responsibility for oversight of subcontractors as well as direct contractors. *Handbook for Armed Private Security Contractors in Contingency Operations*, p. I-4.

[31] Michael N. Schmidt, "The Interpretive Guidance on the Notion of Direct Participation in Hostilities: A Critical Analysis," *Harvard National Security Journal* 1 (5 May 2010), pp. 5–44; Gomez del Prado, "The Privatization of War."

The expansion of tasks contractors are undertaking also complicates the question of direct participation. In the US context, reliance on contractors for intelligence functions and the maintenance and even operation of complex weapons systems, including drones, has raised questions about where the line should be drawn between "direct participation" and support functions. The US military has chosen to distinguish between tasks that are "inherently governmental" and must be carried out by government personnel (e.g., soldiers) and those that do not rise to this level.[32] This may help clarify tasks that clearly can be contracted out, but US policy choices regarding this distinction do not eliminate all the ambiguities regarding direct participation. Notably, US policy places armed guarding outside "inherently governmental" functions, and the government relies heavily on PSCs to provide guarding services and security details. Such guards are authorized to use force in self-defense and to defend those they are protecting.[33] The Blackwater team that killed seventeen civilians in Nisoor Square was a State Department personal security detail, for example. The ICRC determined in 2009 that if contractors were performing "continuous combat function(s)," such as protecting diplomats or convoys, then they would likely be considered combatants, not civilians. This would make them lawful targets in combat, but as civilians, they could still be prosecuted as criminals if they harmed civilians.

It is worth noting that the modern international legal framework governing war was formulated for a different environment: that of 20th-century military practice. Certainly, military forces relied on private actors in previous wars, as the CAF designation implies. But IHL does not account for private actors using force in the service of states, separate from militias.[34] Anna Leander also argues that private military companies have been artificially invested with the authority of the state, by virtue of their claims both to further the government's aims and of expertise. This has blurred the distinction between the state and private companies in terms of who exercises the force that is the state's monopoly, in Weber's understanding of the state. Instead, a "shared monopoly" of the use of force has emerged, in her view, which has hindered efforts to prevent PMSCs from acting as quasi-soldiers.[35] In an alternate view, Elke Krahmann has argued it is a mistake to categorize PMSC employees as CAFs. Rather, she argues that

[32] This reflects broader US policy. The White House, "Memorandum: Government Contracting," 4 March 2009, http://www.whitehouse.gov/the_press_office/Memorandum-for-the-Heads-of-Executive-Departments-and-Agencies-Subject-Government/, accessed 11 February 2010.

[33] Corn, "Contractors and the Law."

[34] Leander, "Paradoxical Impunity of Private Military Contractors."

[35] Leander, "Paradoxical Impunity of Private Military Contractors," p. 483.

contractors represent a new model of soldier, and militaries need to evaluate the implications of this model for civil-military relations.[36] What this means for status under IHL remains unclear. Each of these perspectives highlights tensions with the existing international legal framework governing soldiers and war.

Training

Because contractors are hired by a wide range of corporations, their knowledge and training in IHL varies. First, many PMSC employees are former soldiers, and it can be assumed that those from Western militaries received training in IHL during their military service. It is less clear, however, whether "third country nationals" hired from places such as Chile, Fiji, and Uganda have similar training in IHL. Second, companies hire not only soldiers but also contractors with police and other domestic law-enforcement backgrounds. This is partly because the preferred pool of former soldiers with extensive special forces training was largely tapped out by the industry's expansion. It also reflects the growing need for policing, rather than military skills. Blackwater, for example, acknowledged as early as 2004 that up to 30 percent of its employees in Iraq lacked prior military training.[37] There is no reason to assume that contractors with police backgrounds received previous training in IHL.

A more important point is whether the training that PMSC employees receive from their employers clarifies their current status and obligations under IHL. The key is whether company training emphasizes to former soldiers their changed status under IHL, since they are no longer lawful combatants. A recent survey of contractor self-perceptions suggests that at least some companies do give employees appropriate training for their missions, including instruction regarding applicable "rules of engagement."[38] Survey data suggests, however, that a significant fraction of armed contractors undertook offensive measures in Iraq.[39]

[36] Krahmann, "New Model Soldier and Civil-Military Relations," p. 261.

[37] Schmidt, "Humanitarian Law and Direct Participation in Hostilities," p. 515. See also Krahmann, "New Model Soldier and Civil Military Relations."

[38] Volker Franke and Marc von Boemcken, "Outsourcing Security: Attitudes, Values and Professional Self-Conception of Private Security Contractors," Paper Presented to the Annual Convention of the International Studies Association, New Orleans, LA, 16–20 February 2010, p. 15.

[39] Sarah K. Cotton, Ulrich Petersohn, Molly Dunigan, Q. Burkhart, Megan Zander-Cotugno, Edward O'Connell, and Michael Webber, *Hired Guns: Views about Contractors in Operation Iraqi Freedom* (Washington, DC: RAND, 2010), pp. 29–30.

Contractors and the Use of Force

Under what ROE do PMSC contractors operate? A critical point is that US contractors do not operate under military ROE, but follow "Rules for the Use of Force" (RUF). The US Joint Forces Command, in seeking to clarify appropriate oversight for contractors, stresses that the two terms are not interchangeable, and states that "ROE refers to rules of force during military combat operations while RUF usually refers to the use of force required while conducting security or noncombat operations." The ROE are intended to guide the military, and allow the use of lethal force against the state's enemies, while RUF allow the use of force to complete missions and protect civilians, and are based on the state's authority to protect citizens.[40]

The Iraq situation muddied the waters, because contractors sometimes found themselves in combat situations.[41] Moreover, multiple forms of guidance governed the behavior of different contractors. Before it dissolved in June 2004, the Coalition Provisional Authority (CPA) established by the US government to govern Iraq after the 2003 invasion issued a memorandum laying out the RUF for contractors. The DOD urged that these guidelines be adopted. The document stated at the outset that contractors had the "inherent right to take action necessary to defend yourself."[42] The use of force was allowed for self-defense, to defend those they were contractually protecting, and "to prevent life threatening offenses against civilians."[43] The CPA guidelines followed standard military practice in requiring the graduated use of force ("Shout, shove, show, shoot"), the use of aimed shots, and avoidance of harm or humiliation of civilians as far as possible. The CPA rules also stated, "You may not join Coalition or Multinational Forces in combat operations except in self-defense or in defense of persons as specified in your contracts."[44] This appears to be in keeping with IHL, which does not prohibit civilians from participating in hostilities, but once civilians engage in activities that are part of hostilities, they lose protection from direct attack.[45]

While the CPA RUF covered contractors working for the DOD and for most other government agencies active in Iraq, contractors working for the State

[40] *Handbook for Armed Private Security Contractors in Contingency Operations*, p. II-6.

[41] Robert Young Pelton, *Licensed to Kill: Hired Guns in the War on Terror* (New York: Crown Publishers, 2006), pp. 147–165.

[42] *Registration Requirements for Private Security Companies (PSCs)*, Annex A, Coalition Provisional Authority Memorandum Number 17, 2004, p. 10.

[43] Ibid.

[44] Ibid.

[45] ICRC, *Privatisation of War: The Outsourcing of Military Threats*, 23 May 2006, www.icrc.org/Web/Eng/siteeng0.nsf/html/privatisation-war230506, accessed 25 May 2007.

Department operated under separate RUF until 2008. These evolved over time, and one shorthand summary of the 2003 guidelines was "If they shoot at you, shoot back."[46] In 2007, the State Department described its policy regarding the use of force by protective details as

> a seven-step process that must be utilized as appropriate under the circumstances: (1) English/Arabic visual warning signs on vehicles; (2) hand/verbal warning signs; (3) use of bright lights; (4) use of Pen flares; (5) weapon pointed at offending vehicle; (6) shots fired into engine block of vehicle; and (7) shots fired into windshield of vehicle. It should be noted that deadly force can be immediately applied provided that it is necessary under the specific situation's circumstances.[47]

It is important to keep in mind that under both CPA and DOS guidelines for the use of force, the graduated steps prior to the use of lethal force could occur quite rapidly, particularly in an environment where contractors feared attacks by suicide bombers in cars. In one incident in which Iraqi civilians were killed by PMSC contractors in Baghdad, on 9 October 2007, the PMSC employees apparently made hand signals and tossed a flare before opening fire on a car approaching close to their convoy, but onlookers saw little space for reaction by the driver between these steps.[48]

Army guidelines governing contractors in the field stress the combatant commander's responsibility to account for PMSC personnel operating in his area, to ensure that they are properly trained on the weapons they are authorized to use. Commanders are also expected to establish RUF for contractors, with the recognition that these may change over time as the situation on the ground changes. The sample RUF provided by the Joint Forces Command closely paralleled the earlier CPA RUF. It more explicitly stated that contractors are noncombatants, and are not allowed to engage in offensive operations alongside troops. Again, the right to self-defense was clearly noted. The guidelines reflected some of the problems that emerged in Iraq, by stressing that contractors must stop at both coalition and local checkpoints, and that they must not point their weapons at either coalition troops or Iraqi police and security forces. The RUF allowed for the use of necessary force, for largely the same reasons stipulated by the CPA RUF, and stressed the importance of graduated force ("shout, show, shoot"). If

[46] Pelton, *Licensed to Kill*, p. 116.

[47] "Private Security Contracting in Iraq and Afghanistan," Statement of Ambassador Richard J. Griffin before the House Committee on Oversight and Government Reform, 2 October 2007.

[48] Joshua Partlow and Sudarsan Raghavan, "Guards Kill Two Women in Iraq," *Washington Post*, 10 October 2007.

force must be used, the RUF also stipulated resort only to aimed shots, avoiding bystanders, and reporting shooting incidents immediately. It underscored both treating civilians with dignity and ensuring appropriate weapons authorization by individual contractors.[49] The guidelines to commanders also stressed that contractors should not be assigned "inherently military" tasks, even if they have the background to carry out such tasks. This appears intended to further reinforce the distinction between combatants and noncombatants.

Legal Accountability

Serious questions exist about the accountability of PMSCs and contractors in the international arena. It is not true that contractors fall outside the law; legal frameworks cover their behavior at several levels. The key question, however, is the effectiveness of these frameworks. As noted previously, few contractors have faced punitive legal sanctions for their actions. This contributed to the perception that PMSC contractors could act with impunity in conflict zones, with no expectation of being held legally accountable under national or international law.

Legal accountability can take several forms via mechanisms at both the domestic and international level. To begin with, when military forces are stationed on another state's territory, the two governments involved generally negotiate a "status of forces" agreement (SOFA) that delineates the legal rights and responsibilities of all parties, including civilians accompanying the armed forces. This clarifies which bodies of law govern the behavior of different actors, and which state has authority if soldiers or CAFs commit crimes on or off their bases.

Iraq and Afghanistan were anomalies in this regard. Before 2009, US and Coalition forces remained in Iraq with UN mandate, at the request of first the transitional Iraqi government and later the elected government of Iraq. Contractors, including PSC employees, were granted immunity from Iraqi law for actions taken in service of their contracts under CPA Order #17 (28 June 2004).[50] One consequence was that, for several years, many contractors came to view Iraq, which was then wracked by insurgencies, as a lawless zone, where the guidelines were "kill or be killed."[51] The aggressive tactics of some companies carrying out diplomatic protection generated the impression that contractors were acting with immunity and impunity. After the 2007 Nisoor Square

[49] *Handbook for Armed Private Security Contractors in Contingency Operations*, p. II-5.

[50] *Status of the Coalition Provisional Authority, MNF-Iraq, Certain Missions and Personnel in Iraq*, Coalition Provisional Authority Order Number 17 (Revised), 2004. CPA/ORD/27 june 2004/17, http://www.cpa-iraq.org/regulations/20040627_CPAORD_17_Status_of_Coalition__Rev__with_Annex_A.pdf.

[51] Pelton, *Licensed to Kill*, p. 116.

incident, the Iraqi government sought to remove contractor immunity, and the SOFA reached between the US and Iraqi governments in December 2008 made contractors subject to Iraqi law.[52] US troop withdrawal from Iraq at the end of 2011 was due in part to the failure to negotiate a new SOFA.

The US troop presence in Afghanistan was codified by a "diplomatic note" exchanged by the two governments in May 2003, rather than a SOFA, and by the UN mandate under which NATO operated in Afghanistan.[53] A "Bilateral Security Agreement" to authorize US troops' presence—and support personnel—after 2014 was reached between the US and Afghan governments in late 2013, as the United States planned to reduce its troop presence. But Afghan President Hamid Karzai had refused to sign the agreement, throwing a wrench in US planning until a new president, Ashraf Ghani, was elected. He authorized the security agreement one day after taking office in September 2014.

The US government sought over the last sixteen years to establish clear legal accountability of civilians supporting US military activities overseas. This involved passage by Congress of the Military Extraterritorial Jurisdiction Act (MEJA) in 2000 to ensure accountability of contractors working for the military overseas,[54] with revisions in 2004 and 2007 to expand its reach from DOD contractors to contractors working in support of any overseas mission, regardless of which agency employed them. These amendments followed apparent abuses by PMSC employees who fell outside the mandate of the existing law, in Abu Ghraib in 2004, and in Nisoor Square in 2007.[55] The US Uniform Code of Military Justice (UCMJ), which holds military troops accountable, was also revised by Congress in late 2006 to make the Code applicable in both declared wars and also "contingency operation(s)"; this was intended to ensure that military commanders had more control over the actions of contractors on the battlefield.[56]

The US government has also sought to improve contractor accountability simply by doing more to oversee the activities of contractors supporting overseas contingency operations. Congress required that DOD, the State Department, and USAID, the main agencies active in Iraq and Afghanistan, establish and maintain common databases to keep track of contractors working in support of contingency

[52] It is not clear whether other members of the Multinational Force in Iraq have negotiated SOFA-type agreements with the Iraqi government.

[53] The NATO mission ended in December 2014. Karen DeYoung, "Only a Two-Page 'Note' Governs US Military in Afghanistan," *Washington Post*, 28 August 2008.

[54] This ambiguity did not cause great concern until the 1990s, since the number of both conflicts in which the United States was involved and contractors was low. Corn, "Contractors and the Law," pp. 167–172.

[55] Julian Borger, "US Military in Torture Scandal," *The Guardian*, 30 April 2004.

[56] Matthews, "Contractor Crackdown."

missions.[57] More generally, Congress established special inspectors general for the Iraq and Afghanistan operations to evaluate use of reconstruction funds in 2004 and 2007 respectively, and charged the Commission on Wartime Contracting to examine waste, fraud, and abuse in contracts in these operations.[58] It is notable that the Afghan position was established six years after US and NATO activities there began, which points to the dearth of oversight previously.[59]

Outside the United States, roughly fifty countries have some form of legislation regarding private security companies, ranging from laws to draft laws. The majority of these focus on the activities of domestic private security companies.[60] Few states have legislation governing the private security industry's global activities. In 1998 South Africa passed legislation requiring PMSCs to get government approval for any contracts to provide services in other countries. Legislation making it a crime for any South African citizen to work in a conflict zone without government permission was passed in November 2007.[61]

A handful of other countries have some regulations addressing the private security industry. Angola, for example, passed laws regulating PMSCs in 1992 and 1994, although these are considered ineffective, and Afghanistan has sought unsuccessfully to develop PSC regulations since 2002.[62] The Iraqi government requires PMSCs to register with the Interior Ministry, and the government insisted that PMSC employees were subject to Iraqi law beginning in January 2009, due to outrage over their immunity under CPA Order 17.[63] Yet, the laws

[57] These were provisions of the National Defense Authorization Act of 2008 (FY2008 NDAA), which led to the creation of the Synchronized Predeployment and Operational Tracker (SPOT), a database containing contractor information about contractors throughout Iraq and Afghanistan. See: H.R. 1585, 2007; John P. Hutton, "Contingency Contracting: DOD, State, and USAID Are Taking Actions to Track Contracts and Contractor Personnel in Iraq and Afghanistan," GAO Report GAO-09-538T, 1 April 2009, p. 2. The SPOT mechanism continues to suffer from gaps in information, however. See: GAO, "DOD, State, and USAID Cannot Fully Account for Contracts, Assistance Instruments, and Associate Personnel," *GAO Report 11-886*, September 2011.

[58] On SIGAR, see: http://www.sigar.mil. See also Schwartz and Church, "Department of Defense's Use of Contractors"; on the Commission on Wartime Contracting, see: https://cybercemetery.unt.edu/archive/cwc/20110929213815/http://www.wartimecontracting.gov/, accessed 7 April 2014.

[59] Bruce Falconer, "Afghanistan: Oversight AWOL?" *Mother Jones*, 16 July 2009, http://motherjones.com/politics/2009/07/afghanistan-oversight-awol.

[60] For a database of existing private security regulation, see Private Security Regulation.Net, http://www.privatesecurityregulation.net/pmsc-regulation-database, accessed September 23, 2011. See also: http://psm.du.edu/national_regulation/index.html, accessed 4 April 2014.

[61] Nathan Hodge, "Army for Hire," *Slate Magazine*, August 3, 2006; Percy, *Regulating the Private Security Industry*, pp. 30–32; Michael Peel and Alec Russell, "South Africa Mercenary Law Attacked," *Financial Times*, 29 May 2007.

[62] Lisa Rimli and Susanne Schmeidl, *Private Security Companies and Local Populations: An Exploratory Study of Afghanistan and Angola* (Bern, Switzerland: Swisspeace, 2007).

[63] Karen De Young, "U.S. Moves to Replace Contractors in Iraq," *Washington Post*, 17 March 2009.

established during the CPA period (2003–2004) remain largely unchanged in Iraq law.[64] The UK studied the question of PSC regulation, and considered a range of regulatory proposals in 2002, though no action was taken for several years.[65] The UK government announced in April 2009 that it intended to rely on an international code of conduct to govern PMSCs' behavior globally, along with industry self-regulation for UK-based PMSCs. This is discussed in the next section.

At the international level, IHL sets standards of behavior for all actors in conflict zones, and its guidelines thus apply to PMSC employees. The ICRC in particular has been adamant in stressing this point, as noted earlier, and it has engaged in dialogue with industry representatives regarding private accountability in conflict zones.[66] A few international instruments proscribe the actions of mercenaries, including the UN Mercenary Convention, opened for signature in 1989, the AU's antimercenary convention, and Additional Protocol I of the Geneva Conventions, signed in 1977. As noted previously, however, these conventions do not clearly apply to PMSCs or their employees.

There is no international convention covering the actions of PMSCs or their employees. The UN Working Group on Mercenaries presented a draft convention in mid-2010, but its reception has been mixed. Those states most reliant on PMSCs, the United States and the UK and other European states, have argued that such a convention is unnecessary. Several regional groups, such as the Organization of the Islamic Conference, the African Group, and the Arab Group of states support the prospect of a PMSC convention, and argued that the draft should be pursued further.[67] The UN's Human Rights Council extended the Working Group's mandate through 2017, with the task of monitoring use of mercenary-related activities as well as private military and security companies.[68]

[64] http://psm.du.edu/national_regulation/iraq.html, accessed 4 April 2014.

[65] Christopher Kinsey, "Regulation and Control of Private Military Companies: The Legislative Dimension," *Contemporary Security Policy* 26, no.1 (April 2005): 84–102.

[66] *Private Military/Security Companies "Acknowledge Humanitarian Law Obligations."* Interview with Melker Mabeck, ICRC, 27 November 2006. www.icrc.org/Web/Eng/siteeng0.nsf/html/private-military-companies-interview-271, accessed 25 May 2007; "International Humanitarian Law and Private Military/Security Companies: FAQ," *ICRC*, 23 May 2006, www.icrc.org/web/eng/siteeng0.nsf/htmlall/pmc-fac-230506?opendocument, accessed January 24, 2007.

[67] International Service for Human Rights (ISHR), "Human Rights Council: Little Support for Proposed Convention Regulating Private Security Companies," 23 September 2010, http://www.ishr.ch/archive-council/909-human-rights-council-little-support-for-new-convention-regulating-private-security-companies, accessed 28 September 2011.

[68] "Working Group on the Use of Mercenaries as a Means of Violating Human Rights and Impeding the Exercise of the Rights of Peoples to Self-Determination," http://www.ohchr.org/EN/Issues/Mercenaries/WGMercenaries/Pages/WGMercenariesIndex.aspx, accessed 6 August 2016.

The challenge confronting both domestic and international law is the difficulty of ensuring that violations of law are reported and prosecuted, when incidents occur thousands of miles from likely jurisdictions. Moreover, as is often true with human rights violations more broadly, potential abuses by PMSCs take place in conflict zones, where witnesses and evidence are hard to find and to transport to foreign courts where jurisdiction over PMSCs exists.

Nonbinding Accountability: Codes of Conduct and Standards

In the absence of comprehensive state regulation or international law, PMSCs have proposed self-regulation, and multistakeholder efforts developed a voluntary international code for the industry.

As discussed in the previous section, the United States is one of only a few countries that have developed regulations governing PMSCs' international activities. In the 2000s, some PMSC representatives argued that self-regulation and codes of conduct can provide an effective means to ensure compliance and accountability. The industry, they argued, can regulate itself. Moreover, they claimed that the private security industry has a strong incentive to do so since a good reputation will affect future business opportunities.[69] Self-regulation is a governance mechanism in which private actors design voluntary guidelines for a particular industry. It is generally intended to quell pressure for state regulation, which has more "teeth" than voluntary regulations do.[70] Companies or industries also may adopt self-regulation for reputational reasons, since a poor reputation can hurt business and provoke state regulatory efforts.[71]

The International Stability Operations Association (ISOA), formerly the International Peace Operations Association (IPOA), is a US-based trade association whose members provide services in fragile environments, and includes many private military and security companies as members. The ISOA

[69] Doug Brooks, "In Search of Adequate Legal and Regulatory Frameworks," *Journal of International Peace Operations* 2, no. 5 (2007).

[70] A. Héritier and D. Lehmkuhl, "The Shadow of Hierarchy and New Modes of Governance," *Journal of Public Policy* 28, no. 1 (2008), pp. 1–17. On self-regulation, see also: A. Prakash, *Greening the Firm: The Politics of Corporate Environmentalism* (Cambridge: Cambridge University Press, 2000); H. Ward, *Legal Issues in Corporate Citizenship* (London: International Institute for Environment and Development, February 2003).

[71] The threat of formal regulation, which is often a stimulus for effective self-regulation, has been too weak to convince companies to invest in a stronger association with the capacity to develop and enforce self-regulatory standards. Renée de Nevers, "Self-Regulating War? Voluntary Regulation and the Private Security Industry," *Security Studies* 18 (2009): 479–516.

established a code of conduct (under the IPOA label) to promote high operational and ethical industry standards.[72] The code was first established in 2001, and was updated periodically, most recently in October 2011.[73] It lays out appropriate activities and behavior for members in areas ranging from respecting human rights to insurance and personnel policies. It references as baseline norms IHL and human rights law, as well as specific documents and treaties regarding the conduct of war. A UK-based organization, the British Association of Private Security Companies (BAPSC), also established a code of conduct for UK-based PMSCs, but failed to generate strong industry support. The UK government instead turned to the Security in Complex Environments Group (SCEG), a subgroup of companies within ADS, a UK industry association representing companies in the aerospace, defense, security, and space sectors, as its partner in developing professional standards for PMSCs.[74] Notably, this coincided with establishment of a voluntary international code of conduct and certification mechanisms for PMSCs. Both governments and industry shifted support to these processes.

Internationally, as reliance on PMSCs skyrocketed in Iraq and Afghanistan in the mid-2000s, the ICRC and the Swiss government initiated an effort to enhance PMSC compliance with IHL. The two, along with scholars at the Geneva Center for the Democratic Control of the Armed Forces, initiated a dialogue with industry and government representatives regarding PMSCs' roles and responsibilities under IHL in the mid-2000s.[75] This resulted in the "Montreux Document on Pertinent International Legal Obligations and Good Practices for States Related to Operations of Private Military and Security Companies during Armed Conflict" (the Montreux Document), published in September 2008 and now endorsed by fifty-three states, which lays out state responsibilities under international law regarding the conduct of PMSCs that they employ or host.[76]

[72] IPOA, "About IPOA," http://ipoaworld.org/eng/aboutipoa.html, accessed 10 June 2009; "ISOA Mission Statement," http://www.stability-operations.org/index.php, accessed 26 September 2011.

[73] "ISOA Code of Conduct," http://www.stability-operations.org/?page=Code, accessed 6 April 2014.

[74] http://www.sceguk.org.uk/about-sceg/, accessed 9 August 2016.

[75] The British government also announced in April 2009 that it intended to rely on international codes of conduct to govern PMSCs' behavior globally as one piece of a regulatory framework for UK-based PMSCs.

[76] "The Montreux Document," 17 September 2008, http://www.eda.admin.ch/etc/medialib/downloads/edazen/topics/intla/humlaw.Par.0056.File.tmp/Montreux%20Document.pdf. See also: "Participating States of the Montreux Document," http://www.eda.admin.ch/eda/en/home/topics/intla/humlaw/pse/parsta.html, accessed 6 April 2014.

The Swiss-ICRC effort also led to a multistakeholder initiative that drafted an "International Code of Conduct for Private Security Service Providers" (ICoC), which was opened for signature on 9 November 2010. The ICoC establishes voluntary standards for the private security industry that are "based on international human rights and humanitarian law, as well as to improve accountability of the industry by establishing an external independent oversight mechanism."[77] The ICoC applies to PMSC activities in "complex environments," which includes conflict zones, weak or failed states, and areas hit by natural disasters, where PSCs may find themselves employed.[78] By September 2013, 708 companies had signed the Code.[79]

Following the drafting of the ICoC, an oversight and governance mechanism, the International Code of Conduct Association (ICoCA) was established in September 2013, as called for in the Code. The ICoCA is working to develop guidelines for monitoring and certification of company activities.[80]

Concurrent with the development of the ICoCA, an American National Standards Institute (ANSI)-recognized management standard for PSCs, the "Management System for Quality of Private Security Company Operations (hereafter PSC.1) was established. The US DOD initiated the ANSI process by contracting ASIS International, an organization of security professionals, to work with stakeholders to establish a "quality assurance management system" that would enable companies to demonstrate that they are meeting international norms in doing their work.[81] An explicit goal of the PSC.1 is to encourage compliance with IHL and human rights law—as well as the ICoC, which is founded

[77] *International Code of Conduct for Private Security Service Providers*, http://www.icoc-psp.org/, accessed 26 March 2012. The ICRC was not involved in its development.

[78] This contrasts with the earlier Montreux Document, a voluntary statement signed by states that seeks to clarify states' existing responsibilities and obligations under humanitarian law that focuses on situations of armed conflict. *The Montreux Document*. As of 1 June 2013, 659 companies from 64 countries had signed the ICoC. http://www.icoc-psp.org/, accessed 23 July 2013. The high number of signatories reflected the requirement that PSCs wishing to join the Security Association for the Maritime Industry (SAMI) must sign the ICoC. See: http://www.marsecreview.com/sami/, accessed 13 February 2013.

[79] http://www.icoc-psp.org/, accessed 5 April 2014.

[80] The Articles of Association are available at http://www.icoc-psp.org/uploads/ICoC_Articles_of_Association.pdf, accessed 24 July 2013. For a discussion of the development of the ICoCA, see Anne Marie Buzatu, *Towards an International Code of Conduct for Private Security Providers: A View from Inside a Multistakeholder Process* (Geneva: Geneva Center for the Democratic Control of the Armed Forces, 2015).

[81] "Quality assurance management" ensures management guidelines that focus on processes intended to meet clear standards, and that employ regular monitoring and feedback to ensure that standards are consistently met. Quality assurance is built into the International Standards Organization (ISO) 9000 codes.

on the same legal frameworks. Notably, the PSC.1 includes requirements for training on these points:

> It is the organization's responsibility that all persons working on behalf of the organization are sufficiently trained, both prior to any deployment and on an ongoing basis, in the performance of their functions and to respect relevant local, national, and humanitarian and human rights laws. . . . Training should specifically include training on the: A) prohibition of torture or other cruel, inhuman, or degrading treatment; B) prohibition and awareness of sexual exploitation and abuse- or gender-based violence; C) recognition and prevention of human trafficking and slavery.[82]

The PSC.1 is a commercial business standard. It establishes "auditable requirements" that will enable third-party certification of company performance. This management system is intended to "provide quality assurance in all security related activities and functions while demonstrating accountability to law and respect for human rights."[83] The PSC.1 is intended to fulfill US legislative requirements passed in 2010 and 2011 that directed the DOD to establish standards and certification for private security contractors under its employ.[84] The DOD incorporated a requirement of compliance with the PSC.1 into the Defense Acquisition Regulation System (DFARS) on 22 May 2012 for contracts for security-related services in combat zones, contingency operations, or other exercises.[85] In addition to the PSC.1's incorporation into the DOD's contracting guidelines, the UK government adopted it as the standard for UK-based PSCs working internationally in December 2012.[86] Additionally, drafting of an ISO

[82] *Conformity Assessment and Auditing Management Systems for Quality of Private Security Company Operations*, ANSI/ASIS PSC.2-2012 American National Standard, p. 63, http://www.acq.osd.mil/log/PS/psc/Item_2010_PSC_standards.2_STD.PDF, accessed 12 June 2012.

[83] *Conformity Assessment and Auditing Management Systems for Quality of Private Security Company Operations.*

[84] ASIS International, "ASIS Awarded Contract with U.S. Department of Defense to Develop Standard to improve Performance and Accountability of Private Security Service Providers," ASIS International News Release, 16 March 2011, http://www.asisonline.org/guidelines/committees/psc.1_std.htm, accessed 28 September 2011; ASIS International, "ASIS International Begins Standards Development to Support the Code of Conduct for Private Security Service Providers," ASIS International News Release, 29 April 2011, http://www.asisonline.org/guidelines/committees/psc.1_std.htm, accessed 26 September 2011.

[85] http://www.acq.osd.mil/log/PS/psc.html, accessed 11 December 2012.

[86] "Written Ministerial Statement," Foreign and Commonwealth Office, 17 December 2012.

standard for PSCs based on the principles of the PSC.1 began in 2013, and an ISO "Security Operations Management System Standard," based on the ANSI PSC.1 standard, was published in September 2015.[87] Certification under the PSC.1 was in trial stages in 2014, and the first certification bodies were licensed in 2014. The first company was certified to be in compliance with the PSC.1 in March 2014.[88]

A key issue in the development of the ICoC was how to evaluate company adherence to the Code, so that it would be more than simply window dressing. The ICoCA is intended to determine whether companies meet the standards and principles of the Code through certification, monitoring, and a complaints process open to individuals claiming violations of the Code. To date, only guidelines regarding certification have been established, and they rely largely on national certification schemes. The ICoC called for national and international standards to be considered as possible certification that companies are in compliance with the Code, reflecting a government preference for a single audit mechanism to certify adherence to the ICoC.[89] The ICoCA recognized the ANSI PSC.1 as a certification standard that is consistent with the Code, when accompanied by additional requirements specified by the ICoCA.[90] It is worth noting that once the ICoCA was established, companies could no longer claim that they were adhering to the ICoC simply by signing the Code, as they had previously; ICoCA membership required accepting certification of the company's adherence. Currently, member companies have committed to seek certification, and presumably this process has begun. As of mid-2016, however, the ICoCA had not certified any member companies as in compliance with the Code.[91]

[87] "ISO Publishes Security Operations Management System Standard Based on ANSI/ASIS. PSC.1:2012," NASDAQ, 24 September 2015, https://globenewswire.com/news-release/2015/09/24/770841/10150527/en/ISO-Publishes-Security-Operations-Management-System-Standard-based-on-ANSI-ASIS-PSC-1-2012.html, accessed 9 August 2016.

[88] See: http://business-humanrights.org/en/olive-group-is-first-private-security-company-to-be-awarded-accredited-certification-to-the-private-security-standard-psc1-a-key-milestone-for-the-company-and-the-industry, accessed 23 July 2014.

[89] Indeed, the UK government statement on the launch of the ICoCA stressed its conception of PSC.1 certification with ICoC Association oversight as the appropriate relationship between the two bodies. Simmonds, "Written Ministerial Statement."

[90] These requirements are laid out in "Annex B", available at the ICoCA website: http://www.icoca.ch/en/certification, accessed 9 August 2016.

[91] For a list of member companies of the ICoCA, see: http://www.icoca.ch/en/membership?private_security_companies=companies&op=Search&view_type=list&form_id=_search_for_members_filter_form, accessed 9 August 2016.

Dilemmas of Effectiveness and Accountability

A central challenge in ensuring that PMSCs and their employees adhere to human rights standards is the limited reach of existing mechanisms seeking to hold companies to human rights principles. Because so few countries have regulations governing PMSC activities overseas, corporations can simply change location in order to dodge state regulations. State regulation is the exception, rather than the rule, and there is a strong need for additional national legislation to govern PMSC activities. The ICoC may help fill the gap in international legislation if it establishes effective certification and monitoring mechanisms. Only six governments are members of the ICoCA, however, and while more states likely support its aims, the Code's reach is difficult to ascertain. More broadly, states have the responsibility to enforce international law, and states employing PSCs accrue some responsibility for their behavior.[92] Indeed, one goal of the Montreux Document was to remind states of their responsibilities regarding contractors in their employ. Efforts to establish an international treaty governing PMSC activities deserve serious consideration, due to the paucity of national legislation in this area, but progress is likely to be slow.

An additional challenge arises from private security companies' reliance on contractors from an increasingly wide range of countries. This raises concerns about the danger of violations of IHL and human rights law, as former soldiers from militaries with little respect for human rights take up jobs in conflict and postconflict zones. What authority governments have over these third country nationals is quite murky. They are accountable under their home government's law, but few states have the resources to enforce this. Finally, the prospect that entrepreneurs in countries with poor human rights records will establish their own PMSCs increases concern about respect for IHL by PMSC employees.

The Geneva Conventions face serious challenges in the 21st century. State authority over actors using force appears to have eroded, as states rely on private actors to further their own ends, and support private actors against governments they oppose. This is not new, but the scope of this outsourcing of the monopoly on the use of force has expanded.

In a world where conflicts remain common, IHL remains valuable. Yet, "fitting" the range of actors on the battlefield into the existing framework has proven complex. One solution with regard to PMSCs is to constrain the tasks that PMSCs are permitted to carry out. Governments that have chosen to rely

[92] Emanuela-Chiara Gillard, "Business goes to war: private military/security companies and international humanitarian law," *International Review of the Red Cross*, no. 863, 9 September 2009, 549–557.

heavily on PMSCs may need to revisit their outsourcing decisions, and to reclaim certain functions as public, rather than private. Indeed, the US government has begun revisiting what are appropriate public and private functions. This is particularly important where the use of force is concerned. And IHL may provide a useful framework for delineating the appropriate breakdown of tasks.

In the absence of international laws or treaties governing the activities of PMSCs, the ICoC and its compliance framework offer some hope of determining, and hopefully increasing, PMSC compliance with IHL. Although incomplete, the framework of the ICoC and evolving compliance mechanisms, via the ICoCA and the PSC.1, may provide a baseline for more effective or enforceable guidelines with global reach. But in the end, the ICoC remains voluntary. Its effectiveness will depend on the willingness of those hiring PMSCs to hire only companies in good standing under the code. The United States's incorporation of the PSC.1 into its contracting requirements, and the UK's adoption of the PSC.1 to certify UK companies, are positive steps. The US government's failure to end business relations with companies that have performed poorly in Iraq and Afghanistan, however, gives cause for concern that states and corporations will honor the code in this way.

12

The Geneva Conventions

Do They Matter in the Context of Peacekeeping Missions?

SIOBHÁN WILLS

Introduction

Until the mid-1990s, although the United Nations accepted that UN forces are bound to respect the "principles and spirit" of the laws of war,[1] more commonly referred to today as international humanitarian law (IHL) or the international law of armed conflict, in practice the United Nations treated the subject "as a political issue and not as a fundamental legal obligation."[2]

Criticism of the inadequacy of this approach first surfaced in a serious way in the early 1990s, when a number of peacekeepers in Somalia that had committed serious crimes, including torture and murder, were acquitted by the courts of the contributing States (despite the fact that it was accepted that the crimes had occurred) on the grounds that IHL did not apply to peacekeepers and that other branches of law were not applicable in the circumstances.[3] In 1995 there

[1] UN Doc A/46/185 of 23 May 1991 [28]; A. Roberts and R. Guelff, *Documents on the Laws of War*, 3rd. ed. (Oxford: Oxford University Press, 2000), pp. 625, 723; D. Shraga and R. Zacklin, "The Applicability of International Humanitarian Law to United Nations Peace-Keeping Operations: Conceptual, Legal and Practical Issues," in *International Committee of the Red Cross Symposium on Humanitarian Action and Peacekeeping Operations*, ed. U. Palwankar (Geneva: International Committee of the Red Cross, 1994), pp. 39, 44; P. C. Szasz, "UN Forces and International Humanitarian Law," in *International Law across the Spectrum of Conflict, Essays in Honour of Professor LC Green on the Occasion of His Eightieth Birthday*, ed. M. N. Schmitt (Newport: US Naval War College, 2000), pp. 507, 516.

[2] R. D. Glick, "Lip Service to the Laws of War: Humanitarian Law and United Nations Armed Forces," *Michigan Journal of International Law* 17 (1995): 53–54.

[3] *R v. Brocklebank* CMAC-383, 2 April 1996; J. Simpson, *Law Applicable to Canadian Forces in Somalia 1992/93: Study Prepared for the Commission of Inquiry into the Deployment of Canadian Forces to Somalia* (Ottawa: Minister of Public Works and Government Services Canada, 1997), pp. 28–30; Judgement of the Belgian Military Court regarding violations of IHL committed in Somalia and

were shocking reports of gross abuses committed by peacekeepers against the inhabitants of Srebrenica by a minority of troops, including allegations of complicity in genocide through assisting in the separation of boys and men from women and girls.[4] At the time, a number of commentators argued that there was no legal regime applicable to UN peacekeepers by which they could be held accountable. Therefore, whether or not the allegations that some members of Dutchbat seriously abused the local population were true, "notwithstanding moral and ethical considerations . . . [a]ccording to the present state of public international law, the Dutch soldiers have not committed a punishable act."[5] In response to these concerns the ICRC began pushing for greater clarity on peacekeepers' legal obligations, focusing on securing a commitment from the UN to apply the rules of IHL as a matter of law and not just policy: but it took until 1999 before the *Secretary-General's Bulletin on Observance by United Nations Forces of Humanitarian Law* (hereafter *Secretary-General's Bulletin*) was ready for promulgation.[6]

One reason for the delay was the fact that from its inception the law of war aimed to grant the parties to the conflict privileges, as well as obligations, so as to facilitate the waging of war between them while curtailing inhumane excesses. It developed as a body of law that was intended to apply extraterritorially as well as within the contracting party's own borders (since wars tend to involve armed forces fighting outside their own state) but was framed so as to be applicable to parties to an armed conflict only (thus constraining the laws of war within some identifiable bounds since borders would not serve). Everyone in the vicinity of the conflict who is not a member of the armed forces of a party to the conflict is a civilian: civilians were not expected to have any role in the waging of the war. So long as civilians refrain from participating in hostilities they cannot be directly targeted and must be protected from the harmful effects of the war. There was

Rwanda Nr 54 AR 1997, 20 November 1997; *Journal des Tribunaux*, 24 April 1998, pp. 286–289 [in French]; M. Cogen, "Comment," *Yearbook of International Humanitarian Law* 1 (1998): 415–416.

[4] Netherlands Institute for War Documentation, *Srebrenica "A Safe Area": Reconstruction, Background, Consequences and Analyses of the Fall of a Safe Area* (Amsterdam: Nederlands Instituut voor Oorlogsdocumentatie, 2002): pt II, ch. 8, sect. 15, "The Extent of Anti-Muslim Behaviour" and ch. 9, sect. 11, "Right-Wing Extremist Behaviour in B-Company." Pressure from the Dutch public led to a number of investigations, none of which was sufficiently thorough to meet the gravity of the allegations. Netherlands Institute for War Documentation, *Srebrenica "A Safe Area"*: ch. 9, sect. 7, "Misconduct," sect. 8, "Back to Square One: Misconduct after All?," and sect. 9, "Conclusions on Misconduct?"

[5] R. C. R. Siekmann, "The Fall of Srebrenica and the Attitude of Dutchbat from an International Legal Perspective," *Yearbook of International Humanitarian Law* 1 (1998): 301–312.

[6] United Nations, *Secretary-General's Bulletin on Observance by United Nations forces of humanitarian law* ST/SGB/1999/13, 6 August 1999.

concern that if the UN asserted that its forces had rights and obligations under IHL but rejected the possibility that they might be legitimately targeted, respect for IHL might be undermined globally. It has long been a "cardinal principle of the laws of war" that members of the armed forces of parties to the conflict are treated equally'[7] bearing the same rights and obligations and carrying the same risks. Therefore the *Secretary-General's Bulletin* asserts that peacekeepers retain protected status as civilians most of the time but if through their "use of force in self-defence" they become "actively engaged as combatants" in "situations of armed conflict," they will lose their protected civilian status and IHL will be applicable to them.[8]

The Bulletin has proved highly problematic conceptually, and is hard to apply in practice because of the difficulty of determining when peacekeepers are "actively engaged" as combatants. Christopher Greenwood has argued that troop-contributing states are likely to treat the threshold between use of force in self-defense or defense of the mandate, and active participation as a combatant in an armed conflict,[9] as a relatively high one, since crossing it removes the troops' protected civilian status under customary IHL.[10] The point has been reiterated many times since.[11] The Bulletin has had virtually no effect on improving accountability for crimes and abuses committed by UN personnel against the host state population.

In the last decade the UN's missions have been given increasingly "robust" mandates authorizing them to use "all necessary means/measures" to carry out certain tasks, principally to protect civilians but also to strengthen host state authority. In 2013 the UN created an Intervention Brigade, within the UN Stabilisation Mission in the Democratic Republic of the Congo (MONUSCO), mandated to carry out "targeted offensive operations" to "neutralize" armed groups.[12] When using force to carry out offensive operations to neutralize parties to an armed conflict, IHL is clearly relevant. However, despite the increasingly robust nature of UN peacekeeping missions, most of the time peacekeepers are

[7] Roberts and Guelff, *Documents on the Laws of War* (n. 1), p. 625.

[8] United Nations, *Secretary-General's Bulletin on Observance by United Nations Forces of Humanitarian Law* (n. 6), Article 1.

[9] R. Murphy, "United Nations Military Operations and International Humanitarian Law: What Rules Apply to Peacekeepers?" *Criminal Law Forum* 14 (2003): 153–177; S. Wills, "The Need for Effective Protection of United Nations Peacekeepers: The Convention on the Safety of United Nations and Associated Personnel," *Human Rights Brief* 10, no. 2 (2003): 26–29.

[10] C. Greenwood, "International Humanitarian Law and UN Operations," *Yearbook of International Humanitarian Law* 3, (1998): 23–25.

[11] O. Engdahl, "The Status of Peace Operations Personnel under International Humanitarian Law," *Yearbook of International Humanitarian Law* 11 (2008): 109–131.

[12] S/RES/2098, 28 March 2013.

not using force against parties to an armed conflict. If IHL is applicable only when peacekeepers "are actively engaged as combatants" in an armed conflict, what international legal frameworks govern UN missions the rest of the time? How are the transitions between the circumstances in which IHL is applicable and the circumstances in which it is not, to be managed? What are the criteria for determining whether one legal framework or another applies in any particular circumstance? To what extent is IHL an effective means of regulating peacekeepers' conduct? To what extent is international human rights law (IHRL) relevant?

In response to increasingly robust mandates, usually adopted under Chapter VII of the UN Charter, the UN has developed its own sui generis approach to use of force by peacekeepers which draws on aspects of both IHL and IHRL but does not comply with either. Under the approach taken by the UN's Office of Legal Affairs, a person that would not be a legitimate target under IHL or IHRL may become an authorized military target of a UN military operation (and therefore killed) provided that the peacekeepers' use of force is pursuant to an authorization in the mission's mandate; is provided for in the mission's rules of engagement (ROE); is proportionate to its aim; and that minimum force is used and only as a last resort.[13] The UN takes the view that provided the mission is explicitly authorized to use "all necessary means" or "all necessary measures" to carry out the mandated task (or such an authority can be implied from the text of the mandating resolution and other relevant documents such as the UN Secretary-General's reports relating to the resolution)[14] the mission may use intentional lethal force to carry out that task regardless of whether or not the person targeted is a member of the armed forces of party to the conflict or a civilian directly participating in hostilities (which are the IHL criteria for intentionally targeting with lethal force); and regardless of whether the person targeted presents an imminent threat to life (which is the principal IHRL criterion for use of lethal force). The UN's understanding of its legal obligations with regard to use of lethal force by its troops is now well established and is relied on for the drafting of mission ROE for all "Chapter VII" mandated missions; but is not set out in any document, not even an internal one.[15]

Since the UN has not published its approach to use of force by its peacekeepers and since ROE are normally classified, host state populations are generally unable to find out what rules govern use of force by peacekeepers operating in their midst. The problem is exacerbated by the fact that mandates routinely

[13] Interviews with two senior advisors from the Office of the Legal Counsel, UNHQ, United Nations, New York, 16 and 17 June 2016 and open meeting with members of the Office of the Legal Counsel UNHQ and some UN Mission Legal Advisors, 24 June 2016.

[14] Ibid.

[15] Ibid.

authorize use of force not only to protect civilians but also to carry out other tasks that are often quite broadly conceived, such as supporting "the national authorities in stabilizing the security situation in the country."[16] Since the UN's understanding of its legal obligations with regard to use of lethal force is not published it has not been subjected to criticism or challenge by lawyers or academics from outside the UN system.

The *Bulletin on Observance by United Nations Forces of Humanitarian Law*

A fundamental customary law rule of targeting, now codified in Protocol I, requires commanders (and anyone else planning or carrying out an attack) to distinguish at all times between combatants and civilians. Civilians may not be targeted unless they are directly participating in hostilities, and even then only while they are actively participating. Civilians who are not participating in hostilities are to be protected from the effects of war as far as possible.[17] In 2009 the ICRC produced an *Interpretative Guidance on the Notion of Direct Participation in Hostilities under International Humanitarian Law* which states, citing Additional Protocol 1, that for the purposes of the principle of distinction all persons who are neither members of the armed forces of a party to the conflict nor participants in a *levée en masse* are civilians and are therefore entitled to protection against direct attack unless and for such time as they take a direct part in hostilities.[18] According to the *Interpretive Guidance* the armed forces of a party to the conflict comprise "all organized armed forces, groups and units which are under a command responsible to that Party for the conduct of its subordinates."[19] In similar vein the ICRC's study on *Customary International Humanitarian Law*, states in its commentary to Rule 4, "all persons who fight on behalf of a party

[16] S/RES 2226, 25 June 2015, paragraph 19 c.

[17] Under Articles 51 and 85 of Additional Protocol 1, attacks against legitimate military targets that may be expected to cause incidental loss of civilian life or injury to civilians that would be excessive in relation to the concrete and direct military advantage anticipated, are prohibited and would constitute a grave breach of the Protocol. Additional Protocol 1, (51)(5) and (85). The ICRC's study *Customary International Humanitarian Law* concludes that the Article 51 rule is now customary law applicable in all types of armed conflict whether or not the belligerents involved are parties to the Protocol. Violation of this rule constitutes a war crime: J. M. Henckaerts and L. Doswald-Beck, eds., *Customary International Humanitarian Law*, vol. 1 (Cambridge: Cambridge University Press, 2005), Rules 1 and Rule 156.

[18] N. Melzer, legal advisor ICRC, *Interpretive Guidance on the Notion of Direct Participation in Hostilities under International Humanitarian Law* (Geneva: ICRC, 2009), pp. 20–36.

[19] Ibid., p. 21.

to the conflict and subordinate themselves to its command" form part of its armed forces.[20] Under these criteria peacekeepers will very rarely form part of the armed forces of a party to the conflict. Under Rule 5 all other persons, other than those involved in a *levée en masse*, are civilians.[21]

The *Secretary-General's Bulletin* recognizes the applicability of IHL to UN forces when they are engaged as combatants but also affirms their protected status as nonparties to the conflict when they are not. The *Bulletin* states that the fundamental principles and rules of IHL are applicable to UN forces "when in situations of armed conflict they are actively engaged therein as combatants, to the extent and for the duration of their engagement. They are accordingly applicable in enforcement actions, or in peacekeeping operations when the use of force is permitted in self-defence."[22]

This is rather an odd collation of concepts since ordinarily rules governing use of force in self-defense and use of force as a combatant are not the same. Self-defense is an inherent right to defend that is unconnected with the privileges associated with combatant status, which permit attack.

The *Secretary-General's Bulletin* has been interpreted as implying that, if *as a matter of fact*, a peacekeeping mission engages in robust use of force where this is necessary to carry a mandated task, IHL may become applicable as a *matter of law* provided a certain threshold level of violence is reached such that the peacekeepers cease being civilians using force in self-defense and become combatants, that is, become parties to an armed conflict.[23] This is conceptually problematic since under IHL "combatant" is a status-based concept; members of the armed forces of a party to the conflict are combatants even if they never fire a shot; everyone else is a civilian however violently they behave. Use of force in self-defense, however robust, does not turn the persons defending themselves or defending others into combatants.

The traditional concept of self-defense as applied to UN forces was expanded quite early on in the history of peacekeeping to enable them to take action to defend not only themselves and civilians, but also to defend the mission (a development triggered largely in response to the difficulties faced by the

[20] Henckaerts and Doswald-Beck, *Customary International Humanitarian Law*, vol. 1 (n. 17), Rule 5.

[21] Ibid.

[22] United Nations, *Secretary-General's Bulletin on Observance by United Nations forces of Humanitarian Law* (n. 6), [1.1].

[23] Murphy, "United Nations Military Operations and International Humanitarian Law"; S. Wills, "Continuing Impunity of Peacekeepers: The Need for a Convention," *Journal of International Humanitarian Legal Studies* 4, no. 1 (2013): 1–8.

UN Mission in the Congo in the 1960s).[24] Secretary-General Kurt Waldheim's 1973 Report on the Implementation of Security Council Resolution 340,[25] which sets out this doctrine has been described by several experts in the field as triggering a "sea change" in UN doctrine on the use of force,[26] since allowing peacekeepers to take positive action in defense of their mission "is no different from allowing them to enforce it."[27] The High-Level Independent Panel on Peace Operations (which reported in June 2015) believes that while the concept of self-defense is well understood, "the concept of "defence of the mandate" requires clarity as to which tasks within the mandate may require the use of force."[28]

Determining the Point at Which Peacekeepers Cease to Be "Actively Engaged as Combatants"

The *Secretary-General's Bulletin* states that once peacekeepers become actively engaged as combatants in a situation of armed conflict IHL is applicable "to the extent and for the duration" of their engagement. Does this mean that once peacekeepers' *active* engagement as combatants ceases, peacekeepers regain civilian protected status; if so, how is cessation of "active engagement" to be determined? Is it after every engagement in combat (thus affording troops protected civilian status in between, which would appear to undermine the cardinal principle that combatants are treated equally)? Or is it only when a certain level of peace has returned? If so, how and by whom is the attainment of that level of peace to be assessed?

The wording of the *Secretary-General's Bulletin* suggests parallels with the temporary loss of protected status of civilians that actively participate in hostilities under customary IHL and codified in Protocol 1. Under Protocol 1, civilians may not be directly targeted except "for such time" as they take "a direct part in

[24] Annual Report of the Secretary-General on the Work of the Organization, 16 June 1960–16 June 1961, 16th Session, U.N. Doc A/4800, 27; A. W. Dorn and D. J. H. Bell, "Intelligence and Peacekeeping: The UN Operation in the Congo 1960–64" *International Peacekeeping* 2, no. 1 (Spring 1995): 11–12; N. MacQueen, *The United Nations since 1945: Peacekeeping and the Cold War* (New York: Addison Wesley Longman, 1999), p. 41.

[25] United Nations, Report of the Secretary-General on the implementation of Security Council resolution 340 (1973), UN document S/11052/Rev.1, 27 October 1973.

[26] T. Findlay, *The Use of Force in Peace Operations* (Oxford: Oxford University Press, 2002), p. 100; S. Chesterman, *The Use of Force in UN Peace Operations*, External Study for the UN Department of Peacekeeping Best Practices Unit (New York: New York Law School, 2003), p. 7.

[27] W. J. Durch, "The UN Operation in the Congo: 1960–1964," in *The Evolution of UN Peacekeeping: Case Studies and Comparative Analysis*, ed. W. J. Durch (New York: St. Martin's Press, 1993), pp. 315, 349.

[28] Report of the High-Level Independent Panel on Peace Operations on Uniting Our Strengths for Peace: Politics, Partnership and People, A/70/95–S/2015/446, 17 June 2015, paragraph 128.

hostilities."[29] Once ordinary civilians cease doing the hostile act that rendered them participants in hostilities they regain protected status: Civilian status is never lost, although the right to protection may be, temporarily. However this cannot be the case for peacekeepers who have become "actively engaged as combatants," since nobody can be a civilian and a combatant at the same time: Hence, once peacekeepers become "actively engaged as combatants" they must lose civilian status. Is it possible to lose and regain civilian status? The ICRC's *Interpretative Guidance on the Notion of Direct Participation in Hostilities under International Humanitarian Law* sets out detailed, albeit controversial, guidance on interpreting the meaning of "for such time" as a civilian takes "a direct part in hostilities."[30] There is no guidance of an equivalent nature, anywhere, on interpreting the meaning of "the extent and duration" of UN forces' "engagement as combatants." The *Secretary-General's Bulletin* appears to be premised on a blurring of an activity-based criterion (active participation as a "combatant") and a status-based criterion (combatant status). This blurring of activity-based and status-based criteria renders any assessment inherently opaque and thus open to differences of opinion.

Relationship of the *Secretary-General's Bulletin* to the Convention on the Safety of United Nations and Associated Personnel

Article 8 of the Statute of the International Criminal Court gives the ICC jurisdiction over serious violations of the laws and customs applicable in international armed conflict including under 8(b) (iii):

> Intentionally directing attacks against personnel, installations, materials, units or vehicles involved in humanitarian assistance or peacekeeping mission in accordance with the Charter of the United Nations, as long as they are entitled to the protection given to civilians or civilian objects under the international law of armed conflict.[31]

[29] Protocol Additional to the Geneva Conventions of 12 August 1949, and Relating to the Victims of International Armed Conflicts [50].

[30] The ICRC's *Interpretive Guidance* (n. 18) rejects "any extension of the concept of direct participation in hostilities beyond specific acts" since this would "blur the distinction made in IHL between temporary, activity-based loss of protection (due to direct participation in hostilities), and continuous, status or function-based loss of protection (due to combatant status or continuous combat function)," p. 45.

[31] 1998 Rome Statute of the International Criminal Court (adopted 17 July 1998, entered into force 11 April 2002) UN Doc A/CONF.183/9.

Under IHL, referenced in the quote above by its alternative title "the international law of armed conflict," protected civilian status extends to everyone who is not a member of the armed forces of a party to the conflict regardless of whether the conflict is international or noninternational.[32]

The *Convention on the Safety of United Nations and Associated Personnel*, which has been ratified by over ninety parties, requires States to criminalize all attacks on UN forces except where they are engaged in a Chapter VII mandated operation in which "any of the personnel are engaged as combatants against organized armed forces and to which the law of international armed conflict applies."[33] If peacekeepers are engaged as combatants in a noninternational armed conflict they remain protected by the Convention.[34] The "law of international armed conflict" referred to in the *Convention on the Safety of United Nations and Associated Personnel* deals with interstate armed conflicts and is a subset of "the international law of armed conflict" referred to in the Rome Statute, which deals with both interstate and internal armed conflicts.

Stephen Lepper, the US delegate to the committee that drafted the *Convention on the Safety of United Nations and Associated Personnel*, notes that, while the US delegates recognized the risks that might accrue from breaching the "cardinal principle of the laws of war that combatant forces are treated equally,"[35] they were nevertheless determined to ensure that the convention would criminalize attacks against all UN forces,[36] except those engaged as "combatants" in an international armed conflict.[37] At one point it was proposed that the Convention would not apply "whenever military personnel of the UN operations were engaged in combat with organized armed forces having an identifiable command structure, carrying arms openly and controlling part of the territory of the host State" but this was rejected.[38] After the traumatic experiences of US forces in Somalia in

[32] Melzer, *Interpretive Guidance on the Notion of Direct Participation in Hostilities under International Humanitarian Law* (n. 18).

[33] Convention on the Safety of UN and Associated Personnel 34 ILM (1995), Articles, 2, 9, and 13.

[34] Ibid.

[35] Roberts and Guelff, *Documents on the Laws of War* (n. 1), p. 625.

[36] Including attacks against forces undertaking a UN authorized operation but that are not UN commanded and controlled through a broad interpretation of "associated personnel." S. Lepper, "Legal Status of Military Personnel in United Nations Peace Operations." *Houston Journal of International Law* 18 (1996): 358. This broad interpretation was not shared by all delegates or subsequent commentators: Roberts and Guelff, *Documents on the Laws of War* (n. 1), p. 722.

[37] Lepper, "Legal Status of Military Personnel in United Nations Peace Operations" (n. 32), p. 358.

[38] Ibid; UN, *Report of the Ad Hoc Committee on the Elaboration of an International Convention Dealing with the Safety and Security of United Nations and Associated Personnel*, 1st Annex, Supp., UN Doc. A/49/22 (1994) para. 12.

1992, the United States feared the possibility that a US soldier captured in an operation similar to those undertaken by the UN Task Force in Somalia, "might someday be considered to fall within the scope of common Article 3 and be subject to its minimal protection."[39] Therefore it insisted that the provisions of the *Convention on the Safety of United Nations and Associated Personnel* "supersede common Article 3," notwithstanding the violation of "the cardinal principle of the laws of war that combatant forces are treated equally."[40]

The literature of the late 1990s and early 2000s suggests that at that time, the ICRC, and a number of other commentators, believed that if peacekeepers' use of force reached a level of violence commensurate with participation in armed conflict the laws of *international* armed conflict would become applicable to them. This would be so even if the conflict in which they were operating had been, prior to their intervention, a purely internal one. It was argued that it "would be a denial of the clear international dimension of such missions if humanitarian law were to be restricted to common article 3 or to Protocol II to the Geneva Conventions."[41] However the ICRC's current view, and that of the majority of academic and political commentators, is that formally the law of international armed conflict applies only to conflicts between the armed forces of States.[42] Hence in most peacekeeping missions today, if IHL is considered applicable at all, it is likely to be the law of noninternational armed conflict.[43]

During the negotiations for the 2005 Optional Protocol supplementing *Convention on the Safety of United Nations and Associated Personnel*, the delegate from Costa Rica proposed a new formula such that the Convention would not apply "to any United Nations operation in which any personnel are engaged as combatants against organized armed forces and to which the international law of armed conflict applies."[44] It was not adopted. Thus it remains the case that implementing the *Convention on the Safety of United Nations and Associated Personnel*

[39] Lepper, "Legal Status of Military Personnel in United Nations Peace Operations" (n. 32), p. 358.

[40] Roberts and Guelff, *Documents on the Laws of War* (n. 1), p. 625.

[41] Murphy, "United Nations Military Operations and International Humanitarian Law: What Rules Apply to Peacekeepers?", citing a statement by the ICRC at the 47th Session of the General Assembly on 13 November 2002.

[42] J. Pejić, "Status of Armed Conflicts," in *Perspectives on the ICRC Study on International Humanitarian Law*, ed. E. Wilmhurst and S. Breau (Cambridge: Cambridge University Press, 2007), p. 90.

[43] Ibid.

[44] Sixth Committee, Report of the Working Group on the Scope of Legal Protection under the Convention on the Safety of United Nations and Associated Personnel, Annex 1 UN Doc/A/C.6/58/l.16 2003, cited in Engdahl, "The Status of Peace Operations Personnel under International Humanitarian Law" (n. 11), p. 129.

may require criminalization of attacks against peacekeepers even in cases where they are engaged as combatants in a noninternational armed conflict.

By contrast, when drafting the *Secretary-General's Bulletin* (a long and controversial process) the ICRC and the UN's legal department were keen to maintain intact the principle that combatant forces are treated equally whatever the nature of the conflict. They were also keen to ensure respect for the *Convention on the Safety of United Nations and Associated Personnel*. As a consequence paragraph 1.2 of the *Secretary-General's Bulletin* has ended up somewhat incoherent. It states:

> The promulgation of this bulletin does not affect the protected status of members of peacekeeping operations under the 1994 Convention on the Safety of United Nations and Associated Personnel or their status as non-combatants, as long as they are entitled to the protection given to civilians under the international law of armed conflict.[45]

How is this paragraph to be interpreted? The *Secretary-General's Bulletin* is an internal document that is binding on UN troops, but it does not in itself create direct legal obligations for States.[46] It cannot alter the terms of a treaty or the obligations of parties to that treaty. As noted previously, "law of international armed conflict" referred to in the *Convention on the Safety of United Nations and Associated Personnel* is a subset of "the international law of armed conflict" referred to in the *Secretary-General's Bulletin*. Thus members of peacekeeping missions engaged as combatants in situations of noninternational armed conflict may not be entitled to the protection given to civilians under the international law of armed conflict (because they are engaged as combatants in an armed conflict) but may have protected status under the terms of the *Convention on the Safety of United Nations and Associated Personnel* (because the protections of that convention are only lost when they are engaged as combatants in an international armed conflict and the terms of a convention cannot be altered by a UN internal document).[47] Under the terms of the *Secretary-General's Bulletin* the law of armed conflict will nevertheless be applicable to peacekeepers for as

[45] United Nations, *Secretary-General's Bulletin on Observance by United Nations Forces of Humanitarian Law* (n. 6), [1.2].

[46] Direct obligations for peacekeepers under IHL arise as a consequence of their participation as combatants, and hence parties to the conflict. Report of Experts Meeting on Multi-National Operations, 11–12 December 2003 (ICRC Geneva), p. 2, http://www.icrc.org/eng/assets/files/other/irrc_853_fd_application.pdf.

[47] A State that is party to the *Convention on the Safety of United Nations and Associated Personnel* may be obliged to "take the appropriate measures under its national law to ensure" that anyone present in its territory that has attacked UN forces in the context of a noninternational armed conflict, is prosecuted or extradited, regardless of whether or not the UN forces in question were actively

long as they are "actively engaged as combatants," whatever the nature of the conflict.[48] Since until recently the UN never acknowledged that its forces had reached the threshold where they became actively engaged as combatants in any kind of armed conflict, the problem of inconsistency between the *Convention on the Safety of United Nations and Associated Personnel* and the *Secretary-General's Bulletin* remained a predominantly theoretical one.

The Implications of the United Nations' Intervention Brigade

On 28 March 2013, the Security Council authorized an Intervention Brigade operating under the direct command of MONUSCO's force commander and mandated "to carry out targeted offensive operations . . . either unilaterally or jointly with the FARDC [Congolese armed forces], in a robust, highly mobile and versatile manner" to neutralize armed groups in the Democratic Republic of the Congo (DRC).[49] This is the first time the UN has explicitly authorized offensive operations by missions serving under UN command and control. The mandating resolution states that the Intervention Brigade is established "on an exceptional basis and without creating a precedent."[50] However, successful innovations tend to be repeated and the establishment of the Brigade, which is equipped with attack helicopters, long-range artillery, armored personnel carriers, special forces, snipers, and drones, "has been hailed largely as a success"[51] because of the effectiveness of its military operations against armed groups. The permanent representative of France to the UN at the time of MONUSCO's mandate's renewal in 2014 stated, "now we have tested our idea, the Intervention Brigade, and it works. So we hope it could be a model when necessary for the future."[52]

Resolution 2098, which was been renewed with minor revisions annually since 2013, states that when carrying out offensive operations the Intervention Brigade must act "in strict compliance with international law, including international

engaged as combatants at the time they were attacked. United Nations, *Secretary-General's Bulletin on Observance by United Nations Forces of Humanitarian Law* (n. 6), [13].

[48] United Nations, *Secretary-General's Bulletin on Observance by United Nations Forces of Humanitarian Law* (n. 6), [1].

[49] S/RES 2098 (2013), 28 March 2013, para 12 (b).

[50] Ibid., para 9.

[51] S. Sheeran and S. Case, *The Intervention Brigade: Legal Issues for the UN in the Democratic Republic of the Congo* (New York: International Peace Institute, November 2014), p. 2.

[52] Permanent Mission of France to the UN, "DRC/CAR/Ukraine: Remarks to the Press by Mr. Gérard Araud, Permanent Representative of France to the United Nations," 28 March 2014, cited in Sheeran and Case, "The Intervention Brigade," (n. 52), p. 4.

humanitarian law."[53] It also states that the creation of the Brigade is without "any prejudice to the agreed principles of peacekeeping,"[54] notwithstanding that the core principles of peacekeeping are difficult to reconcile with offensive operations in support of one party against another.

The Intervention Brigade serves alongside the remainder of MONUSCO's forces under the same force commander. MONUSCO is a peacekeeping stabilization mission that took over from an earlier UN peacekeeping operation—the United Nations Organization Mission in Democratic Republic of the Congo (MONUC)—on 1 July 2010. Only the Intervention Brigade has the authority to carry out offensive operations, but the remainder of the force is mandated to use "all necessary measures" to carry out certain of their Chapter VII mandated tasks, which include protecting civilians within the vicinity of their operations and working in cooperation with the Intervention Brigade to "prevent the expansion of all armed groups, neutralize these groups, and disarm them in order to contribute to the objective of reducing the threat posed by armed groups to state authority and civilian security in eastern DRC and to make space for stabilization activities."[55]

Are peacekeepers serving in the Intervention Brigade considered to be "actively engaged as combatants" only while they are carrying out targeted offensive operations? Do they return to civilian status in-between operations in line with the *Secretary-General's Bulletin*, or is the Brigade a party to the conflict the whole time, since it is mandated to carry out offensive operations at any time? Does the whole of MONUSCO become a party to the conflict with the Intervention Brigade, since all are under the one command, or do the troops that are not part of the Intervention Brigade retain civilian protected status throughout?

The UN ROE for the mission are not publicly available, but there are unconfirmed reports that there is only one set of ROE for the entire UN mission,[56] which would lend support to the view that when the Intervention Brigade is a party to the armed conflict, so is the entire mission. In May 2013 the under-secretary-general for legal affairs, Ms. Patricia O'Brien, made comments that suggest that if the Intervention Brigade becomes a party to the conflict so does the entire mission:

> By virtue of the tasks foreseen for the Intervention Brigade, it would appear that MONUSCO may end up becoming a party to armed hostilities in the DRC, thus triggering the application of international

[53] S/RES 2098, 28 March 2013, para 9.
[54] Ibid., para 9.
[55] Ibid., para 12.
[56] Sheeran and Case, "The Intervention Brigade," (n. 52), p. 11.

> humanitarian law. This would mean that MONUSCO would be required to conduct its operations in compliance with IHL—which may lead to significant practical challenges, particularly if MONUSCO is required to detain large numbers of fighters in its efforts to "neutralize" and "disarm armed groups." In addition, MONUSCO itself would also become subject to the application of IHL.[57]

Ms. O'Brien goes on to state that, while "the law remains somewhat unclear in this area," the fact that MONUSCO is subject to the application of IHL "may mean that military members of MONUSCO, and any persons taking a direct part in hostilities, may lose their protected status under the Convention on the Safety of United Nations and Associated Personnel."[58] However, the conflict in the DRC is noninternational. The protections of the Convention on the Safety of United Nations and Associated Personnel continue to apply when UN peacekeepers are engaged in noninternational armed conflicts. Moreover the Protocol amending the MONUC-Status of Mission Agreement explicitly requires the protection regime of the Convention on the Safety of United Nations and Associated Personnel to be applied in respect of MONUSCO.[59]

If the Convention on the Safety of United Nations and Associated Personnel is applicable, attacks against MONUSCO personnel, including the Intervention Brigade even when it is actively engaged in offensive operations, are prohibited under Article 7(1) and would be considered a crime under Article 9. Arguably therefore the establishment of the Intervention Brigade has undermined "the cardinal principle of the laws of war that combatant forces are treated equally"[60] in ways that neither the UN nor ICRC would have considered acceptable in 1999 when the *Secretary-General's Bulletin* was promulgated. This change follows a trend toward increasingly robust peacekeeping missions in the intervening period. However during the same period peacekeeping missions have also become increasingly complex and are generally mandated to carry out a wide range of tasks that have little to do with armed conflict, generally related to strengthening the authority and security of the host state government. Missions may remain in the country long after a conflict is ended, and occasionally they have been deployed to help stabilize countries where was no armed conflict (as defined in IHL) in the first place.

[57] Patricia O'Brien, statement by the under-secretary-general for legal affairs and UN legal counsel delivered to the International Law Commission, Geneva, 23 May 2013, http://legal.un.org/ilc/sessions/65/Statement%20byTheLegal%20Counsel.pdf.

[58] Ibid.

[59] L. Müller, "The Force Intervention Brigade—United Nations Forces beyond the Fine Line between Peacekeeping and Peace Enforcement," *Journal of Conflict and Security Law* 20, no. 3 (2015): 359–380, at p. 374.

[60] Roberts and Guelff, *Documents on the Laws of War* (n. 1), p. 625.

Missions Deployed to Situations Where There Is No Armed Conflict

Peacekeepers must always use minimum force where possible, but ROE for Chapter VII missions routinely allow for use of force beyond self-defense to achieve certain mandated objectives. The *Secretary-General's Bulletin* states that the applicability of IHL to a UN-mandated operation depends on whether mission personnel are engaged as combatants in "a situation of armed conflict . . . to which the international laws of armed conflict apply." The Security Council's determination that there is a threat to international peace and security that requires the deployment of military forces mandated under Chapter VII does not in itself render the situation in the country one of armed conflict. International humanitarian law does not apply to civil disturbances or criminal violence in peacetime even when lawlessness is especially severe and widespread; nor do they apply in a fragile postconflict peace unless there is a resurgence of the armed conflict. In situations where there is no armed conflict the governing legal framework governing use of force is generally based on law enforcement norms. It cannot be based on IHL because IHL creates rights and obligations for parties to an armed conflict. Law enforcement norms prohibit lethal use of force except in self-defense, which includes defense of others.[61]

Under the approach taken by the UN's Office of Legal Affairs, a person that would not be a legitimate target under IHL or IHRL may become an authorized military target of a UN military operation (and therefore killed) provided that the peacekeepers' use of force is pursuant to an authorization in the mission's mandate; is provided for in the mission's ROE; is proportionate to its aim; and that minimum force is used and only as a last resort.[62] Therefore ROE routinely state that peacekeepers must comply with "the international legal principles of proportionality, the minimum use of force, and the requirement to minimise the potential for collateral damage." However there is no one concept of the principle of proportionality, or of collateral damage, that applies in all the different

[61] Article 9 of the Basic Principles on the Use of Force and Firearms by Law Enforcement Officials, Adopted by the Eighth United Nations Congress on the Prevention of Crime and the Treatment of Offenders, Havana, Cuba, 27 August to 7 September 1990, states, "Law enforcement officials shall not use firearms against persons except in self-defence or defence of others against the imminent threat of death or serious injury, to prevent the perpetration of a particularly serious crime involving grave threat to life, to arrest a person presenting such a danger and resisting their authority, or to prevent his or her escape, and only when less extreme means are insufficient to achieve these objectives. In any event, intentional lethal use of firearms may only be made when strictly unavoidable in order to protect life."

[62] Interviews with two senior advisors from the Office of the Legal Counsel, UNHQ, United Nations, New York, 16 and 17 June 2016 and open meeting with members of the Office of the Legal Counsel UNHQ and some UN Mission Legal Advisors, 24 June 2016.

types of situations to which a Chapter VII mandated peacekeeping operation may be deployed. There is no such thing as "the international legal principle of proportionality": there are several international legal principles of proportionality derived from different regimes of law. The IHL principle of proportionality is very different from the IHRL principle of proportionality. "Collateral damage" is a concept primarily associated with IHL that requires a weighing up of the military advantage gained from a particular course of action as against excessive civilian deaths and injuries that may result. To the extent that the concept of collateral damage exists at all outside of armed conflict it is narrower and military advantage is not part of the calculation at all.

In line with the UN's long-standing practice of requiring UN forces to respect the spirit and rules of IHL whether or not they are parties to a conflict,[63] the *Secretary-General's Bulletin* requires that all SOFAs between the UN and host states must include an undertaking that the United Nations shall:

> ensure that the force shall conduct its operations with full respect for the general conventions applicable to the conduct of military personnel . . . [and also] ensure that members of the military personnel of the force are fully acquainted with the principles and rules of those international instruments

Moreover the *Secretary-General's Bulletin* also states,

> the obligation to respect the said principles and rules is applicable to United Nations forces even in the absence of a status-of-forces agreement.[64]

Consequently under the UN Model Agreement between the United Nations and Member States Contributing Personnel and Equipment to United Nations

[63] The ICRC, in a statement to the General Assembly on 16 November 1995, observed, "the ICRC has always taken the view that all the provisions of international humanitarian law are applicable when United Nations contingents resort to the use of force, whereas the United Nations has held the view that it is bound only by the 'principles and spirit' of the humanitarian law treaties. These respective positions have been restated many times." United Nations, General Assembly 50th Session (1995), Fourth Committee, Agenda item 86, 16 November 1995, statement by the International Committee of the Red Cross; From 1993 SOFAs generally included an obligation to respect the "principles and spirit" of the laws of armed conflict but "spirit" has since been replaced by "rules." Szasz, "UN Forces and International Humanitarian Law," pp. 507, 516; Roberts and Guelff, *Documents on the Laws of War* (n. 1), p. 625.

[64] United Nations, *Secretary-General's Bulletin on Observance by United Nations forces of Humanitarian Law* (n. 6), sect. 3.

Peacekeeping Operations (1991), the United Nations undertakes to "observe and respect the principles and spirit of the general international conventions applicable to the conduct of military personnel."[65] The commitment is at best vague, particularly since "general conventions applicable to the conduct of military personnel" do not exist. The conventions that may be applicable to military personnel at any one time depend on the circumstances: not on the fact that they are military personnel. Clearly, the laws and conventions applicable to UN military personnel sitting in a bar in Belfast or Dublin or Stockholm (where perhaps they may be engaged in joint training exercises) are quite different from those applicable to the same personnel when deployed in mandated operations. Equally clearly, the laws and conventions applicable to UN military personnel deployed on missions in the Central African Republic, where there are several armed conflicts, are different from those applicable to military personnel in Haiti or Liberia, where there is no armed conflict.

Conclusion

Under pressure following criticism of the conduct of UN forces and an apparent gap in the legal frameworks governing peacekeeping missions the United Nations has clarified its position on the applicability of IHL to forces with the promulgation of the *Secretary-General's Bulletin* in 1999. However critical questions of interpretation remain unresolved. The creation of the Intervention Brigade within MONUSCO has complicated the legal situation further and appears to have created a situation in which it is a crime under an international treaty to attack UN forces that are parties to an armed conflict. The Intervention Brigade has been successful in reducing the power and influence of armed groups in the DRC and therefore the UN may be keen to create combat brigades within other UN peacekeeping missions to assist host state governments in stabilizing their states and suppressing the activities of armed groups operating within them.

The huge expansion in the size of UN missions since the end of the Cold War, and the much broader range of mission objectives and situations to which missions are deployed, requires that much more detailed attention be paid to the differences between missions, and the consequent differences in the applicable legal regimes, than is currently the case. The drafting of peacekeeping mandates tends to be done by the "penholder" States, usually those permanent members of the Security Council with economic, political, or strategic interests in the region, sometimes in conjunction with a group of "friend" States that also

[65] UN Doc A/46/185 of 23 May 1991 [28].

have interests in the region.[66] There is little discussion among Security Council members before adopting or renewing most peacekeeping mandates for fear that raising queries might upset the whole carefully balanced arrangement agreed between the permanent members, thus creating a veto risk (and political opprobrium for the State responsible for the upset).[67] What checks are there in place to ensure that ROE, which are normally classified, comply not only with the mandate (drafted by the penholder and other interested parties) but also with international law? Any "law creep" that extends armed conflict powers into nonarmed conflict situations may place peacekeepers in the unenviable position of being perceived by the local population as illegitimate enforcers of the will of the penholder State (and perhaps other parties), thus exacerbating tensions between the force and local communities, and in doing so increasing the scope for mutual misunderstanding, intolerance, and abuse. Therefore the legal differences between armed conflict and nonarmed conflict situations should be addressed at the inception of a mission, and should be regularly reviewed as situations evolve. The ROE and other mission specific rules and codes should be updated accordingly.

A key factor in the promulgation of the *Secretary-General's Bulletin* was concern that peacekeepers fell outside all regulatory regimes, and hence prosecution for crimes and abuses they committed is difficult. However it is possible for civilians to be prosecuted for war crimes.[68] The nexus for determining whether a crime committed in a situation of armed conflict is a war crime is broader in nature than the belligerent nexus that would render a civilian a participant in hostilities. The latter requires a direct causal link between a specific hostile act and the harm caused to a party to the conflict or civilians, and the acts must have been specifically designed to cause that harm.[69] The Appeals Chamber of the International Tribunal for the former Yugoslavia has stated that what "ultimately distinguishes a war crime from a purely domestic offence" is that "the existence of an armed conflict must, at a minimum, have played a substantial part in the perpetrator's ability to commit it, his decision to commit it, the manner in which it was committed or the purpose for which it was committed."[70] Peacekeepers' relationship with the local population, and their power over

[66] Security Council Report "In Hindsight Penholders" http://www.securitycouncilreport.org/monthly-forecast/2013-09/in_hindsight_penholders.php Visited July 28 2016.

[67] Ibid.

[68] Henckaerts and Doswald-Beck, *Customary International Humanitarian Law*, rule 156, p. 573; K. Dormann, *Elements of War Crimes under the Rome Statute of the International Criminal Court: Sources and Commentary* (Cambridge: Cambridge University Press, 2003), pp. 34–37, 391–393.

[69] Henckaerts and Doswald-Beck, *Customary International Humanitarian Law* (n. 17), pp. 57–58.

[70] ICTY, *Prosecutor v. Kunarac* et al., Case No. IT -96-23, Judgment of 12 June 2002 (Appeals Chamber), [58].

individuals within it, is not the result an incidental consequence of the chaos of war but of purposeful deployment by the Security Council in response to the conflict. Thus in most cases, the existence of the armed conflict would "have played a substantial part" in the peacekeeper's ability to commit the crime, his decision to commit it, and the manner in which it was committed, in a way that is different in nature to that of a civilian merely exploiting the breakdown of order. Such a relationship, even if it were to be grossly abused, would not necessarily render IHL "applicable" in the sense of rendering the force a party to the conflict subject to the full range of obligations and privileges of IHL; but it may well be enough to establish a sufficient nexus to the conflict to render violence and abuse of civilians a war crime. However not all abusive treatment of civilians would necessarily qualify as a war crime. Moreover in practice, it is unlikely that peacekeepers would be prosecuted for war crimes outside their home state, unless their conduct is so heinous as to attract the attention of the International Criminal Court.[71]

The development of a specific regime of international criminal accountability for peacekeepers, applicable regardless of whether or not there is an armed conflict, would enhance legitimacy and would be welcomed by host states; but there are considerable practical as well as political hurdles that would need to be overcome and there is little prospect of this happening. The current draft *Convention on the Criminal Accountability of United Nations Officials and Experts on Mission*, proposed in 2006, has limited support and in any case excludes military personnel.[72] However it is possible for improvements to be made without resort to international criminal law. It is more important to establish and maintain a culture of respect for general international law, including IHRL, and to inculcate that from the top. The UN's Human Rights Up Front initative, adopted in 2014, commits the UN to entrenching human rights norms into all aspects of its missions. Although it "is designed primarily for settings where the UN does not have a political or peacekeeping mission" the Secretary-General's 2014 Aide Memoire to the plan states, "its spirit can and should also be applied to 'mission settings'."[73] The High-Level Independent Panel on Peace Operations has recommended that the "entire

[71] M. O'Brien, "Prosecutorial Discretion as an Obstacle to Prosecution of Peacekeepers by the ICC: The Big Fish/Small Debate and the Gravity Threshold," *Journal of International Criminal Justice* 10, no. 3 (2012): 525.

[72] UN Doc A/60/980 (16 August 2006) Appendix III.

[73] "Rights Up Front," May 2014, http://www.un.org/sg/humanrightsupfront/. Although the initiative "is designed primarily for settings where the UN does not have a political or peacekeeping mission," the Secretary-General's 2014 Aide Memoire to the plan (on file with this author) states, "its spirit can and should also be applied to 'mission settings'."

United Nations system commits to the full implementation of the Human Rights Up Front initiative."[74]

It is extremely difficult to maintain appropriate Rule of Law standards if the host state population is not permitted to know what rules govern the UN forces that the Security Council has mandated to assist in providing stabilization and security to their State. It is no doubt hard enough for host state communities to put up with large UN bases taking up valuable land in the country, perhaps blocking access to the beach or the fields or the woods or other places people used to go; and put up with soldiers that dominate the roads in large militarized vehicles; earn more money than most of the rest of the population, and spend it in ways that imbalance the local economy and social life; probably do not speak your language or understand your culture; and are only ever present on time-limited tours of duty (though the mission itself may be there for years, since the UN has not yet developed a coherent approach to exit strategies). The very least people might expect to be entitled to know is what rules govern when those soldiers can shoot at you. The ROE should be made public so that local lawyers and NGOs can keep abreast of developments and push for revisions if circumstances change. Otherwise effective control is left with politicians of the penholder state working with host state representatives, and with local elites, some of whom may have vested interests that they hope to advance through exploitation of the presence of the UN mission. Careful attention should be paid to ensuring legitimacy and transparency through publication of ROE and SOFAs, which should be translated into the languages of the host state.

[74] Report of the High-level Independent Panel on Peace Operations on Uniting Our Strengths for Peace: Politics, Partnership and People, A/70/95–S/2015/446, 17 June 2015, paragraph 81(d) (iii).

13

How the Geneva Conventions Matter

MATTHEW EVANGELISTA

> Agreed limitations on warfare imply rational understandings with an enemy who, if he can be reasoned with, should not be an enemy.
>
> —Michael Howard, "Temperamenta Belli: *Can War Be Controlled?" (1979)*

> Some folks trust to reason, others trust to might
> Some folks look for answers, others look for fights
>
> —Robert Hunter, *"Playing in the Band" (1971)*

It is understandable to expect that socialization and internalization of the norms underpinning the Geneva Conventions should constitute the mechanisms by which states comply with their treaty obligations.[1] These are the means that the treaties themselves prescribe, as in this typical article from the Fourth Geneva Convention (1949) on protection of civilians:

> The High Contracting Parties undertake, in time of peace as in time of war, to disseminate the text of the present Convention as widely as possible in their respective countries, and, in particular, to include

[1] The skepticism expressed in the first epigraph is common. For further elaboration, see Michael Howard, "*Temperamenta Belli*: Can War be Controlled?," in *Restraints on War: Studies in the Limitation of Armed Conflict*, ed. Michael Howard (Oxford: Oxford University Press, 1979), p. 7. Nevertheless, among legal scholars especially, one finds more optimism about socialization and internalization of international legal rules. Among the main theoretical contributions to the literature are: Harold Hongju Koh, "Why Do Nations Obey International Law?" *Yale Law Journal* 106, no. 8 (1997); and Ryan Goodman and Derek Jinks, "How to Influence States: Socialization and International Human Rights Law," *Duke Law Journal* 54, no. 3 (December 2004). Responding to Goodman and Jinks are José E. Alvarez, "Do States Socialize?" and Harold Hongju Koh, "Internalization through Socialization," with a reply by Goodman and Jinks, "International Law and State Socialization: Conceptual, Empirical, and Normative Challenges," all in *Duke Law Journal* 54, no. 4 (February 2005).

> the study thereof in their programmes of military and, if possible, civil instruction, so that the principles thereof may become known to the entire population.[2]

The implication is that through dissemination and instruction, civilian and military populations become socialized into the norms regulating warfare and come to internalize those norms. Eric Posner has associated this approach with what he calls the "'legalist' camp [which] holds that states 'internalize' international law, comply with it as a matter of routine, and violate it only in extreme conditions, such as an emergency."[3] The approach is compatible with Louis Henkin's oft-cited generalization that "almost all nations observe almost all principles of international law and almost all of their obligations almost all of the time."[4] The counterargument comes from "the 'realist' camp [which holds] that states follow their interests come what may: international law plays no role in states' policy choices."[5]

Posner and others seek to reconcile the legalist observation that states frequently adhere to international law with the realist claim that international law in effect does not exist as a factor in policymaking. Posner, for example, posits, "states comply with international law when doing so enhances their security and wealth, but not otherwise."[6] Such a generalization is compatible with the observation that *reciprocity* plays a key role in states' observance of the laws of war. If, for example, both sides in a battle "give no quarter"—that is, refuse to take surrendering combatants alive as prisoners, but kill them instead—neither side's security will benefit. If combatants on both sides expect to die if they surrender, the intensity and ferocity of the fighting will be greater than if the combatants adhere to a convention on prisoners of war (POWs). Thus, although the prohibition against giving no quarter has been codified in the Hague Conventions of 1907,[7] both legalists and realists would agree that it would be in states' interests to abide by such a convention even if there were no specific legal obligation.[8]

[2] Article 144, Convention IV, relative to the Protection of Civilian Persons in Time of War, Geneva, 12 August 1949.

[3] Eric Posner, "International Law and the Disaggregated State," *Florida State University Law Review* 32 (2005): 798.

[4] Louis Henkin, *How Nations Behave: Law and Foreign Policy*, 2nd ed. (New York: Columbia University Press, 1979), p. 47.

[5] Posner, "International Law and the Disaggregated State," p. 798.

[6] Posner, "International Law and the Disaggregated State," p. 803.

[7] Article 23 of the *IV Convention—The Laws and Customs of War on Land.*

[8] James D. Morrow, "When Do States Follow the Laws of War?" *American Political Science Review* 101, no. 3 (2007); Geoffrey P. R. Wallace, *Life and Death in Captivity: The Abuse of Prisoners during War* (Ithaca, NY: Cornell University Press, 2015).

The design of this project was intended to pose a difficult test for compliance, regardless of whether one is inclined toward the legalist perspective, the realist perspective, or Posner's interest-based approach (which, many would argue, is effectively a realist—or better, a "rationalist"—position). If legalists claim that states routinely comply with law, except, as Posner puts it, "in extreme conditions, such as an emergency," then a state whose security is imperiled by war—the ultimate emergency—should not be expected to comply. That is, as the opposing camp would claim, it should not be expected to comply unless there were some mechanism at work—such as reciprocity—that made compliance serve the state's interest. Most of the cases in this book were chosen specifically for the *absence* of such mechanisms. States facing terrorist attacks against civilians, or guerrilla insurgents whose strength stems from hiding their combatant status except when engaging in violence, are unlikely to benefit from reciprocal compliance by their enemies. Our expectation, then, was that compliance would be far from automatic or routine in cases such as the French in Algeria, the Russians in Chechnya, or the United States battling insurgents in Vietnam, Iraq, or Afghanistan, or waging a "global war on terror." It would be something worth explaining.

Given that we have focused on the hard cases—and have highlighted violations of the laws of war—one could argue that the study suffers from a "selection bias."[9] Indeed, following Henkin, it is likely that more states comply with more laws of war more often than this study suggests. Yet the study has shed considerable light on the factors that influence noncompliance as well as compliance—valuable information for understanding how norms and laws function in this domain. In this concluding chapter, I review the evidence from our case studies to highlight major issues that have emerged. The section that follows reviews the types of wars our authors have discussed—in particular, counterinsurgencies and antiterrorist operations—and notes a paradox: The body of law governing such conflicts, even in the wake of the 1949 Geneva Conventions, is relatively sparse, yet the belligerents exhibited some sensitivity to basic norms for treating prisoners and civilians (even while violating the law). The third section disaggregates the issue of compliance and noncompliance at different levels—from the top political and military authorities to the individual soldier—and draws out some occasionally counterintuitive findings from the case studies. Compliance is not simply a matter of training officers and soldiers in the laws of war and making sure they obey. Disciplined troops can carry out illegal orders—or sometimes blow the whistle on their criminal leaders.

[9] Alexander Downes, comments on project at Brown meeting.

It is widely held that the second half of the 20th century—the era following the adoption of the 1949 Geneva Conventions—has seen a growing international respect for law, human rights, and restraint on war. The fourth section assesses the impact of the international system as a constraint on war crimes, but also—when major powers and international institutions adopt double standards—as an occasional enabler. The fifth section focuses on courts as a likely vehicle for internalization of legal norms. Our case studies, however, provide widely divergent assessments. Israel and the United States are typically considered to resemble each other in their democratic political systems and the fact that they are frequently at war. Yet the Israeli Supreme Court issues sophisticated rulings on matters of international humanitarian law (IHL) (including treaties that Israel has not even signed), while US civilian courts—with a couple of notable exceptions—routinely defer to the government when it comes to national security. Given that Israeli and US legal practices regarding warfare do not seem so different, the comparison suggests the counterintuitive conclusion that perhaps courts are not so central to socialization and internalization of the laws of war. The final section revisits some of the methodological challenges facing a study of compliance with IHL and summarizes the creative ways our authors have sought to overcome them.

Wars and Laws

Counterinsurgency wars, where a conventional army confronts irregular guerrilla forces, provide fertile ground for war crimes. Our volume includes several such cases—the French effort to defeat armed Algerians seeking to liberate their country from colonial rule; the Korean War, which pitted United Nations (mainly US) and South Korean armed forces against North Korean regulars, sympathetic South Korean guerrillas, and Chinese "volunteers"; the US war in Vietnam, which entailed fighting both North Vietnamese soldiers and guerrilla forces of the Vietcong in the South; and Russia's war to suppress an armed separatist movement in Chechnya. The US wars in Afghanistan and Iraq turned into counterinsurgency campaigns after resistance emerged in the wake of the initial defeat of the Taliban and Saddam Hussein's army, respectively. Many conflicts degenerated into terrorism, with the female *porteuses de bombes* in the Battle of Algiers and suicide bombers and roadside improvised explosive devices in Afghanistan, Chechnya, and Iraq; or featured terrorist assaults against civilians as a prime modus operandi, as with al-Qaeda's attacks of 11 September 2001 or violent Palestinian opposition to Israeli occupation. Counterinsurgent and counterterrorist forces for their part engaged in torture and abuse of prisoners and indiscriminate bombing of civilians. The conflicts that attended the breakup of Yugoslavia witnessed a mix of irregular and regular armed forces and shocking levels of terror and atrocity. Accusations of war crimes dogged the deployment of private security contractors working for the United States and even troops sent into conflict zones as peacekeepers. South Sudan—in 2011, the world's newest country—promptly acceded to the 1949 Geneva Conventions and the two Additional Protocols, and then plunged into civil war, with horrific levels of violence and atrocity against civilians.[10]

Gary Solis, in his chapter on the US war in Vietnam quotes General George S. Prugh on the extent to which the laws of war were drafted with very different conflicts than these in mind: "In the classic sense, the conventions presume a declared state of war between two or more sovereign states, each fielding a regular army fighting on a readily identifiable battlefront."[11] Few of the wars examined in this volume come close to fitting that model. The closest is probably the ten-year Iran-Iraq War, which nevertheless witnessed more than its share of atrocities and war crimes, including the use of chemical weapons by Saddam Hussein's Iraqi forces. Given the presence of potential mechanisms of reciprocity, rationalist accounts of the laws of war might indeed have expected more compliance. Anicée Van Engeland describes a report from the International Committee of the Red Cross (ICRC) that "claimed in 1987 that Iran had 49,285 Iraqi POWs in 15 camps while Iraq held 12,747 Iranian POWs in 10 camps." With such a structural symmetry, one wonders why reciprocity did not play more of role in fostering mutual restraint. The irony is the drafters of the Geneva Convention believed that by the mid-20th century reciprocity was no longer necessary to ensure compliance. The ICRC commentary Fourth Convention insists that the treaty was not "an engagement concluded on a basis of reciprocity, binding each party to the contract only in so far as the other party observes its obligations. It is rather a series of unilateral engagements solemnly contracted before the world as represented by the other Contracting Parties."[12] Yet even peacekeeping forces (the topic of Siobhán Wills's chapter), let alone insurgents or terrorists, are not contracting parties (even if their home states are) or formally parties to the conflict that they are trying to contain. Thus, in most of our cases, we should not expect the rationalist mechanism of reciprocity to operate.

When examining these cases through the lens of law and seeking explanations for compliance and noncompliance, the first thing one must acknowledge

[10] Human Rights Watch, "South Sudan: Killings, Rapes, Looting in Juba," 15 August 2016, https://www.hrw.org/news/2016/08/15/south-sudan-killings-rapes-looting-juba.

[11] George S. Prugh, *Law at War: Vietnam 1964–1973* (Washington, DC: Department of the Army, 1975), http://lawofwar.org/vietnam_pow_policy.htm.

[12] J. Pictet, ed., *The Geneva Conventions of 12 August 1949: Commentary IV Geneva Convention* (Geneva: ICRC, 1958), Art. 1.

is that for some of these conflicts there was little relevant law in place at all, and in others the belligerents denied the relevance of existing law. Giovanni Mantilla's chapter traces the history of efforts to bring what became known as armed conflicts of a noninternational character under the international regime of the Geneva Conventions—starting with Common Article 3 of the 1949 Conventions through the 1977 Protocols and beyond. Some of the cases covered in this book—the Korean War and the French war in Algeria, for example—broke out only shortly after the drafting of the 1949 Geneva Conventions, before either side had incorporated the rules into military law, let alone "internalized" them. As Raphaëlle Branche points out (and as Mantilla anticipated for many such cases), France denied the applicability of Geneva norms to the Algerian conflict, claiming it an internal affair, given Algeria's status as a French *département*, juridically equivalent to Brittany or Provence. By contrast, as Sahr Conway-Lanz describes, the United States sought to portray itself—sometimes unconvincingly—as compliant with Geneva norms during the Korean War, even though it would not ratify the treaty until 1955, well after the fighting had ended.

In both cases, nevertheless, the Geneva Conventions played a role. In the wake of scandals over torture and summary execution of Algerian prisoners, the French government committed itself to compliance with norms governing prisoners of war and allowed access to the ICRC. In April 1960 the provisional government formed by the Front de Libération Nationale (FLN) sought status as the legitimate representative of the Algerian people by claiming to endorse the Geneva Conventions. The FLN's ongoing terrorist activity belied any serious commitment to the laws of war. As Branche points out, the provisional government would not even make available to the ICRC lists of prisoners under its control. It was the defeat and retreat of the French forces that produced the Evian Accords and secured the FLN the legitimacy it desired. Branche concludes that the Algerian war hindered French acceptance of "any international framework regarding human rights." Even regarding the more narrowly defined laws of war, the experience of the Algerian war influenced France's resistance to ratifying the 1977 First Protocol to the Geneva Conventions because, as Mantilla describes, the document put anticolonial struggles in the same category as international armed conflict as far as the rights of combatants were concerned. France only ratified in 2001.

The experience of the Korean War shaped the way the United States adopted the Conventions into its military law and subsequent military practice. As Conway-Lanz explains, the 1956 US Army field manual on the laws of war embodied the legacy of the war and promoted the formal implementation of the Geneva Conventions. Reflecting the 1949 updating of the laws of war, the manual added a new chapter specifically devoted to the treatment of civilians. So, as with several of the cases covered here, US behavior during and after the Korean

War exhibits both violations of the norms and laws governing warfare, and a willingness to incorporate new rules into military practice. For that process to work, officers and troops must be trained to respect the rules and be disciplined if they fail to do so—the topic of the next section.

Training, Discipline, and Compliance in Hierarchical Systems

A state's general commitment to observing the laws of war is hardly sufficient to ensure compliance by its armed forces. Officers and troops must receive proper training and must be monitored to ensure that the training is reflected in their behavior. Given the hierarchical nature of military organizations, it makes sense to distinguish between levels of command at which compliance might vary. As Ben-Ari and Cohen suggest in their study of Israel, the top level consists of "policy decisions of the supreme command and the civilian masters of the military." Next are the "operational decisions of mid- to upper-level military commanders," followed by the "tactical decisions of specific soldiers or junior officers."

Even given a high-level commitment to comply, much depends on these lower levels. Soldiers' adherence to the laws of war (typically translated into rules of engagement for particular missions) is influenced by such factors as the orders of their immediate commanders and the culture of the specific unit within which they serve. Ben-Ari and Cohen refer to "rituals of rationality"—"a gamut of activities in and around safety and minimizing collateral damage that include briefings and debriefings, formulating and changing rules of engagement, creating 'review boards,' writing new training manuals, and elaborating new guidelines." Yet this type of training, while contributing to the objectives of IHL (especially regarding civilian protection), is not the same as specific education in the Geneva Conventions. Ben-Ari and Cohen make this point in their valuable discussion of DABLA, the Hebrew acronym for the International Law Division of the Military Advocate General (MAG) of the Israeli Defense Forces. Writing of midlevel officers, they claim, "a conscious decision was made not to provide these soldiers with instruction respecting the contents of the Geneva Conventions in the basic officer training." The practice instead is "to introduce IHL with its complex standards only to high level commanders." One consequence, "since DABLA representatives are not involved in the operational decisions of small units," is "that actions at such levels may contradict IHL or what DABLA representatives would have advised."

At the opposite extreme from the legalization of the 21st-century Israeli armed forces is the case of the French in Algeria in the middle of the previous century. There the French authorities denied any applicability of the Geneva

Conventions and treated torture—one of the most heinous of crimes—as "a weapon of war, violence employed by design, in order to win."[13] Torture was not a matter of "collateral damage, committed by some ill-disciplined soldiers," as Branche writes in her chapter. Rank-and-file torturers were trained and provided with equipment to carry out their crimes. Even in such a situation, the distinction between levels of command authority is still useful. As Branche points out, to the extent that civilians received decent treatment at all in Algeria (not from the trained torturers, obviously) it depended not on the laws of war but on the decisions of low-level officers and the instructions they gave their troops.[14]

The US conflict in Vietnam represented varying degrees of compliance at different levels. As Solis points out, some of the high-level decisions were of dubious legality. Establishing free-fire zones, where anyone remaining would be designated a combatant, illegally relieved the US authorities of the obligation to follow the principle of distinction and take care not to harm civilians who were not engaged in hostilities. Creating "strategic hamlets" violated the rules against mass population transfers.

At lower levels, the troops in Vietnam did receive training in their legal obligations, as Prugh's study reports and Solis's chapter summarizes. Yet in recounting the atrocities associated with My Lai, Solis poses the question, "Of what effect, then, were the training, the orders, and directives?" He summarizes the evaluation of General William Peers, who investigated the massacre, that "part of the problem was rooted in the lackadaisical manner in which the training was handled." In Solis's judgment, "My Lai also represents a failure of battlefield and higher command leadership," as well as "prosecutions of questionable effectiveness." Some of these shortcomings were remedied in the wake of the Vietnam War, when the Department of Defense instituted a program of training and education to prevent violations of the laws of war. Directive 5100.77, originally issued in November 1974, stated that all members of the Armed Forces must "comply with the law of war during all armed conflicts, however such conflicts are characterized, and with the principles and spirit of the law of war during all other operations." The directive, reissued in 1979 and 1998, was superseded in 2006 by Directive 2301.01E, with much of same language intact.[15] The program increased the role of the judge advocates general (JAGs) in advising and promoting compliance with the Geneva Conventions.

In describing instances when "high level military and civilian political leadership give orders that violate" the laws of war, Ben-Ari and Cohen suggest,

[13] Raphaëlle Branche, *La torture et l'armée pendant la guerre d'Algérie, 1954–1962* (Paris: Gallimard, 2001), p. 14.

[14] Branche, *La torture et l'armée*, p. 243, and her chapter in this volume.

[15] Available at http://www.usslibertyveterans.org/files/231101p.pdf.

"Compliance or noncompliance at this level is not an issue of knowledge, but of politics." This observation would appear relevant to several of the topics covered by our authors, from torture in Algeria to free-fire zones in Vietnam. It also applies to later US cases, such as the torture of terrorist suspects and other detainees, as approved by President George W. Bush and his top advisors. Incidents such as the abuses at the Abu Ghraib prison in Iraq were initially dismissed as a "kind of Animal House on the night shift" (a reference to the 1978 film about the drunken antics of members of a college fraternity). This interpretation is as unconvincing as the claim that "ill-disciplined soldiers" were responsible for torture during the French war in Algeria. It is clear that the decision to violate US domestic and international legal commitments, including the Geneva Conventions, was taken at the highest level. Then Attorney General John Ashcroft, reacting to detailed discussion of torture techniques with the president and his advisors reportedly asked, "Why are we talking about this in the White House?"[16] The answer is that the White House—and the equivalent location for other countries—is where high-level political decisions that contravene the fundamental practices and training of lower-level officials must take place. It was the leaks of photos and documents by whistleblowers that exposed the illegality—suggesting that at lower levels, at least, norms against such vile practices had indeed been internalized by those who blew the whistles.

A more recent example of high-level politics at work would be the Obama administration's decision to create something that resembles free-fire zones in its use of drone attacks. As the *New York Times* reported, the White House avoided difficult (but legally required) questions of distinguishing between civilian and military targets by counting "all military-age males in a strike zone as combatants . . . unless there is explicit intelligence posthumously proving them innocent." As the article makes clear, aside from the obvious motivation to keep Americans secure from terrorist attacks, the president's policies—and the leak to the *Times* that helped reveal them—clearly had political motives as well: to forestall criticism from Republican opponents by adopting a suitably hawkish position.[17] Unlike during the Bush administration, the leaks evidently came from supporters rather than opponents of the practices. The Obama administration

[16] ABC News, "Bush Aware of Advisers' Interrogation Talks," 11 April 2008, http://abclocal.go.com/kfsn/story?section=news/national_world&id=6076727. For a thorough discussion of the political and legal dimensions of the Bush policies, see Thomas Michael McDonnell, *The United States, International Law, and the Struggle against Terrorism* (New York: Routledge, 2011), esp. chs. 3–5.

[17] Jo Becker and Scott Shane, "Secret 'Kill List' Proves a Test of Obama's Principles and Will," *New York Times*, 29 May 2012. For a review of the Obama administration's counterterror policies, see Matthew Evangelista, "A 'War on Terror' by Any Other Name. . . . What Did Obama Change?" Publication 2012-02, Mario Einaudi Center for International Studies, Cornell University, February 2013, http://einaudi.cornell.edu/node/11529.

later denied that it pursued such an open-ended targeting policy, but the documents it issued in support of its contention failed to convince skeptics.[18]

Limits to the effectiveness of training in the laws of war depend on the degree of seriousness with which the lessons are imparted and received. Soldiers will not take the lessons seriously if their instructors signal a low priority or appear hypocritical. Craig Nation's interviews with veterans of the Yugoslav People's Army (JNA) revealed this pattern clearly: "When asked to describe some of the principles imparted in the instruction, former soldiers and officers often respond in a confused ('What is he asking?') or dismissive ('Oh yes, we had to learn all of that') manner." The Yugoslav case offered further impediments to internalizing the laws of war:

> Conversations with JNA veterans reveal a tendency to conflate training in the law of war with indoctrination in Yugoslav communist ideology. Yugoslav citizens and soldiers were taught that they enjoyed a superior form of political and social order and served a state that could not, by definition, wage aggressive war with illicit means. . . . As was the case elsewhere in the communist world, the contradictions inherent in Yugoslavia's official ideology encouraged cynicism.

As the country broke up, and armed militia units and gangs replaced the regular forces, training in communist ideology and the laws of war was supplanted by a very different kind of indoctrination—"often imbued with an aggressive cult of violence for its own sake, intolerant nationalist extremism, sadism, and racial prejudice." As the Serbian nationalist leadership fanned the flames of war in the former Yugoslav republics of Croatia and Bosnia-Herzegovina, they depended not only on undisciplined gangs but also on better-trained troops—from the Special Forces and Interior Ministry. Their training, in effect, consisted in how to contravene the laws of war, by engaging in atrocities intended to destroy diverse, mixed communities in favor of the nationalists' preferred vision of ethnic purity. Soldiers whose individual moral scruples might have inhibited their participation in such crimes faced an additional obstacle associated with their training. As Nation explains, "soldiers operate within hierarchical command structures that make obedience the most fundamental of obligations. They are subject to the normal human tendency to defer to authority figures even when required

[18] Charlie Savage and Scott Shane, "US Reveals Death Toll from Airstrikes outside War Zones," *New York Times*, 1 July 2016. The relevant document, "Summary of Information Regarding US Counterterrorism Strikes outside Areas of Active Hostilities," is available at http://www.nytimes.com/interactive/2016/07/01/world/document-airstrike-death-toll-executive-order.html. For an earlier assessment based on leaked documents, see Spencer Ackerman, "41 Men Targeted but 1,147 People Killed: US Drone Strikes—The Facts on the Ground," *The Guardian*, 24 November 2014.

to engage in actions that offend the conscience. To a significant extent then, the breakdown of respect for Geneva rules during the Yugoslav wars can be attributed to failures of leadership."

Thus, whereas training is essential for adherence to the laws of war, it is a double-edged sword. Given the importance of discipline to military success, soldiers internalize the requirement to obey orders at least as well as they internalize normative restraints on warfare. As Elisabeth Wood found in her path-breaking work on sexual violence during war, undisciplined troops commit rapes, but so do well-trained troops ordered deliberately to destroy communities and carry out "ethnic cleansing" by sexual violence.[19] Branche's observation on French military training for much of the postwar period clearly applies more broadly: "Very little if any attention was devoted to circumstances within which soldiers would be obliged to listen to the dictates of personal conscience and contemplate the need to question or disobey orders to carry out illegal or unethical actions." Branche points out that "the French army was a conscript army" where military service was "compulsory and every French man had to enlist." The military leadership gave a higher priority to discipline than to individual choice in morally difficult situations. The professional army that was developed in France after 1996, Branche argues, took a different approach. She cites a 1999 document, "Foundations and Principles," to the effect that "ethics are not a question of disciplinary rules but rather a question of individual fulfillment."

Paradoxically, the pursuit of "individual fulfillment" can also contribute, indirectly, to war crimes. As in the French case, the Yugoslav People's Army was a conscript army—yet not everyone served. During the violent breakup of the country, tens of thousands of young men evaded the draft and many fled the country rather than fight.[20] Nation reports that some 300,000 young people left Yugoslavia between 1991 and 1999. As he points out, one possible factor in the high level of atrocities committed by the army during the wars of that era is that people of conscience, who might have resisted the descent into barbarity, rejected the violence altogether and left.

As Renée de Nevers describes in her chapter, private military and security corporations pose unusual problems for training and discipline in the service of compliance with the laws of war. She quotes the US Joint Forces Command manual on "armed private security contractors" to the effect that "the principle vehicle for the commander to exercise control" over the private troops is not a command structure but "the contract." Granted, as de Nevers points out, many

[19] Elisabeth Wood, "Variation in Sexual Violence during War," *Politics and Society* 34, no. 3 (September 2006).

[20] UN High Commissioner for Refugees, *Situation of Draft Evaders/Deserters from Former Yugoslavia*, 6 February 1995.

private security employees are former soldiers from Western militaries who should have received training in IHL during their military service. "It is less clear, however, whether 'third country nationals' hired from places such as Chile, Fiji, and Uganda have similar training." Moreover, "companies are hiring contractors with police and other domestic law enforcement backgrounds" who may never have encountered the laws of war.

Nevertheless, it would be incorrect to claim that private military contractors fall outside the law. As de Nevers explains, "legal frameworks cover their behavior at several levels." The high-profile cases of "Iraq and Afghanistan are anomalies in this regard." The US-led Coalition Provisional Authority deliberately sought immunity for the contractors under Iraqi law. Normally a Status of Forces Agreement between the United States and a host government determines under whose jurisdiction violations of the law should be handled. Since 2000, the US government could also prosecute civilian employees of the Department of Defense for crimes under the Military Extraterritorial Jurisdiction Act (MEJA). To supplement reliance on the MEJA, the US Congress revised the Uniform Code of Military Justice in late 2006 "to bring all contractors accompanying the armed forces under its purview."

Thus, as with regular armed forces, the extent to which private contractors abide by their legal obligations depends not only on training and discipline but also on high-level political decisions. The same is true, as Wills describes, for peacekeepers. Yet, in this case, the high-level decisions are not only taken by states but also shaped by international organizations, such as the United Nations. Given that peacekeeping missions emerged following the drafting of the UN Charter, and were not covered by the Geneva Conventions, the status, obligations, and rights of the soldiers participating in such missions have received little attention until recently. Regarding their own behavior—with examples of torture and murder by peacekeepers of civilians in Somalia and widespread sexual exploitation of the local population by peacekeepers throughout the world—it hardly represents the soldiers' internalization of the Geneva norms.

As the studies in this volume have indicated, it is not always easy to identify evidence of internalization of the laws of war. One means of detecting it is to examine the contrast between what soldiers at the middle and lower levels of the command hierarchy automatically consider the right thing to do and what their superiors order them to do. Perhaps one of the best examples of internalization of the Geneva Conventions is the US armed forces' approach to treatment of people captured on the battlefield whose status—soldier or civilian—is unclear. The Third Geneva Convention of 1949 provides rules for handling captives who may not enjoy the full rights of POWs. As Article 5 indicates, in case of doubt about their status, "such persons shall enjoy the protection of the present Convention until such time as their status has been determined by a competent tribunal." Along with most provisions of IHL, these ones have been incorporated into US military law and practice. US military regulations defined a competent tribunal as a panel of three US commissioned officers familiar with the circumstances under which the person was taken prisoner. The use of such tribunals, and their provenance in the Geneva Conventions, had become so familiar to US military officers that they referred to them as "Article 5 tribunals." The 2002 edition of the US Army's Operational Law Handbook spells out the obligation in a paraphrase of the Convention (referring to "prisoner of war" as PW): "When doubt exists as to whether captured enemy personnel warrant continued PW status, Art. 5 Tribunals must be convened."[21] US armed forces made extensive use of Article 5 tribunals during the 1991 Gulf War, conducting 1,196 of them during Operation Desert Storm. The process resulted in 310 individuals receiving POW status. The others were determined to be civilians.[22]

Arguably having internalized the norm, the Pentagon was well prepared to carry out Article 5 Tribunals when the US-led coalition defeated the Taliban and disrupted the al-Qaeda network in Afghanistan in 2002. It took a high-level decision to undermine the standard operating procedures. As Elizabeth Grimm Arsenault describes in her chapter, the initial orders from Central Command to U.S. forces in Afghanistan in October 2001 specified the use of Article 5 Tribunals, as per standard practice. These orders were countermanded at the very top of the US political system, when, as she delicately puts it, "policymakers in Washington assessed that defeating al-Qaeda required new ways of thinking." Starting in January 2002, US authorities transported over five hundred prisoners to the Guantánamo base, never revealing the exact numbers or providing their names. The first public US commentary on the status accorded to the detainees came from then Secretary of Defense Donald Rumsfeld on 11 January. He declared that the detainees "do not have any rights under the Geneva Convention." Bypassing the Article 5 requirements, the Bush administration declared its detainees illegal "enemy combatants" and "international terrorists," not soldiers.[23] The legal basis for the policy was the Military Order

[21] US Army, Operational Law Handbook (2002), quoted in Adam Roberts, "The Laws of War in the War on Terror," in *International Law and the War on Terror*, ed. Fred L. Borch and Paul S. Wilson (Newport, RI: US Naval War College, 2003). My discussion owes much to Roberts's reconstruction and interpretation of the US developments.

[22] US Department of Defense, *Conduct of the Persian Gulf War: Final Report to Congress*, April 1992, p. 663. The report was prepared under the auspices of then-Undersecretary of Defense for Policy Paul Wolfowitz, and directed by his deputy, I. Lewis Libby. The report is available at http://www.ndu.edu/library/epubs/cpgw.pdf.

[23] The discussion here draws on the analysis and some of the language in Matthew Evangelista, *Law, Ethics, and the War on Terror* (Cambridge, UK: Polity, 2008), pp. 62–64.

regarding the Detention, Treatment, and Trial of Certain Non-Citizens in the War against Terrorism, issued under the president's name on 13 November 2001. Although premised on the claim that al-Qaeda had carried out attacks against the United States "on a scale that has created a state of armed conflict that requires the use of the United States Armed Forces," the military order made no reference to the Geneva Conventions or any aspect of the law of armed conflict.[24]

It was not always thus. As Gary Solis points out, US troops dealing with insurgents during the Vietnam War were highly attentive to the issue of status and treatment of prisoners. Solis notes that in the years following the war, a principle US argument against ratification of Additional Protocol I (1977) to the Geneva Conventions related to its Article 44.

> That provision requires ratifying states to give captured enemy fighters who do not meet all four of the traditional requirements for POW status to nevertheless provide captured enemy fighters "protections equivalent in all respects to those accorded to prisoners of war." Some ask, "But is that not what you did in the Vietnam war—treat captured North Vietnamese guerrillas as POWs?" Yes, we did.

The United States also treated South Vietnamese guerrillas, members of the Vietcong, as prisoners of war—a practice that earned US authorities praise from the ICRC.[25]

One can understand such a decision in terms of rational self-interest on a number of grounds. It was bureaucratically more efficient to put all captives in one category rather than spend time making fine distinctions (aside from a basic distinction between combatant and noncombatant). It also took off some of the pressure of international public opinion, much of which was harshly critical of US involvement in Vietnam. But other elements of the practice are harder to explain on rational grounds.[26] Solis points out, for example, that there was no hope of reciprocity from North Vietnam, whose judgment about the war blurred the categories of *jus ad bellum* and *jus in bello*: North Vietnam refused to treat US soldiers as POWs because they were involved in a war of aggression and committing crimes against humanity. By its practice regarding captured

[24] http://www.law.cornell.edu/background/warpower/fr1665.pdf.

[25] Michel Veuthey, *Guérilla et droit humanitaire* (Geneva: Comité International de la Croix-Rouge, 1983), pp. 231–232.

[26] For a recent study drawing on new archival materials, see Brian Cuddy, "Wider War: American Force in Vietnam, International Law, and the Transformation of Armed Conflict, 1961–1977," PhD dissertation, Department of History, Cornell University, 2016.

US troops, the North Vietnamese government itself committed war crimes. As Solis explains:

> Even if captured Americans were not considered by the North to be POWs, their unlawful treatment was prohibited by the fourth Geneva Convention regarding civilians. That is because, in the law of war, there are but two classifications of individuals on the battlefield: combatants and civilians. If US captives were viewed as lawful combatants they merited POW status and treatment in accord with the third Convention; if not viewed as combatants they were necessarily civilians protected by the fourth Convention, as well as common Article 3, which requires humane treatment of all who are *hors de combat*.

This is the same legal regime that governed US policy in the wake of the 9/11 attacks and the invasion of Afghanistan—even without US endorsement of the greater protections afforded by the First Additional Protocol. To evade it, the Bush administration established an alternative system of military commissions to supplant both the Article 5 tribunals, which the US armed forces were prepared to implement to determine the status of their captives, and the regular system of courts-martial to try suspected war criminals. In this case, we can get a sense of the degree of internalization by considering what was necessary to undermine the expected behavior.

As we have seen, violations in IHL—and failure to punish them—can stem from poor or inadequate training at low and middle levels or from high-level decisions taken on political or strategic grounds. They can also result from more prosaic considerations related to material shortcomings. In Vietnam numerous limitations hindered the optimal operation of the military judicial system, as Solis points out—lack of interpreters, electricity, and transport. Arsenault attributes some lapses in efforts to protect civilians in Iraq and Afghanistan to technical limitations—such as "reliance on close air support and the inability to effectively deploy critical weapons systems that would limit civilian casualties." Perhaps if the Obama administration had been able reliably to distinguish between terrorists and innocent people who happen to be near them—it would have been less likely to declare any male in a drone's target area a terrorist.[27]

[27] Defining everyone killed by a drone as an enemy is not a convincing way to demonstrate compliance with international law. Yet this is essentially the approach taken by defenders of the drone strikes, such as Michael Hayden, the retired US Air Force general and former CIA director. He acknowledged rare mistakes in killing innocent people and admitted attacking locations where the presence of the intended target was only suspected, and so others were killed instead. "We made no excuses about killing lower-ranking terrorists," he wrote, because "in warfare it is

Finally, it should not be assumed that military exigencies always influence states toward noncompliance with legal obligations. As Arsenault points out, the shift in US policy in Afghanistan and Iraq toward "a population-centric counterinsurgency mission" pushed in the opposite direction: Noncompliance with the Geneva Conventions—to the extent that it caused harm to civilians—"equated to mission failure."

The International System: Constraining and Enabling

The cases examined here display a range of ways that the international system—including what some have characterized as an emerging global regime governing human rights—has influenced compliance with the laws of war. During the French war in Algeria, General Raoul Salan established special camps for captured members of the Algerian National Liberation Army. Instead of referring to the detainees as prisoners of war (POW) he acknowledged their combatant status by calling them *PAM*: they were ***pris** les **armes** à la **main**,* taken armed (with arms in hand).[28] As Branche describes, Salan "made it very clear: the inmates 'should not be considered prisoners of war. The Geneva conventions did not apply to them.'" Yet establishing the internment camps marked a step toward the international norm—especially if the alternative was summary execution.

As countries came to adhere more consistently to the Geneva Conventions their behavior came to influence not only an international audience of their peers but also an internal, domestic audience. As Conway-Lanz assesses the impact of the Geneva Conventions on the Korean War, he also considers the war's impact on the conventions—for the United States and the world: "The Geneva Conventions," he argues, "underwent a process of legitimatization for Americans and a broader international community during the Korean War that laid a foundation for the future expansion of humanitarian protections. In 1955, the United States chose to ratify the conventions that had gained a new visibility during the war."

Another aspect of the international system that some of our authors consider is the growing worldwide process of legalization. Ben-Ari and Cohen find "the increasing intrusion of judicial considerations into various sectors of societies, including the military" to have influenced Israeli compliance with the Geneva

regrettably necessary to kill foot soldiers, too." Michael Hayden, "To Keep America Safe, Embrace Drone Warfare," *New York Times,* 19 February 2016.

[28] Veuthy, *Guérilla et droit humanitaire,* p. 228.

Conventions, for example. They also point to the role of international institutions, nongovernmental organizations, and a global media. They cite the views of Désirée Verweij, who "suggests that part of the restraint on military action results from an internalization by the military of the 'gaze' of other—the media, social movements, and NGOs, for instance. It is for this reason, that there is now widespread talk about how the armed forces of the industrial democracies operate 'under the shadow' of judicial proceedings." This formulation bears considerable similarity to Harold Hongju Koh's concept of *transnational legal process*: "the theory and practice of how public and private actors—nation-states, international organizations, multinational enterprises, non-governmental organizations, and private individuals—interact in a variety of public and private, domestic and international fora to make, interpret, enforce, and ultimately, internalize rules of transnational law."[29]

Building on Verweij's suggestions, and consistent with Koh's approach, Ben-Ari and Cohen propose "more than a simple model of external influences on soldiers' morality and action." They describe a three-phased process whereby the " 'gaze' of (various) others is first internalized in the rhetoric" of the armed forces; second, the rhetoric comes to be "adopted into the organizational structures and practices" by which the military forces operate; and third, the rhetoric comes to reflect the "soldiers' and officers' self-image as military professionals and as human beings." This is an ideal model, one that cannot be expected to operate universally or consistently, but one that finds a solid basis in the research of psychologists and the popular aphorism that if you "talk the talk," you eventually come to "walk the walk."[30]

The case of Russia, and particularly its military actions in the secessionist republic of Chechnya and elsewhere in the North Caucasus region, poses a problem for this model, however, and in general for explanations that focus on the impact of international institutions. Although post-Soviet Russia is hardly the most open country in the world, the end of communist rule there brought a huge increase in engagement with the outside, and, in particular, an acceptance of a number of international obligations associated with human rights and war—along with integration into key institutions such as the Council of Europe. A small, but energetic and committed community of activists maintained pressure on the government and armed forces to adhere to its obligations in areas directly related to war and the human-rights abuses associated with it, such as torture, hostage-taking, "disappearances," collective punishment

[29] Harold Hongju Koh, "Transnational Legal Process" (1996), Faculty Scholarship Series, Paper 2096, http://digitalcommons.law.yale.edu/fss_papers/2096.

[30] For discussion of this point in relationship to compliance with international law, see Goodman and Jinks, "International Law and State Socialization," pp. 995–996.

(e.g., the Committee of Soldiers' Mothers, Demos, Memorial, Human Rights Watch). Yet Russia's military practices in Chechnya and its overall adherence to IHL appeared to show little effect from either international engagement or the efforts of human-rights activists at home.

The International Committee of the Red Cross represents a particularly strong example of the contrast between level of activity and impact. The ICRC stepped up its activities in Russia and the other former Soviet republics in the wake of the dissolution of the USSR in 1991. By 2008, it could boast of a number of achievements. As the article from the Fourth Geneva Convention I quoted at the outset showed, the ICRC has always aspired to disseminate its principles of respect for the laws of war more widely than just among military forces. It is striking, then, that Russia after the fall of the USSR was the only country in the world that had allowed the ICRC to establish a curriculum on "human values" for school children ages 11–17 (although Anicée Van Engeland describes something similar more recently in Iran). Those in the cohorts of 15–17 years old took a compulsory course in IHL and an exam on the topic. According to François Bellon, who served as the Moscow-based director of the ICRC for the former Soviet region (before heading the ICRC delegation to NATO and the European Union), the program reached 20 million children. The Russian government also allowed the ICRC to provide curricula for law schools, which require mandatory courses in humanitarian law, and for schools of journalism. Regarding the armed forces, starting in 1996 the Russian minister of defense had signed a "plan of action" with the ICRC on a yearly basis—something not done in other countries, and which, in the view of the ICRC director, reflected high-level interest. Yet, as Bellon admitted, the plans failed to match the reality in the field: "We lost that battle."[31]

Regarding Russia's war in Chechnya, the ICRC had informed the government of its obligations early on when a delegation met with officials of then-President Boris Yeltsin's administration at the end of December 1994. The delegation conveyed its assessment that the military action constituted an armed conflict "not of an international character," governed by Common Article 3 of the 1949 Geneva Conventions.[32] Although the ICRC continued to maintain

[31] Author's interview with François Bellon, ICRC headquarters, Moscow, 20 May 2008. For an example of the agreed program of activities: *Rossiiskaia Federatsiia: Kalendar' meropriiatii MKKK, Oktiabr'–dekabr' 2006* [Russian Federation: ICRC calendar of events, October–December 2006], in the author's possession.

[32] A collective memoir by Yeltsin's advisers acknowledges that one of them met with officials of the ICRC and accepted their assessment. See Iu. M. Baturin, A. L. Il'in, V. F. Kadatskii, V. V. Kostikov, M. A. Krasnov, A. Ia. Livshits, K. V. Nikiforov, L. G. Pikhoia, and G. A. Satarov, *Epokha El'tsina: Ocherki politicheskoi istorii* [The Yeltsin Epoch: Sketches of a political history] (Moscow: Vagrius, 2001), p. 625.

its assessment for many years thereafter, the Russian government only accepted it for the period from 1994 until Russian troops withdrew from Chechnya in 1996. From the time Russia reinvaded the republic in 1999, the government considered its subsequent actions as part of an "antiterrorist operation." Although the Russian forces violated many provisions of Common Article 3, as Kramer's chapter describes, they did allow the ICRC access to prisoners up until 2004 (the Chechen side allowed access to its captives only during the first war). Neither the Russian government nor the local Chechen regime under Ramzan Kadyrov allowed access to the "disappeared."[33]

In a certain sense, by rejecting the obligations of the Geneva Conventions, and failing to declare a state of emergency—which would allow for derogation of some of its human-rights obligations—Moscow has unintentionally invited scrutiny by human-rights observers and action by the European Court of Human Rights. The Court heard scores of cases related to Russian policy in the North Caucasus and ruled against Russia in the vast majority of them.[34] Moscow reacted by paying the modest compensation required by the court to victims or families of deceased victims. It barely investigated any of the cases even when the Court identified specific perpetrators of the crimes.[35] Frustrated by lack of progress, some activists picked up on a suggestion of the Parliamentary Assembly of the Council of Europe to advocate creating a special tribunal along the lines of the ones formed to deal with the conflicts in Rwanda and former Yugoslavia.[36] Others have continued to adopt the frame of human rights rather than the laws of war to address the widespread use of torture and "disappearances."[37] Indeed, the early 21st century has witnessed a blurring or overlap between international humanitarian law and human-rights law, with an extension of individual rights beyond the Geneva Conventions for those involved in armed conflict. It is significant already that a European Court of *Human Rights* would hear cases regarding a conflict that the ICRC considers to fall under Common Article 3 of the Geneva

[33] Bellon interview.

[34] Sergei L. Loiko, "In Russia, Some Seek Justice in European Court of Human Rights," *Los Angeles Times*, 22 March 2012.

[35] Author's interview with Tatiana Lokshina of the Demos human-rights groups, Moscow; "Chechen Cases at the ECtHR," European Center for Constitutional and Human Rights (n.d.).

[36] "Promoting the Proposal on Establishment the International Tribunal on Chechnya—The First Steps." The undated report (probably August 2007), in the author's possession, was prepared by Stanislav Dmitrevskii, the managing director of the Russian-Chechen Friendship Society, on behalf of a number of groups, including Memorial, and the Committee against Torture, in anticipation of a meeting in Nizhny Novgorod, planned for October 2007 to honor the journalist Anna Politkovskaia on the first anniversary of her murder.

[37] *Russian NGO Shadow Report on the Observance of the Convention against Torture and Other Cruel, Inhuman or Degrading Treatment or Punishment by the Russian Federation for the period from 2001 to 2006* (Moscow, November 2006).

Conventions. Even more noteworthy is that the judges have ruled consistently against Russia, perhaps setting a precedent for applying the higher standards of human-rights law to an area heretofore considered the *lex specialis* of the laws of war.[38] Although cold comfort to the victims of Russian or Chechen violence, promoters of human rights and restrictions on warfare might view such developments as progress.

In assessing states' compliance with the laws of war, we typically think of the effect of the "international community"—represented, say, by the United Nations or the European Union—as a positive one. Europeans are often given credit, for example, for such initiatives as the Rome Statute for an International Criminal Court and the treaties banning antipersonnel landmines and cluster bombs.

Anicée Van Engeland's chapter on Iran provides a reminder, however, that the international community—by its inaction or double standards—can contribute to undermining respect for international law. She describes how the UN Security Council's refusal to denounce Iraq's poison-gas attacks against Iran and against its own Kurdish citizens during the Gulf War of 1991 undermined the credibility of international humanitarian law in the eyes of Islamist leaders who were already suspicious of international institutions dominated by the West. Undoubtedly Iran's leaders themselves revealed a degree of hypocrisy in denouncing violations of a body of international law that they claimed—in regard to their own behavior—was superseded by Shari'a law as they chose to interpret it. But for international bodies to accuse Iran of using chemical weapons, rather than identify Iraq as the real culprit, as Van Engeland reports, surely did little to bolster the Islamic Republic's respect for the law.

Iran's interest in international law revived in the wake of the Iran-Iraq War, following a pattern well established in the 20th century—with the 1925 Geneva Protocol limiting the use of poison gas signed in reaction to the widespread deployment of that weapon in World War I; the 1949 Geneva Conventions (particularly the new fourth convention intended to protect civilians) following the devastation and genocidal crimes of World War II; and the 1977 protocols inspired by the Vietnam War and wars of anticolonial struggle.[39] The attacks of 11 September 2001 and the subsequent US invasion of Iraq also provided an impetus for an Iranian reconsideration of the merits of international law: By

[38] William Abresch, "A Human Rights Law of Internal Armed Conflict: The European Court of Human Rights in Chechnya," *European Journal of International Law* 16, no. 4 (2005): 741–767. See also the chapter by Charles Garraway in Matthew Evangelista and Henry Shue, eds., *The American Way of Bombing: Changing Ethical and Legal Norms, from Flying Fortresses to Drones* (Ithaca, NY: Cornell University Press, 2014).

[39] See David Wippman's discussion in David Wippman and Matthew Evangelista, *New Wars, New Laws? Applying the Laws of War in 21st Century Conflicts* (Ardsley, NY: Transnational, 2005), pp. 1–3.

endorsing the Geneva Conventions, Iran was seeking to distinguish itself from the lawless terrorists of al-Qaeda and was reacting to the fact that neoconservative officials in the Bush administration such as Paul Wolfowitz clearly had Iran in their gun sights (until the disastrous occupation of Iraq distracted their attention). However instrumental Iran's embrace of the Geneva Conventions, it has the potential, as Van Engeland claims, to become internalized.

Internalization and the Role of Courts

Scholars of international law who favor explanations for compliance that rely on mechanisms of socialization to dominant norms necessarily focus on the level of domestic politics and legislation. Koh, for example, describes "judicial internalization," which "occurs when litigation in domestic courts provokes judicial incorporation of international law norms into domestic law, statutes, or constitutional norms."[40] Yet, at the international level legalization of norms governing warfare is still relatively underdeveloped. The International Court of Justice in The Hague has weighed in on some issues related to the laws of war, most notably in a case brought by Nicaragua against the United States for the latter's support of the Contra forces seeking to overthrow the Sandinista government,[41] and regarding the legality of nuclear weapons.[42] More relevant is the Rome Statute that established the International Criminal Court, whose mandate includes prosecution of war crimes, genocide, aggression, and crimes against humanity. Yet some of the world's major military powers—for example, the United States, Russia, China, and India—are not parties to the treaty. Ad hoc courts have been established to administer justice in the face of war crimes during particular conflicts. The International Criminal Tribunal for the former Yugoslavia (discussed in Nation's chapter) and Rwanda are notable examples. And, although not mandated to deal with IHL, the European Court of Human Rights, as we have seen, has issued many judgments regarding Russia's war in Chechnya, and earlier on British conflict with the Irish Republican Army and Turkey's war against Kurdish separatism.

The Rome Statute, whose definition of war crimes tracks closely with the language of the Geneva Conventions, could have an indirect effect on states that do not formally participate in its institutions. Such states do not necessarily expect that their troops or commanders accused of war crimes will come before the

[40] Koh, "Why Do Nations Obey International Law?" p. 642.

[41] http://www.icj-cij.org/docket/index.php?sum=367&code=nus&p1=3&p2=3&case=70&k=66&p3=5.

[42] http://www.icj-cij.org/docket/index.php?p1=3&p2=4&k=e1&p3=4&case=95.

International Criminal Court. Through the principle of "complementarity," the original Rome Statute provides that national legal authorities have the primary obligation to investigate war crimes. Only if national courts are unwilling or unable to do so does the international court come into play.[43]

So even with the establishment of the International Criminal Court, much of the action should still take place at the domestic level. Military courts-martial of course routinely handle violations of military law by members of the armed forces. As Solis points out in his discussion of the Vietnam War, the violations are not called war crimes or grave breaches of the Geneva Conventions but violations of the relevant national military law—in the US case, the Uniform Code of Military Justice.

Domestic civil courts are typically reluctant to intervene in the area of national security, granting the political authorities wide latitude. A notable exception is the Israeli Supreme Court, which has issued judgments regarding such controversial issues as targeted killings and harm to civilians during military operations. Ben-Ari and Cohen date the Israeli court's activism in matters related to international humanitarian law to the year 2000. "First, the court has expanded its jurisprudence to include application of the fourth Geneva Convention. In recent cases, the court even based some decisions on the First Additional Protocol to the Geneva Conventions (which Israel, like the United States, is not party to), justifying its action on the grounds that some of the norms in this protocol are considered Customary International Law." They point out, "the Israeli Supreme Court may be the only judicial body in the world that has demonstrated a willingness to enforce IHL on the army *ex ante*, that is, before an action is taken, or even while a military operation is in progress." Although they stress "nonintervention is still the norm," they suggest that "the 'shadow' of possible judicial intervention lies over almost every military operation undertaken." The Israeli Defense Forces are thus obliged constantly to take the laws of war into consideration.

US courts rarely involve themselves in matters related to national security, and when they do so their actions do not always uphold the laws of war. Conway-Lanz writes, for example, of the US Supreme Court's overturning a court-martial conviction of a US airman charged with murdering a Korean prisoner on the grounds that the defendant had "been discharged from the Air Force when he was tried." In what he describes as "a collateral attack on the military conviction," Solis reports that a Georgia federal district court overturned the conviction of Lieutenant William Calley, the instigator of the My Lai massacre (a decision later reversed by the Federal Court of Appeals, by which time Calley was granted parole). There are many instances where neither military nor civilian judicial

[43] William A. Schabas, *An Introduction to the International Criminal Court* (Cambridge, UK: Cambridge University Press, 2007).

authorities have pursued cases of documented war crimes because the perpetrators had left the armed forces and were difficult to locate.[44]

A notable exception to US civilian courts' deference on matters of national security occurred during the Bush administration's "global war against terror." In the cases of *Hamdan v. Rumsfeld* (2005)[45] and *Boudmediene v. Bush* (2008), for example, the Supreme Court rejected the administration's policies on detention of terrorist suspects. In the latter case, the majority wrote:

> In considering both the procedural and substantive standards used to impose detention to prevent acts of terrorism, the courts must accord proper deference to the political branches. However, security subsists, too, in fidelity to freedom's first principles, chief among them being freedom from arbitrary and unlawful restraint and the personal liberty that is secured by adherence to the separation of powers.[46]

During the Obama administration, the courts became arguably more compliant with the president's wishes. In a number of cases the White House intervened in defense of Bush administration officials. In December 2009, for example, Obama's Department of Justice successfully "asked an appeals court to dismiss a lawsuit accusing former Bush administration attorney John Yoo of authorizing the torture of a terrorism suspect, saying federal law does not allow damage claims against lawyers who advise the president on national security issues."[47] The previous month a federal appeals court had dismissed the case of Maher Arar, a Canadian citizen whom the United States arrested as part of its "extraordinary rendition" program and sent to Syria, where he was tortured. As one news report summarized, "the Second Circuit Court of Appeals ruled that victims of extraordinary rendition cannot sue Washington for torture suffered overseas, because Congress has not authorized such lawsuits." Although the Canadian government had declared Arar innocent of any connection to terrorism and apologized for providing the faulty intelligence that led to his arrest, the US government refused to apologize, but instead kept Arar's name on a "watch list" of suspected terrorists.[48] A common practice during the Obama

[44] Michael Sallah and Mitch Weiss, *Tiger Force: A True Story of Men and War* (New York: Little, Brown, 2006). This point was made by David Kaiser at our Brown workshop.

[45] David Cole, "Why the Court Said No," *New York Review of Books* 53, no. 13 (10 August 2006).

[46] http://www.law.cornell.edu/supct/html/06-1195.ZS.html.

[47] Bob Egelko, "White House Wants Suit against Yoo Dismissed," *San Francisco Chronicle*, 8 December 2009.

[48] "Appeals Court Rules in Maher Arar Case: Innocent Victims of Extraordinary Rendition Cannot Sue in US Courts," *Democracy Now* (radio program), 3 November 2009, http://www.democracynow.org/2009/11/3/appeals_court_rules_in_maher_arar.

administration, especially favored by the Central Intelligence Agency, was simply to declare the topic of a given law suit—say the targeted killing by drones of innocent civilians—secret on grounds of national security and render the judicial process impossible. As one critical evaluation put it, the policy served "not to protect legitimately classified information from disclosure, but to shield controversial decisions from public scrutiny and to spare officials from having to defend their policies in court."[49]

Assessing the Impact of the Geneva Conventions

Is the glass half full or half empty? Given the methodological hurdles confronting a study of the impact of the Geneva Conventions, or IHL more broadly, it seems unrealistic to pose a question any more ambitious than that one. Granted we have chosen "hard cases"—where one might expect minimal compliance by states fighting terrorists or insurgents who violate the laws of war by design. But that hardly means we can declare the violations we have encountered anomalies. For that reason we have sought to investigate the domestic and international institutions that should be in place and functioning if states are serious about their obligations.

Still, much of our evidence is subject to varying interpretations. Ben-Ari and Cohen found, for example, that between 2000 and 2007 the Israeli Defense Forces indicted just 10 percent of soldiers suspected of criminal offenses against Palestinians. That seems to them a low number. Renée de Nevers described a few high-profile crimes committed by private contractors, but points out that the "bulk of these contractors likely conduct their missions without incidents such as those highlighted here." At the same time, she observes, at the time of writing, "few private security contractors working in Iraq have been charged with committing crimes" and "only one has been prosecuted for actions in Afghanistan." In the infamous case of September 2007, where five employees of Blackwater were charged with manslaughter for killing seventeen civilians in Nisour Square in Baghdad, the charges were initially dismissed due to prosecutorial errors.

Gary Solis reveals the methodological challenges to accounting for war crimes in his close examination of the Vietnam War. How many US war crimes went undetected by military authorities is unknowable. Even the numbers

[49] Jameel Jaffer and Nathan Freed Wessler, "The C.I.A.'s Misuse of Secrecy," *New York Times*, 29 April 2012. Whether the Obama administration's actions represent a permanent "rollback" of rights or a temporary wartime expedient is addressed in Sidney Tarrow, "War, Rights, and Contention: Lasswell v. Tilly," in *Sovereignty, Citizenship, and Cosmopolitan Alternatives*, ed. Sigal Ben-Porath and Rogers Smith (Philadelphia: University of Pennsylvania Press, 2012).

of alleged crimes investigated cannot be known because of records missing or never kept. That said, Solis presents the evidence available and develops a clever technique for assessing the justice of the punishment meted out in those cases that were discovered and prosecuted. He compares them to the nearest equivalent in domestic law—cases of murder and manslaughter. His conclusion is that "court-martial sentences for Vietnam-era war crimes were substantial, even heavy, even when compared to sentences imposed in civilian courts. Nor were there discernible differences in court-martial sentences for the murder of Americans and those imposed for Vietnamese victims." His conclusion: "It is fair to say that Vietnam-era military courts fully executed their responsibilities in light of the 'effective sentencing' envisioned by the Geneva Conventions." Of course this assessment does not apply to other types of US military behavior in Indochina—such as aerial bombardment of civilian areas—that some would deem war crimes.[50] But it does offer a rather hopeful image of compliance with the laws of war.

Conway-Lanz's research into US treatment of civilians during the Korean War reveals heretofore little-known atrocities, such as a deliberate policy to fire on refugees on the suspicion that they might be harboring guerrilla fighters in disguise. Yet, even here he finds reason for hope. "Americans involved in the brutal refugee control policy did display a sensitivity to the norm against harming civilians even in the absence of a public spotlight." He cites as evidence the concern expressed in Ambassador John Muccio's 1950 letter to the secretary of state; a recommendation, contained in military orders to shoot at fleeing refugees, to "use discretion" in the case of women and children; and one captain's refusal to fire on refugees, despite his orders.

Yet if we observe progress, we also must recognize some substantial steps backward. The Bush administration's endorsement of torture, and its successors' unwillingness to investigate or prosecute the crimes, is one obvious example, but there are others. Conway-Lanz's chapter describes the sorry state of a hospital under US military authority, treating refugees in South Korea. "Staffed by five doctors and eighteen nurses with facilities for about 120 patients" at one point it "contained 817 patients with many lying on grass mats on the floor." One visitor wrote that the people "are forced to live worse than any animal kept by an American farmer." More than a half-century later, one might be tempted to say the same about US-held detainees at prisons such as Bagram in Afghanistan or Abu Ghraib in Iraq—and about patients in hospitals. At least that could be the reaction to headlines such as this one from August 2012: "Congressional

[50] For a multidisciplinary analysis of the morality and legality of aerial bombardment, see Evangelista and Shue, *The American Way of Bombing*, particularly Neta Crawford's discussion of the Vietnam War as a turning point.

Probe Reveals Cover-Up of 'Auschwitz-Like' Conditions at U.S.-Funded Afghan Hospital."[51]

These examples come from countries, such as Israel and the United States, commonly considered law-abiding democracies. The evidence in chapters by Craig Nation and Mark Kramer, on former Yugoslavia and Russia, respectively, paint an even bleaker picture of the state of the Geneva regime. From the standpoint of scholarship, however, Nation has done us a service by enumerating the factors that led to such widespread noncompliance in the Yugoslav case. And despite Russia's brutal practices in fighting Chechen separatism, the fact that human-rights activists have brought them worldwide attention—at great personal cost—inspires admiration. Their efforts have arguably contributed to a broadening of the scope of legal protections for civilians caught in armed conflict, as we saw with the rulings of the European Court of Human Rights.

One of our authors has described the US struggle with adherence to the Geneva Conventions as "part of a broader process of international consensus-building on minimizing the destructiveness and human costs of war."[52] Consensus was most easily achieved "in the relatively noncontroversial convention provisions that governments around the world agreed conformed to their military and political interests and their notions of military necessity, such as the immunity of doctors and hospitals from attack or the hundreds of mundane regulations for the humane operation of internment camps for prisoners of war and civilian detainees." These are areas where we would expect self-interest and the rationalist mechanism of reciprocity to operate. Perhaps the absence of reciprocity in the "unequal wars" that the United States has fought in Iraq and Afghanistan, for example, accounts for some of the serious lapses in adherence to even these noncontroversial provisions.[53] Conway-Lanz observes that "the protections for war victims that clashed the most with perceived military and political interests failed to even make it into the 1949 conventions, like noncombatant protections from bombing." Yet some of those provisions appeared in the 1977 Geneva Protocols, in treaties banning landmines and cluster munitions, and in the Rome Statute for the International Criminal Court—despite the opposition of the United States and some of the other major war-fighting powers. The study of the laws of war, as this volume has demonstrated, is full of such paradoxes. Despite the methodological difficulties it is a study well worth pursuing.

[51] *Democracy Now*, 1 August 2012, http://www.democracynow.org/2012/8/1/congressional_probe_reveals_cover_up_of.

[52] The quotations are from Sahr Conway-Lanz's chapter, in this volume.

[53] Alessandro Colombo, *La guerra ineguale: Pace e violenza nel tramonto della società internazionale* (Bologna: Il Mulino, 2006).

INDEX

Note: Page references followed by a *t* indicate table.

The manufacturer's authorised representative in the EU for product safety is Oxford University Press España S.A. of El Parque Empresarial San Fernando de Henares, Avenida de Castilla, 2 - 28830 Madrid (www.oup.es/en or product.safety@oup.com). OUP España S.A. also acts as importer into Spain of products made by the manufacturer.

Printed and bound by CPI Group (UK) Ltd, Croydon, CR0 4YY

14/09/2026

02216304-0017